1 CORINTHIANS 1–4

1 Corinthians 1–4

*Reconstructing Its Social and Rhetorical Situation
and Re-Reading It Cross-Culturally for Korean-
Confucian Christians Today*

OH-YOUNG KWON

WIPF & STOCK · Eugene, Oregon

1 CORINTHIANS 1–4
Reconstructing Its Social and Rhetorical Situation and Re-Reading It Cross-Culturally for Korean-Confucian Christians Today

Copyright © 2010 Oh-Young Kwon. All rights reserved. Except for brief quotations in critical publications or reviews, no part of this book may be reproduced in any manner without prior written permission from the publisher. Write: Permissions, Wipf & Stock, 199 W. 8th Ave., Suite 3, Eugene, OR 97401.

Wipf & Stock
An Imprint of Wipf and Stock Publishers
199 W. 8th Ave., Suite 3
Eugene, OR 97401
www.wipfandstock.com

ISBN 13: 978-1-60899-432-8

Manufactured in the U.S.A.

Contents

Foreword | *vii*
Acknowledgements | *ix*
Abbreviations | *xi*

Introduction | 1

1 A Critical Review of Recent Scholarship on the Problems Paul Addresses in 1 Corinthians 1–4 | 14

2 The Rhetorical Background of Roman Corinth | 59

3 The Social Background of Roman Corinth | 89

4 A Rhetorical Analysis of 1 Corinthians 1–4 | 133

5 A Social Analysis of 1 Corinthians 1–4 | 151

6 Summary of the Rhetorical and Social Analysis of 1 Corinthians 1–4 | 189

7 Cross-Cultural Hermeneutics of 1 Corinthians 1–4 for Korean-Confucian Christians Today | 198

Conclusion | 238

APPENDIX 1 *Cicero: Rhetorical Theories* | 249
APPENDIX 2 *T'oegye: Life and Wisdom* | 255

Bibliography | 265

Scripture Index | 289
Author Index | 295
Subject Index | 301

Foreword

ON FIRST HEARING, AT a postgraduate seminar, an outline of the project contained in this work, I recall exclaiming to a colleague, "There are three doctorates here, not one!" Now that the project is complete, I can only marvel at the synthesis of so many aspects of New Testament scholarship that Oh-Young Kwon has managed to bring together—and not only bring them together but invite them to engage in conversation with each other in a mutually illuminating way.

Oh-Young Kwon describes his work as setting up a dialogue table to which four parties are invited. The four parties are in the first place Paul, as author of his First Letter to the Corinthians, especially of 1 Corinthians 1–4; the community of believers at Corinth, the original audience addressed in the letter; then Oh-Young Kwon himself as twenty-first century reader and interpreter of Paul; and finally twenty-first century Korean Christians, contemporary recipients of his own mediation of Paul in a particular historical and cultural context where the Confucian heritage remains strong. Not only are these four parties engaged in dialogue at the table, but behind them stand two other figures as cultural representatives: the Roman orator Cicero and the sixteenth century Korean Confucian teacher T'oegye.

Setting up and facilitating this four-way dialogue means going beyond the traditional historical-critical paradigm to adopt and employ two contemporary approaches to biblical interpretation: socio-cultural analysis, on the one hand, and the audience-orientated approach of rhetorical criticism, on the other. What draws these two together is the fact that patronal structures were particularly significant in shaping the social situation in Roman Corinth. Such structure involved networks of power and influence that were particularly reflected in the kind of rhetorical devices that are so much the target of Paul's critique in the early chapters of 1 Corinthians, especially around the language of *sophia* and *logos*. The advantage of this audience-orientated approach for project in hand is that it moves the focus away from the theology of Paul—the traditional focus—towards that of the believing community, a re-orientation particularly suitable for bringing to the dialogue table the concerns and cultural presuppositions of Korean Christians today.

All this means, of course, that Oh-Young Kwon, besides engaging in a basic historical-critical examination of the intricacies of the Greek text, has had to master several more recent approaches to the study of the New Testament and the vast array of secondary literature accompanying each. The critical control of such literature displayed in the work is truly amazing. One's admiration is only increased on realizing that, beyond the New Testament itself, the bringing of Cicero to the table as a key witness of ancient rhetorical technique involves an excursus well beyond the discipline of New Testament, to that of Classical Studies in the Latin tongue. Only those familiar with the Korean background will be able to assess the author's achievement in that area and its significance for on-going Christian life in that context. However, granted what he has brought together in the Western tradition of biblical and classical learning, one can only presume even greater efficiency in his own cultural and historical milieu.

While not his doctoral supervisor, it has been my privilege to accompany Oh-Young Kwon at various stages in the production of this work. That role has also given me the pleasure of coming to know his wife, EJ (Eun Jung), and their infant son, Derrick, who came into the world and brought delight to all as the long project was nearing completion. My hope and expectation is that, beyond a significant contribution to Pauline studies, it will serve as a model of a highly creative combination of interpretive approaches seeking to give biblical voices fresh resonance today.

Reader, take your place at the table!

Brendan Byrne, SJ.
Professor of New Testament,
Jesuit Theological College,
Melbourne College of Divinity

Acknowledgements

THIS BOOK IS A revised version of my doctoral dissertation submitted to the Melbourne College of Divinity under the excellent supervision of Dr. Keith Dyer, Professor of New Testament at Whitley College in Melbourne, Australia. I express my deep gratitude to him for his supervision, friendship, and mentorship.

For the successful completion of my doctorate and publication of this work I am indebted to a number of friends whose encouragement, financial support, scholarship, constructive criticisms, and spiritual advice need to be acknowledged here. My sincere appreciation is sent to Dr. Brendan Byrne who has helped me a lot in different parts of my studies and family life and willingly agreed to write a foreword for this publication, and to Dr. Anne Elvey who has always expressed her heartfelt wishes to my studies and academic development.

I send my deep appreciation to my former Whitley colleagues—Rev. Dr. Frank Rees, Principal of Whitley College; former Principal Rev. Dr. Geoff Pound; Dr. Ross Langmead; Rev. Dr. Simon Holt; Dr. Mark Brett; Rev. Marita Munro; Mr. Bill Ford and his wife Christina Bell; and to Professor Paul Beirne, Dean of the Melbourne College of Divinity; Rev. Alan Marr, Director of Ministry of the Baptist Union of Victoria; and Rev. Meewon Yang.

I offer thanks to Wipf and Stock Publishers and especially Mr. Christian Amondson and Ms. Diane Farley for their help to publish this book.

Finally, I give special thanks to my Australian parents Dr. Lindsay and Barbara Herbert for their unconditional love and financial support, and express indescribable love and uncountable thanks to my wife, EJ

(Eun Jung), and son, Derrick (Hyuk), for their long-term sacrifice and patience, and all my family members, relatives and friends in Korea for their ongoing support and prayer. Without my family's endurance and encouragement, this publication would not have happened.

Abbreviations

AB	The Anchor Bible
ABR	*Australian Biblical Review*
ANTC	Abingdon New Testament Commentary
BA	*The Biblical Archaeologist*, a publication of the American Schools of Oriental Research
BAGD	W. Bauer, W. F. Arndt, F.W. Gingrich, and F. W. Danker. *A Greek English Lexicon of the New Testament and Other Early Christian Literature*. 3rd ed. Chicago: the University of Chicago, 2000
BAR	*Biblical Archaeological Review*
BASOR	*Bulletin of the American Schools of Oriental Research*
BCE	Before Common Era
BECNT	Baker Exegetical Commentary on the New Testament
BI	*Biblical Interpretation*
BNTC	Black's New Testament Commentaries
c.	Circa
CBQ	*The Catholic Biblical Quarterly*
CE	Common Era
CIL	*Corpus Inscriptionum Latinarum*
DPL	*Dictionary of Paul and His Letters*. Edited by G. F. Hawthorne, R. P. Martin, and D. G. Reid. Illinois; Leicester: InterVarsity, 1993.
EC	Epworth Commentary

ECGNT		*The Exhaustive Concordance to the Greek New Testament.* John R. Kohlenberger III, Edward W. Goodrick, and James A. Swanson. Grand Rapids: Zondervan, 1995
ExpT		*Expository Times*
FeH		*Fides et Historia*
GNA		Good News Australia
GNS		Good News Studies
GOTR		*Greek Orthodox Theological Review*
HTR		*Harvard Theological Review*
IBC		Interpretation: A Bible Commentary for Teaching and Preaching
ICC		The International Critical Commentary
JBL		*Journal of Biblical Literature*
JETS		*Journal of the Evangelical Theological Society*
JNT		Jewish New Testament
JSNT		*Journal for the Study of the New Testament*
JSNTS		Journal for the Study of the New Testament Supplement Series
JTS		*Journal of Theological Studies*
KJV		King James Version
LXX		Septuagint
MNTC		The Moffatt New Testament Commentary
Mig		*De Migratione Abrahami*
NCamBC		The New Cambridge Bible Commentary
NCenBC		The New Century Bible Commentary
NEB		New English Bible
NIBC		The New International Biblical Commentary
NICNT		The New International Commentary on the New Testament
NIGTC		The New International Greek Testament Commentary
NIV		New International Version
NKJV		New King James Version
NovT		*Novum Testamentum*
NTS		*New Testament Studies*
RBL		*Review of Biblical Literature*
RSV		Revised Standard Version

RTR	*Reformed Theological Review*
SBLDS	Society of Biblical Literature Dissertation Series
SJT	*Scottish Journal of Theology*
SNTSMS	Society for New Testament Studies Monograph Series
TNTC	Tyndale New Testament Commentary
TynBul	*Tyndale Bulletin*
TZfT	*Tübinger Zeitschrift für Theologie*
WBC	Word Biblical Commentary
Wis	The Wisdom of Solomon
ZNW	*Zeitschrift für die neutestamentliche Wissenschaft*

Introduction

> I appeal to you, *brothers and sisters*, by the name of our Lord Jesus Christ, that all of you agree and that there be no dissensions among you, but that you be united in the same mind and the same judgment for it has been reported to me by Chloe's people that there is quarreling among you, my *sisters and brothers*. What I mean is that each one of you says, "I belong to Paul," or "I belong to Apollos," or "I belong to Cephas," or "I belong to Christ."
>
> 1 Cor 1:10–12, RSV (italics mine)

THESE PAULINE VERSES EXPLICITLY demonstrate that by the time Paul wrote 1 Corinthians the Corinthian Christian community had critical problems with schisms (*schismata*, e.g., 3:1–9, 21–23; 4:14–21; 11:18). Furthermore, the entire text of 1 Corinthians 1–4 appears to exhibit that a number of broader cultural phenomena underlay these factions: the issues of *sophia* (1:17—2:16; 3:18–20) and *sophia logou* (1:17; 2:4); social hierarchical structures and social stratification (1:26–28; 4:8–13); and ethnic diversity (1:14–16, 22–24). These factors seem to have been endemic in the social situation of the Corinthians to whom Paul wrote 1 Corinthians. As well as these broader issues, there are particular triggers of schisms found in the rest of the letters: immorality (5:1–12), litigation (6:1–11), marriage (7:1–40), idolatry (8:1—10:22), household cults (10:23—11:1), discrimination at the Lord's Supper (11:17–34), spiritual gifts (12:1—14:40), and the nature of the resurrection body (15:1–58).

Nonetheless, this work narrows its attention to the issues that Paul describes in the first four chapters of 1 Corinthians. These four chapters comprise multiple rhetorical elements. Therein, Paul frequently uses rhetorical terminology such as *sophia* and its equivalent *sophos* and *logos*. He also employs distinctive phrases which are closely related to rhetorical strategies, such as *sophia tou kosmou, sophia aiōnos, sophia logou, logos sophias* and *sophia anthrōpōn*. These rhetorical elements appear to reflect the rhetorical environment of the Corinthian Christian community in Paul's day. This Pauline text also contains a diversity of social indicators. These are expressed particularly in 1:26–28: "not many of you were wise (*ou polloi sophoi*)," "not many were powerful (*ou polloi dunatoi*)," "not many were of noble birth (*ou polloi eugeneis*)," "what is foolish in the world (*ta mōra tou kosmou*)," "what is weak in the world (*ta asthenē tou kosmou*)" and "what is low and despised in the world (*ta agenē tou kosmou kai ta exouthenēmena*)." These expressions seem to represent the social situation of the Corinthian Christians. In addition, in 1:22–24 Paul refers to ethnic groups such as Jews (*Ioudaiois*), Greeks (*Hellēnes*) and Gentiles (*ethnē*). This biblical reference would be an indication of the ethnic composition of the Corinthian Christians.

Because of such rhetorical elements and the social indicators recorded in 1 Corinthians 1–4, the Pauline text will be investigated primarily from social and rhetorical perspectives. These perspectives satisfy my attempt to reconstruct the rhetorical and social situation of 1 Corinthians 1–4. It is especially significant to employ rhetorical analysis in such a work as this for two particular reasons.[1]

One reason is that rhetorical analysis is based on an audience-oriented interpretation because the situation of the audience is understood as a primary concern to a writer or speaker. In that Paul's letters are explicitly intended to be read aloud to the communities addressed (e.g., Rom 1:7; 1 Cor 1:2–3; 2 Cor 1:1–2), they can be analyzed using rhetorical analysis as if Paul was speaking directly to the gathered community. The writer or speaker finds that he or she is "obliged to speak at a given moment to respond appropriately to the situation" of the audience.[2] This means that the writer to a great extent has to give his or her response to

---

1. Rhetorical analysis has been the dominant method used by many scholars recently in the study of 1 and 2 Corinthians. For 1 Corinthians, see Winter, *Philo*; *After*; Smit, "Apollos"; "Disposition"; Given, *True*; Anderson, *Theory*, 245–76; Erickson, *Traditions*; Welborn, *Politics*; Litfin, *Paul's*; Pogoloff, *Logos*; Wire, *Women*; Mitchell, *Reconciliation*. For 2 Corinthians see Dicicco, *Ethos*; Peterson, *Eloquence*. For detailed introductions to New Testament rhetorical analysis, see Kennedy, *Interpretation*; Classen, *Criticism*.

2. Pogoloff, *Logos*, 78.

the current situation of the audience rather than simply to present his or her thoughts or theology. In rhetorical analysis, it is also assumed that the role of the audience is not passive but active in some sense. In other words, the audience is not simply seen as a group passively hearing the discourse, but a group of individuals that are influenced by the discourse such that they take decisive action for change. From this it becomes apparent that in rhetorical analysis two points must be emphasized: the appropriate response of a writer or speaker to the current situation of the audience and the audience's participation in taking action for change.

While 1 Corinthians 1–4 is interpreted in terms of rhetorical analysis, it should be considered important that the Pauline text is not just some kind of reflection of his thought or theology, but rather it is his response to the Corinthian situation, and particularly to the critical problem of *schismata* among the believers. Therefore, in order to urge the Corinthian Christians to be reconciled in the crucified Christ, he seeks to persuade them to take action to change their behavior. Furthermore, rhetorical analysis is the appropriate method for this study because it helps turn the direction of our primary focus from a potential over-emphasis on the thought and theology of Paul to the rhetorical and social situation of 1 Corinthians 1–4 and the wider Greco-Roman rhetorical and social culture with which the Corinthian audience identified themselves.[3] That is why this method is called an audience-oriented perspective, and why the modern audience needs to begin with an examination of the social and rhetorical situation of 1 Corinthians 1–4. In particular, the modern audience needs to give full attention to the Corinthian audience's understanding of such distinctive words as *sophia, logos, dynatos, eugenēs* (1:26), *kauchēma* (1:29, 31; 4:3), and *mimētēs* (4:16; 11:1) as a reflection and manifestation of their Greco-Roman rhetorical and social environment.[4]

The second major reason for the appropriateness of this approach is that when using rhetorical analysis the modern audience is also encouraged to dialogue between the Pauline text and the situation of the readers in our own time. Pogoloff claims that "a text which functions

3. This is helpfully and neatly expressed in the saying that the "rhetorical situation . . . allows us to move from the world of the text of Paul to the world of the Corinthian community without ever leaving the world of the reader," ibid., 83.

4. This approach is helpful and relevant not only to biblical hermeneutics but also to homiletics because it challenges preachers to focus their preaching on the appropriate response to the current situation of the audience rather than just on theological input.

rhetorically in the original situation will continue to do so if a reader interprets it as addressing his or her attitudes or actions within the new situation."[5] This means that in the ongoing process of rhetorical analysis we can re-read the Pauline text in the eyes of our own situation—not in a naïve way, but informed by the rhetorical strategies and responses of the implied author and audience. In other words, for example, the modern audience may interpret *sophia*, as addressed in 1 Corinthians 1–4, in terms of rhetorical and social perspectives and then evaluate its interpretation from a Korean-Confucian Christian context for contemporary Korean readers in terms of a collective methodology of social, historical, and contextual approaches.

In this evaluating process, however, a rhetorical method is not employed because, unlike the Corinthians in the first-century Greco-Roman world, Koreans do not emphasize the importance of eloquence and relate it to social privilege. They consider written documents and exams more important than oral ones. In Korean society, in order to elevate one's social status and take leadership positions, one should obtain good marks in the exams that the Korean government provides or those of the giant private companies. Most of these exams comprise written exams, not oral ones. Hence, the modern audience neither employs a rhetorical method in this process nor includes an investigation of Corinthian eloquence, as such, from a Korean-Confucian context.

Nevertheless, a major task in this work is to attempt to dialogue between understandings of Corinthian *sophia* in the original rhetorical situation and understandings of Korean wisdom (*jeehye* or *sulgi*) in the Korean Confucian situation.[6] In doing this, we bring together two distinctive cultures, the Corinthian culture in the first century Greco-Roman world and twenty-first century Korean Confucian culture. At the same time, we make the two horizons, the Pauline text and our current Korean-Confucian Christian context, meet and inform each other.

---

5. Ibid., 80–81. Similarly, D. Flemming states, "in order for the Christian message to be meaningful to people it must come to them in language and categories that make sense within their particular culture and life situation. It must be contextualized" (Flemming, *Contextualization*, 13).

6. Both words *jeehye* and *sulgi* refer to wisdom in the Korean language. The word *jeehye* is originally taken from the Chinese word *chi* which means wisdom in the Chinese language. The word *sulgi* is a true Korean word. The two words alike are used here in relation to the Greek word *sophia*.

In reading Paul's writings, and especially 1 Corinthians cross-culturally, it is important to invite both Paul and his Corinthian audience to our dialogue table and let all parties continue to talk to each other and dialogue with us and our readers, twenty-first century Korean Christians. This is, so to speak, at least a four-party dialogue. The four parties—Paul, his Corinthian readers, ourselves, and the Korean church (with Cicero and T'oegye lurking in the background as cultural representatives)—ask different questions and give various suggested answers to the questions from both forward and backward in time. In this regard, it is correctly stated that "people in different cultural settings do not simply give different answers to the same questions, they ask different questions."[7]

In recent Pauline scholarship, and especially Korean scholarship on 1 Corinthians, this obviously involves a re-reading of 1 Corinthians 1–4 that comprises an awareness of the social and rhetorical milieu of Corinth in the mid-first century Greco-Roman world, and explores possible analogies with contemporary Korean Christianity today. Thus far, no Korean scholars have investigated wisdom traditions at Corinth as described in 1 Corinthians 1–4 in terms of a social and rhetorical method, nor have any attempted to dialogue between Corinthian *sophia* and Korean *jeehye*.[8] Yet, Ik-Su Park tackles briefly the issue of wisdom as addressed in 1 Corinthians 1:18–24 in terms of a theological approach and analyzes the behavior of Protestant Korean Christians in parallel with that of the Corinthians. Nevertheless, he does not give much attention to the study of the social and rhetorical milieu of first-century Corinth.[9] Furthermore, in recent Korean scholarship on Paul's epistles Johann D. Kim examines Romans 9–11 from a social and rhetorical perspective, although he does not investigate the problems Paul addresses in 1 Corinthians 1–4 or does not attempt to evaluate the Pauline message from a Korean Christian context today.[10]

Nonetheless, in recent Pauline scholarship this sort of intercultural hermeneutics of Paul has been advocated by scholars such as C. H. Cosgrove, H. Weiss and K. K. Yeo. In their work *Cross Cultural Paul:*

---

7. Cosgrove, Weiss and Yeo, *Cross-Cultural*, 32.

8. The following Korean commentaries on 1 Corinthians are acknowledged here, but they take a more traditional approach to the text: Y. O. Kim, *Korindojeonseo*; J. C. Kim, *SongseoJuseok Korindojeonseo*; K. S. Kim, *Baulseoshin*.

9. Park, *Nuga guayen cham*.

10. Kim, *God*.

Journeys to Others, Journeys to Ourselves, these scholars use a historical-critical approach because this approach, as they argue, helps the writers "distinguish Paul in his culture from (them) in (theirs)."[11] They further state that "connecting Paul with our (the writers') own cultural settings . . . calls for analogical reasoning, finding ways to do fair comparison by noting similarities and differences."[12] Their historical-critical perspective enables readers to read Paul cross-culturally and explore analogies between the biblical contexts of his letters and their own cultural contexts in terms of theological and ecclesiological issues that might potentially apply in both contexts. But this is only part of the hermeneutical process required to read cross-culturally.

Dachollom Datiri also uses a historical-critical exegetical method to attempt an intercultural reading of 1 Corinthians from an African context.[13] He draws analogies between the problems Paul addresses in 1 Corinthians and those that African Christians face today. Based on this comparison, he critiques the latter from the perspective of Paul's message in 1 Corinthians. For example, in reaction to the problem of divisions in the African church, Datiri comments, "In Africa, we frequently witness church divisions based on factors such as age, education, loyalty to the pastor. Such divisions are wrong, for God's way of handling differences maintains unity of the body even as it addresses difficult issues."[14] Such an approach at least recognizes the importance of cross-cultural issues in biblical hermeneutics, but the tendency is to concentrate more on the cultural context surrounding the text in order to extract spiritual principles to apply today. The often invisible culture of the reader is seen as the target of such principles rather than a dialogue partner in the process.

Similarly, Sigurd Grindheim argues that such historical-critical analysis alone cannot provide "the evaluations Paul would have given of cultures across the world" but is in danger of misleading readers into attempting to extract a pure Pauline message from "the (Greco-Roman) cultural packaging with which Paul furnishes it" and to juxtapose it with

---

11. Cosgrove, Weiss, and Yeo, *Cross-Cultural*, 272. In this book each of these writers provides "a chapter on Paul from his own cultural perspective *Anglo-American, Chinese and Argentine respectively* and also a cross-over chapter on Paul from a cultural perspective not his own *African American, Russian and Native American*," ibid., 5; [italic's mine].

12. Cosgrove, Weiss, and Yeo, *Cross-Cultural*, 272.

13. Datiri, "1 Corinthians," 1377–98.

14. Ibid., 1379.

issues and problems that contemporary readers face in their Christian lives.[15] This is a good beginning to intercultural hermeneutics but does not go far enough.

For these reasons, such historical-critical analysis does not fit into my primary concern to investigate the social and rhetorical background of 1 Corinthians 1–4 in dialogue with Korean-Confucian Christianity. In these chapters in particular, Paul demonstrates his message in reaction to the Corinthian Christians' behavior that would have been profoundly influenced by Greco-Roman social and rhetorical conventions. Therefore, a special emphasis on rhetorical and social approaches fits this investigation. We will then re-read some of Paul's critique of Greco-Roman culture within our Korean-Confucian Christian context and let the fourfold dialogue begin. For this, as mentioned earlier, a collective methodology of social, sociological, historical, and contextual approaches will be used, both of the biblical text and context, and to a lesser extent, the Korean context.

Nevertheless, this work could be helpfully informed by the postcolonial hermeneutics favored by scholars in recent biblical scholarship.[16] Such an approach is indeed relevant for the issue of "Comfort Women." The important question of "Comfort Women" can be regarded as an ongoing post-colonial issue in Korean society. During the Japanese occupation, the Japanese government recruited young single Korean women by force and sent them as sex slaves to the battlefields where Japanese soldiers fought, to entertain and cheer these soldiers. This issue can be connected, in a sense, to the problem of sexual immorality at Corinth and the presence of on-going victims of abuse within the Christian community (see 1 Cor 5:1–13; 6:12–20; 11:2–16). Against Jennifer A. Glancy, who states that "the thought that an (enslaved) prostitute might be a member of the Christian body seems almost absurd," it is claimed that Paul is aware of the continuing abuse of some slaves within the community, but proclaims them washed and holy (1 Cor 6:11) with all other members of the body—while sternly forbidding any continuing abuse within the community.[17] To name them specifically would be to shame them further. Such an argument—and its implications for Korean

---

15. Grindheim, "Reviews on *Cross-Cultural*, 1–4."

16. For more details about this approach see Pui-lan, *Imagination*; Sugirtharajah, *Third*.

17. Glancy, *Slavery*, 65.

"Comfort Women"—requires an extended treatment of its own and cannot be developed further here.

Nevertheless, this sort of postcolonial hermeneutics will be employed in the second part of chapter 7 below: "Shinto Shrine Worship," where we will deal with the situation of Korean Christians who were compelled to worship a Japanese emperor during Japanese imperialism from 1910 to 1945. Japanese colonization in Korea, however, was relatively short in comparison to countries such as India and the Philippines.[18] The thirty-five years of Japanese colonization was not long enough for Japanese culture to penetrate so profoundly into Korean culture. That is why it is argued that this postcolonial perspective does not fit our investigation of the fundamental influences on the behavior and mentality of Korean Christians today—namely, Confucianism. If accepted in biblical scholarship, a "post-World War II" approach would be more relevant to the social and political situation of the Korean peninsula where the ongoing issue of the reunification between the two Koreas is crucial among all Koreans, whether Christian or non-Christian today.

Moreover, the perspective of liberation theology and Minjung theology does not fit our interest in this study either.[19] Certainly liberation theology and Minjung theology approaches are useful for interpreting the social and political environment of Korean Christians who were oppressed and persecuted during the times of Japanese occupation (1910–1945), the Korean War (1950–1953), and the dictatorship of military governments in South Korea (1960s–1992) and in North Korea now. But Minjung theology has gradually become an out-of-date theology in Korean Christianity today. It has lost its cutting edge in the spiritual atmosphere of twenty-first century Korean Christianity where (sadly) there seems to be more interest in individual spiritual welfare and church growth than in social justice and political issues. Minjung theology first came out of the socially, economically, and politically difficult situation of South Korea in the 1960s–80s, right after the Korean War. So it embraced the grief, sorrow, and suffering of Korean Christians in those days. During this period, Koreans grieved over the loss of loved ones in

---

18. India was colonized by the British for about 200 years and the Philippines was occupied by the Spanish for about 370 years and then ruled by the United States for about forty years.

19. Minjung theology is an indigenous Korean theology. The Korean word *minjung* means ordinary people, compared to the wealthy, elites, and political and social leaders (see Suh, *Minjung*).

the Korean War and over the division of the Korean peninsula into two countries. They suffered economically from extreme poverty and were politically oppressed under the dictatorship of former military governments. Many Koreans fought against these governments for freedom, human dignity, and democracy.[20] This was called the "democratization movement" in which Minjung theologians such as Byong-Moo Anh and Ik-Hwan Moon were actively involved and took leadership roles.

Nonetheless, Minjung theology does not attract the attention of many Korean Christians today. In the last two decades (late 1980s to early 2000s), South Korea has changed quickly in terms of social, economic, and political structures. Korean society became globalized and individualized and influenced more by Western life patterns. The Korean economy has grown so rapidly that no Koreans complain about a shortage of food and shelter any more. Democracy is widespread all over South Korea. Not many Koreans have great interest in issues of social justice and human rights. This distinctive change in Korean society over the last few decades has heavily influenced the lives of Korean Christians. Korean churches have become mega churches in terms of growth and finance and now send a good number of missionaries overseas. The success of such churches tends to be measured by numerical growth. Christians prefer to move from small churches to larger churches to share in the benefits of their social success. Prosperity theology appears to replace Minjung theology. Wealthier Korean Christians tend to project their social position and privilege into churches and claim leadership positions.

It is an important part of this work to investigate the profound causes of such mentality and behavior among Korean Christians and to evaluate it in the light of Corinthian behavior and Paul's reaction to it as addressed in 1 Corinthians 1–4. Aspects of such behavior appear to be strongly influenced by Korean Confucianism that has deeply penetrated the life of Korean society for a long time, in a way that is analogous to how the conduct of some of the Corinthian Christians was affected by Greco-Roman social and rhetorical conventions. The analogy is imper-

---

20. Jinseoung Woo reads the Bible, particularly Titus, Romans, and Psalms, from the standpoint of the social and political situation of the military dictatorships in Korea in the 1980s and his imprisonment experience during this time (see Woo, "Bible," 169–76). This is still a powerful contextual reading and essential for understanding the Korean church, but already it relates more to a reconstruction of the past rather than addressing the present context.

fect and messy, but a rich one to explore because of the multiple levels on which it operates.

In order to reconstruct the rhetorical and social situation of 1 Corinthians 1–4 and evaluate this reconstruction from a contemporary Korean-Confucian Christian context, two proponents of wisdom most representative of the wider culture in each context will be focused upon. We propose that Cicero (106–43 BCE) and his rhetorical handbooks comprise the best example of the thinking that influenced, to some extent, the behavior and mentality of the Corinthians in the mid-first-century Greco-Roman world. Though he lived in the Roman Republic of the first century BCE (see further below), it is neither possible nor necessary to argue a direct connection between Cicero, Corinth, and Paul. Rather, as the greatest exponent of the Romanization of Greek wisdom in his world and for long after, he best encapsulated the kind of rhetoric and boasting that Paul encountered and critiqued in the Roman colony of Corinth.

In a similar way, we will use T'oegye (1501–1570) and his Confucian thought as one of the most influential foundation stones for the mentality of contemporary Koreans, though he lived in the sixteenth century CE (see further below). It is necessary for us to use Cicero and T'oegye to embody wisdom thought in this way to avoid an exhaustive overview of Greco-Roman and Korean wisdom traditions. It also serves to sharpen the dialogue to follow by focusing on it as a discussion between the implied Cicero, Paul, and T'oegye in the social and rhetorical contexts of Corinth and Korea. For these reasons we will briefly outline the thought of these two paradigms of wisdom, as a basis for later reflections (see further below).

Recent Pauline scholars sometimes refer to Cicero's writings and letters in order to understand the social and rhetorical background of 1 Corinthians.[21] Yet none of them specifically employs Cicero's rhetorical handbooks, as recorded in his *De Inventione*, to reconstruct the social and rhetorical situation of 1 Corinthians 1–4 or to defend the position that this Pauline text as a whole is a rhetorical unit. None of them

---

21. See Erickson, *Traditions*, 43–72; Litfin, *Paul's*, 91–100; Pogoloff, *Logos*, 45–69; Welborn, *Fool*, 44, 82, 86, 129, 142–43, 251; Dutch, *Educated*, 108 n. 58, 190 n. 136. Cf. Juhana Torkki refers to Cicero's *De Natura Deorum* to examine the philosophical background of Paul's speech addressed in Acts 17:16–34. He draws parallels between Cicero (and Stoic thought), and Paul's speech in Athens (Acts 17) (see Torkki, *Dramatic*, 56–68, 94–100).

point out that his rhetorical handbooks—owing much to Aristotle and Isocrates—may have influenced to some degree the mentality and behavior of the Corinthians in the first century CE.[22] None of them find explicit similarities between Cicero's understandings of wisdom (*sapientia*) and eloquence (*eloquentia*), as depicted in his *De Oratore*, *De Inventione*, and *De Officiis*, and some of the Corinthians' understandings of wisdom (*sophia*) and eloquence (*logos*) as addressed in 1 Corinthians 1–4. Moreover, none of them claim that the way Cicero had boasted (*gloriatur*) and had encouraged the Romans to imitate (*imitator*) his rhetorical traditions, was analogous to the way the Pauline opponents boasted and urged other Corinthian Christians to imitate them. These approaches were in turn subverted explicitly by Paul (*kauchaomai*, 1 Cor 1:29, 31; 4:3; *mimeomai*, 1 Cor 4:16; 11:1). In this study, such arguments are a significant part of the analysis of the Corinthian situation.

It will be investigated later in this work that the influence of Cicero's legacy of rhetoric is revealed in the language of Paul in 1 Corinthians 1–4. Cicero's theories of rhetoric are glimpsed in Paul's use of rhetoric in his own writing, and particularly in 1 Corinthians 1–4. Here Paul employs and subverts some of the rhetorical elements that Cicero suggested in his rhetorical handbooks. This is attested in the fact that there are similarities between the language of Cicero in *De Officiis*, *De Oratore*, and *De Inventione*, and that of Paul in 1 Corinthians 1–4, despite Cicero's use of Latin. It is not difficult, for example, to see parallels between the way Cicero had boasted (*gloriatur*) and the way some of the Corinthian Christians boasted, which is inversely related to Paul's ironic boasting (e.g., 1 Cor 1:28; 5:6; 9:15, 16; 15:31; cf. 2 Cor 11:18, 21; 12:1). It is suggested that just as Corinthians in the broader civic society imitated Cicero and others, so some members of the Corinthian congregation took them as their model rather than the way of Christ and Paul, and imitated Cicero in the way he had encouraged the Romans to imitate their ancestors (e.g., 1 Cor 4:1, 16). These patterns of social behavior were in turn subverted explicitly by Paul in 1 Corinthians 1–4. It is a major task of this study to explore the background of these words and of Corinthian wisdom, and their relation to *schismata* in the Corinthian congregation as recorded in 1 Corinthians 1–4.

---

22. Though, as Litfin indicates, "his life-span brackets the time of Paul," (Litfin, *Paul's*, 88).

It will also be claimed that Cicero's legacy of wisdom and eloquence influenced the social behavior of the Corinthians, and their social and worldly understandings of wisdom. Moreover, Cicero's legacy can be seen in the mentality and conduct of some of the Corinthian Christians as addressed in 1 Corinthians 1–4. Some (but "not many") of the Corinthian Christians were, according to worldly standards, wise, wealthy, powerful, and of noble birth (see 1 Cor 1:26). They continued to express their wealth, high social status, and patronal hierarchies within the Christian community (e.g., 9:1–27; 11:22). They understood the Christian church to be more of a sort of social club (*collegia*) where patron-client systems played a vital role in interconnecting between patrons and clients of various social levels within the *collegia* (8:1—10:22; 15:29). Furthermore, they valued social and worldly understandings of wisdom and eloquence more highly than Christ crucified as the wisdom of God (1:18—3:22), according to Paul. Such attitudes caused divisions in the Corinthian Christian community (1:10–13; 11:17–19).

In order to comprehend the problem of schisms and the nature of *sophia* that Paul addresses in 1 Corinthians 1–4, we will also undertake a social analysis and investigate carefully the following questions: What ethnic groups in particular existed in the Corinthian congregation? What social classes did the Corinthian Christians belong to? How many major parties existed in the Corinthian Christian community? Who played an influential and leading role in opposing and criticizing Paul at Corinth? What particular points did Paul's opponents argue about with him?

I am not intending to adopt a sociological or social-science approach in this study, though we do make use of the results of those studies in some places. Rather than using sociological modeling, I am operating more in the area of applied social theory. That is, I aim to focus on the social and cultural manifestations of that which is valued most in Corinthian society—that which shapes the daily lives of ordinary or common people. Again, whereas philosophy and religion were undoubtedly profoundly important in shaping Greco-Roman city life, I do not intend to add to the significant studies already undertaken in this area.[23]

Rather, I aim to focus on popular culture and the powerful influence of patriarchal hierarchies (particularly the patronal system) and the popular wisdom that supported them (particularly as shown in speech-making and public rhetoric). I do this by asking how Paul's first

---

23. See Strom, *Reframing*, 103–41; Winter, *Philo*, 180–255; Welborn, *Fool*, 44–250.

letter to Corinth would have been heard at a public reading in such a context. I will not attempt to describe all the variations on the methods of rhetorical analysis in biblical exegesis today, since our interest is in the earliest hearers of the letter and how such a reconstruction (with all its uncertainties and imaginative re-creations) might inform the Korean listeners of the Corinthian correspondence today. So our attempt is to span two very different (but surprisingly similar) cultures nearly two thousand years apart.

Furthermore, Corinthian understandings of *sophia* and *logos*, and other social and rhetorical indicators addressed in 1 Corinthians 1–4, will be investigated; then, any insights will be re-read in light of a Korean-Confucian Christian context, especially in parallel with Korean Confucian wisdom, in which shaping T'oegye played an important role. It is not surprising, then, that I, as a Korean-Confucian Christian, should attempt to read and interpret the biblical message from the perspective of my own Korean-Confucian Christian context. As part of such an attempt, we will try to examine from a Korean-Confucian Christian context the Corinthian wisdom and the rhetorical and social situation of mid-first-century Corinth as indicated in 1 Corinthians 1–4. In particular, the cultural manifestations of wisdom traditions that become evident in relation to imperial cults, domestic ancestor cults, social hierarchies, and ethnic identity, are particularly fruitful areas of dialogue between the Korean-Confucian Christian context and Paul's first letter to the Corinthians. Reflections on these areas constitute a major part of the final chapter of this work; but first, we now turn to a critical review of recent scholarship on the problems Paul addresses in 1 Corinthians 1–4.

1

A Critical Review of Recent Scholarship on the Problems Paul Addresses in 1 Corinthians 1–4[1]

IN RECENT PAULINE SCHOLARSHIP, there is a wide range of scholarly opinion about the reconstruction of the Corinthian situation and Paul's relationship to it.[2] Scholars differ when identifying who Paul's opponents were in 1 Corinthians and when describing what the Pauline opponents based their wisdom on. Indeed, Pauline scholars have hotly disputed these issues for decades. Among the major hypotheses about Paul's opponents and their viewpoints are the following, summarized by the catchphrases: over-realized eschatology (postulated by Albert Schweitzer, N. A. Dahl, P. H. Towner, B. J. Oropeza, Anthony C. Thiselton, and John L. Hiigel); proto- (or incipient) Gnosticism (proposed by Walter Schmithals, Ulrich Wilckens, Dieter Georgi, Hans Conzelmann, Charles H. Talbert, Frederick F. Bruce, Elaine H. Pagels, and Todd E. Klutz); Hellenistic Jewish wisdom tradition (Birger Albert Pearson, James A. Davis, and Richard A. Horsley); the Petrine party (F. C. Baur, Gerd Lüdemann, and Michael D. Goulder); and rhetorical conventions or patterns (Bruce W. Winter, Peter Marshall, Timothy H. Lim, Stephen M. Pogoloff, Ben Witherington III, Duane Litfin, Joop F. M. Smit, Mark D. Given, and Richard B. Hays).

---

1. A modified version of this section is published in *Currents in Biblical Research* (See my "Critical Review").

2. For the history of recent Pauline scholarship on 1 Corinthians see Adams and Horrell, *Christianity*, 1–240.

In addition to the mainstream of scholars, there is a minor group of scholars who hypothesize that the identification of the Pauline opposition lies in Jewish apocalyptic thought, though their hypothesis has much in common with those of Hellenistic-Jewish sapiential tradition, especially in terms of the examination of Jewish literature.[3] Alexandra R. Brown analyzes Jewish literature in detail, such as Sirach, Baruch, Wisdom of Solomon, and Philo of Alexandria and apocalyptic literature such as 1 Enoch, 4 Ezra, 2 Baruch, and Qumran literature (1QH 1:11–13, 21; 4:27–28; 1QS 4:19–26; 5:21; 6:14; 9:17; 11Qpsa 18:3; 19:2).[4] She asserts that in 1 Corinthians there is terminology which reflects apocalyptic thought such as the "Wisdom of God" versus "Wisdom of this age" (2:6–8), "mature/perfect" (2:6), "see" and "hear" (2:9), "Spirit of God" versus "Spirit of the World" (2:10b–14), "the revealing power of God (2:10), "the *psychikos*" versus "the *pneumatikos*" (2:14–15) and "the mind of Christ" (2:16).[5] She thus suggests that Corinthian *sophia* was grounded in Jewish apocalyptic teachings. In addition, it is worth noting that Ronald Herms explores similarities of rhetorical elements between 1 Corinthians 3 and 1 Enoch 50.[6] Nevertheless, Paul's opponents' perception of *sophia* appears to have been rooted in Greco-Roman rhetorical traditions rather than Jewish apocalyptic thought. This will be firmly defended in the following chapters.

Some scholars such as H. H. Drake Williams, John Paul Heil, Margaret M. Mitchell, and J. C. Hurd avoid mentioning Paul's Corinthian opponents at all. Neither Williams nor Heil tackle directly the issue of the Pauline opposition in Corinth but pay full attention to examining the function and role of Scripture that Paul employs in 1 Corinthians in order to admonish the Corinthian Christians.[7] Mitchell does not state her position on the opposition to Paul but asserts that 1 Corinthians should be understood as "Paul's response to Corinthian factions, not opponents."[8] In addition to Mitchell, Hurd claims that there is no evidence of the existence of opponents who came into the Corinthian Christian church

---

3. For a detailed explanation of this position see Brown, *Transformation*; cf. Scroggs, *Christology*; "Sophia," 33–55.

4. Brown, *Transformation*, 36–64.

5. Ibid., 105–148.

6. Herms, "Saved," 187–210.

7. Williams, *Wisdom*; Heil, *Scripture*.

8. Mitchell, *Reconciliation*, 302.

from outside, for instance, teachers of gnostic thought and those who attacked Paul and drew the Corinthians away from him.[9]

Aware of the existence of such scholarly views, in the following section I will examine carefully and evaluate critically the major scholarly positions on the Pauline opposition and the basis of their *sophia* using the hypotheses listed above. I will then suggest what seems to be the most persuasive hypothesis to give an appropriate explanation for these matters.

OVER-REALIZED ESCHATOLOGY

The hypothesis that some Corinthian Christians were subject to an over-realized eschatology is still employed and defended by many scholars such as P. H. Towner, B. J. Oropeza, A. C. Thiselton, Christopher Mearns, and John L. Hiigel. Such scholars interpret the opposition to Paul in 1 Corinthians in terms of the consequences of an over-realized eschatological outlook, and I will evaluate the work of A. C. Thiselton as the best and most recent exponent of this viewpoint.[10]

Thiselton, based on the works of predecessors like Albert Schweitzer and N. A. Dahl, presents his argument that the Corinthian eschatological enthusiasts misunderstood Paul's teaching of a partly realized eschatology which stressed both the already and the not-yet as equal in importance. They thus misinterpreted it as an over-realized eschatology, over-emphasizing the already and neglecting the not-yet. On this basis, they justified their behavior such as the eating of meat offered to idols (8:1–13), sexually immoral conduct (6:12–20), the self-interpretation of the Lord's Supper as feasting, and revelry (10:14–33; 11:17–33, esp. 21–22) and of understanding of the resurrection as having fully and finally taken place (15:1–58).[11]

---

9. In the early twentieth century, Kirsopp Lake and Morton S. Enslin characterized Paul's opponents as the spirituals, "denying that they are Judaizers." Rudolf Bultmann, Ernst Käsemann, and Erich Dinkler saw them as reflecting a "Hellenistic and mystic pre-Christian Gnosis." On the other hand, Hans-Joachim Schoeps put an emphasis on "the Jewishness of Paul's opponents at Corinth," and Jacques Dupont especially regarded their wisdom as deriving mainly from "charismatic Jewish-Christians from Palestine" (Hurd, *Origin*, 107).

10. Thiselton, "Realized," 510–26; *Corinthians*, 357; Towner, "Gnosis," 95–124; Oropeza, "Apostasy," 69–86; Mearns, "Eschatological," 19–35; Hiigel, *Leadership*, 81, 90.

11. Thiselton, "Realized," 515–16, 520–23; "Meaning of *Sarx*," 204–27; Dahl, "Church," 313–35; Schweitzer, *Mysticism*, 177–204.

According to Thiselton, a futuristic eschatological perspective is clearly evident in the Pauline language of 1 Corinthians 1–4, which Paul wrote particularly to counteract the Corinthians who adhered to an over-realized eschatology. Paul employs this future eschatological viewpoint in speaking of "the assessment of individual ministers" in chapters 3-4 in particular.[12] In support of this, Thiselton cites the following texts:

> So do not pronounce judgment on anything before the proper time, until the Lord comes, who will shed light upon the hidden things of darkness and will disclose the hidden motivations of our lives. Then (*tote*) will recognition come for each from God (4:5). The work of each will become apparent, for the Day shall reveal it (3:13a) . . . the fire will test what kind of work each has done (3:13b). Each will receive their reward in accordance with their own labor (3:8b).[13]

Such examples affirm for Thiselton that Paul criticized the Corinthians who over-emphasized the already and neglected the not-yet and that he reminded them that the last days and the day of the Lord's judgment had not been revealed yet (e.g., 4:3–5).[14]

Thiselton further asserts that Paul inserted a futuristic eschatological perspective in tackling the Corinthians' catchwords of "power, discernment, especially wisdom (1:18—2:16, 3:18-20, 4:10), and spirituality (2:10—3:4)."[15] Arguing against the Corinthians who identified with these catchwords and preferred an over-realized eschatology, Paul instead stressed "a less finished but more dynamic perspective of being on the way to salvation (1:19)."[16] On the basis of such observations, Thiselton believes that Paul emphasized this futuristic eschatological perspective in the writing of 1 Corinthians 1–4 precisely because he wished to correct the Corinthians who adhered to an over-realized eschatology.

Furthermore, in 1 Corinthians 1:7 Thiselton affirms that there is evidence of over-realized eschatology and neglect of the double perspective of already and not-yet. In the phrase "wait for the public revealing of our Lord Jesus Christ" at 1:7 Paul insists that for Christians, especially

---

12. Thiselton, "Realized," 514.
13. Thiselton, *Corinthians*, 295–96, 318.
14. See Thiselton, "Realized," 513, 515.
15. Ibid., 514. Surprisingly, Thiselton does not mention the word *schismata* (1:10), though it is one of the most crucial words in 1 Corinthians 1–4.
16. Ibid., 514.

the Corinthian Christians, all has not yet arrived or been revealed, so that they have to wait for the revealing of Jesus Christ.[17]

In 4:8–13, according to Thiselton, Paul speaks explicitly of such an over-realized eschatological tendency in the Corinthian congregation. Some of the Corinthians or the "strong" (4:10; cf. 1:27) mistakenly behaved or acted as if they had already arrived or been filled. So they looked down on the apostles as well as the others or the "weak" (4:10; cf. 1:27) who seemed still to struggle in situations of difficulty, hardship, danger, and conflict (vv. 11–13).[18]

Moreover, Thiselton convincingly argues that the word "already" (*ēdē*) used in 4:8 is a definite signal of the Corinthian adherence to an overly realized eschatology, particularly in conjunction with the phrase "without us." Borrowing Schrage's idea, Thiselton then understands the word *ēdē* in close relation to the themes of resurrection (e.g., 1 Cor 15) and the Holy Spirit (e.g., 1 Cor 12). He claims that here Paul points out the Corinthians' over-emphasis on "triumphalism" as "the illusion of the enthusiasts" and on the Holy Spirit, so that they overlook "the realities of continuing sin and struggle and the need for discipline and order."[19] They behaved as if "the age to come" had already been consummated and they "had already taken over the kingdom (Dan 7:18)."[20] Likewise, in their mentality there is only the perception of the already realized eschatology, not of the not-yet. In reaction to them, Paul affirms that the victory has not yet come to them as a fulfilled reality.

For these reasons, Thiselton goes on to argue against the oft-stated claim that only at 4:8 in 1 Corinthians 1–4 as a unit is there seen a glimpse of the over-realized eschatological viewpoint.[21] He states that "it is quite misleading to imply that in the first four chapters this perspective can be found only at 4:8,"[22] since there is clear evidence of the Corinthian tendency to an over-realized eschatology and of Paul's correction of their misunderstanding of his teachings.

---

17. In this regard, Thiselton refers to Oscar Cullman and George E. Ladd's arguments (Thiselton, *Corinthians*, 99).

18. Ibid., 99.

19. Ibid., 358.

20. Ibid., 358.

21. "Already (*ēdē*) you are filled! Already (*ēdē*) you have become rich!" (4:8a) (RSV).

22. Thiselton, "Realized," 515; *Corinthians*, 357.

In spite of Thiselton's repeated emphasis of this position, there are clear criticisms to be made at several points. First, as mentioned earlier, Thiselton sees the main theme of 1 Corinthians 1–4 as the problem of the Corinthian attitude towards ministry. Within this framework, he argues, the issues of *sophia* and divisions have to be discussed. However, this viewpoint does not convince all because the matter of ministry is addressed only in the third chapter of 1 Corinthians as a whole. And this matter rather has to be understood in terms of the broader issues of *sophia* and schism which are widespread throughout 1 Corinthians 1–4 (e.g., *sophia*, 1:18–25; 2:1–13; 3:18–20; 4:10; *schismata*, 1:10–12; 3:1–4, 22; 4:6). In the first four chapters, Paul appears to deal mostly with the Corinthian misuse of rhetorical conventions in which the understanding of *sophia* is of importance, and which underlie the *schismata* in the Corinthian congregation (see further below).

Second, Thiselton understands the Corinthian behavior as shaped particularly by their catchwords: power, discernment, wisdom, and spirituality.[23] With respect to this understanding, we should note that rather than re-focusing the Corinthians on what will happen in the future, especially "at the eschaton," Paul drew attention to what had in fact been happening in the Corinthian congregation at the time of his writing.[24] Consequently in 1 Corinthians as a whole, Paul addresses practical and growing problems such as internal schisms, social hierarchies, patron-client networks, underlying Greco-Roman rhetorical understandings, and ethnic discrimination. In this respect the Corinthian catchphrases can best be interpreted as being addressed predominantly from a present-time perspective rather than a futuristic eschatological perspective. In other words, these are best seen as factors which caused the disturbances and factions within the Corinthian community at Corinth and that Paul addresses in the present, rather than from the renewed perspective of a futuristic eschatology. Clearly Paul retains a future dimension to his eschatology, but the re-assertion of this does not

---

23. Thiselton, *Corinthians*, 514.

24. Crocker, *Reading*, 93. In addition, Crocker states that in reading 1 Corinthians we readers need to find, "new possibilities from the world of the text for *our* world in front of the text. As such, the text is more for *us* than a window into the Corinthian setting; *we* also allow it to function as a mirror of *our* own world and to challenge *us* to understand *ourselves* and *our* world in new ways," ibid., 46; [italic's mine]. Similarly, the text of 1 Corinthians 1–4 is re-read in terms of a Korean-Confucian Christian context (see further below).

appear to be his over-riding concern in 1 Corinthians. Paul's concerns are predominantly ecclesiological rather than eschatological.

Third, as stated earlier, Thiselton asserts that the use of the word *ēdē* particularly at 4:8 points to an over-realized eschatology at Corinth. The word *ēdē* occurs 4 times in 1 Corinthians as a whole (twice in 4:8; once in 5:3; once in 6:7). Apart from 4:8, the other references do not have any hint of the over-realized eschatology in their use by Paul. Therefore, it would be inappropriate to interpret in terms of this perspective only the problems or issues as described in the whole book of 1 Corinthians, and particularly the problems of schisms and the matter of *sophia* in chapters 1–4.

Hays also rejects this position, remarking that "the over-realized eschatology hypothesis rests on only the scantiest evidence" in 1 Corinthians as a whole. Moreover, he denies that in 4:8 there is any evidence to support the over-realized eschatological view, but there is rather a close link with "philosophy and rhetoric."[25] In agreement with Hays, it is noted that this over-realized eschatological view does not give a persuasive explanation for the issues surrounding schisms and *sophia* in 1 Corinthians 1–4, although it may be possible to see a glimpse of it in 4:8 because of the sarcastic use of the word *ēdē* by Paul.

The limits of using over-realized eschatology as an explanation for the Corinthian problems are thus exposed. A social and rhetorical analysis, however, is better able to provide an adequate explanation for the social consequences of *sophia* as addressed in 1 Corinthians 1–4. This is because in the Pauline language of these chapters there is a lot of evidence that Paul's opponents were influenced by rhetorical and sophistic conventions. They valued highly *sophia* and its equivalents, like *sophia logou* (which is translated as "eloquence"), because in the rhetorical situation of first century Corinth those people who possessed *sophia* and eloquence were understood as being well educated, of a high level of intellect, and ranking high in the social hierarchy (e.g., 1 Cor 1:26–31; 2 Cor 1:13–17; see below). In reaction to such thoughts, however, Paul put a heavier stress on Christ the wisdom (*sophia*) of God than on the social and cultural values of *sophia* and eloquence (e.g., 1:18–24).

---

25. Hays, "Conversion," 391–412, esp. 407–8; *Corinthians*, 70.

PROTO-GNOSTICISM

The Gnostic hypothesis was initially formulated by Wilhelm Lügert in 1908. Then its more influential and bolder formulations were made by Walter Schmithals and Ulrich Wilckens in the second half of the 1950s. Between the 1960s and 1980s this hypothesis was advocated and modified by such New Testament scholars as Hans Conzelmann, C. K. Barrett, Dieter Georgi, Charles H. Talbert, Frederick F. Bruce, and Elaine H. Pagels.[26] Of them, such scholars as Conzelmann, Talbert, and Bruce were more careful to describe Paul's opponents in 1 Corinthians as "proto-Gnostic," because it is anachronistic to name them Gnostics when Gnosticism proper appeared from the second century CE onwards rather than in the days of Paul.[27]

Subsequently, this general proposal (the Gnostic Hypothesis, or GH) was criticized and modified by a number of scholars, notably Gerd Theissen, who asserted that Paul's epistles, especially 1 Corinthians, could be interpreted much more persuasively in terms of a sociological perspective. Although Theissen himself went on to formulate a version of the GH, he provided a helpful social corrective to an overemphasis on the history of ideas in the study of Corinthians.[28] Together with this lack of social context, the most telling reasons for recent scholarly objections to the GH approach were the "uncertainties both about the boundaries of Gnosticism itself and its existence prior to the second century."[29]

Despite such scholarly objections, in recent Pauline scholarship there continue to be modifiers of this perspective. Amongst them, Todd E. Klutz suggests that there are significant similarities between the contents of 1 Corinthians and those of the *Gospel of Philip* of the Nag Hammadi texts. These shall be more carefully investigated below. Prior to a closer examination of Klutz's article, the traditional Gnostic hypothesis of Walter Schmithals and earlier modifiers of his view, particularly Elaine H. Pagels, will be briefly reviewed.

26. Schmithals, *Gnosticism*; Wilckens, *Weisheit*; Georgi, *Opponents*; Conzelmann, *Corinthians*; Barrett, *Corinthians*; Talbert, *Reading*; Bruce, *Corinthians*; Pagels, *Gnostic*. A more recent and carefully stated form of this hypothesis is found in Todd E. Klutz, "Re-Reading."

27. Bruce, *Corinthians*, 21; Talbert, *Reading*, xxii; Conzelmann, *Corinthians*, 15: Yamauchi, "Gnosis," 350–54.

28. See Theissen, *Social*.

29. Klutz, "Re-Reading," 194–96.

Schmithals sees Paul's opponents in Corinth as Jewish Gnostics who, "[having] resided among the Diaspora, identify themselves . . . as Palestinian Jews . . . without having lost the inward and outward connection with the Palestinian homeland."[30] With regard to the origin of Gnosticism, Schmithals goes on to assert that it was "a phenomenon of the syncretism which was widespread in the period around the birth of Christ."[31] In addition, he contends that as "an understanding of human existence" it is older than the "religio-historical phenomenon of Gnosticism" because the idea that the Gnostic sees himself or herself to be "imprisoned in this world as in an evil and alien world" and "the body as prison of the soul," was presupposed in both "the anthropological dualism of Hellenism and the cosmological dualism of the religion of Zarathustra."[32]

Regarding Christology, which is a key theological issue in 1 Corinthian 1-4, Schmithals claims that "the Christology of the Corinthian 'Christians' expressed in the *anathema Iēsous* ('Jesus be cursed') in 1 Corinthians 12:3, is a genuinely Gnostic Christology" that is rooted in Corinthian wisdom in contrast with the wisdom of God and Paul's gospel (1 Cor 1-4).[33] In their Christology, Gnostics strongly rejected "a close connection between the heavenly Pneumatic-Christ and the man Jesus" and disputed that "the Messiah had come in the flesh (1 Cor 4:2),

---

30. Schmithals, *Gnosticism*, 113-16. He says that it is undoubted that in the Corinthian community "there were Judaizers" and "Paul is dealing with Judaizers in the Corinthian epistles," ibid., 118-19. It seems likely that by "Judaizers" he means those Jews who try to subjugate Gentile converts (or Christians) to the law, and try to make Gentiles or Gentile believers into Jews by circumcision and other works of law. This sort of understanding continues to be favored by recent scholars such as Thomas Schreiner (*Romans*), Seyoon Kim (*Perspective*), D. A. Carson, Peter T. O'Brien and Mark A. Seifrid (*Variegated*), Waters (*Justification*), Das (*Law*), and Piper (*Future*).

Nonetheless, this understanding is challenged by scholars who are advocates of the New Perspective on Paul such as N. T. Wright (*Fresh*), Terence L. Donaldson (*Gentiles*), Brad H. Young (*Jewish*), and James D. G. Dunn (*Galatians*). These scholars argue that the traditional Lutheran understanding of Judaizers can no longer be maintained in that the term refers to Gentiles who try to live like Jews by adopting or copying Jewish customs and that in the term there is no sense of forcing Gentile converts to be like Jews (see Barclay, *Obeying*, 36 n. 1; also Howard, *Crisis*, 7-11, 39).

31. Schmithals, *Gnosticism*, 25-26.

32. Ibid., 26. For Hellenism and Zoroastrianism see E. Ferguson, *Backgrounds*, 211-49; S. Ferguson, *Dictionary*, 290-91, 735-36.

33. Schmithals, *Gnosticism*, 129.

when they denied Jesus."[34] Gnostics "confessed Christ, but not Jesus as the Christ," because the man Jesus was cursed (cf. 12:3) and crucified (cf. 2:2).[35] On this basis it is quite understandable why Paul's opponents opposed Paul, who was putting a strong emphasis on the crucifixion of Christ (1:23; 2:2; cf. 1:13), because of their Gnostic-oriented wisdom or knowledge that the man Jesus cursed on the cross should be separated sharply from "the heavenly spiritual being Christ."[36]

In a further development, based on Schmithals' work, Elaine H. Pagels contends that Paul wrote his letters, especially 1 Corinthians, so as to make an assault on Gnosticism and to oppose Gnostic Christians and refute their claims of "secret wisdom."[37] Paul preached the kerygma of Christ crucified, the wisdom of God (e.g., 1 Cor 2:2; cf. 1:18–25), and warned of the coming judgment (e.g., 3:12–14). He further strongly insisted on the priority of love over knowledge (*gnōsis*) (e.g., 1 Cor 13) and proclaimed the resurrection of the body (e.g., 1 Cor 15). In speaking of these matters Paul intended to demonstrate his truly Christian attitude over his Corinthian Gnostic opponents.[38]

According to Pagels, however, rather than repudiate Paul as their most critical and "obstinate opponent," later Gnostic writers claimed the Pauline epistles, and 1 Corinthians in particular, as "a primary source of Gnostic theology."[39] Pagels argues that evidence for this is found in the Nag Hammadi documents. For instance, the Naassenes and Valentinians in fact revered Paul as one of the apostles who initiated Gnostic theology.[40] This partly underlies Klutz's comparisons and conclusions (see below).

These traditional Gnostic arguments, however, have been critiqued by other Pauline scholars at several points. R. McL. Wilson had earlier warned of the danger of reading 1 Corinthians through the eyes of second century Gnosticism. He maintained that "to speak of Gnosis in Corinth, and then to interpret the teaching of Paul's opponents by a wholesale introduction of ideas from the second-century Gnostic systems, is to run

34. Ibid., 127.
35. Ibid., 127.
36. Ibid., 128.
37. Pagels, *Gnostic*, 1.
38. Ibid.
39. Ibid.
40. Ibid.

the risk of seriously distorting the whole picture."[41] Edwin Yamauchi argues that there is no evidence to prove clearly that in the first century or before, a "pre-Christian Gnosticism" existed and, moreover, he disagrees that there would be a "fully developed Gnostic system" early enough to have influenced the New Testament writers like Paul in 1 Corinthians.[42]

Stephen J. Chester further criticizes those scholars who project Gnostic influence upon the Corinthians by stating that they have indiscriminately mixed their sources. Chester claims that they have made a false assumption that "Gnosticism and the mystery cults are essentially the same phenomenon."[43] In fact, according to Chester, the two were quite different because there are few specific references to the mystery cults in Gnostic texts; though, as "the syncretistic religious movement *par excellence*," Gnosticism owed something to them.[44]

Furthermore, Peter Marshall critiques the GH in the light of Greco-Roman hospitality and conventions of friendship and enmity. He attempts to provide an alternative social explanation of the status of Paul's enemies (or opponents) in the Corinthian epistles. He critiques strongly the hypothesis of Gnostic opponents in the Corinthian Christian church, because it does not make sense to him that Gnosticism, which is supposedly "so central to 1 Corinthians," is "absent in 2 Corinthians."[45] He suggests rather that Paul's enemies should be investigated not from the perspective of Gnosticism but of "hybrists" who were the wealthy and powerful and belonged to the upper ranks of social strata in Corinth and "constituted the major threat to Paul's apostolic authority in Corinth."[46] He maintains that in order to explain with satisfaction the behavior of the Corinthians, "the notion of *hybris* and related ideas" should be applied to the passages that have usually been accepted to have a connotation of

---

41. Wilson, *Gnosis*, 52; "Gnostic," 71.

42. Yamauchi, "Pre-Christian," 25. Very similarly, Gordon D. Fee argues that "none of the essential phenomena of Gnosticism is present in this letter (or 1 Corinthians) . . ." (Fee, *Corinthians*, 11). In addition, Wesley Carr strongly denies that there is evidence of Gnostic influence in 1 Corinthians, particularly 2:6–8. He defines the *archontes* as human rulers such as Pilate and Herod rather than as angelic or demonic beings in a Gnostic sense. Then, he concludes that "we may no longer see any Gnostic hints behind the obscure reference to the rulers of the age" (Carr, "Rulers," 28, 35).

43. Chester, *Conversion*, 223.

44. Ibid.

45. Marshall, *Enmity*, 404.

46. Ibid., 214.

Gnostic influences.[47] This observation anticipates some of our own findings about the social consequences of rhetorical elitism in Corinth.

Consequently, it is difficult to conclude that in the Corinthian Christian community there existed clear Gnostic tendencies which deeply influenced the Pauline opponents and played a critical and substantial factor in causing the congregation to be split into factions. Therefore, this traditional Gnostic hypothesis cannot be regarded as adequate to explain the social situation of 1 Corinthians and the factions caused by the Pauline opposition. More recently, nevertheless, T. E. Klutz re-investigates and defends this Gnostic proposal in another way, from a socio-cultural perspective. He initially takes ideas from both G. Theissen and Michael A. Williams.[48] Ironically, these two scholars both argue against the Gnostic hypothesis in general.[49]

Klutz derives from both scholars rich and significant ideas to help him reconstruct the Corinthian situation in terms of a Gnostic perspective. He seeks to re-read 1 Corinthians from a socio-cultural perspective, understanding the behavior of Paul's Corinthian opponents in the light of their wider socio-cultural environment. He does this by a comparative analysis of the extant texts of 1 Corinthians and one of the Nag Hammadi tractates. So Klutz demonstrates behavioral similarities between Paul's Corinthian opponents and the implied author of the *Gospel of Philip*, which was "probably composed in Greek during the second or third century and perhaps influenced by Valentinian circles."[50]

Furthermore, Klutz shows that there is a parallel between the usage of the Greek word *gnōsis* in the *Gospel of Philip* and in 1 Corinthians. He notes that several occurrences in the former echo one or another passage of the latter. For instance, there is an impressive similarity between the viewpoints on knowledge, freedom, and love in 1 Corinthians 8:1–13 and the *Gospel of Philip* 77:15–30. The former says,

> We know that all of us possess knowledge. Knowledge puffs up, but love builds up . . . we are no worse off if we do not eat, and no better off if we do . . . only take care lest this liberty of yours somehow become a stumbling block to the weak . . . by your knowledge this weak man is destroyed . . . sinning against your brethren and wounding their conscience when it is weak, you sin

---

47. Ibid., 218.
48. See Theissen, *Social*; Williams, *Rethinking*.
49. Klutz, "Re-Reading," 193 n. 1, 202.
50. Ibid., 207.

against Christ . . . I will never eat meat, lest I cause my brother to fall (RSV).

And the latter says similarly,

> He who has knowledge of the truth is a free man, but the free man does not sin, for he who sins is the slave of sin . . . knowledge of the truth merely makes such people arrogant . . . it even gives them a sense of superiority over the whole world. But "love builds up." In fact, he who is really free through knowledge is a slave because of love for those who have not yet been able to attain the freedom of knowledge. Knowledge makes them capable of becoming free.[51]

Likewise, at other points the Gnostic text has much in common with the Pauline epistle—sometimes sharing the perspective of Paul (as here), but more often the assumptions of Paul's opponents. Hence, Klutz highlights that like Paul, the implied author of the *Gospel of Philip* clarifies an ambivalent perspective of *gnōsis* and freedom by promoting "the disposition of love over both of these possessions."[52] And as implied in the Pauline text, the *Gospel of Philip* denotes that those who possess *gnōsis*, and its accompanying freedom, are arrogant and do not build up others who do not possess *gnōsis*. Furthermore, in at least partial agreement with Paul, the implied author of the Gnostic tractate regards "freedom as something that, paradoxically, mutates into a proper Christian servanthood when it is tempered by love for those who lack knowledge."[53] Based on the similarities between these two texts, therefore, Klutz argues that there is an analogy between Paul, and the behavior of Paul's opponents or the strong in 1 Corinthians, and the situation addressed by the implied author of the *Gospel of Philip*.

Klutz goes on to re-examine 1 Corinthians in the light of this socio-cultural approach. He describes Paul's Corinthian opponents as the Corinthian strong, the knowers, or the patrons. Klutz investigates their behavior in terms of their wider civic social and cultural environment. He describes them as being probably ranked higher than Paul in the social pyramid and as most likely holding "aristocratic ideals of friendship similar to those espoused by Aristotle and Plutarch."[54]

51. Ibid., 209.
52. Ibid.
53. Ibid.
54. Ibid., 210.

Due to their interest in social status or position, and knowledge itself, the Corinthian strong did not follow Paul's own practice of "psychagogic adaptability."[55] In other words, unlike them, Paul was enthusiastic about the sharing of the gospel of Christ to all, not to them alone, and making more converts among all people regardless of social status and education (e.g., 1 Cor 9:19–23; 10:32–33, "I might win the more" in 1 Cor 9:19). He further "esteemed the cultivation of friendship with people of widely divergent types and to this end valued interpersonal adaptability over constancy and steadfastness."[56] In contrast, the Corinthian strong, unlike Paul, regarded more highly those friendships which could help them elevate their social status. In their mentality this elevation or promotion of social status would be achieved through making interpersonal friendships and social relationships with people of socially high standing and of superior knowledge.[57]

According to Klutz's argument, a similarity to such a Corinthian tendency as described in 1 Corinthians is found in the mentality and language of the implied author of the *Gospel of Philip*, despite his occasional similarities to Paul's position. In a similar way to the Corinthian strong, he ranked knowledge and truth highly in a hierarchical pyramid of values and shows a steadfast commitment to them. Moreover, he understood those who possess *gnōsis* of the truth as superior to others who lack it. That is why he does not commend "anything like an ethic of adaptability" to people of *gnōsis* of the truth; rather, he urges those people who lack *gnōsis* to change.[58] And he, like the Corinthian strong, did not show any generosity, consideration or "protean sensibility" to other fellow Christians, but ignored their deficient views of *gnōsis* of the truth. Due to such similarities, Klutz claims that there is a significant analogy between the Corinthian strong of 1 Corinthians and the implied author of the *Gospel of Philip* in the matter of adaptability.

Finally, Klutz goes on to raise the issue of intra-Christian strife or discord in order to present another notable analogy between 1 Corinthians and the *Gospel of Philip*. In these texts a similar proclivity towards intra-Christian conflict is found. Like Paul's Corinthian strong of high status and knowledge as addressed in 1 Corinthians, the implied

55. Ibid.
56. Ibid.
57. Ibid.
58. Ibid., 211.

author of the *Gospel of Philip* showed a corresponding tendency towards harmonious relations with the wider social community. Hence, he would apparently seek concord with other people in his wider social milieu. This is attested in the fact that in the voice of its implied author there is not found any sign that he experienced conflict with outsiders in the wider civic society. Rather, he displays discord with other Christians who were of lower standing in the hierarchical social structure (e.g., *Gos. Phil.* 55:23–31; 56:15–19; 56: 26—57:21; 66:7–20; 69:1–3; 76:17–21; 80:16–22). This experience is in accord with that of the strong of the Corinthian congregation who had a high degree of strife and conflict with other fellow Christians.[59] In this matter, Klutz accepts Craig S de Vos's argument that at Corinth "while there is a lack of conflict between the *ekklēsia* and outsiders there is also abundant evidence of conflict within the *ekklēsia*."[60] Consequently, Klutz claims that on the issue of internal discord in a Christian community, there is an apparent similarity between 1 Corinthians and the *Gospel of Philip*.

Thus, in terms of their socio-cultural environments, Klutz compares the Corinthian strong in 1 Corinthians and the implied author of the *Gospel of Philip* with particular reference to issues of knowledge, adaptability, and intra-Christian discord. He then arrives at the conclusion that there is "a significantly high degree of ideological continuity between the Corinthian elites and the implied author of the *Gospel of Philip*" and that, in spite of "their many divergences," the strong of the Corinthian Christian community and the implied author of the *Gospel of Philip* probably exhibit "very similar human types."[61] With these statements, Klutz argues for textual interconnection between 1 Corinthians and the *Gospel of Philip* and ideological continuity between the Corinthian strong and the implied author of the *Gospel of Philip*.

Klutz also explores, helpfully, the problem of internal conflict and strife in the Corinthian congregation in the light of the social and cultural milieu of the Corinthian Christians. His insights into the strong are also helpful for understanding the nature of the Corinthians' improper behavior which was closely linked with that of outsiders in the wider civic community at Corinth.

---

59. Ibid., 211–14.
60. Ibid., 213; de Vos, *Church*, 214.
61. Klutz, "Re-Reading," 215, 216.

Nonetheless, Klutz's proposal can be challenged at several points. He argues that the relatively frequent occurrences of the word *gnōsis* (ten times in 1 Cor; cf. six times in 2 Cor), and its initial appearance in the greeting and thanksgiving (1:5), indicates that it is a key theme of 1 Corinthians and that it is related more directly to his audience in particular than some other concepts.[62] This argument can be criticized at two significant points. One is that at the simple level of word statistics, the words *logos* (seventeen times) and *sophia* (seventeen, and *sophos* eleven times) occur more frequently than the word *gnōsis* in 1 Corinthians. Furthermore, the word *gnōsis* appears in 1:5 for the first time and is then found nowhere until 8:1.[63] Then, it suddenly disappears until 12:8 where, thereafter, it occurs three times (13:2, 8; 14:6). In contrast, the words *logos* and *sophia* continue to appear in the first three or four chapters. Thereafter, they are missing in the following chapters as well until they occur again in 12:8 where the word *logos* is found twice. On this basis it is clear that as we interpret 1 Corinthians we should consider these three important words together and treat them as a unit and relate them directly to the situation of Paul's opponents.

In careful consideration of such an observation, therefore, it is difficult to agree with Klutz's assertion that the word *gnōsis* "emerges as a salient motif in the letter by virtue of its relatively frequent repetition and patterns of occurrence."[64] Rather, it is better to argue that in the entire epistle of 1 Corinthians there is an underlying motif which is intimately linked to the three frequently occurring words *logos*, *sophia*, and *gnōsis*. That motif would be closely related to the rhetorical situation of first-century Corinth where those three words were of equally great importance. Accordingly, it is likely that rather than Gnostic tendencies as such, there is a concern to address certain rhetorical influences or patterns in 1 Corinthians. Moreover, Klutz himself implicitly supports this view that there is evidence of the misuse of rhetorical conventions in the Corinthian congregation. This is because he sees some of the Corinthian

---

62. Ibid., 207.

63. It is used more frequently in chapter 8 than any other chapter, where it is used five times (vv. 1 [twice], 7, 10, 11). Thereby, it can be assumed that particularly in chapter 8 Paul speaks of a significant and crucial matter which is closely related to the word *gnōsis*. In that particular chapter Paul had tensions with some of the Corinthians over the understating of meat offered to idols (e.g., vv. 12, 13). Here the word *gnōsis* played a critical role in Paul's perception of the problem.

64. Ibid.

"wise" and "powerful" in 2:6 as having "rhetorical prowess" or "oratorical skill."[65] In this regard, it is assumed that Klutz, to some extent, seems to agree with the argument that in 1 Corinthians Paul argues against his Corinthian opponents who misuse rhetorical skills and highly value the possession of *sophia*, *gnōsis*, eloquence, and oratory rather than the gospel of Jesus Christ who is the *sophia* of God (e.g., 1 Cor 1:17–25; 2:1-5).

The other criticism of Klutz's proposal is that he never deals directly with the issue of *sophia* in chapters 1-4, though he tackles the issue of internal conflict or schism within the Corinthian Christian community that Paul addresses predominantly in the first four chapters (e.g., 1:10–12; 3:3). In those chapters Paul clearly relates the problem of intra-Christian strife to the matter of *sophia* which is found here sixteen times out of the total of seventeen in 1 Corinthians as a whole. It can be assumed, therefore, that there was a relationship between the issues of intra-Christian conflict and the abuse of *sophia* in the Corinthian Christian community. Consequently, it is unlikely that the problem of intra-Christian discord can be dealt with in one way, whilst the issue of *sophia* is tackled in another. Both have to be treated as a single related issue. In other words, *sophia* must be seen as a substantial part of the problem of internal division in the Christian community at Corinth.

So it seems likely that Klutz does not pay adequate attention to examining the problem of intra-Christian discord as implied in 1 Corinthians in relation to the issue of *sophia*, although he appropriately and correctly investigates such a problem in terms of the socio-cultural environment of the Corinthians.[66] This is because he focuses his full attention on seeking the same echoes or similarities with respect to intra-Christian conflict between the Corinthian strong as addressed in 1 Corinthians (1:27; 4:10) and the implied author of the *Gospel of Philip* rather than considering that a fundamental cause of the problem is *sophia*, and not just *gnōsis*.

Having critically examined the traditional Gnostic hypothesis and its more recent modification in Klutz's argument, it would be argued that a social and rhetorical analysis would provide a better explanation of the issues of *sophia* and the problems of schism and social hierarchy in the Corinthian congregation.

---

65. Ibid., 214.
66. Ibid., 211–14.

HELLENISTIC JEWISH WISDOM TRADITIONS

In recent Pauline scholarship on the reconstruction of the Corinthian situation and Paul's relationship to it, Richard A. Horsley, Birger Albert Pearson, and James A. Davis come to the conclusion that the speculations of Hellenistic Jewish wisdom form the most persuasive and convincing background to explain the Corinthian situation addressed by 1 Corinthians.[67] Their arguments will be critically reviewed.

Pearson argues that Paul's opponents at Corinth were "Hellenistic-Jewish-Christian missionaries" and their wisdom was rooted in "Hellenistic Jewish wisdom speculation" or "Hellenistic Jewish speculative mysticism."[68] Pearson focuses his full attention on the *pneumatikos-psychikos* terminology in 1 Corinthians 2:13–14 and 15:44–47 to understand Paul's opponents and his response to them. The origin of the *pneumatikos-psychikos* language, according to Pearson, was the Hellenistic Jewish traditional exegesis of Genesis 2:7 (in the LXX) where the Greek words *pneuma* and *phychē* occur.[69] This exegesis is focused in Hellenistic Jewish literature such as Philo's writings, the Wisdom of Solomon and Qumran and Rabbinic literature.[70] According to Pearson, it is particularly due to Philo's interpretation of Genesis 2:7 that a human being is seen as "a composite creation made up of earthly substance and divine spirit," and that humans are composed both of "the body" as "mortal" and "the mind" as "immortal" at the same time.[71]

Similarly, the *teleios-nēpios* terminology of 1 Corinthians 2:6 and 3:1 arose from Hellenistic-Jewish wisdom speculation. Pearson says,

> For Philo *teleios* is one who has achieved the highest religious attainments, especially wisdom. The metaphor is that of adulthood over against infancy: Those who have achieved wisdom have arrived at a higher plane of existence, in contrast to babes who still need to be fed a milk diet (e.g., *Migr.* 28 ff.). The solid food of wisdom is for the *teleioi* who live according to the propensities of the mind or spirit within them, the heavenly nature given to Adam in creation (cf. *Leg. Al.* 1.90 ff.; *Agr.* 8 ff.).[72]

---

67. Horsley, "Wisdom," 228; "Gnosis," 32–33; "Pneumatikos," 269–88; cf. "Consciousness," 574–89; *Spiritual*.
68. Pearson, *PNEUMATIKOS-PSYCHIKOS*, 2, 82.
69. Ibid., 11–12, 18.
70. Ibid., 18–23.
71. Ibid., 18.
72. Pearson, "Hellenistic-Jewish," 52.

Paul's opponents believed that the *pneumatikos* (or *teleios*) is superior to the *psychikos* (or *nēpios*), and that they had the potentiality to become *pneumatikoi* (1 Cor 3:1) and *teleioi* (2:6) by virtue of having "the divine spirit," the *logos* (as in Philo) or *sophia* (as in the Wisdom of Solomon) granted by God, and that in cultivating *sophia* they would "rise above the earthly and psychic level of existence and anticipate heavenly glory."[73] On the contrary, Paul argued that "in the wisdom of God, the world did not know God through *sophia*, it pleased God through (the crucified Christ) who preached to save those who believe" (1 Cor 1:21).

Pearson's argument, therefore, is that the Pauline opponents at Corinth were Hellenistic Jewish Christians whose wisdom was grounded in this Hellenistic Jewish wisdom speculation originating from Genesis 2:7. This plays the most important factor in discerning or distinguishing between heavenly or spiritual things and earthly or physical things. Accordingly, this sort of interpretation becomes foundational for interpreting those passages requiring a religio-theological perspective, for instance 1 Corinthians 15:44–54 where Paul talks about the resurrection body.

Pearson's analysis may help us to understand part of the thinking and worldview of some in the Corinthian community, but it does not explain how this thinking is related to the specific range of social issues that Paul addresses in this letter. In 1 Corinthians there is clearly a wider range of issues of a more practical nature. For instance, there are the problems of internal schism and social hierarchy in the Corinthian congregation (1 Cor 1:10—4:21). These demand that we interpret the text also with reference to the social and cultural environment of first-century Corinth, and not just those intersections between Judaism and the wider world of Hellenistic wisdom. Pearson's distinctions assist in understanding part of the issue in 1 Corinthians 15, but do not seem to be fruitful for the examination of the Corinthian schisms or the other ethical problems in 1 Corinthians. In this regard, a social and rhetorical hypothesis can be argued to be the most persuasive and satisfactory approach to re-construct the wider Corinthian situation of 1 Corinthians, and especially chapters 1–4.

Nevertheless, James A. Davis also asserts that *sophia* at Corinth in the time of Paul was closely linked to "some form of later sapiential

---

73. Pearson, PNEUMATIKOS, 20, 39.

Judaism."⁷⁴ Davis attempts to find analogies between the Corinthian Christians' concept of *sophia* and Jewish sapiential traditions in later Jewish wisdom literature or pre-Christian Jewish sapiential literature. These include the book of Sirach, the scrolls of Qumran, and the Wisdom of Solomon, and the Philonic literature. The most striking point in Sirach is that the content of wisdom is essentially and ultimately rooted in the Torah, or the law. Thus, in order to attain to a higher sapiential level one must study the law constantly. But one needs the divine spirit to help achieve success in the full comprehension of the Torah. In this consideration, as ben Sira believed, it is the scribes only who could acquire the potentiality of becoming the sage.⁷⁵

At Qumran, as in Sirach, it seems clear that wisdom finds its primary locus in the Torah in which the wisdom of God has been revealed, that there is a close relationship between the comprehension of the Torah and the obtainment of wisdom, and that the acquisition of wisdom is closely related to the assistance and activity of the Spirit of God. In the Qumran community it was believed that more understanding of the law could lead one to a "higher degree of wisdom" and a "higher spirituality."⁷⁶ In Philo, in a similar sense as in Sirach and in the Qumran community, the wisdom-law relation and the wisdom-Spirit link still appear. He says further that it is an attribute of the wise person that by the help or aid of God's Spirit he will purify his soul to be able to receive "the higher wisdom of allegory" and to experience "a mystical transport into the divine presence."⁷⁷ So we can see that in the later Jewish sapiential tradition in the Greco-Roman era it was a common understanding that in order to attain a higher level of wisdom, or a higher sapiential status, one needed to comprehend the law and continue to experience inspiration by the divine spirit.

Davis goes on to apply such an analysis to understanding *sophia* at Corinth as addressed in 1 Corinthians 1:18—3:20. He logically and carefully demonstrates a close relationship between the nature of the Corinthian wisdom and the Jewish sapiential tradition, arguing that through such a Jewish wisdom tradition some of the Corinthians have adversely affected the community. They identify themselves as the wise

74. Davis, *Wisdom*, 81.
75. Ibid., 26.
76. Ibid., 43–44.
77. Ibid., 61.

(1:18–19) and as having the highest sapiential status (2:6). In response to them, Paul replaces their wisdom rooted in the Jewish sapiential tradition by the christ centerd or christological wisdom of God, its core being the crucifixion of Christ (1:22–24). He also substitutes the "natural" person, obtaining wisdom by the study of the law (2:14), with the person receiving the Spirit of God who brings wisdom (2:12–13).[78] Again, Davis's work is a helpful explanation of the general background of *sophia* in Hellenistic Judaism, which is particularly related to the Torah, and how this might impact on Hellenistic Jewish Christians in Corinth.

Nonetheless, Davis's proposal can be criticized at the same point as Pearson's, in that he crucially fails to present the Pauline text in its wider historical and social context, and especially fails to give a satisfactory explanation of the situation of the Corinthian factions.[79] Critically, the following question may be asked: To what extent can an explanation of Hellenistic Jewish wisdom help us to understand the social and ethical tensions of a mixed community in a Roman colony in Greece? It is, rather, argued that for a clearer understanding of the problems of schisms (*schismata*) that Paul addresses in 1 Corinthians 1–4, a wider social and rhetorical perspective has to be taken into account. This is because the Corinthian schisms were inevitably linked to the wider social and rhetorical situation of first-century Greco-Roman Corinth, and especially the Corinthians' understanding of *sophia* and the influence of rhetorical conventions and patron-client relations.

Last, just as Pearson and Davis have argued, so R. A. Horsley confidently contends that the Corinthian perception of *sophia*, in opposition to Paul's gospel in 1 Corinthians 1–4, is apparently rooted in the Hellenistic Judaism represented by Philo of Alexandria and the Wisdom of Solomon.[80] According to Horsley, there are a few distinct similarities between 1 Corinthians 1–4 and the Hellenistic Jewish literature. At first glance, it is acknowledged that both in Hellenistic Jewish literature (Wis 8:8, 12–18) and the first four chapters of 1 Corinthians, the Greek word *sophia* plays a prominent and important role.[81] As Horsley observes, in the Hellenistic Jewish tradition *sophia* is the core and essential "agent of

---

78. Ibid., 143, 144, 147.

79. So argues William Baird, "Reviews: *Wisdom*," 149–51. More recently, Florian Voss agrees with Davis's Hellenistic Jewish sapiential hypothesis (see Voss, *Wort*).

80. Horsley, "Wisdom," 228; *Wisdom*, 27.

81. Ibid.; Towner, "Gnosis," 99.

religion" and, moreover, it is accepted as the sole "means and content of salvation."[82] In 1 Corinthians it is demonstrated that the Corinthians understood *sophia* as being proportional to spiritual status. In other words, it seems to them that some who possess *sophia* become the *pneumatikoi*, and achieve spiritual perfection, but others who do not obtain *sophia* become the *psychikoi* and are essentially different from the former (cf. 1 Cor 2:6—3:4; 15:44–45).[83]

Furthermore, from this *pneumatikos-psychikos* contrast Horsley attempts to find analogies between the language of 1 Corinthians 1–4 and that of Philo. He states that even though in Philo's writings there is no actual use of the *pneumatikos-psychikos* language, Philo employs the analogous terminology of "*teleios-nēpios*" ("perfect"-"child") which is closely paralleled to the *pneumatikos-psychikos* contrast and the distinction between "solid food" and "milk" in 1 Corinthians (3:2; 2:6—3:4; 15:44–45).[84] In Philo the *teleios-nēpios* contrast has the connotation of different levels of "religious endowment" or "soteriological achievement," thereby "perfection" (*teleios*), just as the descriptor *pneumatikoi* (1 Cor 2:13) should be seen as the spiritual perfection that is attained through the most intimate relationship with *sophia*.[85]

Finally, and more helpfully, Horsley suggests that in 1 Corinthians 1–4, and in this Hellenistic Jewish culture, eloquent (or persuasive) speech (*logoi sophias*) is very important.

> The close association of eloquent "speech" with wisdom is most strikingly paralleled in the Hellenistic Jewish wisdom-devotion ... Hellenistic Jews readily fused the importance of eloquence in Hellenistic public discourse and philosophy with the high evaluation of speech in the Jewish wisdom tradition (e.g., Prov 1:2–7, Sir 6:5; 18:28–29; 38:33; 39:1–6). Most striking in connection with chapters 1–2 is Wis 8:8, 12, 18, where turns of speech and skill in public discourse are important benefits of a personal relationship with *sophia*. Philo elaborates the connection between eloquence and a close relationship with *sophia* in a number of images paralleled later in 1 Corinthians.[86]

---

82. Horsley, "Wisdom," 228. In Philo's treatises the equivalent *logos* is preferred, but has no difference in function to *sophia* in the Wisdom of Solomon (Horsley, "Wisdom," 228; "Consciousness," 575).

83. Horsley, "Consciousness," 575; "Pneumatikos," 280.

84. Horsley, "Pneumatikos," 280–81.

85. Ibid.

86. Horsley, *Corinthians*, 47.

Philo valued highly eloquent speech as part of God's gifts and as necessary for spiritual perfection, and he emphasized its important role in the religious life of the wise and its proper use in communication (*Mig* 70–80). For him it is an important means for the soul to express his or her intimate relationship with *sophia*.[87] In the Corinthian language addressed in 1 Corinthians 1–4, as Horsley says, and in accordance with the Philonic idea that the Corinthians considered eloquent speech as part of "the key gifts of wisdom" granted on the wise (*sophos*), it is not surprising that they saw these gifts as an integral manifestation of the perfect and highest spiritual status (cf. 1:17, 26; 2:4–5).[88] This interest in eloquent speech foreshadows the later developments that have occurred in social-rhetorical analysis that is even more helpful than the religio-historical analysis of Hellenistic Jewish wisdom for interpreting 1 Corinthians.

Consequently, Horsley argues that because of the Corinthians' self-understanding of spiritual perfection, Paul sharply rejects *sophia* as the soteriological means (1:21–24). Instead, he strongly argues that the crucified Christ (1:23) is the foundation of salvation (1:18) and also the power of God and the wisdom of God (1:24). He rejects *sophia* as persuasive speech (*logoi sophias*) (2:1–5) and, instead, he presents "the demonstration of the Sprit and of power" (2:4).[89] Based on Horsley's argumentation it seems that there are analogies between the language of Hellenistic Jewish wisdom traditions and that of the Corinthian religiosity addressed in 1 Corinthians 1–4. Both consider *sophia* as the most essential factor to maintain their religious and spiritual identity. Horsley also pays more attention than Pearson and Davis to the examination of the wider Corinthian situation in terms of its social and cultural environment or milieu.

In his more recent works, Horsley shows even more interest in studying the social and cultural situation of first-century Corinth. Particularly, he gives much attention to the study of the Roman imperial order and such aspects as the imperial cult, patronage, and rhetoric

---

87. Horsley, "Wisdom," 226–27, 229, 236.

88. Ibid., 228, 235–36.

89. Ibid., 237. Furthermore, Horsley attempts to find the "Hellenistic Jewish background of the Corinthian polemical situation" in chapters 8–10, for instance, regarding the matter of eating of idol-meats (for details see Horsley, "Consciousness," 574–89; "Gnosis," 32–51).

which were the essential elements of Greco-Roman culture in the days of Paul. Furthermore, Horsley states significantly that:

> First Corinthians, which features so many parallels to public rhetoric, should thus be read in the context of the functions of public rhetoric in the Roman imperial order... Paul's own arguments display a composite rhetoric. He used the standard forms and devices of Greco-Roman rhetoric.[90]

Thus, Horsley indicates that there is clear evidence of composite rhetorical usage in the language of Paul in 1 Corinthians. This is consistent with the argument that in the Corinthian Christian community there were also influences of rhetorical patterns and conventions which deeply affected the Corinthian behavior. Moreover, Horsley remarks that rhetorical criticism can give an adequate explanation of the Corinthians' lives in relation to the dominant imperial order.[91] It seems that Horsley has moved from his earlier position to see that rhetorical criticism provides a more appropriate method to explain the Corinthian situation of 1 Corinthians than simply the philosophical or religio-historical category of *sophia* itself.

It appears, however, that the religio-theological proposals of Pearson, Davis, and Horsley give a persuasive and logical explanation of the Hellenistic Jewish background to *sophia* at Corinth as addressed in 1 Corinthians 1–4. These hypotheses are helpful for explaining some aspects of the causes of serious tensions within the Corinthian factions (e.g., 1:10–12; 3:4, 22)—insofar as Jews are involved—and as background to the resurrection debate (1 Cor 15). Furthermore, the more recent developments in Horsley's method and arguments are valued more highly.

Nevertheless, this Hellenistic Jewish sapiential hypothesis has recently faced sharp criticism from S. J. Chester who argues that this proposal has a few significant weaknesses. Chester's criticism is summarized as follows. First, as noted already, the specific *pneumatikos-psychikos* terminology which is considered important by Pearson and Horsley in their arguments, is found in the Pauline language of 1 Corinthians but is used nowhere in Philo's writings. Second, this hypothesis "rests upon an extremely narrow exegetical base," because its proponents attempt to interpret 1 Corinthians as a whole in the light of "a Philonic ontological

---

90. Horsley, "Empire," 82; see "Introduction," 17–19.
91. Horsley, "Empire," 101.

distinction concerning the origins of two different kinds of humanity."[92] As argued earlier, this kind of interpretation may be more appropriate for interpreting 1 Corinthians 15:44–54 than the rest of the letter of 1 Corinthians. Finally, Chester challenges Pearson and Horsley when they argue that Apollos, as an Alexandrian Jew and an advocate of Philo's view, introduced to the Corinthian Christian community his philosophical thoughts, especially his ontological perspectives on humanity. Chester casts doubt on such an argument with his question as to how this fits the image of Apollos as "an enthusiastic advocate concerning the things of the Spirit with strong opinions to impart," though "Apollos knew only the baptism of John" (Acts 18:24–26).[93]

Moreover, it would be critically observed that this general Hellenistic Jewish sapiential hypothesis on its own fails to take into account the influence of the Greco-Roman social system and conventions on the Christian community at Corinth. The former must have had a profound impact on the latter, so that the rhetorical culture and the patronage system penetrated deeply into the life of the Corinthian Christians and became one of the direct causes of the tense relations between Paul and his Corinthian opponents.[94] In order to comprehend this background to the Corinthian situation and the wisdom issues addressed in 1 Corinthians, a rhetorical and social analysis is a necessary corrective to those explanations which examine *sophia* using religio-historical and philosophical categories.

THE PETRINE PARTY

In the scholarly debate over the identity of the Pauline opposition and the nature of *sophia* in 1 Corinthians, the hypothesis of Petrine opposition has been advocated by scholars such as G. Lüdemann, W. Wuellner, W. Carr, Y. M. Gillihan and M. D. Goulder. This proposal was initially postulated by J. E. C. Schmidt and then developed by F. C. Baur one and a half centuries ago. After a careful evaluation of the arguments representative of these scholars, the major criticisms of this position will be outlined.

First, Gerd Lüdemann claims in a recent development re-working Baur's proposal, that in 1 Corinthians 1–4, and more certainly chapters

---

92. Chester, *Conversion*, 224–25.
93. Ibid., 225.
94. So also Chow, *Patronage*, 38–166.

9 and 15, the Pauline opposition was the party of Cephas. He argues that in such references as 1:12; 3:4, 6; 4:6 the party slogans indicate that the advocates of "anti-Paulinism" were a group who expressed their solidarity with Cephas by claiming that "I belong to Cephas" (1 Cor 1: 12).[95]

On the other hand, argues Lüdemann, the slogan that "I belong to Apollos" (1:12; 3:4) does not reflect any explicit polemic against Paul for the following reasons. The groups who described themselves as belonging both to Apollos and Paul identified themselves with Paul as the founder of the Corinthian Christian community. In 3:6 and 4:6 Paul describes his close relation to Apollos. Here he speaks of Apollos and himself in a positive manner since Apollos is his co-worker in building the Christian community (cf. 3:16–17), so it is doubtful that the followers of Apollos attacked Paul.

On the other hand, in 3:10–17, Paul indirectly polemicizes against the Cephas party, and he explicitly mentions the name of Cephas. Paul speaks of a definite person in verses 10–17 in parallel with the proceeding context (vv. 6–9), in all probability referring to Cephas. This is certainly evident in the immediate context (vv. 18–23). In verses 22–23 in particular, Paul once again tackles the issue of the factions in the Corinthian congregation. There, alongside Apollos and himself he speaks of Cephas. This is because he intends to polemicize against the party of Cephas which formed in Corinth after Paul's departure.

Therefore, Lüdemann's argument can be summarized as the view that in the Corinthian church there was a Cephas party which formed after his departure and that sharply criticized Paul.[96] This proposal, however, has to be criticized at two significant points. On the matter of the existence of a Cephas party at Corinth, many scholars throw doubt on the claim that Cephas was present at Corinth in the days of Paul. Thus, they assert that Cephas's party was not an actual entity. Rather they maintain that the slogan "I belong to Cephas" (1 Cor 1:12) was used by Paul merely to reflect the special esteem which some Jewish Christians exhibited to Cephas as a respected Christian leader at the time (see below).

The other significant point is that Lüdemann himself concludes that the first four chapters of 1 Corinthians provide "the weakest indications" of an "anti-Paulinism" among the Cephas party.[97] It is inevitable that he

95. Lüdemann, *Oppositio*, 75–76.
96. Ibid., 75–78.
97. Ibid., 78.

should say so, because in these chapters it is not clear that Paul describes the divisions in the Corinthian church that existed between the Pauline party and the Cephas party. He no longer speaks of the Cephas party as such after 1:12; though in 3:22 he mentions once the name of Cephas along with Paul and Apollos, as he warns the Corinthians not to boast. On the other hand, Paul does explicitly speak of the party of Apollos who opposed and criticized him. This idea is attested in such verses as 3:4–5 and 4:6. Thereby, Paul possibly indicates that there were serious tensions between the followers of Apollos and those of himself, although Paul also regarded Apollos and himself as God's fellow co-workers (3:9). As such then, as Lüdemann concedes, there is no clear indication of anti-Paulinism by the Cephas party in 1 Corinthians 1–4. In addition, in his proposal Lüdemann does not provide an adequate explanation of the fundamental cause of the schism in the Corinthian church as described in 1 Corinthians 1–4, which is closely related to the issue of *sophia*. This is one of the weakest points in his hypothesis.

Michael D. Goulder is one of the major recent advocates for the Petrine hypothesis. Goulder comes to the strong and bold conclusion, in employing Baur's and Schmidt's language, that the opponents at Corinth were definitely the Petrine (or Cephas) party.[98] In other words, they were Jewish Christians, but a "less radical group" than the Judaizers in Galatia because they did not try to "impose the law on Pauline converts and have them circumcised."[99] He states correctly that for a proper interpretation of 1 Corinthians 1–4, it is a significant matter to disclose the nature of *sophia* at Corinth against that which Paul argues because there is a close relation between the issue of wisdom traditions and the problem of schisms (*schismata*) that existed in the Corinthian church as addressed in 1 Corinthians 1:12–17, 3:1–17 and 3:22–23.

In the Corinthian congregation, Goulder asserts, rather than three (3:22) or four groups (1:12), there were only two. One group was composed of the converts of Paul and Apollos, the other comprised the followers of Cephas who identified as *christou* ("of Christ"). Goulder bases this hypothesis on his two predecessors, Schmidt and Baur.[100] Baur, especially, says that "there is no difference between the party of Peter and that

---

98. Peter (Petrine) and Cephas are used interchangeably here in identifying the same person (see Allison, "Cephas," 489–95).

99. Goulder, "*Sophia*," 519; *Competing*, 1, 26, 47; Baur, "Corinthians," 258–307.

100. Goulder, "*Sophia*," 516; *Competing*, 5–15.

of Christ, just as those of Paul and of Apollos did not essentially differ."[101] Goulder explains that the claim of the Petrine party regarding oneness with Christ is based on them understanding themselves as having the same authority as Peter their leader who was chosen by "the historical Christ," so they might also say "I belong to Christ" (1:12).[102] He goes on to argue that rather than competitors, Paul and Apollos were colleagues. This is clearly attested in Paul's own language (3:5–9) where the phrases "I planted" and "Apollos watered" (v. 6) denote a companionship between Paul and Apollos in "working on God's field, God's building" (v. 9) which is the Corinthian church.[103] Thus, in this church the opposition must be between the people of Paul and Apollos together and the Cephas party. This is explicitly stated when Baur concludes that "the opponents of the apostle Paul belonged to one class with the adherents of the party of Peter."[104]

It is proposed by Goulder that this opposition or *schisma* (1:10) between the two parties is primarily rooted in the issue of apostolic authority. The Cephas party did not admit, in the eyes of Goulder, that Paul and Apollos possessed the full and genuine apostleship authorized from the Jerusalem church because their teaching was so different from the gospel of Peter. Nor did they speak "words of wisdom."[105]

Furthermore, in Goulder's discussion it is important to note that *sophia* means "the Torah (or *nomos*, the law)" which, "written in the Pentateuch and expounded by the sages," was "the word of God and the essential basis of salvation," while the "word (*logos*)" refers to "sayings," or "rulings" by "Jewish sage(s)."[106] The combined words *logoi sophias* (words of wisdom) make the "OT prescriptions into a practical way of life."[107] So it follows for Goulder that the *logoi sophias* have to do with a message of salvation for Jewish Christians in Corinth.

101. Baur, "Corinthians," 267.
102. Goulder, *Competing*, 16.
103. Ibid., 21.
104. Baur, "Corinthians," 269.
105. Goulder, *Competing*, 23.

106. Ibid., 48, 89. "Where there were many Jews, as in Antioch, or Asia Minor, or Rome, Torah was naturally thought of as law; in other European cities like Corinth there were fewer Jews, and in discussion with Gentiles, as in the church, it was presented as *sophia*" (Goulder, "Sophia," 522).

107. Goulder, *Competing*, 74.

Goulder goes on to claim that such a meaning of *sophia* is drawn into 1 Corinthians 1–3. Especially, in 1:17—2:16 it appears that "the word of the cross" (1:18) in the Pauline gospel fundamentally contrasts with *logoi sophias* among the Petrine Christian leaders (1:17–18). Paul rejected *logoi sophias* and instead proclaimed Christ as the power of God and the wisdom of God (1:24), while "they spoke of the Torah as wisdom and of the specific rulings of the sages as words of wisdom."[108] In other words, Paul proclaimed "the cross of Christ" as the only way to obtain salvation, but the party of Peter claimed the "halakah" as the "means to salvation."[109] It is clear, then, that for Goulder there was opposition between the Petrine party (or Jewish Christians) in claiming the Torah as wisdom and the party of Paul and Apollos in proclaiming Christ as the wisdom of God.

Other scholars such as Wilhelm Wuellner and Wesley Carr also take this line. In a similar sense, they both concur that there is exhibited a Jewish tendency in the Corinthian *schismata* which Paul records in 1 Corinthians 1–4. Wuellner in particular contends that the troubles or bickerings at Corinth were caused and inspired by "halakic and haggadic discussions" which were currently prevalent in the Jewish Christian community at Corinth as elsewhere throughout the Diaspora.[110]

Yonder M. Gillihan asserts convincingly that the Christian gatherings at Corinth were overwhelmingly influenced by Jewish concerns and laws consistent with the Jewish community, although he is primarily interested in illicit marriage (7:12–16). This is also supported by references to circumcision in 7:18 and food purity in 8:1–6 because there were a number of prominent Jewish members becoming converted to Paul's gospel, such as Crispus and Sosthenes who were the Corinthian synagogue leaders (1:1, 14; the same as mentioned in Acts 18:8–17). Paul, as a Jew and having known "Jewish law thoroughly, would have been able

---

108. Ibid., 89.

109. Ibid., 74; Goulder, "*Sophia*," 521, 523.

110. Paul employed "Jewish literary genres" in 1 Corinthians, like "haggadic synagogue sermons which Paul had heard, hymnic traditions or wisdom psalms, popular proverbial wisdom, (and) rabbinic wisdom teaching" (Wuellner, "Haggadic," 203; Carr, "Rules," 30–31). Carr himself admits that this hypothesis has a weak point in that there is not evidence enough to prove that the Corinthian Christians were overwhelmingly dominated by "Jewish concerns" (Carr, "Rulers," 31). However, another scholar (Yonder M. Gillihan) strongly argues for an overwhelming Jewish influence on the Christian community at Corinth (see below).

to advise concerned believers about halakic issues and to expect at least some of them to understand halakic argumentation when he made it."¹¹¹ It is likely, therefore, according to Y. M. Gillihan, that Paul contrasts his gospel message with the Jewish traditional desire for miracles (and, of course, the Greek concern for wisdom) (1:22), stressing that the cross on which Christ died, as the Power of God and wisdom of God, is able to lead them to salvation (23–25).¹¹² It appears, however, that Gillihan's proposals pay more attention to a minority of Jewish members in the Corinthian church, who adhered to their own Jewish customs and legal responsibilities and demanded signs and miracles different to the Greeks who sought wisdom (1 Cor 1:22). Consequently, Gillihan does not examine the issue of the words *sophia* and *logos* in terms of the wider Greco-Roman rhetorical understandings and culture, and thereby misses the major thrust of Paul's concern about accommodation to the surrounding dominant culture. These two words are the most frequently occurring words in 1 Corinthians 1–4 which comprises a diversity of rhetorical elements (see further below).

As analyzed above, Goulder describes the issues of the Pauline opposition and of *sophia* at Corinth as addressed in 1 Corinthians 1–4 in terms of a speculative reconstruction involving connections with Palestinian Judaism. A tense atmosphere in the Corinthian congregation was fuelled by a dispute over apostleship between the Party of Paul and Apollos who possessed no "proper authorization from Jerusalem," and the Cephas party who was representatives of the Jerusalem church (cf. 1 Cor. 15:1–10; 2 Cor. 10–11).¹¹³ Goulder also argues that there was a close relationship between the Corinthian opponents belonging to the Petrine party and the Galatians as Judaizing Jews, because of their links with the apostle Peter (and possibly James and John) (Gal 2:1–10).¹¹⁴ So he maintains that *sophia* in 1 Corinthians 1–4 has to do with the Torah or the law as addressed in both Galatians and Romans.¹¹⁵

---

111. Gillihan, "Laws," 712–13, 713 n. 6.

112. Ibid., 713 n. 6. In addition, Peter Richardson recently provides an appropriate explanation of the relationship between the Jewish community and the Christian community at Corinth ("Judaism and Christianity," 42–66). Cf. P. W. Barnett, who insists on Paul's opponents as "Jews, Jerusalem Jews, Judaizing Jews" ("Opposition," 5).

113. Goulder, *Competing*, 23.

114. Ibid., 26, 47.

115. Ibid., 48–63.

Nevertheless, this proposal cannot avoid severe criticism at some points. As briefly stated earlier, there is a growing consensus in recent Pauline scholarship that it is difficult to know whether Peter had ever been present in Corinth,[116] and that a Peter (or Cephas) party might not have existed as a real party created by Peter in the Corinthian church.[117]

Furthermore, it does not make sense that Goulder claims that in the Christian community at Corinth there was something like a Judaizing movement, although it was less radical than the significant phenomenon in the Christian communities at Galatia and Rome. This, however, does not fit the problems of the Corinthian church as described in 1 Corinthians. There, Paul nowhere deals with Gentiles who claimed to live like Jews, while in Paul's language in Galatians and Romans the word Judaizing or Judaizers refers to Gentiles who adopted "a (characteristically) Jewish way of life,"[118] or lived like Jews, rather than Jewish Christians who forced Gentiles or Gentile Christians to Judaize or follow their Jewish tradition.[119] Furthermore, the issue central to Galatians and to some extent in Romans—namely circumcision—appears only in passing in 1 Corinthians (1 Cor 7:18–19).

Last, as examined above, Goulder employs a religio-theological approach to provide an explanation of the identity of the Pauline opposition and the background of wisdom traditions at Corinth. However, such a method is not adequate to give a satisfactory description of the social and cultural situation of Corinth in the first-century Greco-Roman world. There, the Roman imperial order, and characteristics such as patronage, rhetoric, and imperial cults deeply influenced the civic life of the Corinthians in the days of Paul. Accordingly, it is impossible to speak of the identity of Paul's Corinthian opponents and the nature of their wisdom traditions which were closely related to the schism in the Corinthian congregation unless we reconstruct the Corinthian situation in its social

---

116. Fee, *Corinthians*, 55; Morris, *Corinthians*, 40. On the other hand, Margaret E. Thrall claims the possibility of Peter's visit to Corinth, concurring with C. K. Barrett (Thrall, "Initial Attraction," 72–73).

117. Witherington, *Conflict*, 130; similarly Hays, *Corinthians*, 22. Some critics against this view argue that rather than the party of Peter, Paul had a tense relationship with that of Apollos at Corinth (Pogoloff, *Logos*, 173–96; Witherington, *Conflict*, 130–31).

118. Dunn, *Galatians*, 129.

119. Ibid., 9 n. 2. Cf. Francis Watson describes Paul's opponents in Galatia as "agitators" rather than "Judaizers" because "to judaize is to convert to Judaism oneself, rather than to encourage others to do so" (*Judaism*, 112 n. 35).

and cultural environment. It would, thus, be better to reconstruct the situation of 1 Corinthians in terms of a rhetorical and social analysis.

THE MISUSE OF RHETORICAL CONVENTIONS

The phrase "rhetorical conventions" here refers to the influence of the oral expressions of wisdom on the social and secular systems of Corinth, which caused the disturbances within the Christian community. At the time of Paul's writing of 1 Corinthians, Greco-Roman rhetorical conventions and patron-client networks were foundational in the wider civic community at Corinth. Many scholars thus view rhetorical patterns and patron-client relations as producing the tensions and movements opposing the purposes which Paul intended for the church at Corinth. Arguments of these scholars shall be briefly investigated below.

The Corinthian *ekklēsia* at Corinth clearly experienced schism (*schismata* in 1 Cor 1:10) and bickering (*eris* in 1 Cor 1:11; 3:3; 2 Cor 12:20; *zēlos* in 1 Cor 3:3; 2 Cor 12:20) caused by issues concerning *sophia*. For a proper comprehension of the background of such problems, a rhetorical and social approach is proposed as the most appropriate method. This is because the factions at Corinth (e.g., 1 Cor 1:12) can best be explained and understood as resulting from the inappropriate use of Greco-Roman rhetorical conventions and patron-client relations.[120] These were two of the most significant elements in first-century Greco-Roman culture (see further below). Of course, Paul himself used rhetorical conventions in order to persuade and impress his Corinthian audience (e.g., 1 Cor 1–4).[121] So it is essential that prime consideration is given to a rhetorical and social perspective when 1 Corinthians 1–4 is read. Furthermore, this approach holds the promise of providing an accurate description of the identity of Paul's Corinthian opponents and the underlying Corinthian understandings of *sophia*.

This approach is also in accordance with a growing consensus in recent Pauline scholarship on 1 Corinthians. A growing number of Pauline scholars have used this social-rhetorical method to analyze the problems at Corinth as addressed in 1 Corinthians 1–4 in particular; although,

---

120. See Grindheim, "Wisdom for Perfect," 689. For introductions to Greco-Roman rhetoric see Fiorenza, "Rhetorical Situation," 386–403; Wire, *Women*; Walton, "Criticism," 4–9; Eriksson, *Traditions*; Peterson, *Eloquence*; and Olbricht and Sumney, *Pathos*.

121. Witherington, *Conflict*, 45.

technically speaking, some scholars prefer a purely social method,[122] whereas others concentrate on a rhetorical approach.[123] Among these scholars, Bruce W. Winter and Stephen M. Pogoloff will be examined more carefully as representatives of this position. Their hypotheses also help dialogue between the value of wisdom (*sophia*) in the rhetorical situation of first-century Corinth and that of wisdom (*jeehye* or *sulgi*) in a Korean Confucian context of our time (see below). Prior to this examination, such scholars as Stephen J. Chester, Gerd Theissen, Peter Marshall, David G. Horrell and Margaret M. Mitchell are briefly reviewed.

Many scholars understand Paul's opponents and the division at Corinth using sociological methodology, where social stratification is a major concern. For example, Stephen J. Chester states that an inner social stratification was a significant factor in the life of the Corinthian Christian community.[124] In many ways such scholars base their arguments on Gerd Theissen's contention that the Corinthian Christian community was composed of a few powerful upper status members and a majority of lower status members.[125] Peter Marshall argues that the Corinthian opponents of Paul were "hybrists" who belonged to the upper classes in the social pyramid of Corinth in Paul's day.[126]

John K. Chow understands the identity of the opponents at Corinth primarily in terms of the patronal linkages in the first-century Greco-Roman world. He argues that Paul's opponents at Corinth were the rich and powerful patrons in the Christian community. They "who kept their contact with pagans, namely the immoral man, the litigants and the idolaters, may have been people who by their social status within Corinth were able to exercise influence" in the Corinthian church."[127]

122. See Theissen, "Social Structure," 65–84; Meeks, *Urban*; Engberg-Pedersen, "Gospel," 557–84; Chow, *Patronage*; Barclay, " Thessalonica," 57–73; Clarke, *Secular*; Mitchell, "Rich," 562–86; Martin, *Body*; Horrell, *Ethos*; Tomlin, "Christians and Epicureans," 51–72; Hays, *Corinthians*; de Vos, *Church*; "Stepmothers, Concubines," 104–44; Sanders, "Paul," 67–83; and Meggitt, *Poverty*; Dutch, *Educated*.

123. See Munck, *Salvation*, chapter 5; Betz, "Rhetoric," 16–48; Marshall, *Enmity*; Welborn, "*Mōros*," 421–35; "Discord," 85–111; "Conciliatory," 320–46; Lim "Persuasive," 137–49; Pogoloff , *Logos*; Mitchell, *Reconciliation*; Litfin, *Paul's*; Witherington, *Conflict*; Lanci, *Temple*; Winter, "Paul," 28–38; *Welfare*; Thiselton, *Corinthians*; Grindheim, "Wisdom"; Smit, "Apollos"; Given, *True*.

124. Chester, *Conversion*, 222.

125. Theissen, *Social*, 69–119.

126. Marshall, *Enmity*, 214.

127. Chow, *Patronage*, 123, 130, 139.

David G. Horrell also argues that the leading people of the division opposing Paul at Corinth were among "the socially prominent members of the community" who were "the people who had cause to consider themselves wise in the world's eyes and who sought to maintain and further their social standing."[128]

Margaret M. Mitchell argues distinctively that "the wisdom of the world . . . in 1 Corinthians 1:18—4:21 refers to . . . the norms and values of human politics" rather than religious speculations. She understands the Christian community at Corinth as a political body (*ekklēsia*), where division was caused by ethnic diversity, such as one group of Greeks and the other of Jews (1:22-24). She argues that it was not "monetary wealth and propertied status" but an "ethnic diversity" that was the major factor causing Corinthian factions.[129] Mitchell's argument that there was a diversity of ethnic groups such as Greeks, Jews, and Romans in the Christian *ekklēsia* at Corinth is correct, as far as it goes, and this was certainly one of the factors which caused the divisions at Corinth. But there were also other factors which caused the factions, such as social hierarchies, rhetorical influences and patron-client bonds. Given these, Bruce W. Winter's argument is now carefully analyzed.

Bruce W. Winter investigates the nature of Corinthian *sophia* addressed in 1 Corinthians 1-4 in the light of "the sophist movement" in the first-century Greco-Roman world.[130] He asserts that the Pauline opponents at Corinth were sophists and their wisdom was rooted in sophistic rhetorical conventions. In order to defend this argumentation, Winter seeks to establish two major supporting theses.

In Winter's reconstruction, first, it is important to note that the Christian community at Corinth was profoundly influenced by the secular sophistic educational conventions such as the secular "disciple-teacher relationship" and "professional competitiveness among teachers."[131] At the time of Paul's Corinthian correspondence it was of the nature of the secular pupil-instructor relationship that students imitated not only their sophist's oratorical and rhetorical style and accent but also his style of walking and dressing with elegant attire. Elegance in appearance was

---

128. Horrell, *Ethos*, 131.

129. Mitchell, *Reconciliation*, 88-89, 94.

130. For a detailed explanation to the sophist movement in Alexandria and Corinth in the first century CE, see Winter, *Philo*, 17-140.

131. Winter, *After*, 31-32, 36.

an important factor for successful orators. Students were challenged and motivated to show extreme zeal (*zēlos*) for their own sophist teacher by "demonstrating their exclusive loyalty" to him and "promoting his professional attributes (and) educative prowess."[132] At the same time, they openly ridiculed and made sharp criticisms of the deficiencies of other teachers.[133] Furthermore, among the sophists in first-century Corinth there existed a spirit of rivalry and competitiveness; and they were full of quarrels and strife (*eris*) in order to attract and train a good number of disciples in their schools. This secured their public honor and guaranteed exceedingly high fees from their students.

Winter asserts that 1 Corinthians 1–4 indicates that the Corinthian Christians behaved in a thoroughly secular way (*kata anthrōpon peripatein*) (1 Cor 3:3) in imitating and following such sophistic fashions.[134] The *schismata* in the Christian community at Corinth reflected the influence of secular conventions in the Christian community which was overwhelmingly dominated by the secular conceptions of student-sophist relationships and a competitive spirit among sophists (1:10–12; 3:3–4). Just as the contemporary secular disciples treated the sophists, so the Corinthian Christians treated their teachers, Paul and Apollos—in a way that demonstrated their loyalty (which is closely related to *zēlos* and *eris* in 3:4) to one teacher. They also praised the rhetoric of their teacher, at the same time as they trenchantly criticized the other teacher due to his rhetorical deficiencies and weak appearance (1 Cor 2:1–5; 3:3–4; 4:6; 2 Cor 10:10).[135]

In contrast to this, Paul describes Apollos and himself in terms of a functional and comparative working for the body of Christ rather than in terms of social status. The Corinthian Christians had imported such social status distinctions into the Christian *ekklēsia* from their contemporary secular Corinthian context. Instead, Paul puts a strong emphasis on exclusively belonging to Christ (3:21–23) rather than zealous loyalty to individual instructors (1:12; 3:3–4). Rather than puffing up the social

---

132. Ibid., 39.

133. Ibid., 39–40.

134. Winter, *Philo*, 173; *After*, 40. This Greek phrase is interpreted as "walking in a secular way." The concept of walking metaphorically referred to "living or acting." The phrase *kata anthrōpon* describes "the fact that they were operating in the same way as the rest of Corinthian society" (Winter, *After*, 40)

135. Ibid., 41.

elite and the promotion of professional achievement, Paul insists on different gifts and careful stewardship in building up the body of Christ. He describes Apollos and himself as laboring workers, despised in a Corinthian society influenced by Greco-Roman rhetoric, and expresses this in terms of agricultural language, i.e., planting and watering. So he declares them to be "the servants of Christ and stewards of the mysteries of God" (4:1). As seen above in 1 Corinthians 1–4, the Pauline language is definitely anti-sophistic and his ministry was conducted in absolute opposition to the sophistic conventions in which the Corinthian ideas of *sophia* were grounded.

Second, in Winter's argumentation, 1 Corinthians 2:1–5 and 1 Corinthians 9 (which will not be tackled fully here) are significant evidence of the anti-sophist nature of Paul's writings.[136] In 2:1–5 Paul attempts to differentiate his "*modus operandi*" of coming to Corinth and establishing a Christian *ekklēsia* from the typical visit to a city by a sophist who has tried to establish a reputation as a speaker by using rhetorical conventions and oratorical speech or wisdom (2:1). Paul distinguishes his oratory (*logos*) and message (*kērygma*) from the sophist's eloquent speech which takes "the form of the persuasiveness of rhetoric," that is, "the art of persuasion" (2:4a).[137] Paul stresses that his proclamation of the crucified Christ was undertaken in the "demonstration (*apodeixis*) of the Spirit and of Power" (2:4b).[138]

Winter says that 2:3 describes the main reason why Paul was severely attacked by his "opponents" and failed to be a persuasive orator—because in his proclamation he did not employ the rhetorical techniques, *ethos* and *pathos*, which an effective persuader usually used in his oratory. So it is natural that the Corinthian audience regarded Paul as inferior to others. Paul's presence as a persuasive orator did not match "the fine figure of the orator" which was recommended in "rhetorical handbooks."[139] That is why Paul could not help confessing (perhaps ironically overstating!) that due to his inferior figure compared with other sophists he was in the midst of them in "weakness (*en astheneia*), fear (*en phobō*), and much trembling (*en tromo pollō*)"(2:3).

---

136. Winter, *Philo*, 143, 148.

137. Ibid., 143, 148, 158.

138. The Greek word *apodeixis* means "a clear proof, a method of proving what is not certain by means of what is certain," ibid., 149.

139. Ibid., 158–59.

Winter further says:

> The whole purpose of Paul's renunciation of the conventions (*ethos*, *pathos*, and *apodeixis*) surrounding the coming of an orator was designed to ensure that the Corinthians' "proof" (*pistis*) or "faith" . . . might not rest in the wisdom of men but in the power of God (2:5).[140]

Paul, by employing "a method of preaching" rather than following a sophistic oratorical fashion, intended to remind the Corinthians of having faith not in human *sophia* but in the power of God and the crucified Christ (1:24; 2:5).[141] Paul's policy of an "anti-*ethos*, anti-*pathos*, and anti-*apodeixis* argument" elucidates his anti-sophistic stance and at the same time challenges the sophistic orientation of *sophia* at Corinth.[142] By means of such a policy, he clearly differentiated his preaching of the crucified Christ from the sophists' oratory with its rhetorical elements. He intentionally rejected the sophistic strategy of taking a persuasive form of *sophia* which the Corinthians favored and regarded as superior to Paul's preaching. Instead, Paul proclaimed Jesus Christ in the "demonstration of the Spirit and of power" (2:1, 4), which was opposite to the Corinthians' expectation.

It appears, therefore, that Winter's reconstruction of 1 Corinthians 1–4 in the light of the sophist movement of the first century Greco-Roman world is essential for a proper understanding of the Pauline opposition at Corinth and the nature of Corinthian wisdom. As examined earlier, there are clear similarities between the sophistic fashions and the Corinthian behavior as indicated in 1 Corinthians 1–4, such as the student-teacher relationships and similarly patron-client relations, a spirit of competitiveness and rivalry, the preference for rhetorical abilities, and the high value given to *sophia*. Such ideas have to be kept in mind and to be considered important as 1 Corinthians 1–4 is interpreted.

Furthermore, in terms of intercultural dialogue and cross-cultural hermeneutics, Winter's hypothesis challenges and helps make a bridging point between the cultural context of the Corinthian Christians in the first-century Greco-Roman era and that of Korean Christians in our time. A similarity in these two cultures is that just as the sophistic fashions penetrated deeply into the life of the Christian community at

---

140. Winter, "Sophists," 30.
141. Winter, *Philo*, 159.
142. Ibid.

Corinth in first-century Greco-Roman culture, so Confucianism has had a profound influence upon the life of Korean Christians in twenty-first century Korean-Confucian culture (see below).

Stephen M. Pogoloff, similarly to Winter, reconstructs the Corinthian situation of 1 Corinthians 1–4 in the light of its rhetorical setting. So he employs rhetorical criticism as the most convincing method to give more accurate information about the identity of Paul's Corinthian opponents and the nature of their wisdom as indicated in 1 Corinthians 1–4.[143] He argues that the entire Greco-Roman culture and society to which the Corinthian situation of Paul's time belonged was profoundly influenced by first-century Greco-Roman rhetorical conventions. Early Christian communities were not able to avoid such influences, so there is no doubt that this influence penetrated the life of the Christian *ekklēsia* in first-century Corinth. In this regard, therefore, the situation to which Paul responded in 1 Corinthians 1–4 should be studied carefully in the light of such rhetorical conventions.[144]

Pogoloff then turns to the issues of *schismata* ("divisions" [NIV 1:10]) and *sophia logou* ("eloquent speech" [RSV 1:17; 2:4]) that Paul refers to. He also argues that the divisions in the Corinthian Christian *ekklēsia* were most likely related to the problem of *sophia logou* or rhetoric and social status (1:26–28; cf. 11:18–22). At first glance, the words *sophia logou* simply mean "clever or skilled or educated or rhetorically sophisticated speech."[145] But in the first-century Greco-Roman world they frequently meant more than such. They had the connotation of "a whole world of social status related to speech," in which the word *sophia* in particular described implicitly the "educated or cultural characteristics of persons of high social standings."[146] On this basis, Pogoloff gives a further explanation:

> In the Greco-Roman milieu of Corinth, one who was described as speaking *en sophia logou* would have been understood to be an educated, cultured individual who could speak to a group about a subject in a manner which persuaded them by evidence and argument presented in a suitable style . . . such speech communicated not just the subject matter, but also explicitly or implicitly

143. For a detail explanation of rhetorical criticism, see Pogoloff, *Logos*, 77–80.
144. Ibid., 1–3, 8, 44, 52, 84.
145. Ibid., 110.
146. Ibid., 113.

> communicated the character and authority (*ethos*) of the speaker. This *ethos* was ... intimately tied to issues of social status, boasting, and rivalries ... Although Paul shows no sign of finding primary or secondary education a source of problems, there are very clear indications that he had thrown himself into a total confrontation with those who espoused the reigning values of higher education.[147]

From this it is clear that by the time he wrote 1 Corinthians, Paul had serious tensions with those members (the *teleios* in 2:6) in the Christian community who had boasted of themselves as belonging to a better *sophos* possessing greater *sophia* (2:6) and speaking *en sophia logou* (1:17; *en sophias logois* in 2:4). He, moreover, was unintentionally and unconsciously driven into the spirit of contest and competition in *sophoi logoi*, which was a part of classic rhetoric and of the Hellenistic culture in which the Corinthians lived. Such competition eventually led to bitter divisions, for instance, between one philosopher and another, or one rhetor and another.

The same tendency had apparently invaded the Corinthian Christian *ekklēsia* which Paul founded. It is likely, therefore, that the Corinthians had considered whether Paul was among those "persuasive speakers" and whether to regard him as a "persuasive rhetor, i.e., as *sophos*," just as in other secular communities.[148] Pogoloff goes on to claim that in the Christian community at Corinth there were only two groups, although there are four names given as the leaders of each party, as mentioned in 1 Corinthians 1:12. This is because:

> Paul and Apollos garner far more attention than the other two (3:4–9, 22; 4:6; cf. 16:12). Those "of Apollos" and those "of Paul" are singled out as the target of Paul's rhetoric (4:6). For these reasons, the slogans "I am of Paul" and "I am of Apollos" dominate the exigence. The other two slogans may be read as no more than hyperbole.[149]

From this statement it is assumed that one group comprised people who still accepted Paul as an adequate rhetor, whereas the other included those who preferred Apollos as a *sophos*.[150] "Apollos's Alexandrian

---

147. Ibid., 54.
148. Ibid., 173–78.
149. Ibid., 178.
150. Ibid.

origin" should have appealed to the Corinthians because Alexandria was well known for its rhetorical education and "any educated Alexandrian" like Philo was well disciplined and trained in rhetoric and in skilful and persuasive speech.[151]

Pogoloff, however, differentiates Paul's rhetoric from Apollos's in a distinctive way. The former was appealing more to the educated and sophisticated people, while the latter to the less educated and cultured. This affirms that there were divisions of social status in the Christian community. These levels were not about "lines of class or income" but of "education and culture."[152]

Furthermore, Pogoloff asserts that the relationship of Paul with the higher status and more educated members in the Corinthian Christian *ekklēsia* is attested in his discussion of baptism (1:14–16) and patronal relations. He baptized Crispus, Gaius, and the household of Stephanus. These were patrons of the Christian *ekklēsia* at Corinth, as well as Phoebe (called *prostatis* in Rom 16:1–2). Therefore, Pogoloff concludes that such members belonging to the Pauline group were of higher status than those of the Apollos group. The latter might be strong in number, but the former were the strongest in terms of status in the community.[153] Yet, according to Pogoloff, although Paul's rhetorical ability appealed to the higher status and more educated, that is, "the strong," he took the position of "the weak" (1 Cor 8; 10:23–30) in order to parody those followers of Apollos, his opponents, who highly valued *sophia* as representing education and high social status from the perspective of first-century Greco-Roman rhetoric.[154]

In a reverse way, therefore, Pogoloff argues that in order to challenge the Corinthians to change their values and attitudes which were overwhelmingly influenced by the secular rhetorical conventions and social standards, Paul employed the narrative of the crucified Christ which had

---

151. Ibid., 180–87.

152. Ibid., 189.

153. This is a significant weakness in Pogoloff's argument. Paul clearly identifies himself with the Corinthian Christians who were poorer and of lower social-status. This is explicitly described in 1 Cor 4:10–13. It should be also understood that Paul names those three baptized members in 1 Corinthians 1:14–16, as representatives of each ethnic group: the Greeks, the Jews, and the Romans rather than as the highest social-status members in his faction of the Corinthian congregation (see further below).

154. Ibid., 190–93.

been preached and had become the foundation of the Christian *ekklēsia*. He reminded them of the crucified Christ, the power of God and the wisdom of God (e.g., 1 Cor 1:18–25).

Pogoloff consistently and satisfactorily explains the background of the divisions and the Corinthian wisdom addressed in 1 Corinthians 1–4 in terms of first-century Greco-Roman rhetorical traditions. His unique points are as follows: first, Pogoloff is interested in the Corinthians' social values and behavior as influenced by Greco-Roman rhetorical conventions rather than as the cause of the divisions in themselves. Second, in the light of the rhetorical situation of 1 Corinthians 1–4, he has a unique understanding of *sophia* as representing those of socially high status and education, and further relates such an understanding to the emergence of the divisions in the Corinthian Christian community, where the followers of Apollos opposed Paul's rhetorical ability. What is unique is that in the Corinthian congregation, according to Pogoloff, Paul's rhetorical ability, in fact, appealed to the higher status and more educated people than those who preferred Apollos. These points ought to be born in mind as the situation of 1 Corinthians 1–4 is reconstructed in the light of its rhetorical situation. Moreover, in terms of a cross-disciplinary approach, Pogoloff's proposal has to be considered important for an attempt to dialogue between the rhetorical situation of first-century Corinth and the contemporary Korean-Confucian Christian context of our time because in these two contexts the word "wisdom,ᆞ (*sophia* in the former and *jeehye* or *sulgi* in the latter) signifies social standing and education (see further below).

As observed above, Winter and Pogoloff's hypotheses are the most persuasive and helpful for one to reconstruct the situation of 1 Corinthian 1–4, especially in terms of its rhetorical situation. Both convincingly argue that Paul's opponents at Corinth were some of the Corinthian Christians who were deeply influenced by Greco-Roman rhetorical conventions seen as a fundamental element of first century Greco-Roman culture. These Corinthians highly valued wisdom and eloquent speech. They esteemed such rhetorical influences even more than the message of the gospel Paul preached to them. And they also continued to practice uncritically in the Christian community such customs as patron-client systems and a spirit of competitiveness and rivalry. Furthermore, the majority preferred Apollos's rhetorical ability, rather than Paul's, because of his Alexandrian origin. That is why in the Corinthian congregation there were tense relations between the people of Paul and those of Apollos. Later on, these developed into factions among the Christians.

Thus far, a wide range of recent Pauline scholars' proposals about the identification of the Pauline opposition at Corinth and the reconstruction of the nature of its *sophia* has been investigated. Of those proposals, rhetorical and social approaches appear to be the most appropriate method for an adequate description of the background of Corinthian wisdom traditions as addressed in 1 Corinthians 1–4. There are two apparent reasons. One is because the shaping of wisdom traditions at Corinth occurred in intimate relation to first-century Greco-Roman culture, including the prominence of rhetoric and patronage. So it was that in many areas of life such as social relations, education, thinking systems, moral behavior, and social systems, the Corinthian Christians were deeply permeated by these aspects of Greco-Roman culture.

The other reason for a rhetorical and social approach is because the overall shape of 1 Corinthians 1:10—4:21 as a unit is dependent on the characteristics of Greco-Roman rhetoric. This is clearly evident in Paul's frequent use of rhetorical terminology such as *sophia* and its equivalents (which appear twenty-six times in chapters 1–4) and *logos* (nine times). In recent Corinthian scholarship, therefore, many scholars have attempted to interpret 1 Corinthians 1–4 in terms of its rhetorical situation (see above). Pogoloff especially claims that the rhetorical situation should connect the issue of *sophia* with the existence of divisions in the Christian community at Corinth and also with the issues of social status (1 Cor 1:26–28; cf. 11:18–22).[155] Furthermore, Charles A. Wanamaker asserts that in 1 Corinthians 1–4 Paul uses "a rhetoric of persuasion" to reclaim the Corinthian congregation from the grips of schism and to unify the Christian *ekklēsia*.[156] For these reasons, it is apparent that such rhetorical and social methods should provide the most persuasive answers to questions about the problems of wisdom as described in 1 Corinthians 1–4. So before undertaking a thorough social and rhetorical analysis of the Pauline text, some possibilities for a Korean-Confucian reading of the text will be briefly outlined.

---

155. Pogoloff, *Logos*, 119.
156. Wanamaker, "Power," 115–37.

CONCLUSION

The Rhetorical Situation of 1 Corinthians 1–4 from a Korean-Confucian Context

As stated earlier, Winter and Pogoloff's hypotheses provide the most helpful methods for one to attempt to dialogue between the two extremely different horizons, the first-century Corinthian Christian context and the twenty-first century Korean-Confucian Christian context.

Korean Christians have been profoundly influenced by Confucianism, which has dominated Korean culture since its introduction (see further below), just as the Corinthian Christians were overwhelmed by the sophistic movement and its rhetorical strategies which prevailed in Corinthian culture in the time of Paul. In both cases it is apparent that Christians in every generation and everywhere are profoundly influenced by the prevailing and dominating culture, whether secular or religious, in which they think and live. Christians are not able to isolate and segregate themselves totally from such cultural influences and domains.

Accordingly, in order to contextualize the biblical message in our time we need to observe thoroughly, study, and examine the prevailing culture surrounding us, and very carefully analyze similarities and differences between insights into the culture and the biblical message. We then need to attempt to dialogue between these two horizons.

Furthermore, Pogoloff's position suggests ways to re-read the biblical text in the context of Korean-Confucian Christianity. As indicated above, the Corinthian conception of wisdom (*sophia*) was shaped and strongly inspired by the social and cultural values of Greco-Roman rhetoric which was an essential part of the first century Greco-Roman culture. Similarly, it is understood that Korean perceptions of wisdom (*jeehye*) are overwhelmingly influenced by Korean Confucian teaching, especially T'oegye's teaching on wisdom (see Appendix 2). It is further seen that Korean culture has much to do with Korean Confucian influences, just as first-century Corinthian culture had much to do with Greco-Roman rhetorical influences as well as patronage systems. Such bridging points encourage one to think deeply about these parallels and to bring the two together in dialogue.

Pogoloff's understanding that Paul did not reject Greco-Roman rhetoric but, rather, he himself used it in his persuasion is a very helpful perspective. Nevertheless, Pogoloff further argues that Paul rejected the cultural and social values of wisdom as they were enacted in the

Corinthian church. This is because these values took over the life of his Corinthian converts more than the message of the gospel he had proclaimed.[157] In a very similar sense Paul W. Gooch argues:

> Paul's first-prong attack is against the misuse of reason *or philosophy* resulting in self-deception and boasting . . . it cannot follow that all philosophical activity is rendered illegitimate by his attack . . . Paul's critique cuts not at *philosophy* itself but its inflated pretender- intellectual conceit . . . the attack on rhetoric is against the deliberate misuse of words to convince beyond the proper bounds of knowledge . . . *we* distinguish the general target from *philosophy* by calling it "worldly wisdom" . . . the same distinction needs to be made between "worldly persuasion" and rhetoric or style. It need not follow for Paul that all worldly persuasion expresses the speaker's own conceit [italic's mine].[158]

In this statement Gooch contends that since the words *philosophy* and *reason* do not appear in 1 Corinthians 1–4, in referring to worldly wisdom, that Paul did not directly oppose philosophy or reason *per se* against faith, but human misuse of it in pride and conceit which obstructs one the attainment of the true knowledge of God and the wisdom of God.[159]

Gooch's ideas provide some significant pointers to one to re-read the Pauline message from a Korean-Confucian Christian context. Korean Christians do not necessarily have to reject the influence of Confucianism in their Christian lives, which has shaped Korean culture as a whole. However, Korean Christians may question and challenge those social and cultural values wedded to Confucianism, which may have taken over the life of Korean Christians and churches more than the message of the gospel. The social values rooted in Confucian teaching oftentimes distort the message of the gospel and make divisions of social status, hierarchy, and discrimination in the Korean churches (see further below). In this regard, these particular teachings should be critiqued in the life of Korean Christians, just as in 1 Corinthians Paul rejected the social values wedded to certain Greco-Roman philosophies and their conventions. In other cases the practice of Confucian wisdom and teachings ought to be encouraged as part of the essential culture of Korean Christianity in our time.

---

157. Pogoloff, *Logos*, 121.
158. Gooch, *Knowledge*, 34–49.
159. Ibid., 28, 40–42.

For this reason, consistent with contemporary biblical hermeneutics, an intercultural reading of the Corinthian *sophia* addressed in 1 Corinthians 1–4 will be made below. Such scholars as Cosgrove, Weiss, and Yeo encourage contemporary readers to engage in cross-cultural readings of the Pauline epistles and interpret Paul's teaching and message "sensitively" from their own cultural perspective. In this process they can learn how "cross-cultural interpretation can be a journey to others and a journey" to themselves.[160]

Using the methods of rhetorical analysis, Corinthian understandings of *sophia* will be investigated, then any insights will be re-read in a Korean-Confucian Christian context, especially in parallel with Korean Confucian wisdom. In so doing, Paul's gospel and teachings can be re-born and clothed in a Korean-Confucian Christian context. In this process Korean Christians can more clearly understand and recognize the importance of dialogue between the message of the gospel and the culture within which they live and into which they were born and have breathed and lived. Such an attempt is part of the major concern in this work; but, first, we now turn to a more detailed rhetorical and social analysis of 1 Corinthians 1–4.

---

160. Cosgrove, Weiss, and Yeo, *Cross-Cultural*, 5.

2

The Rhetorical Background of Roman Corinth

THE APPLICATION OF RHETORICAL and social approaches to grasping the background of Roman Corinth in the time of Paul enables a plausible description of the Corinthians' social and cultural understandings of wisdom and eloquence, and their social manifestations. In 1 Corinthians 1–4 Paul frequently uses rhetorical terminology such as *sophia* and its equivalent *sophos*, which occur twenty-six times in chapters 1–4 (twenty-eight times in 1 Cor as a whole), and *logos* which appears nine times (occurring seventeen times in 1 Cor). He also employs distinctive phrases which are closely related to the idea of rhetoric such as *sophia tou kosmou* (1:20, 21: 3:19), *sophia aiōnos* (2:6), *sophia logou* (1:17), *logos sophias* (2:4; cf. 12:8), *anthrōpinēs sophia* (2:13) and *hē sophia anthrōpōn* (2:5; cf. *sophia sarkikos* in 2 Cor 1:12).

Furthermore, the Corinthian wisdom and eloquence which Paul sharply criticized in 1 Corinthians 1–4, appear to have been rooted in Greco-Roman rhetorical traditions as exemplified in Cicero's rhetorical handbooks. Wisdom and eloquent speech were hallmarks of education and high social status in the Roman Empire including Roman Corinth in Paul's time (see below). In establishing this social phenomenon, Cicero would have made part of the most substatial contribution, though he lived in the Roman Republic of the first century BCE. Nevertheless, it is neither possible nor necessary to argue a direct connection between Cicero, Roman Corinth, and Paul. Yet it is proposed that Cicero would have best encapsulated the sort of rhetoric and boasting that Paul encountered and critiqued in Roman Corinth. Therefore, in order to comprehend the nature of Corinthian wisdom as described in 1 Corinthians 1–4, it is demanded to investigate the influence of Cicero's rhetorical legacy in the wider civic communities of Roman Corinth in the mid-first century CE.

CICERO'S RHETORIC

Cicero was "the greatest Roman orator and the most important Latin writer on rhetoric."[1] The name of Cicero itself represents rhetoric and eloquence in Rome. Plutarch regards him as "the best orator," and Quintilian (ca. 35–95 CE) views him as "the best producer and teacher of eloquence" among the Romans.[2] No Roman can be compared with him in terms of his influence on Roman mentality and culture and his contribution to the development of rhetoric in the Roman world.

Cicero was among the very first group of Romans who regarded rhetoric itself as useful and honorable and who "devoted themselves to it as a defence and for glory."[3] Tacitus (ca. 55–120 CE) acknowledged Cicero's initial commitment to the development of rhetoric and oratory in the Roman world. He states, "Cicero was "the first to give its proper finish to oratorical style . . . (and) the first to adopt a method of selection in the use of word, and to cultivate artistic arrangement."[4]

Cicero put an equal emphasis on the importance of rhetoric and eloquence, and on philosophy. He devoted himself to the study of philosophy and the practice of eloquence at the same time, considering these essential in his life. He thus confesses in his *De Officiis* that he spent his life aspiring to "the orator's peculiar ability to speak with propriety, clearness, and elegance."[5]

Before Cicero's beliefs and contributions were embraced by Rome, rhetorical conventions had not been previously popularized among the Romans. Rhetoric had only been regarded as a Greek cultural heritage. The study of rhetoric had been first introduced to Rome decades before Cicero's birth (in 106 BCE), yet the actual practice and study of rhetoric did not consistently take place at Rome because of a decree by the senate

---

1. Kennedy, *Classic*, 101; also Litfin, *Paul's*, 91.
2. Plutarch, *Cicero*, 2.4; Quintilian, *Institutio Oratoria*, 10.3.1.
3. Suetonius (*c.* 75–140 CE), *De Rhetoribus*, 1.
4. Tacitus, *Dialogue de Oratoribus*, 22.2–3.
5. Cicero, *De Officiis*, 1.1.2.

in 161 BCE and an edict of the censors in 92 BCE.⁶ Because of these reasons, wealthy young Romans travelled to Greece and Athens to study philosophy and rhetoric in the time of Cicero, who was also one of these young Romans.⁷ In his teenage years, Cicero studied at the school of Philon of Larissa the academic, in Rome. Cicero admired Philon for his eloquence and character,⁸ and afterwards travelled to Greece and Athens to study philosophy and rhetoric.⁹

While in Greece and Athens, Cicero was inspired and influenced by Greek philosophers and rhetoricians: Socrates (469–399 BCE), Isocrates (436–338 BCE), Plato (429–347 BCE), Demosthenes (384–322 BCE) and Aristotle (384–322 BCE).¹⁰ This is clearly supported by Quintilian's comments: "Cicero, who devoted himself heart and soul to the imitation of the Greeks, succeeded in reproducing the force of Demosthenes, the copious flow of Plato, and the charm of Isocrates."¹¹

Nonetheless, Isocrates and Aristotle influenced Cicero more than the other intellectual masters did.¹² These two Greeks strongly influenced Cicero's conviction that philosophy and rhetoric should be seen as closely related sciences, not as separated ones. They also affected the

---

6. In 161 BCE, the senate declared that philosophers and rhetoricians were not permitted to reside in Rome at all. In 92 BCE, the censors made an edict that Latin rhetoricians were prohibited from opening and running schools at Rome, and students were not permitted to attend their schools (see Suetonius, *De Rhetoribus*, 1).

7. See Plutarch, *Cicero*, 4.1.

8. Ibid., 3.2.

9. See Cicero, *De Oratore*, 1.4.13.

10. Plutarch, *Cicero*, 3.3.

11. Quintilian, *Institutio Oratoria*, 10.1.108. Even Cicero describes himself as a follower of Socrates and Plato (*De Officiis*, 1.2.2). A description of Aristotle's influence on him will be given below.

12. Cicero was also inspired so much by the other Greek masters. Yet this inspiration was limited to either philosophical aspects or that of oratory and eloquence: Socrates and Plato would have mostly influenced Cicero's philosophical thought (see Cicero, *Academica*, 1.4.16-19), while Demosthenes would have mainly influenced his skills of oratory and eloquence. Quintilian and Plutarch alike compare Cicero's eloquence with that of Demosthenes (see Quintilian, *Institutio Oratoria*, 10.1.108-110; Plutarch, *Demosthenes*, 3.1-4; Plutarch, *Demosthenes and Cicero*, 1.1—3.7). In spite of this, Cicero critiqued both Plato for his lack of willingness to engage in oratory and Demosthenes for his discontinuation of philosophical studies: "if Plato had been willing to devote himself to forensic oratory, he could have spoken with the greatest eloquence and power: and . . . if Demosthenes had continued the studies he pursued with Plato and had wished to expound his views, he could have done so with elegance and brilliancy" (Cicero, *De Officiis*, 1.1.4).

formation of his theory of rhetoric and improved his skills of oratory and eloquence. Consequently, Cicero adapted the theories of both Isocrates and Aristotle and fused them together in his rhetorical handbooks.[13] H. M. Hubbell supports this and observes that Cicero "definitely announces his work, *De Oratore*, as an adaptation of the theories of the greatest two ancient masters, Isocrates and Aristotle."[14] Therefore, Cicero was, as it were, an Isocrates and Aristotle in Rome.

Yet Cicero acknowledged that the older Greek masters up to Socrates, had combined "with their theory of rhetoric the whole of the study and the science of everything that concerns morals and conduct and ethics and politics."[15] In this acknowledgment, Cicero desired to restore the former connection of philosophy with rhetoric, following the ancient masters' approach, and wished to combine the study of philosophy with the practice of oratory, relating one to the other.[16] This is indicated in Cicero's *De Officiis*, which he wrote for his son, "I (Cicero) have always combined Greek and Latin studies—and I have done this not only in the

---

13. Cicero, *De Inventione*, 2.2.8. Cicero acknowledges that as contemporaries, Isocrates and Aristotle opposed each other. He comments that Isocrates and Aristotle, "each of whom, engrossed in his own profession, undervalued that of the other" (Cicero, *De Officiis*, 1.1.4).

14. Hubbell, *Influences*, 16. "*Aristotle was* busy with philosophy, but devoting some attention to the art of rhetoric as well, the other *Isocrates* . . . devoted to the study and teaching of oratory . . . ."(Cicero, *De Inventione*, 2.2.8; [italic's mine]).

Their approach, however, was very different from Socrates and Plato, who refused to relate and connect philosophy to rhetoric. Cicero states: "Socrates . . . in his discussions separated the science of wise thinking from that of elegant speaking . . . The compositions of Plato . . . from which has sprang the undoubtedly absurd and unprofitable and reprehensible severance between the tongue and the brain, leading to our having one set of professors to teach us to think and another to teach us to speak" (Cicero, *De Oratore*, 3.16.60–61). Nonetheless, Cicero recognizes that Socrates initially considered valuable the study of oratory. Yet he did not like to use oratory and eloquence in the context of politics and public life. Afterwards, Plato used Socrates's idea to defend that philosophy had to be separated from rhetoric (see Cicero, *De Oratore*, 3.16.59–60).

15. Cicero, *De Oratore*, 3.19.72.

16. See Hubbell, *Influences*, 22; also Cicero, *De Oratore*, 3.16.60. In addition, Hubbell states that "Isocrates opposed those who rejected rhetoric altogether and substituted other pursuits, hence he emphasized the value of *legein*; while Cicero opposed the rhetors who refused to admit that philosophy had any relation to rhetoric, hence he emphasized . . . the necessity of a wide knowledge if one would attain success as an orator" (Hubbell, *Influences*, 23). As such, Isocrates and Cicero alike laid an emphasis upon the necessity and importance of philosophy and rhetoric.

The Rhetorical Background of Roman Corinth 63

study of philosophy but also in the practice of oratory."[17] Cicero further states, "My dear Cicero, I cordially recommend you to read carefully not only my orations but also these books of mine on philosophy . . . I have attempted . . . both."[18]

Cicero admired Isocrates for his rhetorical ability and especially his excellence in eloquence. He considered Isocrates as one of those ancient masters who were professional orators and teachers of oratory, and who were equipped with philosophy, wisdom, and the talent of oratory.[19] Cicero also describes Isocrates as "the Master of all rhetoricians," "a great orator, and ideal teacher" and "a great and famous teacher of oratory."[20] These descriptions indicate that Cicero derived from Isocrates in particular, his idea of oratory, the ideal model of an orator, and the high value of eloquence.[21] This attitude was certainly different from that of philosophers in the Platonic and Socratic tradition.[22] Adopting Isocrates's attitude, Cicero comments, "Socrates . . . all the Socratic schools and the philosophers looked down on eloquence and the orators of wisdom, and never touched anything from the side of the other study"— namely rhetoric.[23] Due to Isocrates's strong influence, Cicero aimed to become a good orator and was devoted to improving his ability in oratory and eloquence.[24] As a result, Greek and Latin writers in the first and second century CE depicted him as the best orator and best producer of eloquence (*eloquentia*) among the Romans.[25]

---

17. Cicero, *De Officiis*, 1.1.1.
18. Ibid., 1.1.3.
19. Cicero, *De Oratore*, 3.16. 59.
20. Cicero, *De Oratore*, 2.3.10; 2.22.94; *Brutus*, 8.32; *De Inventione*, 2.2.7.
21. See Cicero, *De Oratore*, 1.5.17; 1.8.31–34; 3.19.72; 3.20.76; also Hubbell, *Influences of Isocrates*, 16–20.
22. Plato disliked rhetoric and saw it as a means of persuasion (see Plat, *Gorgias*, 453–54). He certainly distinguished philosophers from sophists. He identified himself with the philosophers and disliked sophists such as Isocrates (Litfin, *Paul's Theology*, 46–47). Clearly, in the dialogue between Socrates, Gorgias and others, Plato identifies himself with Socrates as a philosopher who is a pure lover of knowledge and learning, and of knowing the truth, and at the same time Plato distinguishes himself from Gorgias who is described as a rhetorician or sophist (Plato, *Gorgias*, 449, 453, 436).
23. Cicero, *De Oratore*, 3.19.72; see also *De oratore*, 3.16.59–60.
24. See Cicero, *De Officiis*, 1.1.2.
25. Plutarch, *Cicero*, 2.4; Quintilian, *Institutio Oratoria*, 10.3.1.

Aristotle also had a strong influence on Cicero, particularly on the formation of his concept of rhetoric. Cicero referred to Aristotle's rhetorical handbook to understand the definition of rhetorical genres, and developed his idea of rhetoric based on Aristotle's writings.[26] In his late teenage years, Cicero wrote *De Inventione*, some of which seems to have been quoted directly from Aristotle's theory of rhetoric in his *Rhetoric* (*technē rhētorikē* or *peri rhētorikēs*), because there are similarities in the definition of rhetorical genres between these two writings.[27] It is clear that Cicero developed his idea of rhetoric based on Aristotle's *Rhetoric* (see Appendix 1).

In summary, Cicero was of great significance in Greco-Roman rhetoric. He was a person who introduced Greek/Hellenistic rhetoric to the Romans and contextualised it in the Roman setting. Cicero adapted the rhetorical theories of Greek/Hellenistic masters such as Aristotle and Isocrates and fused them together in his rhetorical handbooks such as *De Inventione*. Moreover, he played an important role in developing rhetoric in the Roman world and became the best orator among the Romans. These points lead me to argue for the great importance of Cicero for rhetoric in the Roman world. We now turn to briefly investigate Cicero's understandings of wisdom.

CICERO'S WISDOM

Wisdom (*sapientia*) was what Cicero most desired to possess. He asserted that people must seek wisdom.[28] The high value he placed on wisdom is revealed clearly in his rhetorical handbooks. In his *De Officiis*, *De Re Publica*, *De Legibus*, and *De Inventione* Cicero employs the word *sapientia* frequently. Cicero's perception of wisdom was influenced strongly by Plato and Aristotle's understandings of wisdom.[29]

Cicero views wisdom as "the foremost of all virtues": wisdom (*sapientia*), justice (*iustitia*), courage (*fortitudo*), and temperance (*temperantia*). Because of this, the duty carried out by a person who possesses

26. For a brief description of Aristotle's rhetorical genres, see Appendix 1.

27. The idea of Cicero's rhetorical genres are found in his *De Inventione* (see Appendix 1). The *De Inventione* was written by Cicero in *c.* 89 BCE (Kennedy, *Classic*, 101). Some of the material in Aristotle's *Rhetoric* derived from his lectures at Athens in the mid-fourth century BCE and from Plato's principles of rhetoric in the *Phaedrus* (Stern, *Greek*, 75).

28. See Cicero, *De Invetione*, 1.36.65.

29. "Wisdom—what the Greeks call *sophia*" (Cicero, *De Officiis*, 1.43.153).

wisdom is the most important and highest duty in his or her civic society.[30] Cicero also sees wisdom as "the knowledge (*scientia*) of things human (*humanarum*) and divine (*divinarum*), which is concerned with the bonds of union between gods and humans and the relations of person to person."[31] Cicero describes wisdom as the highest knowledge and the truest knowledge because by wisdom people are able to know all things, divine or human, because by wisdom people know the primary and the highest principles and causes which regulate and control those things.[32]

Cicero describes wisdom as "the knowledge of what is good, what is bad, and what is neither good nor bad."[33] This wisdom comprises three faculties: memory (*memoria*), intelligence (*intellegentia*), and foresight (*providentia*). Memory is the faculty through which the mind remembers what has occurred.[34] Intelligence is the faculty by which it makes sure of what is now. Foresight is the faculty by which the mind foresees what is going to happen before it happens.[35]

Cicero regards wisdom as the noblest part of philosophy. He argues that philosophy is nothing other than the pursuit of wisdom. Cicero defines a philosopher as "the lover of wisdom" and as a person who searches for wisdom itself.[36] Because of this, Cicero emphasizes both the study of philosophy and the pursuit of wisdom. He states, "If one ought to desire wisdom, it is proper to study philosophy."[37] In addition, Cicero says, "If the person would belittle the study of philosophy, I quite fail to

---

30. This viewpoint is similar to Plato claiming wisdom as the noblest of the virtues (see Plato's *The Republic*, 4: 428, 433; *Protagoras*, 329–30).

31. Cicero, *De Officiis*, 1.43.153.

32. Cicero, *De Officiis*, 2.2.5. This is similar to Aristotle describing wisdom as "the highest degree of universal knowledge" and "the most divine science" (Aristotle, *Metaphysics* A.1. 982a23; *Metaphysics* A.1. 983a5). Aristotle maintains that wisdom deals with "the first causes and principles of things" (*Metaphysics* A.1. 981b29–982a1).

33. Cicero, *De Inventione*, 2.52.160.

34. This is similar to Aristotle arguing that a human being produces experience from memory (see Aristotle, *Metaphysics* A.1. 980a28–981a12. In his *Metaphysics*, Aristotle refers to wisdom (*sophia*) often and relates it to the words *gnōsis*, *philosophia* or *philosophos*, and *protē philosophia* (*Metaphysics* A.1. 981a27; 981b10, 28; A.2.982a1, 2, 6, 16, 17, 20; A.9. 992a24; also Reale, *Concept*, 46).

35. Cicero, *De Inventione*, 2.53.160.

36. Cicero, *De Officiis*, 2.2.5. This is in accord with Plato defining philosophy as the love of wisdom and the love of knowledge (see Plato, *Phaedrus*, 278; *Cratylus*, 391).

37. Cicero, *De Inventione*, 1.36.65.

see what in the world he would see fit to praise."[38] This makes clear that for Cicero the study of philosophy and the possession of wisdom should come together. It is not that to study philosophy is one discipline and to pursue wisdom is another, but that the two occur at the same time.

Cicero insists on the necessity and significance of wisdom in public affairs. In his *De Re Publica*, Cicero asserts that it is the noblest function and the highest duty of wisdom that it makes a person who possesses it useful to his State.[39] Cicero maintains that wisdom and eloquence are, alike, needed for people who handle public affairs for the good and benefit of the State. Yet the role of wisdom is more important than that of eloquence because "from eloquence the state receives many benefits, provided only it is accompanied by wisdom, the guide of all human affairs."[40] In other words, a person who is involved in public affairs has to combine the study of philosophy and the pursuit of wisdom with the possession of eloquence. Cicero thus contends that a person who lacks either wisdom or eloquence should not be allowed to handle public affairs.[41]

Cicero also asserts that wisdom is of importance in private affairs and social life. Under the guidance of wisdom, a person knows and discerns between what is good and bad. He gives the example that Lucius Brutus, who was a pre-eminent man of wisdom "freed his fellow citizens from the unjust yoke of cruel servitude."[42] As the guidance for all human affairs, wisdom provides people benefits in their private affairs.[43] Cicero states, "wisdom urges us to increase our resources, to multiply our wealth, to extend our boundaries. Wisdom urges us also to rule over as many subjects as possible, to enjoy pleasures, to become rich, to be rulers and masters."[44] Cicero also believes that wisdom is intimately

---

38. Cicero, *De Officiis*, 2.2.5.

39. Cicero, *De Re Publica*, 1.20.33.

40. Cicero, *De Inventione*, 1.4.5.

41. Ibid., 1.3.4. Clearly, such ideas were taken from Plato's writings. Plato states that wisdom is the most important and necessary element of the things that a ruler or king of State must have and that the peaceful and orderly nature of the State depends on whether or not there are people who possess wisdom (see Plato, *Statesman*, 294, 309). Plato goes on that a person who wishes to become a good and noble guardian of the State should study philosophy and seek wisdom and true knowledge. This person can become a good counselor for the people (see Plato, *The Republic*, 2:376; 4:428, 433; *Protagoras*, 329–30).

42. Cicero, *De Re Publica*, 2.25.46.

43. Cicero, *Laws*, 1.22.4.

44. Cicero, *The Republic*, 3.15.24.

related to sociability. Guided by wisdom, defined as the knowledge of all things human and divine, a person knows how to build good social relationships with others and how to keep good fellowship with a god.[45] Wisdom, therefore, is part of the most necessary and important elements a person should possess in order to shape a good personality and sociality, become wealthier, and become a ruler.

Aware of the necessity and importance of wisdom in private and public affairs, Cicero asserts that "if wisdom is to be sought above all things, then folly is to be avoided above all things."[46] He thus devoted himself to the study of philosophy and the pursuit of wisdom. He believed firmly that wisdom made him all he was. Furthermore, Cicero encouraged and motivated Romans to devote themselves to studying philosophy and seeking wisdom, for this was their duty.[47]

To sum up, wisdom is the most desirable one of all virtues that Cicero wished to possess. As a politician and orator Cicero gave high value to the importance of wisdom in public affairs and social life as well as private affairs. He especially encouraged his people to attain wisdom, for in his belief this wisdom would provide them benefits and social securities such as wealth and high social status. These elements in Cicero's understandings of wisdom help me to draw analogies between the way Cicero gave high value to wisdom and the way some of the Corinthian Christians regarded worldly/human wisdom more highly than Christ the wisdom of God as indicated in 1 Corinthians 1–4 (1:18—2:16; see below). We now move on to an examination of Cicero's idea of eloquence.

CICERO'S ELOQUENCE

Cicero was an icon of Roman eloquence (*eloquentia*). The name Cicero itself represents Roman eloquence, of which it is impossible to speak without dealing with Cicero's legacy. Plutarch claims that Cicero was the only Roman who made the Romans know "how much eloquence does grace and beautify that which is honest."[48]

It is no exaggeration to claim that Cicero devoted his adulthood to possessing and practicing eloquence.[49] After finishing his boyhood stud-

---

45. Cicero, *De Officiis*, 1.43.153.
46. Cicero, *De Inventione*, 1.37.66.
47. Cicero, *De Legibus*, 1.24.63.
48. Plutarch, "Cicero," 77.
49. See Cicero, *De Officiis*, 1.1.2.

ies, Cicero went to Greece and Athens to learn Greek oratory and eloquence. In Cicero's day Greece was the centre of eloquence, and Athens was the place where "the supreme power of oratory (or eloquence) was both invented and perfected."[50] There, Cicero was inspired by the reputed eloquence of Greek orators: Isocrates and Demosthenes. He esteemed Isocrates's eloquence most highly and referred to him as an "eminent father of eloquence."[51] Cicero was influenced by Aristotle and Plato's ideas of eloquence as well. These Greek philosophers spoke of eloquence at length in their philosophical and rhetorical handbooks.[52]

Similarly, Cicero insists that oratory has great power. He states, "The power of oratory (or eloquence) in the attainment of propriety is great."[53] Cicero maintains that this oratory is employed in "pleadings in court" and in "popular assemblies and in the senate."[54] In his *De Optimo Genere Oratorum*, Cicero speaks of the power of eloquence in private affairs. For instance, eloquence is used to defend a person at trial in court and to plead a private case before referees.[55] In his *De Inventione* Cicero further claims that eloquence is of importance in public life: assemblies and in the senate. He acknowledged that a person who desired to succeed in public and political life had to possess eloquence.[56] Plutarch supports this in his *Demosthenes and Cicero*. He states, "It is necessary, indeed, that a political leader should prevail by reason of his eloquence."[57]

---

50. Cicero, *De Oratore*, 1.4.13.

51. Cicero, *De Officiis*, 1.1.4; also *De Oratore*, 1.5.17; 1.8.31–34; 2.3.10; 2.22.94; 3.19.72; 3.20.76; *Brutus*, 8.32; *De Inventione*, 2.2.7; also Hubbell, *Influences*, 16–20.

52. Plato acknowledges the importance of eloquence in rhetoric and its power in public meetings. He sees rhetoric as the art of eloquent speech itself (see Plato, *Phaedrus* 268, 270). Aristotle's insistence on eloquence is evidenced in his *Rhetoric* and *Rhetoric to Alexander*. Aristotle sees eloquence as the most important topic in rhetoric and explains how to make an eloquent speech (*Rhetoric* 1:2 1358a36—3 1359a29; 2:18 1391b1–1392a8; 3:1 1403b5–7; *Rh. Al.* 1420a8; 1 1421b9; 1420a 13–14; 22 1434a33–39; 1434b28–29).

53. Cicero, *De Officiis*, 1.37.132, where eloquence and oratory are used interchangeably in this literary context.

54. Ibid., 1.37.132.

55. See Cicero, *De Oratorum*, 4.10.

56. Cicero, *De Inventione*, 1.4.5.

57. Plutarch, *Demosthenes and Cicero*, 2.1. Plutarch here talks about Cicero's speeches and his boasting and self-praise of his eloquence. On the other hand, Plutarch argues against Cicero and claims that it is "ignoble for him to admire and crave the fame that springs from his eloquence (*logos*)" (*Demosthenes and Cicero*, 2.1).

The Romans in Cicero's day also believed that a person's eloquence could provide benefits, interests, and protection to the country and community where that person belonged.[58] This is clearly evidenced in Cicero's language, "the man who equips himself with the weapons of eloquence . . . defends the welfare of his country . . . He will be a citizen most helpful and most devoted to . . . interests of his community."[59] Cicero further states, "from eloquence the state receive many benefits . . . from eloquence those who have acquired it obtain glory and honour and high esteem. From eloquence comes the surest and safest protection for one's friends."[60]

It is evident that Cicero's political success was related, to some extent, to his eloquence. Cicero's eloquence gave a good impression to the Romans of his time, and his Roman contemporaries acknowledged Cicero's excellent eloquence. Apparently, "crowds used to gather to hear the eloquence of Cicero," as F. R. Cowell says.[61] Plutarch informs us that even Julius Caesar "praised Cicero's eloquence."[62] Furthermore, Dio Cassius (ca. 150–ca. 235 CE) describes an incident that demonstrates a relation between Cicero's eloquence and his political success. At the time Julius Caesar was assassinated (44 BCE), Rome was in political chaos. The senate was divided into factions. Cicero, with his excellent eloquence, persuaded the senators to be united. The senators valued and followed all Cicero's advice. He thus protected the senate from factionalism.[63] Afterwards, Cicero took control of the senate. At this time, his

---

58. See Cicero, *De Officiis*, 1.21.70, 73; 1.37.132.

59. Cicero, *De Inventione*, 1.1.1. Cicero describes eloquence as an art and a gift of nature. This eloquence arises from "most honorable causes and continues on its way from the best of reasons" (*De Inventione*, 1.1.2).

60. Ibid., 1.4.5.

61. Cowell, *Cicero*, xiv.

62. Plutarch, *Cicero*, 39.5. Here is an example of the effect of his eloquence: "Caesar said to his friends: 'what is to prevent our hearing a speech from Cicero after all this while, since Legarius has long been adjudged a villain and an enemy? But when Cicero had begun to speak and moving his hearers beyond measure, and his speech, as it proceeded, showed varying paths and amazing grace, Caesar's face often changed color and it was manifest that all the emotions of his very soul stirred; and at last, when the orator touched upon the struggle at Pharsalus, he was so greatly affected that his body shook and he dropped from his hand some of his documents'" (Plutarch, *Cicero*, 39.7).

63. "Cicero by the foregoing speech persuaded the senate to vote that no one should bear malice against anyone else. While this was being done, the assassins also promised the soldiers that they would not undo any of Caesar's acts" (Dio Cassius, *Roman History*, 44.34).

power reached its greatest height in the city of Rome, so that even young (Octavianus) Caesar feared his power.[64] Clearly, Cicero's eloquence was intimately connected to his political success. It is no wonder that Cicero obtained fame, glory, and high esteem in Rome, where the people valued his eloquence highly.

Cicero insisted on the importance and necessity of eloquence for the welfare of Rome and urged the Romans to study eloquence carefully. He states, "persons ought . . . to devote themselves to the study of eloquence although some misuse it both in private and public affairs."[65] Cicero further claims that the Romans "should study eloquence the more earnestly in order that evil men may not obtain great power to the detriment of good citizens and the common disaster of the community."[66]

Finally, Cicero contends that a person should equip himself with both eloquence and wisdom and keep them in balance for the benefit and advantage of State. He believes that "wisdom without eloquence does too little for the good of states, but eloquence without wisdom is generally highly disadvantageous and is never helpful."[67] Cicero argues that a person must practice eloquence in combination with the study of philosophy and moral conduct, so that they can then provide beneficial and useful contributions to the country. If he "neglects the study of philosophy and moral conduct, which is the highest and most honorable of pursuits and devotes his whole energy to the practice of oratory, his civic life is nurtured into something useless to himself and harmful to his country."[68] Cicero's legacy of eloquence had a great influence on the Romans of the succeeding generations.[69]

---

64. See Plutarch, *Cicero*, 45.4–6.

65. Cicero, *De Inventione*, 1.4.5.

66. Ibid., 1.4.5; *De Officiis* 1:156. Seneca the elder (ca. 54 BCE–ca. 39 CE) encouraged Romans to study eloquence as well. He states, "Do study eloquence. You can easily pass from this art to all others; it equips even those whom it does not train for its own ends (Seneca the elder, *Controversies* 2. Preface 3, in *the Elder Seneca*, which is taken from Peterson's *Eloquence*, 60).

67. Cicero, *De Inventione*, 1.1.1. This emphasis on eloquence and wisdom in Cicero's mind is similar to the conduct of some of the Corinthian Christians as addressed in 1 Cor 1–4 (see below).

68. Ibid., 1.1.1. This equal importance of eloquence and wisdom in Cicero's idea of rhetoric is in accordance with the Corinthian conception of rhetoric as addressed in 1 Cor 1–4 (see below).

69. For an example, see Plutarch, *Cicero*, 49.5.

Furthermore, Seneca the Younger (ca. 4 BCE–65 CE), a first-century rhetorician and philosopher in Rome, was inspired by Cicero and his legacy of eloquence. He confesses, "I have simply been following the practice of Cicero."[70] Seneca referred to Cicero as "the greatest master of eloquence" and called him "the eloquent Cicero."[71] He thus recommended his Roman readers to read and study Cicero's rhetorical handbooks. Seneca states, "Read Cicero; his style has unity."[72] Cicero's rhetorical handbooks were indeed favored and read by philologists, scholars, and followers of philosophy in Rome of Seneca's time and the mid-first century CE.[73]

Quintilian, a first-century teacher of rhetoric and oratory in Rome, also acknowledged Cicero's eloquence. Quintilian claims, "the name of Cicero was not regarded as the name of a man, but as the name of eloquence itself."[74] Cicero was "the best producer and teacher of eloquence" among the Romans.[75] Quintilian goes on that it was Cicero "who shed the greatest light not only on the practice but on the theory of oratory; for he stands alone among Romans as combining the gift of actual eloquence with that of teaching the art."[76]

Due to these reasons, Quintilian regarded Cicero as the pride of Roman eloquence and oratory in comparison with Greek eloquence. In his *Institutio Oratoria* Quintilian compares Cicero proudly to Demosthenes (384–322 BCE).[77] Quintilian depicts Demosthenes as "by far the most perfect of Greek orators," while he describes Cicero as "the perfect orator."[78] Hence, Quintilian referred to Cicero as the perfect model of eloquence and of "oratorical excellence."[79] Quintilian highly

---

70. Seneca, *Epistulae*, cv 2.10. In addition, Seneca says, "I shall quote Cicero's actual words," and "The word which Cicero used seems to me most suitable," ibid., xc 7.3; cx 1.2.

71. Ibid., c 9; cv 2.10; cx 8.1.

72. Ibid., c 7.

73. "When Cicero's book *On the State* is opened by a philologist, a scholar or a follower of philosophy, each man pursues his investigation in his own way," ibid., cv 8.30.

74. Quintilian, *Institutio Oratoria*, 10.1.112.

75. Ibid., 10.3.1.

76. Ibid., 3.1.20.

77. "It is our orators, above all, who enable us to match our Roman eloquence against that of Greece for I would set Cicero against any one of their orators without fear of refutation," ibid., 10.1.105.

78. Ibid., 10.2.24, 28.

79. Ibid., 10.2.24, 28.

recommended that all Romans should learn from Cicero and admire him for his eloquence. Quintilian said to his students, "Cicero, in my opinion, provides pleasant reading for beginners and is sufficiently easy to understand: it is possible not only to learn much from him, but to come to love him."[80] He further states, "Let us . . . fix our eyes on him, take him as our pattern, and let the student realise that he has made real progress if he is a passionate admirer of Cicero."[81]

Cicero's eloquence was highly esteemed by the Romans of the next generations through to the first century CE. Plutarch shows that Cicero's fame for eloquence abided to his time of the late first century and early second century CE. As such, it is clear that Cicero was an icon of Roman eloquence and that many Romans were inspired by his eloquence, not only in his time and the first century BCE but also in the first century CE. These Romans would possibly have included some members of Roman origin in the Corinthian church (see below).

In summary, Cicero was regarded as a great master of eloquence in the Roman world. The Romans acknowledged and admired his excellent eloquence. Cicero insisted on the great importance of eloquence in public and private affairs. He believed that people who possessed eloquence were beneficial not only for their country but also for themselves and that eloquence was a weapon to defend the welfare of the State and to bring fame and glory to individuals. That's why he urged his people to devote themselves to the study of eloquence and equip themselves with it. Moreover, Cicero's ideas of eloquence were highly favored by the Romans in succeeding generations. They took Cicero's eloquence as their pattern and followed his practice of it. These Romans included Seneca the Younger (4 BCE–65 CE), Quintilian (ca. 35–95 CE) and Tacitus (ca. 55–120 CE) who were contemporaries of the Christians in the first century CE (see below).

Seneca the Younger especially lived in the same era as Paul and the Corinthian Christians in the mid-first century, and was a significant figure in Roman eloquence at that time. Plutarch states, "Seneca proved that his eloquence profited others more than himself."[82] The Romans praised eloquence and believed that a person could "rescue himself or herself

---

80. Ibid., 2.5.20.
81. Ibid., 10.1.112.
82. Plutarch, "Seneca" in *Lives of Noble Greeks*, 998.

from mortality by the composition of glorious works of eloquence."[83] This notion helps understand better the mentality and behavior of some of the Corinthian Christians who were connected to some extent to the rhetorical situation of mid-first century Rome. Of the Corinthian Christians, we know that Priscilla and Aquila lived in Rome and moved to Corinth. Phoebe took Paul's letter to the Roman Christians (Rom 16:1–2). It seems plausible that Priscilla and Aquila would have heard about Cicero's legacy of rhetoric and eloquence in Rome from Roman rhetoricians and orators like Seneca the Younger who was inspired by Cicero (see above). So we turn now to an examination of Cicero's legacy in Roman Corinth in Paul's day.

CICERO'S LEGACY IN ROMAN CORINTH

Roman Corinth in the mid-first century was "a significant Greco-Roman city which partook in, an ordinary way, of the features of Greco-Roman culture."[84] These features included patronal networks, social stratification, the imperial cult, and the influence of rhetorical systems. They all had a role to play in shaping the social and cultural milieu of mid-first century Corinth where Paul established the Corinthian congregations (see further below).

In particular, rhetorical conventions seem to have played an integral part in shaping the life of Corinthian civic society and had a continuing impact on the Corinthians' mentality and social behavior. Furthermore these rhetorical conventions would have been to some extent shaped by and related to Cicero's rhetorical ideas as described in his handbooks such as *De Officiis*, *De Oratore*, and *De Inventione*. In other words, Cicero and his rhetorical handbooks are the best examples we have of the thinking that influenced, to some extent, the social behavior and mentality of the Corinthians in the mid-first century Greco-Roman world, though he lived in the first century BCE. It is neither possible nor necessary to argue a direct connection between Cicero and the Corinthians, nor

---

83. Seneca the Younger, *De Consolatione*, 2.6.

84. Litfin, *Paul's*, 143. Scholars have already argued that rhetorical conventions were widespread at Roman Corinth in the mid-first century (see above). It is not my purpose here to repeat this scholarly argument but to argue specifically for the special significance of Cicero's legacy of rhetoric and eloquence in Roman Corinth in the mid-first century.

between Cicero and Paul, but merely to show the continuing legacy of Cicero's thought in the wider Roman Empire.[85]

It is proposed that Cicero and his rhetorical handbooks would have influenced the Corinthians through three different channels after Corinth was rebuilt in 44 BCE. First, the first generation of Roman colonists may well have brought Cicero's handbooks from Rome when they came to Corinth following the orders of Julius Caesar, but probably his influence would have arrived with them. Yet, Graham Tomlin argues that when the Rome colonists came into Corinth they brought Epicureanism from Rome. He states,

> . . . it was the Epicurean philosophy which held the field in Italy . . . Seneca . . . gives grudging testimony to the widespread popularity of Epicurean teaching in the mid-first century. In 45 BCE Cicero . . . admitted that it was the most popular philosophy in Rome at the time.[86]

Tomlin further argues that the Corinthian Christians were influenced by the teachings of Epicurus (341–270 BCE) and his follower Lucretius (90s–55 BCE). Nonetheless, Tomlin appears to overlook that Seneca and Cicero acknowledged that the Stoics were also regarded as a popular philosophical school at Rome.[87] For this reason, Juhana Torkki argues for a Stoic, not Epicurean, influence on Paul and particularly in his Areopagus speech (Acts 17:16–34). He states, "Paul is well at home in the Stoic tradition, while Epicureanism is foreign to him."[88] Similarly, Michelle V. Lee claims the influence of Stoicism on Paul and his use of body language in 1 Corinthians 12.[89] It seems likely that the Epicureans and the Stoics were like philosophical schools under the influence of

---

85. Cicero travelled to Roman colonial cities such as Athens, Ephesus, Galatia, and Tarsus (see Quayle, "Cicero," 709). He never visited Corinth, for Cicero lived between the periods of the destruction and rebuilding of Corinth. Greek Corinth was destroyed by Roman forces in 146 BCE, several decades before his birth (106 BCE). The city was then rebuilt as a Roman colony in 44 BCE (the year in which Julius Caesar was assassinated), one year before Cicero's death (43 BCE) (see Dio Cassius, *Roman History*, 50.3–5). Cicero saw the re-founding of Corinth, but he did not visit the city. Cicero does briefly mention Corinth in his writings: "I wish they had not destroyed Corinth" (Cicero, *De Officiis*, 1.11.35). "I have got his works on the constitutions of Corinth and Athens at Rome" (Cicero, *Epistularum ad Atticum*, 2.1).

86. Tomlin, "Epicureans," 54.

87. See Cicero, *De Inventione*; Seneca, *De Constantia Sapientis*, 15.4.

88. Torkki, *Dramatic*, 141.

89. See Lee, *Stoics*, chapters 3–5.

rhetorical conventions at Rome. Furthermore, Tomlin finds similarities between Epicurean teachings and the problems of the Corinthian church (1 Cor). Nevertheless, he fails to provide a plausible description of the nature of Corinthian wisdom as addressed in 1 Corinthians 1–4 in relation to the Epicurean idea of *sophia*. Tomlin simply states that in Epicurean texts there was an idea of *sophia*. He does not demonstrate how the Epicurean idea of *sophia* had impact on the Pauline opponents at Corinth and why they esteemed wisdom more highly than Christ as the wisdom of God and how this caused the problem of divisions in the Corinthian congregation. In spite of this, his argument that "wisdom can be explained within a more pure Greek Gentile context, rendering the Jewish background . . . unnecessary" is plausible enough to take into account.[90] Yet it would be better to substitute the words "Greek Gentile context" by the phrase "Greco-Roman culture." This is because Corinthian wisdom, as addressed in 1 Corinthians 1–4, should be investigated in terms of the influence of Greco-Roman culture in which rhetorical conventions and particularly Cicero's rhetorical handbooks were so characteristic.

By the way, from the first years of its re-founding, Roman Corinth was repopulated by Roman colonists. These colonists comprised a diversity of people groups: freed people, slaves, Caesar's army veterans, and other Romans who possessed full Roman citizenship. Many of these Roman colonists may well have known of Cicero's eloquence and have read his rhetorical handbooks. Some would have received Cicero's teaching on rhetoric and eloquence while they resided in Rome.[91] These Roman colonists would have been inspired and influenced by Cicero and his rhetorical legacy because, as indicated earlier, in the mid-first century BCE Cicero was the most influential man in Rome in terms of his contribution to the development of rhetoric and eloquence and his Romanization of Greek rhetoric (see above).

Second, what we know of the re building of Corinth and its culture supports the widespread use of rhetorical conventions in the civic society of first century Corinth and the influence of Cicero's rhetorical handbooks. Roman Corinth was one of the most Romanized cities within the

---

90. Tomlin, "Epicureans," 67.

91. This is supported by Cowell claiming that Roman crowds gathered to hear Cicero's eloquence (see Cowell, *Cicero*, xiv). Quintilian also describes Cicero's teaching in Rome (see Quintilian, *Institutio Oratoria*, 10.3.1).

entire Roman Empire. According to the Roman policy of colonization, Corinth took on a Roman look not only in its architecture but also in its social, cultural, and political systems when it was rebuilt (see below). This is supported by Augustus's homogeneous policy during his reign (31 BCE–14 CE), whereby the entire Roman Empire had an increasingly homogeneous culture regardless of regions. The empire was envisioned as having no cultural differences between Rome the capital of the Roman Empire and its colonies. Rome and its colonial cities were encouraged to develop the same social and cultural systems, such as the imperial cult, patronage, social hierarchies, and rhetorical conventions.[92]

Due to this Roman propaganda, we first investigate the rhetorical situation of Rome in the first century in order to grasp to some degree the similar culture of first-century Roman Corinth. First-century Rome had become a leading centre of rhetoric within the Greco-Roman world. Rhetorical conventions were such a significant part of the civic life of the Romans that Rome had a number of rhetorical schools in the first century CE.[93] In first-century Rome, Seneca the Younger (ca. 4 BCE–65 CE), Quintilian (ca. 35–95 CE), and Tacitus (ca. 55–120 CE) were distinguished rhetoricians and orators.[94] They were, alike, inspired by Cicero, Seneca, and Quintilian in particular, acknowledged Cicero's excellent eloquence. They encouraged their students to admire Cicero for his eloquence and read his rhetorical handbooks as their rhetorical pattern.[95] So, although Seneca and Quintilian were both respected and admired for their rhetorical abilities by the Romans in the first century CE, they themselves encouraged the Romans to learn rhetorical patterns from Cicero and his rhetorical handbooks.[96]

As a wealthy, prosperous, and luxurious city, Roman Corinth would not only have been inhabited by a large number of people and a diversity of people groups (for the demographic composition of Corinth, see further below), but would also have been influenced by rhetoricians and

---

92. See Cook, *Cambridge Ancient History*, 209.

93. See Quintilian, *Institutio Oratoria*, 10.1.112. In the time of Cicero, Athens had been the center of oratory and eloquence in the Mediterranean world (see Cicero, *De Oratore*, 1.4.13).

94. In 71, Quintilian became the first man called to a chair in rhetoric at Rome. Tacitus was one of the most admired orators in Rome in the first century (Kennedy, *Classic*, 118).

95. See Quintilian, *Institutio Oratoria*, 2.5.20; 10.1.112.

96. See ibid., 10.1.112; Seneca, *Epistulae*, cv 2.10.

orators who came from Rome and admired Cicero for his excellent eloquence. As stated earlier, Seneca the Younger was a contemporary of the Corinthians addressed in 1 Corinthians. It is worth noting that Gallio, proconsul of Corinth in Paul's time, was the elder brother of Seneca.[97] So there is no doubt that the Corinthians in the mid-first century would also have been influenced by Cicero and his rhetorical ideals, though they may not have had a direct connection with him or with Seneca the Younger.

Most educated Romans spoke Greek fluently and even preferred Greek cultural traditions to their own Latin ones. Thus, in their literature and art they preferred to use Greek instead of Latin. This phenomenon was evident in the colonial cities like Corinth even more distinctively than in Rome.[98] Given that Cicero had made Greek philosophy so popular in Rome and, thereby "had a great influence on intellectual life" and was "a prime source for Greek thought and the status of philosophy at the close of the Roman Republic,"[99] we would expect this influence to be strong in Roman Corinth also.

It can also be argued that the influence of Cicero's legacy reached out to people of other origins such as Jews and Greeks in the Greco-Roman world of the first and second century CE. Plutarch (ca. 45–120 CE), a Greek writer, confirms that Cicero's fame for eloquence abided to the day of Plutarch.[100] Pogoloff also indicates the extent to which a rhetorical education had become the norm throughout the people groups of the empire:

> In the Greco-Roman schools education was almost exclusively education in rhetoric, which the ancients considered an adequate preparation for the life of free men . . . the concept of rhetoric dominated the schooling of the time in Greek and Roman education, and it was conspicuous in Jewish schools also.[101]

---

97. Seneca, *Epistulae Morales*, 104.

98. See Newsome, *Greek*, 260. Similarly, James B. Rives states, "Greek culture, already widespread thus became the culture of the elite throughout the . . . Mediterranean (region). Roman conquests helped spread Greek culture still further, since Roman rulers regarded cities of the Greek type as essential to their governance and so encouraged their foundation" (Rives, *Religion*, 55).

99. E. Ferguson, *Backgrounds*, 359; see also Cicero, *De Officiis*, 1.1.1–3.

100. Plutarch, *Cicero*, 2.5.

101. Pogoloff, *Logos*, 49, 49 n. 54.

Assumably, in this Greco-Roman rhetorcial education, Cicero's rhetorical handbooks such as *De Inventione* and *De Oratore* would have been used as textbooks. For these reasons, Cicero's rhetorical theories will be used as the principal guide for our rhetorical analysis of 1 Corinthians 1–4 and will help classify the type of rhetorical discourse in the Pauline text.

IMPLICATIONS FOR THE STUDY OF 1 CORINTHIANS 1–4

Cicero's rhetorical handbooks, and especially *De Inventione*, will be here compared with the Pauline text of 1 Corinthians 1–4, a text that comprises a diversity of rhetorical elements (see above). This involves considering which type of rhetorical genre this biblical text is, deliberative, epideictic, or forensic.[102] Furthermore, for a better understanding of the rhetorical situation of the Pauline text, it's needed to find out the influence of Cicero's rhetorical legacy on the conduct of some of the Corinthian Christians, which is glimpsed in positive and negative ways in Paul's use of rhetorical language.

Before doing so, several indications of the general influence of Cicero's rhetorical legacy in the wider New Testament will be briefly examined. Of course, this legacy is not specifically Cicero's alone, but belongs to the wider Hellenistic rhetorical traditions. It may well be that Paul was shaped more by the latter, and the Corinthians by the former. But Cicero cannot be, and must not be, removed from the equation altogether. However, first, Paul uses in 2 Corinthians the three moods of proof—*ethos, pathos,* and *logos*—that Cicero popularized in Roman culture through his *Oratore, De Oratore,* and *De Inventione*. He employs these three modes in 2 Corinthians 10–13, in particular.[103] Second, Paul employs theories of rhetorical genre in his epistles that are thoroughly consistent with those outlined by Cicero. For example, the atmosphere of forensic rhetoric is abundantly evident in Galatians. In other words, Galatians is an apologetic letter, where Paul views the addressees as the jury, Paul as the defendant, and his Galatian opponents as the accusers. So argues Hans Dieter Betz.[104] F. F. Bruce appreciates Betz's argu-

---

102. For more details on Cicero's description of rhetorical genres see Appendix 1.

103. See DiCicco, *Ethos,* 77–268; Cicero, *Orator,* 21.71; *De Oratore,* 1.5; *De Inventione,* 1.14.20; 1.50.92–3.

104. Betz, *Galatians,* 14, 25.

ment.[105] Richard N. Longenecker disagrees with Betz in general. He argues that Galatians "appears to be a case of mixed rhetorical genres," but he admits that forensic rhetoric dominates 1:6—3:7 and 4:8–11.[106] Ben Witherington disagrees with Betz, seeing Galatians as deliberative rhetoric.[107] James D. G. Dunn concludes that Galatians does not accord closely with any type of rhetorical genre.[108] The extent of forensic rhetoric in Galatians may be disputed, but no other rhetorical type can explain so adequately the diversity of Paul's arguments in defense of his gospel.

Third, Paul certainly uses the functions of the *exordium* (beginning) and *peroratio* (end or conclusion) in Romans, which Cicero describes in his *De Inventione* and popularizes for a Roman context. Johann Kim argues that Romans 1:1–13, 15 functions as *exordium*, and 15:14—16:27 serves as *peroratio*.[109] Douglas A. Campbell also claims that the influence of Cicero's rhetorical theories is glimpsed in Romans 3:21–26.[110] Lastly, there is a striking similarity between the description of Jesus in Hebrews 3:1 ("fix [*katanoeō*] your thoughts on Jesus") and that of Cicero in Quintilian's *Institutio Oratoria*, 10.1.112 ("Let us fix our eye on him [Cicero], take him as our pattern").

Furthermore and more specifically, 1 Corinthians 1–4 is clearly a rhetorical unit for it comprises several rhetorical elements, such as *inventio, dispositio, elocutio, memoria,* and *pronuntiatio*, that Cicero describes in his *De Inventione*. Paul employs the function of *inventio* (discovering valid arguments) in the following passages: 1:10–13a, in which the issue of *schismata* is tackled, and 1:13b–25 and 2:1–5, where the issues of wisdom (*sophia*) and eloquence (*sophia logou*) are addressed. These are the issues Paul mostly raises in 1 Corinthians 1–4 to argue against his Corinthian opponents who caused the problem of divisions in the Corinthian Christian community. Paul puts these issues in proper arrangement and order (*dispositio*), when he addresses concretely the causes of *schismata* (1:26–31; 3:1–17; 4:1–21) and the differences between worldly (or human) wisdom and the wisdom of God (2:6–16;

---

105. Bruce, *Galatians*, 58.
106. Longenecker, *Galatians*, cv, 185.
107. Witherington, *Grace*, 27.
108. Dunn, *Galatians*, 20.
109. See Kim, *God*, 58–89; Cicero, *De Inventione*, 1.15.20–21, 24; 1.52.98–100.
110. Campbell, *Righteousness*, 80–99.

3:18-23). Such is evidence that the function of *dispositio* (arrangement) occurs in 1 Corinthians 1-4.

Paul includes the function of *elocutio* (expression) in his letter where he quotes the slogans of some of the Corinthian Christians: "I belong to Paul," "I belong to Apollos" (1:12; 3:4), "wise," "powerful," "noble birth" (1:26), "wisdom," and "eloquent speech" (2:1-5).[111] For the function of *memoria* (recalling shared memories), 4:1-12 is an example. Paul reminds the Corinthian Christians of the ministry to which he devoted himself while he stayed in Corinth. Lastly, with regard to the function of *pronuntiatio* (delivery or tone of voice—implied only, in a letter, but already intended by Paul; see 1 Cor 5:3-4), it is taken as an example that in 1 Corinthians 1-4 Paul describes the Corinthian correspondents differently depending on the tone appropriate for each issue. He refers to them as *adelphoi* (1:10, 26; 2:1; 3:1; 4:6), as *sarkinois* (3:1), as *nēpiois en christō* (3:1), and as *tekna mou agapēta* (4:14). In using such different expressions, Paul seems to encourage the Corinthian audience to pay more attention to what he is saying and to respond emotionally to each label as given. For instance, in describing them as his beloved children in 4:14, Paul as their father commends them to stop factionalism and urges them to imitate him (4:14-16). This is clear evidence that 1 Corinthians 1-4 as a whole contains these distinctive rhetorical elements.

Cicero's rhetorical theories suggest that the Pauline text of 1 Corinthians 1-4 comprises characteristics of both deliberative and epideictic rhetorical genres, although in recent Pauline scholarship on 1 Corinthians most scholars define 1 Corinthians 1-4 as either deliberative or epideictic.[112] Jeremy Corley, however, argues that it is not easy to regard clearly 1 Corinthians as either an example of deliberative or epideictic rhetoric because it comprises characteristics of both. Hence, it is better to view 1 Corinthians as a piece of both deliberative and epideictic rhetoric

---

111. "Many scholars point to Paul's comments in 1 Corinthians 2:1-5 as evidence of his self-styled rhetoric, wherein he deliberatively eschews his rhetorical skills in order to advance the gospel" (Johnson, "Epistolary," 500 n. 49).

112. The following scholars view it as deliberative: Mitchell (*Reconciliation*, 20-23), Lanci (*Temple*, 51), Witherington (*Conflict*, 46), Welborn ("Discord," 89), Kennedy (*Interpretation*, 87), Fiorenza ("Rhetorical," 393, 399), and Wanamaker ("Power," 123).

These scholars refer to 1 Corinthians 1-4 as epideictic: Wuellner, ("Function," 46-77; "Rhetorical," 448-63), Humphries (Wire, *Women*, 198), Hester (Wanamaker, "Power," 123), and Smit ("Epideictic," 3-32; "Apollos").

Some scholars do not mention either position: Pogoloff (*Logos*), Anderson (*Ancient*, 245-76), Litfin (*Paul's*), Wire (*Women*), and Winter (*After*; *Philo*).

than of either of the two.[113] In agreement with Corley, it is argued that the Pauline text is partly epideictic because Paul deals with the present situation and the problem of schisms that the Corinthian Christians had when he wrote 1 Corinthians 1–4. In these chapters, Paul addresses the ongoing problems of factions (1:12; 3:3; cf. 11:18–19). These were caused by some of the Corinthian Christians' misuse of rhetorical conventions (1:17; 2:1–4), and by them giving a higher value to worldly understandings of wisdom and eloquence than to the wisdom of God and the gospel message (1:18–25), and by continuing expressions of high social status, wealth, and patronal hierarchies within the Christian community (1:26–29; cf. 11:22). These Corinthian Christians syncretized their social cultural practices, particularly their dependence on rhetorical conventions and patronal networks, with the practices of their Christian community and thereby discriminated against other Christians of lower social status. Paul also tackles explicitly the associated social issues of Corinthian wisdom (3:18–20), wealth, noble birth, and power (1:26; 4:8–13). In response, he wishes to describe the Corinthian church as a whole as one body (*sōma*) and the body of Christ (1 Cor 12:12–31). These are some of the issues that the Corinthian Christians faced when Paul wrote 1 Corinthians and censured them, denouncing some of their worldly-wisdom-oriented behavior (3:1–3). This clearly demonstrates some of the characteristics of an epideictic discourse as Cicero, among others, describes in his rhetorical handbooks.

Nonetheless, 1 Corinthians 1–4 also comprises some elements of deliberative oratory. The Pauline text implicitly includes the underlying themes of benefit and advantage, and the need for future-oriented decisions. These features are consistent with the characteristics of deliberative discourse as Cicero suggests in his *De Inventione*.[114] Paul refers to Apollos and himself as examples of servants of God. He then insists that both are God's fellow workers and of equal importance (3:5–8) and that between God's servants there should not be jealousy or boasting or conflict (4:1–7). He challenges the Corinthians to have the attitude of humility and sacrifice for the sake of Christ as both he and Apollos have, rather than the spirit of rivalry and competition (4:8–9).

Furthermore, Paul appeals to the Corinthians that if the leaders would have such a humble attitude, they would stop the quarrelling

113. Corley, "Authorship," 258.
114. See Cicero, *De Inventione*, 2.4.13; 2.5.18; 2.51.156; 2.52.157; 2.55.166.

and boasting which caused the problem of divisions (1:28–31). He then reclaims the Corinthian congregation from the grips of factionalism and urges them to be united in Christ. Moreover, he appeals that they love one another as brothers and sisters in the household of God (e.g., 13:1–13), just as he, as their spiritual father, loves them as his children (4:1–21). In doing this, Paul challenges some of the Corinthian Christians to stop assuming that they can take control of the Christian community by continuing to express their high social standing, wealth, and patronal hierarchies and by humiliating and discriminating against other Christians of low social position (1:18–25; 3:8). Paul does this by challenging them to stop valuing the social and cultural understandings of wisdom and eloquence more highly than Christ crucified as the wisdom of God who is the foundation of the Corinthian Christian community and the essence of the gospel message (1:18–25; 2:1–4). Paul then encourages and motivates them to make a decision to stop such worldly-wisdom-rooted conduct for the future benefit and advantage of the whole congregation. He says, "What do you wish (*ti thelete*)? Shall I come to you with a rod, or with love in a spirit of gentleness?" (4:21). Such descriptions include all the deliberative rhetorical categories of "appealing to benefit," "future response," "proof by example," and "subjects of factionalism and concord."[115]

Furthermore, Cicero describes in his *De Inventione* that in employing deliberative speech, an orator seeks in his or her audience friendship, rank, glory and influence. These possess their own intrinsic merit and bring about advantages as well.[116] These four elements are all found in the mentality and behavior of some of the Corinthian Christians as addressed in 1 Corinthians and 1–4. They built patronal relationships with other Corinthian Christians of lower classes. These relationships were beneficial for both patrons and clients. The two parties exchanged resources for mutual benefits. So they seemingly appear to be friendships between the patrons and the clients. Yet they were in fact hierarchical and unequal relationships between the two parties. They were like a relationship of a ruler and the ruled (see 1 Cor 4:8; 11:22). So these relationships did not necessarily include loving each other. In reaction to these patronal relationships, Paul appeals to the Corinthian Christians to build true friendship between themselves. In this friendship "love" is the

---

115. Mitchell, *Reconciliation*, 20–225.

116. Cicero, *De Inventione*, 2.55.166; also Appendix 1 further below.

most important element. Paul says, "Love is not arrogant or rude. Love does not insist on its own way" (1 Cor 13:4). Paul commends, "Make love your aim" (14:1). Paul took himself as an example for love. He called them brethren (e.g., 1:10; 2:1; 3:1; 10:1; 12:1). Some of the Corinthian Christians possessed wealth and power and ranked highly on the social scale (see 1:26). They were held in honor and respect (see 4:8, 10). By using their social power and wealth they influenced other Corinthian Christians of low classes to join their party and opposed Paul (1:12; 3:4). They desired glory and boasted of what they possessed in terms of worldly standards. They boasted about their wisdom, eloquence, wealth, high social status, and social power. They gave glory to themselves rather than to Christ crucified as the wisdom of God (1:29; 4:7; 5:6; cf. 2 Cor 11:18, 21, 30; 12:1). As such, 1 Corinthians 1–4 demonstrates characteristics of deliberative as well as epideictic rhetoric.

Yet, the elements of forensic rhetoric are not so clearly found in 1 Corinthians 1–4. They can be absorbed or collapsed into those of epideictic and deliberative orations. In spite of this, the mood of defense and apology which fits forensic rhetoric is glimpsed in 1 and 2 Corinthians as a whole. Paul uses the Greek word *apologia* once in each letter (1 Cor 9:3; 2 Cor 7:11). Paul exhibits explicitly that he uses 1 and 2 Corinthians as apologetic letters to defend himself. He says, "This is my defense (*apologia*) to those who would examine me" (1 Cor 9:3). This clearly accords with Cicero suggesting that the defendant defends himself or herself by using a letter or written form of apology "so as to support his or her own case and develop from the written word something that is not expressed."[117] Furthermore, Paul appears to have been aware of the frequent use of forensic rhetoric in the wider Corinthian civic society of his time. This is reflected in 1 Corinthians 6:1–8 where Paul addresses the issue of the Corinthian believers going to law courts against their fellow believers before unbelieving juries.

So, 1 and 2 Corinthians can be understood this way: Paul is the defendant, some of the Corinthian Christians and his Corinthian opponents are the accusers (1 Cor 1:26; 4:8–10, 18; 8:7–12; 2 Cor 10:1—13:10), and the rest of the Corinthian Christians are the jury. By using 1 and 2 Corinthians as his self-apology delivered in written form rather than in person, Paul defends himself. This is because Paul had better rhetorical skills in written form than in speech ("His letters are weighty and strong,

117. Cicero, *De Inventione*, 2.48.142–3.

but . . . his speech [is] of no account" [2 Cor 10:10]; "I am unskilled in speaking" [2 Cor 11:6]). Paul defends his own case by explaining why he did not adapt to the social and cultural conventions that prevailed in the wider civic society of Roman Corinth in the first century CE: Paul did not use his rhetorical skills in the proclamation of the gospel because he might have distorted the essence of the gospel message (1 Cor 1:17; 2:1-5; 2 Cor 10:1—11:33). He did not build patronal relationships or accept financial support in order that he might preach the gospel free of charge (1 Cor 9:1-23; 2 Cor 11:7-11; 12:11-14). He did not boast about his wisdom, rhetorical skills, and high social status because he boasted only of Christ Crucified as the wisdom of God (1 Cor 1:29-31; 4:6-13; 2 Cor 1:12; 10:13-18).

Finally, for a proper understanding of 1 Corinthians 1-4, it is important to note that there are more specific similarities between the language of Cicero in his rhetorical handbooks and the Pauline language of 1 Corinthians 1-4. These parallels are evident in their usage of the word "boast" (Latin, *gloriatur*;[118] Greek, *kauchaomai*). Cicero employs the word "boast" frequently in his rhetorical handbooks when he boasts about himself and the glorious traditions of Greek rhetoric.[119] Paul seems to play on this use of boasting and glory in 1 and 2 Corinthians when he reflects on the behavior of his Corinthian opponents' boasting about social and rhetorical understandings of wisdom rather than the wisdom of God (1 Cor 1:29; 3:21). It would be argued, therefore, that in order to grasp the background of the issue of boasting in 1 Corinthians 1-4, Cicero's idea of boasting and glory within his Greco-Roman world ought to be carefully examined.

In Cicero's thirty-one writings, the Latin word *gloriatur* and its equivalents occur 151 times.[120] In these occurrences, Cicero describes how boasting was a social phenomenon of the Roman society of his time. He states, "The professors and masters of rhetoric . . . boasted (*gloriatus*) before an audience . . . (about) their knowledge of literature

---

118. Its equivalents are "*gloria*" and "*glorior*" meaning "boasting,ʽ "praise,ʽ "glory,ʽ "fame," and "distinction." In addition, the Greek word *kauchaomai* is translated as *gloriatur* in the Vulgate or Latin Bible.

119. See Cicero, *Epistulae ad Familiares*, 4.8.2; *De Officiis*, 2.17.59.

120. For example, it appears thirteen times in *De Oratore*, twenty times in *Epistulae ad Familiares*, thirteen times in *Epistularum ad Atticum*, twenty-six times in *Pro T. Annio Milone Oratio*, seven times in *Epistulae ad Brutum*, fifteen times in *Pro Publio Quinctio*, and eighteen times in *Pro Sexto Roscio Amerino*.

and poetry, and the doctrines of natural science."[121] Cicero gives further examples: "For all the world like C. Caesar, as he himself often boasts."[122] "Asellus was boasting [or bragging, *gloriaretur*] that his military service had taken him over every province."[123] "I (Cicero) have often heard my own father and my wife's father say that our people . . . desired to win high distinction (*gloria*) in philosophy."[124]

Consistent with this social phenomenon, Cicero encouraged Romans to seek and pursue fame and glory. He says, "in the rest of my life, I admit that I eagerly pursued whatever might be a source of true glory (*gloria*)."[125] "Bear in mind that we are now striving after a *gloria* that remains to be won . . . but fighting for a *gloria* already ours—a *gloria* which it was not so much our object in the past."[126] "Do your utmost to surpass yourself in enhancing your own glory (*gloria*)."[127] "Each man is a partaker in the good. Is he also deserving of boasting (*gloriari*) . . . or does anybody boast about (*gloriando*) . . . his success in getting pleasure? You actually make a habit of boasting (*gloriari*) that you did so."[128] "My dear Plancus, apply yourself with all your energy to the decisive completion of war . . . (and) the culmination of your popularity and glory (*gloria*)."[129]

Cicero boasted about his oratory, political success, fame, and reputation in Roman society. This is evidenced in his language: "If anyone violently accuses me . . . for the very thing which is the boast and triumph of speech . . . that is not my fault . . ."[130] "In the very city in which I (Cicero) was richly blessed in popularity, influence, and fame (*gloria*)."[131] "I (Cicero) may boast (*gloriatur*) about myself . . . for in comparison with the eminence of the offices to which I was unanimously elected at the earliest legal age . . . the outlay in my aedileship was

---

121. Cicero, *De Oratore*, 3.32.127.
122. Cicero, *Epistulae ad Familiares*, 10.32.2.
123. Cicero, *De Oratore*, 2.44.258.
124. Ibid., 3.33.133.
125. Cicero, *Epistulae ad Familiares*, 15.6.13.
126. Cicero, *Epistulae ad Quintum Fratrem*, 1.1.43.
127. Cicero, *Epistulae ad Familiares*, 12.7.2.
128. Cicero, *Paradoxa Stoicorum*, 1.1.15; 1:4.32.
129. Cicero, *Epistulae ad Familiares*, 10.19.2.
130. Cicero, *In Catilinam*, 2.3.
131. Cicero, *Epistulae ad Familiares*, 4.8.2.

very inconsiderable."[132] He goes on to claim that "I should be returning in three days' time with the greatest glory (*summa cum gloria*)."[133] Moreover, Plutarch confirms that:

> Cicero's immoderate boasting of himself in his speech (*logos*) proves that he had an intemperate desire for fame . . . at last he praised not only his deeds and actions, but also his speeches (*logos*), both those which he delivered himself and those which he committed to writing, as if he were impetuously vying with Isocrates and Anaximenes the sophists, instead of claiming the right to lead and instruct the Roman people.[134]

As evidenced above, glory and boasting were a prominent part of the culture and mentality of Romans in the first century BCE. Cicero desired *gloria* and boasted about his eloquence, his influence, and his fame in his Roman society. He further encouraged the Romans to seek fame and glory. It can be argued, therefore, that Cicero's ideas of glory and boasting may well have affected to some degree the mentality and social behavior of the Corinthians in the mid-first century CE. As they imitated Cicero and his wisdom and eloquence, and the way he had boasted (*gloriatur*) and glorified himself, they were simply following the way Cicero had urged the Romans of his time to imitate his ancestors.

In his rhetorical handbooks Cicero employs the Latin word *imitator*, and its equivalents, often. For example, "Messalla is an excellent consul . . . for me (Cicero) he expresses admiration and respect, and shows it by imitating (*imitator*) me."[135]

> Let this then be my first counsel, that we show the students whom to imitate (*imitetur*) and to imitate (*imitabitur*) in such a way as to strive with all possible care to attain the most excellent qualities of his model. Next, let practice be added, whereby in imitating (*imitando*) he may produce the pattern of his choice and not portray him as time and again I have known many imitators (*imitatores*) do, who in imitating (*imitando*) hunt after such characteristics as are easily imitated or even abnormal and possibly faulty. For nothing is easier than to imitate (*imitari*) a man's style of dress, pose, or gait.[136]

132. Cicero, *De Officiis*, 2.17.59.
133. Cicero, *Epistulae ad Quintum Fratrem*, 1.4.4.
134. Plutarch, *Demosthenes and Cicero*, 2.1.
135. Cicero, *Epistularum ad Atticum*, 1.14.6.
136. Cicero, *De Oratore*, 3.22.90, 92.

Cicero insisted that to serve the State, the Romans should imitate the way their ancestors lived. He states, "Truly a citizen born to serve the State, mindful of the name he bears, and an imitator (*imitatoremque*) of the ancestors! For our ancestors' longing for liberty . . . was not so great as ours should be to retain it now."[137]

Paul is not opposed to the idea of *mimesis* (imitation) as such, but he wishes to offer a different "role-model,": not the wealthy and eloquent but Christ himself. Paul uses the word *mimētēs* twice in 1 Corinthians (4:16; 11:1): "be imitators of me" (4:16), and "be imitators of me, as I am of Christ" (11:1). In this way Paul subverts the imitation of the Roman ideal of glory, and offers instead the glory of the crucified Christ and his suffering followers (1 Cor 4:8–13).

It is not difficult to see parallels between the way Cicero had boasted (*gloriatur*) and the way the Pauline opponents boasted and to see how this is inversely related to Paul's ironic boasting (e.g., 1 Cor 1:28; 5:6; 9:15, 16; 15:31; cf. 2 Cor 11:18, 21; 12:1). Possibly, as other Corinthians in the broader civic society imitated Cicero and others, so these Pauline opponents took them as their model rather than the way of Christ and Paul and imitated Cicero and Seneca in the way they had encouraged the Romans to imitate their ancestors (e.g., 1 Cor 4:1, 16). These approaches were in turn subverted explicitly by Paul in 1 Corinthians 1–4. This is evident in his frequent use of the Greek word *kauchaomai* and the word *mimētēs* in 1 and 2 Corinthians.

Paul employs the word *kauchaomai* and its equivalents frequently in his writings, just as Cicero did in his rhetorical handbooks. These words occur thirty-nine times in 1 and 2 Corinthians (ten times in 1 Corinthians [1:29, 31 {twice}; 3:21; 4:7; 5:6; 9:15, 16; 13:3; 15:31], and twenty-nine times in 2 Corinthians) out of the fifty-nine times in the entire New Testament.

These occurrences indicate that by the time Paul wrote 1 and 2 Corinthians, boasting was one of the critical issues which was causing factions (*schismata*) in the Corinthian Christian community. Some of the Corinthians and the Pauline opponents probably imitated (*mimeomai*) the way Cicero had boasted (*gloriatur*) of himself and his eloquence and political success and urged his Romans to imitate (*imitator*) their ancestors. These Corinthians then boasted (*kauchaomai*) of themselves in their wisdom, eloquence, and high social status rather than of Christ as

---

137. Cicero, *Philippica*, 3.4.8.

the wisdom of God and the gospel message (e.g., 1:29–31; 3:21). Such arguments will be part of the major investigation which follows herein.

In summary, the Pauline text of 1 Corinthians 1–4 demonstrates many rhetorical features according to Cicero's theories of rhetoric. Clearly, it comprises the characteristics of both deliberative and epideictic rhetorical genres. Moreover, there are more specific similarities between Cicero's rhetorical handbooks and Paul's language of 1 Corinthians 1–4 in terms of their use of the words, boasting, and imitator. It is a major task in this work to find out backgrounds of these words and of Corinthian wisdom in general and their relation to *schismata* in the Corinthian congregation as recorded in 1 Corinthians 1–4. We now turn to a careful examination of the social background of Roman Corinth.

3

The Social Background of Roman Corinth

GIVEN THE RHETORICAL BACKGROUND of Roman Corinth in Paul's time, three elements of the social environment of the city must be carefully investigated: 1. the ethnic and social composition of the wider Corinthian civic community; 2. its patronal networks; and 3. the ethnic and social makeup of the Corinthian Christians. So, we now turn to an examination of Greco-Roman patronage.

PATRONAGE

Patronage was an integral part of the Roman social system in the Greco-Roman world of the first century CE. At the time Paul wrote 1 Corinthians, the patronage system was foundational in shaping and maintaining Roman Corinth's civic life. D. Flemming states that patronal networks were "essential to the fabric of life in Roman Corinth."[1]

The initial form of patronage emerged in Roman society in the early Roman Republic (509–31 BCE), but it extended out to the Roman colonial provinces by the late Republic and more significantly in early imperial times. The patronage of this time is glimpsed in Cicero's books and letters such as *Epistularum Ad Atticum* and *Epistulae Ad Familiares*. As L. L. Welborn argues, "Cicero's speeches and letters provide ample documentation of the way aristocrats used patronage to garner political support."[2]

---

1. Flemming, *Contextualization*, 194; also Chow, *Patronage*, 30–82; Silva, *Honor*, 94–156.
2. Welborn, *Politics*, 25.

In the Roman Empire, patronal networks appear to have existed at two different levels. Initially, patronage involved formal and legal bonds. In early Roman law patron-client relations were clearly referred to as the "ex-master-libertus relationship."[3] By these patronal systems, a governor and the city, or a former master and his freed persons, were interconnected as patrons and clients. But patronage also developed as informal and quite subtle ties arose between the emperor and his officials and between wealthy patrons and their literary friends. In these relationships, patrons and clients exchanged simultaneously different kinds of resources.[4] R. Saller describes the nature of this kind of patronage:

> First, it involves the reciprocal exchange of goods and services. Second, to distinguish it from a commercial transaction in the marketplace, the relationship must be a personal one of some duration. Third, it must be asymmetrical, in the sense that the two parties are of unequal status and offer different kinds of goods and services in the exchange—a quality which sets patronage off from friendship between equals.[5]

It is clear that patronal relationships contained three essential elements: first, patron-client relations were personal relationships similar to friendships, but vertical, asymmetrical, or hierarchical friendships. They existed between social unequals: between a patron of wealth and higher social status and poorer, lower-status clients. It must be stressed, therefore, that there were distinct social divisions between patrons and their clients within the patronal structures of the Roman imperial era. A patron could be called *rex* (king) by the clients,[6] so that the relationship between a patron and his or her clients was something like the relationship between a ruler and the ruled. It was strictly a hierarchical relationship. Nonetheless, this patronal relationship was established on a voluntary basis. A patron and his or her clients build voluntary relationships for mutual help and benefit.[7]

---

3. "When Herennius invoked his patronage duty in his refusal to testify against Marius in the late second century BCE, the (patron-client) relationship still had some legal content..." (Saller, "Friendship," 50).

4. Chow, *Patronage*, 81.

5. Saller, "Friendship," 49.

6. Martin, *Body*, 66.

7. Johnson and Dandeker, "Patronage: Relation," 221; Malina and Rohrbaugh, *Science*, 74; Elliot, "Clientage," 144.

Second, patronal systems included the reciprocal or simultaneous exchange of goods and services between a patron and his or her clients. The patron who has wealth, political power, and social influence provides scarce resources that are not easily accessible to the clients such as financial support, protection, favor, and benefit. The clients in return offer political support, honor, "promises and expressions of solidarity and loyalty," and personal service and assistance.[8]

Third, patronal networks may be metaphorically described as symbiotic relationships because they provide a strategy for survival and livelihood for clients, and a means of exercising and practicing power and influence in society for the patrons.[9] For example:

> Clients could contribute to their patron's social status by forming crowds at his door for morning *salutatio* (Tacitus, *Annals*. 3.55) or by accompanying him on his rounds of public business during the day and applauding his speeches in court. In return, (clients were due one meal a day a*nd*) could expect handouts of food or *sportulae* (small sums of money, customarily about six sesterces in Martial's day) and sometimes an invitation to dinner ... (but) Martial warns that the *sportulae* were not enough to live on. They must have been just one of the possible supplements to the grain dole (Martial, *Epigrams*. 3.7 and 8.42) ... (Humiliation of clients was frequent and little recourse was available. Patrons who provided more were considered gracious) ... Martial's verses and other evidence ... leave no doubt that the *salutatio* and other patronal customs continued to characterize life in Rome throughout the Principate.[10]

In addition, Jeffers states,

> ... a client might be invited to a patron's banquet table simply to witness the latter's wealth and power, not out of genuine friendship. In such cases the client could expect to be the butt of jokes and to receive food and wine far inferior to that of honored guests, as Juvenal laments (*Satires* 5).[11]

It is obvious that by means of patronal relationships, patrons showed off their social status such as economic wealth and social power, whereas

---

8. Neyrey, *World*, 248; see also Chow, *Patronage*, 81–82.

9. See Stambaugh and Balch, *Environment*, 112.

10. Garnsey and Saller, *Empire*, 151; see also "Power," 99–100; Malina and Rohrbaugh, *Synoptic*, 75.

11. Jeffers, *Greco-Roman*, 192.

clients were inevitably involved in these relations in order to survive in the Roman society in which reciprocal exchange friendships were so popular that they became a social convention.

Clearly, patronal relationships widely and deeply influenced a society that comprised a majority of poor and lower social-status clients and a minority of wealthy and higher-status patrons. So, in considering the social composition of Roman Corinth, a Romanized colony, it is apparent that such patronage networks existed in the city and interconnected high social-class persons (patrons) and lower-status persons (clients). People of these extreme social classes lived together having reciprocal exchanges and relationships to meet mutual needs.[12]

Patron-client structures also had an effect on the mobility between social classes in the Roman world. Regardless of social status, many people strove to rise to higher positions, especially those of the lower classes such as slaves, who sought manumission. Stambaugh and Balch states, "the most common and also the most dramatic rise in status came about in the manumission of slaves. Roman citizens set their slaves free in remarkably large numbers, and each manumitted slave became . . . a *libertus* (freedman) or *liberta* (freed woman)."[13] This manumission was "normally the reward for years of loyalty and obedience" and depended heavily on favorable patronal networks.[14] Due to this sort of manumission, a majority of the population in cities like Roman Corinth in the first century CE comprised the social class of freed men and freed women, though slaves occupied a great number of the population of the major cities, as B. Witherington states, "at least a third, if not a half, of the population of Rome was slaves."[15]

As such, for promotion in social standing and the eventual successful acquisition of Roman citizenship, clients of lower-status positions were advised to have a good friendship and patronal relationship with patrons of higher status, who undertook the role of mediation for their lower-status clients. These sorts of patronal relationships appeared at nearly every level of social standing, not only in the upper classes but also in the lower ones. The patron-client bonds that enabled some social mobility were found between the emperor and prosperous provincial

---

12. See Chow, "Patronage," 110–13.
13. Stambaugh and Balch, *Environment*, 115.
14. de Vos, "Slave," 98.
15. Witherington, *Testament*, 321.

governors, between local governors and local aristocracies, between local aristocracies and wealthy freed people, and between former masters and their manumitted slaves.[16]

Almost every case of a rise in status or promotion to higher social standing generally came about by means of recommendation and appointment by patrons.[17] For instance, when a prosperous person aspired to the local aristocracy in the civic community of Corinth, he would make the acquaintance of a patron who was in authority and possessed a socially influential position and establish a patronal relationship. At the request of the client, the patron undertook sponsorship and wrote a letter of recommendation to the emperor or governor on behalf of his client, and then the emperor or governor appointed the candidate to the local council in agreement with the patron's recommendation.[18]

Patron-client bonds could also be seen in terms of a political system in the Roman Empire especially between the ruling class or nobility and the ruled—the mass of the people. Through these patronal relations, the ruling elites maintained their dominance over the people and kept them subjected, though such relations were based on *fides* and personal connections or links of dependence and obligation.[19] For this reason patronal networks became essential for the integration of the vast Roman Empire. All the colonial provinces were interconnected and interrelated to the capital of the Roman Empire by patronal systems. By means of this imperial patronage, the emperor was able to reign and maintain his authority and domination over the Roman Empire. He was directly related not only to major officials in Rome but also to his appointed rulers of various ranks in the Roman colonies. In doing this, the emperor acted as the supreme and universal patron, and the imperial officials were his clients.[20]

---

16. So argue Stambaugh and Balch, *Environment*, 114–15.
17. See ibid., 114.
18. See Stambaugh and Balch, *Environment*, 114–15.
19. Wallace-Hadrill, "Patronage," 68.
20. See John K. Chow, "Patronage," 105; cf. Saller, *Patronage*, 205. Many examples of imperial patronage are evident in the writings of Cicero: "As for Gabinius, Cicero . . . could count on him absolutely as an adherent . . . and especially Piso, because of . . . his kinship with Caesar" (Dio Cassius, *Roman History*, 38.16.1). So also in the letters of Pliny: Pliny had a close relationship with Trajan the emperor. He petitioned the emperor to grant full Roman citizenship to his three slaves. His letter reads: "Gaius Pliny to the emperor Trajan. Valerius Paulinus, sir, has left a will which passes over his son Paulinus and names me a patron of his Latin freedmen. On this occasion I pray

In the case of those provinces, where the authority and power of the emperor did not directly reach due to distance, he sent imperial officials (such as proconsuls, imperators and delegates) to act on his behalf. These imperial officials were seen as representatives of imperial power in these regions where they acted as imperial patrons on behalf of the emperor. The provincial rulers and citizens were their clients. When imperial patronage was embraced enthusiastically by local people, the Roman officials and proconsuls were no longer regarded as foreign conquerors but as friends and benefactors.[21] For example, Cicero was a proconsul of Cilicia in 51–50 BCE. During his proconsulate, he was the imperial patron of the province[22] and provided for the Cilician people certain benefits. In return they offered their loyalty to the Romans. Cicero writes, "those who had had clear proof of my clemency and probity, had now become more friendly to the Roman people; and that Cilicia, moreover, would be confirmed in its loyalty if allowed to share the fruits of my equitable administration."[23]

Further, in this system of imperial patronage imperial officials often took on the role of patronal mediators between the emperor and the provincials. In this way, these provincials became both the imperial officials' clients and the emperor's clients. They were all under the ruling power of the emperor and his influence and benefaction. The emperor in fact extended his patronal relationships from major imperial officials through local elites and notables down to the populace and even slaves. They were potentially the recipients from the emperor of a wide range of benefits such as official positions, financial assistance, full Roman citizenship, and "the right of tapping the water supply."[24] They in return offered to the emperor as their supreme patron, deference, reverence, respect, and loyalty. As an expression of such reverence, the local people honored

---

you to grant full Roman citizenship to three of them only: it would be reasonable, I fear, to petition you to favor all alike, and I must be all the more careful not to abuse your generosity when I have enjoyed it on so many previous occasions (Pliny, *Epistles* 10.104)" (Elliott, "Clientage," 144). This is a typical example of how imperial patronage operated between the emperor and his client.

21. Garnsey and Saller, *Empire*, 152. David Braund provides examples for this (see Braund, "Dysfunction," 137–52).

22. See Cicero, *Epistulae Ad Familiares*, 15.1–15.

23. Ibid., 15.1.3.

24. Garnsey and Saller, *Empire*, 148–52; see also Chow, "Patronage," 105; Malina and Rohrbaugh, *Synoptic*, 75.

the emperor and members of the imperial family with the titles "patron," "benefactor," "savior," "lord," and "son of a god," suggesting their "greatly superior status."[25] This imperial patronage was reinforced by imperial cults. In Roman imperial times, the populace was increasingly compelled to participate in the imperial cult and emperor worship.[26]

Imperial patronage also appeared in the procedure whereby imperial officials were recruited. In Roman imperialism "patronal support was essential in the recruitment of the imperial elite because no bureaucratic mechanisms were developed to supply the next generation of aristocratic officials."[27] So, in order to recruit his officials the emperor had to rely largely on letters of recommendation written by his imperial officials.[28] These imperial officials acted as mediators between the emperor as recipient and the candidates as recommended. In doing this, the recommender acted as the emperor's client and a patron of the recommended at the same time.[29]

As stated above, patron-client structures initially emerged in Roman society in the early Roman Republic, but by the late Republican and more distinctively early imperial times they extended out to the provinces. During this period, Roman culture and social systems rapidly dominated the Roman colonies and, consequently, Roman patron-client

---

25. Examples of this include the title of patron given to Marcus Agrippa and Lucius Caesar, son of Augustus; of "benefactor" to Marcus Agrippa, Augustus, and Tiberius; of "Savior" to Marcus Agrippa, Augustus, Gytheum, and Tiberius; of son of a god or god to Augustus, Tiberius, Caligula, and Claudius (Chow, "Patronage," 105, 105 n. 5; see also Winter, *After*, 285).

26. See Jeffers, "Slaves," 127–33.

27. Garnsey and Saller, *Empire*, 153.

28. The letters were "a form of introduction," "to publicly acclaim a citizen," "a testimony to the character of a person on trial," and "to recommend favored athletics by the emperor or Roman of high status" (Marshall, *Enmity*, 92, 96, 92 n. 10).

29. See Marshall, *Enmity*, 91–129, esp. 115, 120, 123. Here is an example of a similar recommendation: "I recommend to you M. Ferdius, a Roman knight, the son of a friend of mine, a worthy and hard-working young man, who has come to Cilicia on business. I ask you to treat him as one of your friends. He wants you to grant him the favour of freeing from tax certain lands which pay rent to the cities—a thing which you may easily and honorably do and which will put some grateful and sound men under an obligation to you (*as Familiares* 8.9.4)" (Braund, "Dysfunction," 141).

The Greco-Roman custom of recommendation is also evident in the Pauline communities. Paul recommended Phoebe to the Roman Christians (Rom 16:1–3). The phrase "letters of recommendation" occurs in 2 Cor 3:1–2. Paul recommended Onesimus to Philemon for his forgiveness and acceptance (Philemon vv. 1–21).

relationships and patronal networks were firmly embedded in the wider Mediterranean social structures. In other words, rather than other earlier social systems, patronal relationships became more powerful and influential in the social fabric of the Roman colonies including first century Corinth, and they then played a vital role in increasing Roman domination in such colonies.[30] That is why it is said that patron-client relationships were "a distinctive and central element in Roman culture and ideology" and that they "represented a vital part of conscious Roman ideology, of their own image of how their world both was and ought to be."[31] In this regard, it is apparent that such patron-client relations as an expression of Roman culture and ideology played an especially significant role in shaping and maintaining the civic society of Roman Corinth because it was a Romanized colony since its re-establishment in 44 BCE. Moreover, such patronal networks may well have influenced the conduct of the Corinthian Christians, as addressed in 1 Corinthians (e.g., 1 Cor 1:10–13; 3:1–4; 11:18–19).

THE SOCIAL SITUATION OF ROMAN CORINTH

Paul arrived at Corinth from Athens (Acts 18:1). There he established the Corinthian Christian *ekklēsia* while staying for a year and six months (Acts 18:11).[32] He then went to Ephesus where he wrote the first letter to the Corinthian Christians in the mid fifties (1 Cor 16:8).[33] By this time,

30. Hendrix, "Benefactor/Patron," 40; Garnsey and Saller, *Empire*, 151; see also Horsley, *Empire*, 91, 93.

31. Wallas-Hadrill, "Patronage," 65, 71.

32. There is disagreement in recent Pauline scholarship about the year of Paul's arrival at Corinth. Some scholars argue that Paul arrived at Corinth in late 49 CE (Murphy-O'Connor, *Corinth*, 159; Engels, *Corinth*, 107), while others support early 50 CE (Thiselton, *Corinthians*, 18; Witherington, *Conflict*, 5). The precise date of Paul's arrival at Corinth need not bother one too much here. Most scholars concur that Paul stayed in Corinth for eighteen months (Horsley, *Corinthians*, 29).

33. The exact date is still debated by scholars. Witherington suggests "early in 53 or 54" (Witherington, *Conflict*, 73). Hays agrees with Fee on 53–55 (Hays, *Corinthians*, 5; Fee, *First Corinthians*, 4–5). Barrett argues for "the early months of 54, or possibly towards the end of 53" (Barrett, *Corinthians*, 5). Thiselton concurs with Murphy-O'Connor, arguing for "May" or "the early part of 54" (Murphy-O'Connor, *Corinth*, 173; Thiselton, *Corinthians*, 31). Bruce, Robertson, and Plummer prefer 55 CE, the last year of Paul's residence in Ephesus (Bruce, *Corinthians*, 25; Robertson and Plummer, *Corinthians*, xxxi). Conzelmann goes for the Spring of 55 (Conzelmann, *Corinthians*, 12–13; Thiselton, *Corinthians*, 32). Talbert argues that the year is probably around the first half of the fifties (Talbert, *Reading*, xviii), Morris "the mid fifties" (Leon Morris,

Roman Corinth was the largest and most prosperous city in Roman Greece,[34] with a population of approximately 100,000–130,000 in the years the Christian community was founded.[35] There were several factors why Roman Corinth increased its population to such a number in the Roman era. First-century Corinth enjoyed great economic prosperity. It was one of the most successful cities in the Roman Empire in terms of economic achievement, and was a wealthy, prosperous, and luxurious city. It is interesting that Murphy-O'Connor parallels Corinth to "San Francisco in the days of the gold rush."[36] Donald Engels claims that Roman Corinth was crowded with a large number of inhabitants and a diversity of people groups such as merchants; traders; ship workers; artisans; travellers; pilgrims; philosophers; rhetoricians and orators; envoys; veterans; and government officials.[37] Of these groups, the merchants played the most important role in Corinth's economic prosperity, making money through trade for the city of Corinth. As a result, they became wealthy and, at the same time, a major factor in causing the complex social strata in Corinth. They possessed high social status because their wealth ranked them highly in the social pyramid. It was commonly accepted in the Roman world that the wealthy people could gain status through using their money.[38]

Corinthians, 31). The Gallio inscription is often used to help date the writing of 1 Corinthians (cf. Acts 18:12–17) (for details see Thiselton, *Corinthians*, 29–32; Winter, "Gallio's," 213–24; Slingerland, "Acts," 439–49; Murphy-O'Connor, "Gallio," 315–17). But even this is not conclusive. So there is no unanimous agreement in Pauline scholarship for dating the writing of 1 Corinthians but the range 53–55 CE seems most plausible. The exact date is not important for our discussion.

34. Greek Corinth was destroyed by Roman forces in 146 BCE. But Julius Caesar ordered it to be rebuilt as a Roman colony in 44 BCE (Strabo, *Geography*, 8.6.23; Pausanias, *Guide to Greece*, 2.2; Dio Cassius, *Roman History*, 50.3–5; Cook, *Cambridge*, 206). Later it became the capital of the Roman province of Achaia which was formed in 27 BCE by Augustus Caesar (Horrell, *Ethos*, 65; Engels, *Corinth*, 19).

35. de Vos, *Church*, 185. Engels proposes that it was about 100, 000, consisting of the urban areas and 20,000 in the rural areas (Engels, *Corinth*, 84; cf. Murphy-O'Connor, *Corinth*, 31).

36. Murphy-O'Connor, "Saint," 147.

37. Engels, *Corinth*, 50–51. Dio Chrysostom (ca. 40–ca. 120 CE) includes some of these people groups (*Discourse*, 37.8).

38. In addition, de Vos states that "a substantial part of Corinth's wealth appears to derive from its extensive manufacturing industries, e.g., Corinthian bronze, dyeing, marble-carving, pottery, and it may have been the main center for the slave-trade in the region" (de Vos, *Church*, 186; cf. Engels, *Corinth*, 10, 35–38, 42). Particularly noteworthy was the contribution of the bronze sculpture industry to the economic development

From all over the Roman world a variety of people groups immigrated into Roman Corinth because the city was able to provide them with many opportunities for business and trade, running schools, and goods for luxurious living.[39] It is not surprising then that Paul visited Corinth with his personal interest in proclaiming the gospel (Acts 18:1, 4, 5, 11).

The city of Corinth's economic prosperity deeply influenced the life of all Corinthians, Christian and non-Christian, and especially in the area of social status. Wealth would be a major factor causing serious social stratification between the rich and the poor, the powerful and the powerless, in the broader civic communities. We should not expect the Christian community at Corinth to be an exception from these social phenomena. In the Christian *ekklēsia*, just as in the other communities to which the Christians belonged for social relationships as well, there were certainly factions or divisions between the wealthy and the poor, the upper classes and the lower classes. This is attested in 1 Corinthians in 1:10, 26–28; 3:3 and, moreover, in Paul's discussion of the Lord's Supper (1 Cor 11:17–34) where it is written, "there are divisions . . . factions among you . . . when you meet together . . . (at) the Lord's Supper . . . one is hungry and another is drunk . . . do you despise the *ekklēsia* of God and humiliate those who have nothing?" (vv.18–22).[40]

Another reason for the growth in Corinth's population was its geographical location that drew travellers and tourists, and merchants and traders. In the days of Paul, a large number of travelers and tourists visited the city of Corinth because it was regarded as a central and significant transit point from east to west or from Asia to Rome.[41] This is because, as Strabo (63 or 64 BCE to ca. 24 CE) notes,

---

of Corinth. They were exported to Rome at a high price (Cook, *Cambridge*, 403). This is evidenced further by Seneca the Younger (ca. 4 BCE–65 CE) recognizing the good quality of Corinthian bronzes (see Seneca, *De Tranquillitate Animi*, 9.5).

39. Engels, *Corinth*, 44–45, 82.

40. For a detailed discussion of this matter, see de Vos, *Church*, 179–232; Pickett, *Cross*; Lampe, "Eucharistic," 1–15.

41. E. Ferguson, *Backgrounds*, 64. This is apparently evident in the *Discourse* of Dio Chrysostom an eyewitness of Roman Corinth and Paul's contemporary. Dio Chrysostom says that " . . . upon my second visit to Corinth . . . you did your best to get me to stay with you . . . you accorded me this honor, not as to one of the many who each year put in at Cenchreae as traders or pilgrims or envoys or passing travelers, but as to a cherished friend . . . " (Dio Chrysostom, *Discourse*, 37.8; also Murphy-O'Connor, *Corinth*, 102).

> It is located on the Isthmus and is master of two harbours, one of which leads straight to Asia, and the other to Italy; and it makes easy the exchange of merchandise from both countries that are so far distant from each other . . . At any rate, to land their cargoes here was a welcome alternative to the voyage to Maleae for merchants from both Italy and Asia. And also the duties on what was exported by land from the Peloponnese (which was one of the great crossroads of the ancient world) as well as on what was imported into it belonged those who held the keys. And to later times this remained ever so.[42]

Such a good location was certainly attractive to those merchants and traders who played the most significant part in Corinth's commercial prosperity. For the traders who were involved in the transit trade between Italy and Asia, Corinth was the most crucial stopover point because ships unloaded their cargoes, goods, and passengers at one end of the Isthmus, the port of Cenchreae, transhipped across the Isthmus, and reloaded at the opposite end, at the port of Lechaeum, or vice versa.[43] In doing so, the merchants and sailors could minimize time and financial loss, avoiding the risk of "the long voyage round the rocky, storm-tossed capes at the south of the Peloponnese."[44] By virtue of these geographical merits, Roman Corinth in the first century was well known as a crossroad for ideas, trade, commerce, and traffic in the eastern Mediterranean world.[45] For these reasons, the population of Roman Corinth increased dramatically during the first century of the Common Era.

Furthermore, it is likely that for Paul as a tentmaker and leatherworker (the same trade as Aquila and Priscilla, Acts 18:3), Roman Corinth should become an attractive and interesting city because of its commercial and geographical importance for his tentmaking business in particular. It also makes sense that a number of the Corinthians in Paul's time would be merchants and traders engaged in the trading business rather than agriculture (Acts 18:3; Rom 16:1; 1 Cor 1:11, 16; 16:15). Some, thus, became wealthy (cf. 1 Cor 1:26). Importantly, Engels

---

42. Strabo, *Geography* 8.6.20; cf. Engels, *Corinth*, 50; Murphy-O'Connor, "Saint," 148; *Corinth*, 53; Hays, *Corinthians*, 3.

43. Engels, *Corinth*, 50–51.

44. Morris, *Corinthians*, 17.

45. Hafemann, "Corinthians," 172. Dio Chrysostom describes Corinth as "the promenade of Greece" and as located at "the cross-roads of Greece" (Dio Chrysostom, *Discourse* 8.5; also Murphy-O'Connor, *Corinth*, 100, 103).

points out that their income possibly made a substantial contribution to the prosperous economy of Corinth.[46] No doubt any in the Christian community who were wealthy would play a significant part as patrons who supported Paul's mission and provided their houses for congregational gatherings. This idea is supported by Luke in Acts where he tells of Aquilla and his wife Priscilla (Acts 18:2; cf. Rom 16:3), and also it is attested in Romans and 1 Corinthians where Paul speaks of Phoebe, Gaius, Erastus, Chloe, and Stephanas (Rom 16:1, 23; 1 Cor 1:11, 16).

The city of Corinth was also seen as "a major center of entertainment" and "a major tourist attraction in itself."[47] The Isthmian games played a substantial role in attracting a large number of tourists to Corinth.[48] The theaters of Corinth were also considered important centers for entertainment and religious festivals during the Roman era.[49]

The Isthmian games were dedicated to Poseidon, the god of the sea, and were regarded as one of the three most important religious and athletic festivals in Greece. The Games were held biennially under the supervision of the city of Corinth, while the Caesarean Games and the imperial Contests were held every four years.[50] Every two years, due to the Isthmian games, Corinth played host to a multitude of pilgrims, visitors, athletes, and delegates, though they were actually held nearby at Isthmia, where the temple of Poseidon was located.[51] In the time of Paul, particularly in the fifties, the Isthmian games became more and more famous and attracted a large number of participants and even dignitaries like Nero who, himself, in later years, visited the games and actually took part in the contests.[52] Furthermore, the Isthmian games reflected and reinforced the importance of social status in Roman Corinth because the person elected as the president of the games was guaranteed to possess great wealth and honor. During the games, the president provided

---

46. Engels, *Corinth*, 51.

47. Ibid., 47, 51.

48. Dio Chrysostom clearly mentions the popularity of the Isthmian games. He says that "when the time for the Isthmian games arrived, and everybody was at the Isthmus . . . " (Dio Chrysostom, *Discourse* 8.6; also Murphy-O'Connor, *Corinth*, 100).

49. Cf. Boatwright, "Theaters," 184–92.

50. See Winter, *After*, 10. For a detailed explanation of the Isthmian games see Broneer, "Isthmian," 2–31; cf. Rothaus, *Corinth*, 84–92.

51. Broneer, "Isthmian," 5.

52. Winter, *After*, 277.

luxurious dinner feasts to which those of higher social standing among the privileged elite of Corinth and its Roman citizens were invited.[53]

Interestingly, these Isthmian games clearly influenced Paul's ideas in 1 Corinthians 9:24–27 where words closely related to athletic contests appear, such as *stadion, trechō, brabeion, stephanos,* and *agōnizomai*.[54] It is probable that Paul, like many of his contemporaries, visited and attended in person the famous athletic festivals and made it a good opportunity to carry on his mission.[55] Oscar Broneer even asserts that for Paul the Isthmian games played "a contributing, if not decisive, role in his choice of Corinth as the chief base of his missionary work."[56] It is plausible, therefore, to imagine that Paul shared the message of the gospel with his neighboring viewers in the crowd during the Isthmian games, just as he did in the synagogue every Sabbath (Acts 18:4).

Roman Corinth was also well known as a city of diverse cults and religions including Judaism and Christianity. In the time of Paul, Corinth had numerous temples, shrines, and ritual sites, numbering at least twenty-six.[57] Craig S. de Vos lists some of the major deities as follows:

> The gods and cults adopted or revived by the Corinthians included Apollo, Aphrodite/Venus, Asclepius, Athena, Athena Chalinitis, Demeter and Kore, Dionysus, Ephesian Artemis, Hera Acraea,

---

53. Ibid., 277, 283.

54. Murphy-O'Connor, "Saint," 149; Broneer, "Isthmian," 17; Stambaugh and Balch, *Environment*, 158. Additionally, in order to help us understand the meaning of the words *phthartos stephanos* ("perishable wreath") and *aphthartos* ("imperishable") in v. 25, we note that in the Isthmian games of Paul's days at the middle of the first century, the Isthmian crown that was made of wild celery which grew in abundance in surrounding areas of Corinth, was awarded to the victors. The wreath of celery did not stay fresh for several days, but it withered quickly. When he wrote verse 25 Paul would keep such an idea in mind. In illustrating the withered crown Paul intended to emphasize "the contrast between the perishable wreath (*phthartos stephanos*) of the athletes with the imperishable (*aphthartos*) prize awarded to those who, like the Apostle, persevered in the exercise of Christian virtues" (Broneer, "Pagan," 186). Thereby, it is likely that Paul was present among the crowd who viewed the Isthmian games, and such an experience inspired him to present the Christian life in terms relevant to Corinthian social circumstances. This idea is more certainly evident in his arguments against the problems of divisions and wisdom in the Corinthian congregation as addressed in 1 Cor 1–4.

55. Stambaugh and Balch, *Environment*, 158.

56. Broneer, "Pagan, 169, 187.

57. Hafemann, "Corinthians," 172–73. For more details on religions in Roman Corinth see Schowalter and Friesen, *Urban*.

Hermes/Mercury, Jupiter Capitolius, Poseidon/Neptune, Tyche/Fortuna and Zeus.[58]

This list indicates the overlapping between Roman gods and Greek ones, or at least in the names used. It also shows that the people of Roman Corinth in general did not worship predominantly a single god or cult. Instead, their religious belief was complex and intricately mixed up with a diversity of gods and cults. Thus, it is difficult to determine which were the most important gods or cults accepted by them,[59] although de Vos has suggested helpfully that:

> According to the number of temples, shrines and statues, and the number of images on coins, the two most important and popular gods were Poseidon/Neptune and Aphrodite/Venus.[60]

Of the temples in Corinth, that of Aphrodite, the goddess of love, beauty, and fertility, located on the summit of the mountain at Acrocorinth was the most famous. That is why a large number of religious pilgrims from all over the Mediterranean world visited the temple, which directly affected the growth of the economy of the city of Corinth.[61] Moreover, the worship of Poseidon, the god of the sea, was of special importance because it was associated with the Isthmian games which also played a decisive role in Corinth's economic prosperity.[62] The importance of this worship for the wider culture is attested in the complex of buildings surrounding the sanctuary of Poseidon. Engels describes it as follows:

> The sanctuary itself consisted of the large Doric temple of Poseidon, a theatre, and a stadium where the literary and athletic contests were held. There were also numerous auxiliary buildings: a bath, stoas, smaller shrines, and a hotel for visiting athletes.[63]

It is apparent that the identification of the Corinthians with the god of Poseidon and the goddess of Aphrodite was of importance for their

---

58. de Vos, *Church*, 192; see also E. Ferguson, *Backgrounds*, 143.
59. Engels, *Corinth*, 95.
60. de Vos, *Church*, 192
61. Witherington, *Conflict*, 12. Many scholars have noted that Strabo claimed that in Corinth there were 1,000 sacred prostitutes practicing at the temple of Aphrodite. Most scholars agree that it is doubtful whether or not such sacred prostitution took place at the temple of Aphrodite in Roman times (Strabo, *Geography*, 8.6.20; Witherington, *Conflict*, 13; Engels, *Corinth*, 226 n. 17).
62. Engels, *Corinth*, 96.
63. Ibid.

religious needs and entertainment as well as for Corinth's economic and commercial prosperity.

The imperial cult also played a substantial role in the economy of Roman Corinth, as well as in increasing its population. The imperial cult, or emperor worship, was firmly established by the time the early Christian *ekklēsia* was beginning. The imperial cult had already existed in some form in the Roman Empire since the reign of Augustus Caesar, decades before the founding of the Corinthian Christian community.[64] In the imperial era, emperors such as Julius Caesar, Augustus, and Claudius (who died in 54 CE) were given divine honors and apotheosized or portrayed as deities. Particularly, Augustus "was transferred among the celestial gods by apotheosis" on his death in 14 CE and "by official act" the senate included him in "the list of Roman deities."[65] Later, temples were dedicated to Augustus during the reign of Tiberius (d. 37 CE) and of Caligula (d. 41 CE). These temples were ordinarily placed at the center of the provincial capitals where the assembly gathered, such as Roman Corinth, the capital of Achaia.[66] Moreover, in the imperial cult the emperors including the reigning and the dead were increasingly adored and honored as deities, and the imperial family elevated to a divine status. Diverse divinities were related to the emperors as their "protectors and helpers."[67] It is clear, therefore, that in the imperial cult the Corinthians worshipped or venerated not only deceased emperors but also the reigning one, and even living members of the imperial family. This cult was closely connected to the Isthmian games, because it was expressed in the form of an annual event taking place on the birthday of the reigning emperor, while the games were combined with this event every second year.[68]

Clearly then, the Isthmian games and the imperial cult played an important role in the life of the Corinthians because they were closely linked to their economic well-being and social status. Only the socially

---

64. Shotter, *Caesar*, 60; E. Ferguson, *Backgrounds*, 197.

65. E. Ferguson, *Backgrounds*, 195–97. In addition, Gaius Suetonius Tranquillus argued that "'Augustus' was both a more original and more honorable title, since sanctuaries and all places consecrated by the augurs are known as 'august'—the word being . . . an enlarged form of *auctus*, implying the 'increase' of dignity thus given such places . . . "(Tranquillus, *Twelve*, 48).

66. E. Ferguson, *Backgrounds*, 198.

67. Ibid., 197

68. Winter, *After*, 271, 273.

privileged were allowed to participate in this cultic festival, because the imperial cult "was conducted by the same officials as were responsible for local government."[69] The imperial cult, furthermore, was intimately related to patron-client relations because this cult was strengthened and popularized by "a large number of private associations that took as their patron the emperor," and because in order to celebrate and fully participate in the cultic festival, a large financial contribution was demanded.[70] This contribution was made by patrons of the city. For example, Gaius Iulius Spartiaticus was a major patron of Roman Corinth and a president of the Isthmian games. He was also Achaia's first high priest who conducted the imperial cult in Roman Corinth.[71] As such, the imperial cult embodied the ideals of the life of the upper-social classes and of patron-client networks in Roman Corinth.

So it is that cults and religious festivals, such as the worship of Poseidon and Aphrodite and the imperial cult, were closely related to the economic prosperity and social stratification of Roman Corinth in the first century. The Corinthians worshipped many different Roman and Greek deities. That is why the city of Roman Corinth consisted of numerous temples and ritual sites (see above). Consequently, the Corinthians did not seem to have a clear preference for a particular deity. In other words, in their mentality there was a plurality of deities and a syncretistic polytheism. This sort of Corinthian attitude toward the deities may have continued to be practiced by some of the Corinthian Christians in the Christian community and to influence their disability to distinguish between God the Creator and Greek and Roman gods. The prevalence of a syncretistic polytheism is apparently reflected in Paul's language in 1 Corinthians 8:4-5, where he says, "'an idol has no real existence' . . . 'there is no God but one' . . . many 'gods' and many 'lords' . . . "(RSV). In reaction to such Corinthian attitudes toward polytheism, Paul puts a strong emphasis on Christ crucified and the wisdom of God and the power of God (1 Cor 1:18-25).

To summarise our overview of the social situation in Roman Corinth, by the time Paul founded the Corinthian Christian community, a wide range of people groups such as merchants, rhetoricians, religious pilgrims, Jews, Greeks, and Romans inhabited the city of Corinth from

---

69. Shotter, *Caesar*, 61.
70. E. Ferguson, *Backgrounds*, 198.
71. Winter, *After*, 274-75.

all over the Roman Empire. As a result, a diversity of cultures, social systems, philosophies, cults, and religions were interwoven and intermingled in the social fabric. Accordingly, it is not unreasonable to expect that the Christian *ekklēsia* at Corinth would be composed of a diversity of people groups and social classes. Such a conclusion is suggested to some extent by 1 Corinthians 12:13, "Jews or Greek, slave or free." We should read the text with an awareness that in the Christian community at Corinth there were issues reflecting social stratification among the members, such as the upper class and the lower class, the wealthy and the poor, the elite and the uneducated, the powerful and the powerless, the free and the enslaved, even though it was a relatively small-sized community.[72] Similarly, there would be a diversity of problems within the Christian community (1 Cor 1–4). That is why the Corinthian correspondence must be read in the light of the complex social situation of the Corinthian community.

THE ETHNIC AND SOCIAL MAKEUP OF ROMAN CORINTH AND THE CORINTHIAN CHURCH

Paul's letters to Corinth confirm that the Christian *ekklēsia* at Corinth was a multi-cultural and multi-ethnic community,[73] reflecting to some extent the wider civic community of Roman Corinth in the first century. In the time of Paul, there was a diversity of ethnic migrant communities at Corinth including Romans, Jews, and Greeks who came from all over the Roman world. So, the Corinthian Christian gatherings would no doubt reflect to some extent the ethnic composition of the wider civic community at Corinth (e.g., Acts 18:1–28; Rom 16 1–3, 23; 1 Cor 1:11, 22, 23; 12:12; 16:12–19).

Nonetheless, the members from Greek and Jewish origins were the majority groups in the Christian community at Corinth. This is the reason Paul speaks of these ethnic groups specifically and gives special attention to them in 1 Corinthians 1:22 and 24.[74] In these verses the word *Hellēnes* appears twice, and the word *Ioudaiois* occurs three times (including v. 23): "for Jews (*Ioudaiois*) demand signs and Greeks (*Hellēnes*)

---

72. The Christian *ekklēsia* at this time had approximately forty to fifty people (see de Vos, *Church*, 203; Murphy-O'Connor, *Corinth*, 182).

73. Cf. de Vos, *Church*, 197.

74. See also 1 Cor 10:32 (*Ioudaiois . . . Hellēsin . . . tē ekklēsia tou theou*) and 12:13 (*eite Ioudaioi eite Hellēnes . . .*).

seek wisdom . . . a stumbling block to Jews (*Ioudaiois*) . . . but to those who are called, both Jews (*Ioudaiois*) and Greeks (*Hellēnes*) . . . "(RSV). It is worth noting that in verse 23, rather than the word *Hellēn* (Greek), Paul employs the plural form of the word *ethnos* (Gentile) to describe the ethnic groups that are distinguished from Jews (*Ioudaiois*). The question here is, do we interpret it as Gentiles referring to all other ethnic groups or do we understand it as simply a different expression for Greeks? The former is more appropriate than the latter. The word *ethnos* occurs four times in 1 Corinthians (1:23; 5:1; 10:20; 12:2) and once in 2 Corinthians (11:26). Can it possibly be understood only in 1:23 as an alternative description of Greeks? In the other occurrences, it is referring to ethnic groups other than Jews in the Christian community at Corinth.[75] This understanding is attested in 10:20 where Paul uses the word as referring to Gentiles who offered sacrifices to demons. Not only Greeks but also people of other ethnic groups such as Romans participated in cults and cultic feasts. Therefore, it is plausible that the plural form of the Greek word *ethnos* in 1:23 is interpreted as referring to people of other ethnic groups at Corinth including Greeks. In addition to the two major ethnic groups of Jews and Greeks, Paul indicates implicitly that the Corinthian congregation comprised other minor ethnic groups such as Romans, Anatolians, Phoenicians, Syrians, Egyptians, Gauls, and citizens from Asia Minor.[76]

It is also clear that the re-established Roman colony at Corinth consisted of a diversity of social classes. This social makeup is apparent in the Pauline language of 1 Corinthians 1:26–28 and 12:13. In 1 Corinthians 1:26–28 in particular, Paul talks about upper or higher classes in the social pyramid such as the "wise," the "powerful" and those who are of "noble birth" (v. 26). In verses 27–28 he speaks of lower classes such as the "foolish," the "weak" and the "low." Such a social composition within the Corinthian congregation is clearly representative of the broader civic community of Corinth. In the imperial world, there existed a diversity of social classes. Moreover, there was a strong social hierarchical structure or social stratification in all civic communities including first-century Corinth. Such a social hierarchy deeply affected the lives of the Christian communities in the New Testament times and especially the Corinthian

75. Tibbs, *Experience*, 159 n. 60.

76. Engels, *Corinth*, 70; de Vos, *Church*, 187; see also my "1 Corinthians 12:12–13," 124.

congregation Paul founded.[77] For these reasons, it is needed to outline the ethnic and social diversity of Roman Corinth in the first century and to investigate a detailed profile of the *ekklēsia* itself using to some extent the evidence of 1 and 2 Corinthians. Prior to this, it is helpful to describe briefly the social hierarchical structure of the wider Roman Empire.

In the wider Roman Empire there existed a strong social hierarchical system, with the emperor at the pinnacle of the social pyramid.[78] On the next level were the senators, numbering about six hundred throughout the whole Roman Empire, who "commanded the armies, administered some of the provinces, contributed to social and cultural projects, and fulfilled ceremonial priesthoods."[79] They, too, exercised great wealth and power.

Below the senators, there was a large group of "equestrians" or "knights" who were wealthy and rich Roman citizens and landowners able "to ride to battle on horseback," and in the imperial era "the order of the knights became an intermediate elite, with certain status symbols and with responsibility for certain duties in the government of city and empire."[80] It was possible, but unusual, for a man of this rank to rise to become Emperor, as did Vespasian.

On a lower level than the knights there was a group of local aristocrats in the provinces and cities. They obtained:

> Wealth and influence through inheritance, business, or appointment (and) exercised political authority by serving as *decuriones*—members of the local council—in cities and towns throughout the Empire . . . Their civic duties included collecting taxes, supervising harbors and markets, and undertaking embassies to governors and kings.[81]

---

77. Cf. Theissen, *Setting*, 70.

78. Stambaugh and Balch (*Environment*) give a very helpful description of social classes in Greco-Roman culture. They observe that there were two main categories, the upper classes and the lower classes in the social pyramid in general, although MacMullen argues that in the Roman Empire between the top and the bottom there was a middle class, "a range of intermediate wealth made up the aristocracy of small cities" (MacMullen, *Relations*, 89). The proposals of Stambaugh and Balch is incorporated with that of MacMullen in the following description.

79. Stambaugh and Balch, *Environment*, 111.

80. Ibid.

81. Ibid.

These members of the upper strata were conspicuous, so that they dominated and controlled the social, economic, and political power of the Empire, though they were relatively few in number. In the New Testament itself, there are very few mentioned from the upper classes, the highest (apart from the named Emperors) being proconsuls like Sergius Paulus in Cyprus (Acts 13: 4, 7) and Gallio in Achaia (Acts 18:12), and local aristocrats like Erastus in Roman Corinth (Rom 16:23) and Dionysius the Areopagite in Athens (Acts 17:34).[82]

On the other hand, the lower social classes included "small landowners, crafts-persons, (merchants), and shopkeepers and also the middle and lower ranks of Roman citizens in the army, from centurions down to ordinary legionary soldiers and veterans."[83] They were people of some moderate means. Some Corinthian Christians like Priscilla and Aquila seem to have belonged to this group.[84]

Below them there were extremely poor people who did not own any property but worked on farms, in construction sites, and at the docks to sustain their living. If such day laborers in Rome possessed Roman citizenship, "they could claim their portion of the monthly grain dole, and there were special provisions made to feed the poor in some other cities."[85] Otherwise, the only hope for the masses was to align themselves in some way with a wealthier patron.

Finally, the lowest legal status of the social pyramid were the slaves. To Greek philosophers they were seen as "less than human," and in Roman law they were treated as "a piece of property."[86] Thousands of slaves were regarded as "nothing but a commodity."[87] They "worked as chattel gangs on ships, farms, road construction, and mining."[88] So they were extremely poor. In contrast to these slaves, there was another category of slaves in Greco-Roman society who took "administrative and managerial positions" and were "active in the world of business and commerce as agents, or as managers of enterprises in which they themselves participated as

---

82. Ibid., 112.
83. Ibid.
84. Ibid.
85. Ibid.
86. Ibid., 113.
87. Ibid.
88. Ibid.

bankers, shopkeepers, traders, or craftspeople."[89] These slaves were hired by wealthy, socially powerful, and influential families and enjoyed great privileges. Moreover, they were often considered quite influential people within the local civic communities because their masters' social power and influence extended to them also.[90] For the servile class, Onesimus is an example in the New Testament (Philemon vv. 1–16).

It appears that in the Corinthian Christian gatherings, as in the wider society, there were far greater numbers from the lower classes than the upper classes. 1 Corinthians 12:13 suggests that there were, in general, two different categories of social status in the Corinthian congregation: the enslaved (*douloi*) and the free (*eleutheroi*). 1 Corinthians 1:26–28 also suggests that the majority of the Corinthian congregation was not from the higher classes. Paul says, "not many of you were wise . . . not many were powerful, not many were of noble birth" (1 Cor 1:26). Yet the very mention of this implies that there were some who were wise, powerful, and of noble birth (as indicated by Rom 16:23).

This is supported to a certain degree by Theissen. He provides good parallel information which sheds light on the possible social composition of the Corinthian congregation. He compares two different types of clubs in antiquity, professional clubs, and religious clubs. The professional clubs were comprised of 1.18 percent senators, 0.60 percent knights, 0.47 percent decurions, 32.75 percent free people, 64.95 percent freed persons, and 0.05 percent slaves. On the other hand, the religious clubs, Jewish and Christian communities included,[91] had no senators or knights, 0.47 percent decurions, 17.25 percent free people, 63.60 percent freed persons, and 18.68 percent slaves. The professional clubs had some very high-ranked people like senators and knights, whereas the religious clubs did not include such high-ranked people, but only decurions. Both types of clubs comprised the class of freed persons (*liberti*) as the majority group, contributing about two-thirds of the total members. In

89. Martin, *Slavery*, 13, 15.

90. Ibid., 17.

91. It is worth noting that some scholars such as Strom and Judge claim that it is anachronistic to consider the first-century Christian community as a separate religious group. To their contemporaries it appeared that the Christian group was the same as the Jewish one and that the legal exemption granted to Jews was applied to the Christians as well (Strom, *Reframing*, 134). The people outside the Jewish and Christian communities regarded the Jewish group irreligious because Judaism was accepted as "a legal cult (*religio licita*)" and because Jews were exempted from obligation to the imperial cult, ibid.

the former, there was a substantially higher percent of free persons but scarcely any slaves, whereas in the latter there was a small number of free persons, but rather a large number of slaves. These figures suggest that the majority of the Corinthian congregation was likely to comprise those who were poor and of lower social classes such as slaves and freed persons, though some of the freed persons possessed wealth and higher social status. Slaves and ex-slaves together would have contributed more than 80 percent of the whole congregation.[92]

Such scholars as R. J. Banks doubt, however, that the majority of members of the Pauline communities, including the Corinthian congregation, belonged to lower social classes. Banks claims that 1 Corinthians 1:26 indicates that "a significant number of people in the Corinthian church came from the more respected levels of society," in other words, the class of "social and political prestige."[93] At a glance, 1 Corinthians 1:26 appears to indicate that there were a few members such as Erastus and Gaius who came from this class (cf. Rom 16:23). Yet this does not seem to support the conclusion that a significant number of Corinthian Christians belonged to this level of high social class but rather that the majority of the Corinthian Christians belonged to lower social status. Having understood this, we now turn to an examination of the diversity of ethnic groups in the broader society of Roman Corinth and the Corinthian Christian community including Jews, Greeks, and Romans, beginning with a description of the Jews in the city.

Jews

A sizable Jewish community had already existed in Roman Corinth long before Paul arrived and established the Christian community. de Vos argues that:

> It is likely that there were Jews among the colonists (in 44 BCE) since Pompey had taken a large number of Jews back to Rome as slaves in 61 BCE, many of whom would have been *liberti* (freed persons) at the time the colonists were chosen (44 BCE) . . . during the civil war between Caesar and Pompey the Jews probably supported Caesar. Thus . . . in reward for this loyalty Caesar designated some as colonists . . . (and) there was a strong Jewish community at Corinth in the first century CE. The Jewish community

---

92. Theissen, "Structure," 76–77; also Meggitt, *Poverty*, 41–180.
93. Banks, *Idea*, 116.

may have been well integrated and on good terms with the wider community since there is no record of any conflict.[94]

On this basis it is likely that in the mid-first century CE there was a substantial Jewish community at Corinth. This idea is supported by Philo's writing in the early forties, where he refers to a Jewish colony in many places including Corinth.[95] It is also evident in the discovery of a Greek inscription reading "synagogue of the Hebrews" at Roman Corinth, probably dating to post-first century CE.[96]

Witherington argues further:

> As many as two thirds of all Jews in Paul's day lived outside Palestine. About seven percent of the Empire's population appears to have been Jewish. They ranged from very sectarian and separatist to very Hellenized, and also from rather wealthy to slaves, though there appear to have been fewer Jewish slaves than slaves of any other ethnic group. The Jewish community of Corinth probably included a few Roman citizens, ship-owners, ship-workers, artisans, merchants and slaves . . . Jewish religion in the Diaspora (was) . . . somewhat more liberalized than in Palestine . . . (for instance) women had prominent roles in Diaspora synagogues.[97]

Consequently, there is no doubt that there existed a substantial Jewish community at Roman Corinth in the days of Paul.

As observed above, in this Jewish ethnic community at Roman Corinth there was also a wide range of social classes. Some possessed Roman citizenship, wealth, and power in the wider civic society, so they were ranked high in the social pyramid. Others were ranked fairly low on the social scale, such as the artisans, slaves, and urban poor.[98] Due to such social stratification, there would have been tensions, divisions, and potentially discrimination and humiliation within the Jewish community itself. Whether the Jews of socially higher classes humiliated

---

94. de Vos, *Church*, 187–88.

95. Philo, *De Virtutibus*, 281.

96. Witherington, *Conflict*, 25–26; Richardson, "Judaism," 52. cf. Stambaugh and Balch, *Environment*, 159.

97. Witherington, *Conflict*, 27. Cf. Meeks, who claims that in the first century "some five to six million Jews" lived in the Diaspora. "There was a substantial Jewish population in virtually every town of any size in the lands bordering the Mediterranean." So Meeks argues for an even higher percentage (about 10–15 percent) of Jews in the wider Empire (Meeks, *Urban*, 34).

98. See Witherington, *Conflict*, 27.

and despised lower-status ones, just as happened in the Christian community at Corinth (1 Cor 11:17-22), is not clear, since the evidence of the dinner parties in 1 Corinthians 11 suggests a thoroughly Hellenized setting for at least some of the divisions.

These investigations of the Jewish community at Corinth in the time of Paul help assume that the Jews (or the members of Jewish origin) in the Corinthian congregation did not comprise the majority of Paul's opponents. This is because Paul did not make many converts among the Jews, particularly the wealthy and those of high social classes in the wider Corinthian civic society because of their hostile attitude towards his evangelism (Acts 18:5-6).

In spite of this, 1 Corinthians 1:22-25 and 12:13 appears to indicate that there were Jewish members in the Corinthian congregation. This idea is attested in 1 Corinthians 7:18-19 where Paul refers to "circumcised believers" in the Corinthian Christian community,[99] and is explicitly evident in Acts 18 where Luke clearly speaks of Jewish members in the Christian community at Corinth, such as Aquila and Priscilla (v. 2; cf. Rom 16:3), Titus Iustus, a God-fearer who lived next door to the synagogue (v. 7),[100] and Crispus the ruler of the synagogue (v. 8; cf. 1 Cor 1:14; cf. Sosthenes the ruler of the synagogue [v. 17; 1 Cor 1:1]).[101] From this evidence, there is no doubt that there were members of Jewish origin in the Corinthian congregation (1 Cor 1:22, 24; 12:13; cf. Acts 18:4).[102] Moreover, some of them were patrons who hosted and supported the Christian *ekklēsia* (e.g., 1 Cor 1:14; 16:19; cf. Rom 16:1-3).

Of those members of Jewish origin, Crispus was one of the first attracted to the Christian faith in Corinth and seems to have been wealthy and of high social standing. He was possibly respected in the wider civic community because of his former career as a ruler of the synagogue.[103] After conversion, he continued to influence other Corinthians and have

---

99. Ibid., 24.

100. Engels, *Corinth*, 107.

101. Augustine Myrou correctly argues that Sosthenes and Crispus in Acts 18 and 1 Cor 1 were the same person, the head of the Synagogue at Corinth. Crispus changed his name on his conversion, just like Paul (Myrou, "Sosthenes," 207-12).

102. See my "1 Corinthians 12:12-13," 127.

103. Thiselton supports this view and argues that " . . . Crispus was ruler of the synagogue (Acts 18:8), this was an honorific title awarded by a community in gratitude for a donation to their place of prayer. Such a one was not a poor man" (Thiselton, *Corinthians*, 141).

a good and respectful reputation in the wider Corinthian civic society (cf. Acts 18:8). He may have helped Paul make converts among the Corinthians, especially the Jews with whom Crispus had a good relationship. So Crispus more likely belonged to the group of higher status members than that of lower class members in the Corinthian congregation. Accordingly, his conversion was of great importance and encouragement for Paul's mission at Corinth.[104]

In addition, Aquila and Priscilla were patrons of Paul (Acts 18:2; Rom 16:3–5; 1 Cor 16:19), and probably Apollos (cf. Acts 18:26). They were possibly freed persons of Jewish origin who came from Rome in 49 CE (cf. Acts 18:1–3).[105] They were co-workers with Paul for the Messianic or Christ-oriented mission to Corinth and beyond, as well as in the tentmaking business (*skēnopoioi*) (Acts 18:3), as artisans, and probably leatherworkers. Because of their occupation, they were probably ranked fairly low in the wider social pyramid, but they in fact were not so.[106] They, rather, were relatively wealthy because they most likely employed workers and slaves to make tents and leatherwork. This is explicitly indicated in the fact that they offered accommodation to Paul, frequently traveled from one place to another, and were patrons of the Christian communities at Corinth, Ephesus, and Rome (Acts, 18: 2, 26; Rom 16:3; 1 Cor 16:19). It seems plausible, hence, that in spite of their lowly occupation as *skēnopoioi*, they were relatively well-off (or "well-to-do"), whereas a great number of artisans would have been among the urban poor at the time they stayed at Corinth.[107]

Paul would normally have made contact with many Jews in religious, political, social, and economic gatherings.[108] But in the Jewish

---

104. Pogoloff, *Logos*, 190; de Vos, *Church*, 198; Theissen, *Setting*, 75.

105. At this time the emperor Claudius closed down the Jewish synagogues in Rome, then he ordered the Jews out of Rome because "they were out of favor with the imperium" (Thiselton, *Corinthians*, 1343; Witherington *Testament*, 261.

106. Horrell, *Ethos*, 99.

107. Fee, *Corinthians*, 835–36; Witherington, *Conflict*, 322. Interestingly, it is said that "the fact that Priscilla's name is mentioned before her husband's name once by Paul (Rom 16:3) and (twice) out of three times in Acts (e.g., Acts 18:26) suggests that she has higher status than her husband" (Horrell, *Ethos*, 99; cf. Thiselton, *Corinthians*, 1344; Meeks, *Urban*, 59), or at least in the church she does. As Peter Lampe argues, "Apparently Priscilla was even more outstanding in her work for the church than was Aquila" ("Roman," 223).

108. Stambaugh and Balch, *Environment*, 159.

community at Corinth, Paul was not highly successful in attracting many to the way of Jesus, although such influential and wealthy Jews as Crispus did join him in the *ekklēsia*. This apparently was because the Jewish community as a whole was hostile to him and his message (Acts 18:5–6).[109] This is understandable as we realize that there were serious tensions and conflicts between Christ-believers and Jewish believers. These tensions and conflicts were casued by Paul. His Messianic or Christ-oriented mission to Gentiles lured into the Christian community those God-fearers and proselytes to Judaism who were often patrons of the synagogues.[110]

In Roman Corinth, according to Peter Richardson's proposal, there was "a variant form" of Judaism such that Egyptian (or Alexandrian) Judaism had a heavy impact upon some of the Corinthian Christians.[111] That this Egyptian Judaism existed in Corinth is evident in the use of the name of "Apollos."[112] In Acts, Luke describes how Apollos, an Alexandrian, came to Corinth and influenced some of the Corinthian Christians after Paul had left the city (cf. Acts 18:24–28; 19:1; 1 Cor 1:12; 4:6). Before conversion, Apollos (Acts 18:24) was possibly influenced by "the Egyptian Therapeutae," and after becoming converted to Christianity might have consciously or unconsciously brought such influences into the Christian communities in Ephesus as well as Corinth (e.g., Acts 18:24—19:1).

Nonetheless, this knowledge about specific Jewish members in the Corinthian congregation suggests that the majority of Paul's opponents in the Corinthian congregation were not members of Jewish origin who possessed wealth and ranked highly in the social pyramid. This small group, rather, seems to have supported Paul. Nor were the Jewish members of low social standing, who might have opposed Paul in some aspects, the key opponents. They neither possessed wealth nor were ranked socially

---

109. Engels, *Corinth*, 108

110. Theissen, *Setting*, 104. In a very similar sense, Witherington says that "synagogue attending Gentiles" were converted to the new Christian faith in Corinth (*Conflict*, 25).

111. Richardson, "Judaism," 53. Interestingly, Richardson points out that at Corinth in the first century onwards there were similarities between Judaism and Christianity, in that just as Judaism began with house-synagogues, so Christianity began with one or several house-communities, ibid.

112. "The name 'Apollos' was a peculiarly Egyptian abbreviation (found rarely outside Egypt) of the name 'Apollonius,'" ibid.

high enough to agitate and instigate many of the Corinthian congregation to oppose Paul.

In the Corinthian congregation, however, there would no doubt have been Jewish members who argued against Paul because of the influence of other non-Christian Jews who lived in the wider Jewish community. As seen earlier (Acts 18:5–7), at Corinth there were conflicts between Paul and some in the Jewish community because of Paul's Gentile mission and its attraction for proselytes. Furthermore, the possible existence of Jewish opposition to Paul in the Corinthian congregation can be seen in terms of patron-client structures. Some Jewish members of socially low status would have been influenced by their wealthy patrons. If their patrons had expressed hostile attitudes towards Paul's ministry in Corinth, these Jewish Christians would certainly have joined the party to which their patrons belonged. Yet they wouldn't have played a leadership role in such a group because of their low social status, nor would they have created the atmosphere of opposition to Paul into the Corinthian congregation. According to Pogoloff and Theissen, these Jewish members were of socially lower classes than the other Jewish members who were hospitable to Paul (cf. 1 Cor 4:10–13).[113] Having said this, we now move on to an investigation of the Greeks in Roman Corinth and of Greek members in the Corinthian Christian community.

Greeks

The Greeks comprised the largest portion of the population in the broader civic community of Corinth by the time Paul founded the Corinthian congregation. These Greeks were descendents of the original indigenous Corinthian inhabitants who were largely destroyed by Roman forces, particularly Mummius in 146 BCE. Interestingly, however, they were not then completely eliminated. Some of them escaped from the enslavement of Mummius's forces and continued to remain in the destroyed city of Corinth during its ecliptic period (146–44 BCE), until the mid-first century CE. Nevertheless, these indigenous Corinthians were ranked low in the social pyramid. Their numbers were supplemented in the first years of the colony by a large number of descendents of those Greeks who had scattered all over the Roman Empire, especially the Mediterranean regions such as Achaia and Greece since 146 BCE, who

---

113. Pogoloff, *Logos*, 193; Theissen, *Setting*, 121–43.

then returned to Roman Corinth because of its rapid commercial development. These people and their descendents inhabited the city by the time the Christian community was founded. Most of these people were poor and ranked lowest in the social hierarchy.[114]

Nonetheless, it is likely that Paul would have made more converts to the Christian faith among these people than any other ethnic group and that they became the majority group in number, but most of them were poor and of socially low class. This is certainly indicated in Paul's description of the social makeup of the Christian gatherings at Corinth (1 Cor 1:26–28). Due to this, they were discriminated against (e.g., 1 Cor 4:10–13; the Lord's Supper, 1 Cor 11:20–22). But among the Corinthian Christians of Greek origin, there would also have been some who possessed wealth and high social positions. These Christians assumed they could be (benevolent) patrons of Paul and the Corinthian Christian community. Yet it seems likely that the majority of Christians of Greek origin did not actively oppose Paul at Corinth, however, but belonged to Paul's party. Nevertheless, it may be that some of these Christians were associated with the party that opposed Paul because in terms of patron-client bonds, they had to belong to the party to which their patrons belonged, but they were not the leaders of such a group.

Furthermore, the Pauline language in Romans and 1 Corinthians certainly supports the existence of Greek members in the Corinthian congregation. Paul names Greeks such as Chloe,[115] Phoebe, Stephanas, and Erastus (Rom 16:1, 23; 1 Cor 1:11, 16). Paul speaks of Phoebe in Romans 16:1–2 and informs us that she was a *diakonos*. Some scholars interpret the Greek *diakonos* here as "servant," "helper," or especially "deaconess." These scholars seem to oppose to the idea of women's active leadership role in the Pauline communities. They instead claim that women simply helped and assisted male leaders or missionaries. These women were

---

114. Engels, *Corinth*, 70; de Vos, *Church*, 186; Witherington, *Conflict*, 6. In addition, first-century Corinth was a bilingual city where the common language was Greek which was spoken in marketplaces and streets, but Latin was used as the official language (see Theissen, *Setting*, 79). It is not surprising that Paul wrote 1 Corinthians in Greek rather than Latin because the majority of the Corinthian congregation was comprised of those Greeks who were ranked fairly low on the social scale (see Theissen, *Setting*, 70–73, 102; also Barclay, "Thessalonica," 57; Thiselton, *Corinthians*, 181; Fee, *Corinthians*, 82; Pickett, *Cross*, 45; Witherington, *Conflict*, 22).

115. In 1 Cor 1:11 Paul names Chloe once, so we do not have much information about her. It is presumed, however, that she was wealthy and a prominent member of the Pauline community at Corinth.

allowed to do only limited pastoral work. They, thus, see Phoebe as a pastoral assistant helping Paul in his mission and giving hospitality to other women and visiting the sick and the poor in the Corinthian Christian community rather than view her as an active leader.[116] This interpretation should be criticized at two points: First, the Greek word *diakonos* is here used in a masculine form rather than feminine.[117] It, thus, should be translated as "deacon" rather than "deaconess." Second, "deaconess" is a later invention.[118] Elisabeth S. Fiorenza claims that some scholars interpret the word *diakonos* as "deaconess" "in terms of the later institution of deaconess."[119] Moreover, the feminine form of *diakonos* occurs nowhere in the New Testament in which the masculine form appears twenty-nine times. This means that women workers were not called "deaconess" as such in Christian communities in the first century. The office of deaconess was institutionalized in the "early post-apostolic centuries."[120] That is why it is not appropriate to translate the word *diakonos* anywhere in the New Testament as "deaconess," even where it is used in reference to women. Therefore, it is unlikely that men leaders were named as deacons and women as deaconesses and that only men took on leadership roles with women as their assistants. Accordingly, it is anachronistic to translate *diakonos* in Romans 16:1 as "deaconess." The word should instead be interpreted as "deacon," referring to Phoebe's leadership role in the Pauline community at Cenchreae, just as it is applied to Paul and Apollos (1 Cor 3:5).[121] This argument is supported by E. S. Fiorenza, B. Byrne, J. D. G. Dunn, B. Witherington, C. H. Talbert, T. R. Schreiner and R. Aitchison.[122] Furthermore, this interpretation challenges Korean churches that are heavily influenced by Confucian conceptions of social hierarchical structure. Korean Christians, whether men or women, tend

---

116. Barrett, *Romans*, 282; Thomas, *Deacon*, 111; Käsemann, *Romans*, 411; my "1 Corinthians 12:12– 13," 126 n. 10.

117. Witherington, *Romans*, 382; Schreiner, *Romans*, 787.

118. Schreiner, *Romans*, 787.

119. Fiorenza, "Missionaries," 62, 71.

120. Thomas, *Deacon*, 112.

121. Cenchreae was one of the two most important harbors for Corinth's commercial and economic prosperity in the first century (Witherington, *Conflict*, 34; Fiorenza, "Missionaries," 63).

122. Fiorenza, "Missionaries," 71; Byrne, *Romans*, 447; Dunn, *Romans*, 888; Witherington, *Romans*, 382; Talbert, *Romans*, 333; Schreiner, *Romans*, 787; Aitchison, *Ministry*, 88.

to devalue the leadership capacity of women in the church and exclude them from leadership positions and decision-making groups. Most Protestant Korean churches tend not to entitle women to be elders (*jangro* in Korean) but only assistants and helpers (*kwonsa*) who support the pastors and elders in the church (see further below).

Phoebe is also described as a *prostatis* whose Latin equivalent, *patronus* technically means "patron." Remarkably, Paul nowhere uses the Greek word *prostatis* except here in Romans 16:2. In 1 Corinthians and Romans, Paul names many prominent members who accommodate and host the whole congregation in Corinth.[123] Of them, only Phoebe is identified as a *prostatis*. E. S. Fiorenza argues that Paul uses the word *prostatis* in terms of "the technical-legal sense of the Greco-Roman patronage system," in other words, patron-client relations.[124] Yet C. E. B. Cranfield claims that "it is doubtful whether Phoebe, as a woman, would have been able to fulfill the legal functions involved. However, it is possible that the word is here used in its most general sense of 'helper.'"[125] His argument appears not to convince all. B. Witherington comments that in the Roman world "women could assume the legal role of *prostates*," and they actually acted as patrons or "benefactors."[126] Interestingly, "one-tenth of the patrons, protectors or donors to *collegia*" (social associations or clubs) were women.[127]

The Pauline description of Phoebe as a *prostatis* suggests two points: first, in the Christian gatherings at Corinth, Phoebe, as a woman, took on a substantial and active leadership role in the Corinthian Christian community. This is supported by Fiorenza claiming that her leadership was "equal to men and sometimes even superior to men."[128] Second, Paul draws attention to her role as patron because it provides a model of Christian patronage that critiques the dominant form practiced by the male elite. As mentioned above, women (most likely widows with sons—thus retaining their husband's wealth) comprised up to 10 percent

---

123. My "1 Corinthians 12:12–13," 126 n. 11.
124. Fiorenza, "Missionaries," 64.
125. Cranfield, *Romans*, 783.
126. Witherington, *Conflict*, 34.
127. Ibid., 34–35; also Dunn, *Romans*, 889; Fiorenza, "Missionaries," 64, 71; BAGD, 718; Pogoloff, *Logos*, 191.
128. Fiorenza, "Missionaries," 63, 65; see also Witherington, *Conflict*, 35; Pogoloff, *Logos*, 191.

of the whole population of patrons or benefactors for *collegia* in the Roman world. Paul has no problem with this.

In his expression of Phoebe as a *prostatis*, Paul may have been gently critiquing the Christian *ekklēsia* at Corinth and other social clubs, associations, and cults where men dominated and there were strong patriarchal structures between patrons and clients.[129] Here, Paul seems to highlight that in the Christian community at Corinth, there should be a different relationship between patrons and clients. All were one in Christ (*hen eisin*, e.g., 1 Cor 3:8). Phoebe was relatively wealthy (or at least independent) and ranked highly on the social scale, if she was the letter-bearer to Rome. She was also a patron of Paul and the whole congregation. Unlike some of the patrons in the *collegia*, she must not have patronized him and the other members in the Christian community at Corinth in an arrogant and elitist way. In Roman 16:2, therefore, Paul explicitly names and commends her to the Roman Christian community as a model of Christian patronage and encourages and urges the Roman believers to imitate her patronage, and thus not to adopt the patronage which was normally practiced in *collegia* within Roman civic society.

As regards to Erastus, Paul mentions his name with his social position as the treasurer of the city of Corinth in Romans 16:23 (cf. Acts 19:22 and 2 Tim 4:20, where it is evident that he stayed in Corinth), unlike Phoebe and Priscilla and Aquila. In naming these three, Paul might have in mind more pastoral concerns because Paul mentions their ecclesial offices in a specific fashion, such as "deacon" and "workers in Christ Jesus" (Rom 16:1,3). But Paul does not need to explain to the Romans something about their social status and careers because Phoebe would be appearing in person bringing with her his letter to them, and Priscilla and Aquila were already known to them since they had stayed with them at Rome (cf. Rom 16:1–3; Acts 18:2). Interestingly, however, in speaking of Erastus, Paul specifies his civil profession as *ho oikonomos tēs poleōs*. This is because the Romans must have known nothing about him. So Paul introduces him to them by mentioning his profession.

Nonetheless, his social status is controversial among scholars because of his position, *ho oikonomos tēs poleōs*. The Greek word *oikonomos* could refer to the same office as the Latin *aedile* in the Roman world. This is a high financial officer, although it is not clear how high it was ranked in the administrative hierarchy. But it is suggested that the office

---

129. Fiorenza, " Missionaries," 65.

is equivalent to that of *quaester*. This position could probably be taken by slaves and freed people. That is why scholars dispute Erastus's social status. But most of these scholars claim that he was a freed man or a descendent of the colonist freed people, rather than a slave. The *aedile*'s main tasks were to maintain public streets, buildings, and marketplaces; to collect revenues for business in such places; and he could be a judge in the local games in other places than Corinth. But the *aedile* was an important officer, especially in wealthy cities like Corinth. By virtue of his office, an *aedile* could obtain considerable wealth and property. On this basis, it is suggested that Erastus would have been ranked highly in the social pyramid of the Corinthian civic society in particular.[130] In addition, Stambaugh and Balch say that "in 1929 and 1947, different pieces of a Latin inscription were discovered. They name an Erastus as donor of the paving east of the theater in Corinth; he offers his pavement 'in return for the office of *aedile*.'"[131] In agreement with Stambaugh, Balch, Witherington, de Vos, and Horrell, it is maintained that the Erastus, who took the office of *aedile* and is named in the inscription at Corinth, was the same person as the Christian of whom Paul mentions in Romans 16:23. Yet, it is noticed that scholars such as D. W. J. Gill and A. D. Clarke claim uncertainty about "the link between the two Erasti."[132]

It is likely, therefore, that the Erastus referred to in Romans 16:23, Acts 19:22, and 2 Timothy 4:20 is the same prominent person who stayed in Corinth and assisted Paul. He was probably a freed man of Greek origin, although he possibly held Roman citizenship (that is why he had a Romanized name) that was granted to him because of his high public office of *aedile*.[133]

This office suggests he was a major magistrate in the local government. Such descriptions mean that he was socially powerful and ranked highly in the social pyramid of Roman Corinth in particular.[134]

---

130. Theissen, *Setting*, 83; de Vos, *Church*, 199–201; Witherington, *Conflict*, 33–34; Dunn, *Romans*, 911; Horrell, *Ethos*, 97; my "1 Corinthians 12:12-13," 126 n. 12.

131. Stambaugh and Balch, *Environment*, 160.

132. Gill, "Erastus," 300; also Clarke, "Erastus," 146–51.

133. So argues Dunn, "the possibility remains (we can put it no more strongly) that Erastus was a Roman citizen . . . of some wealth and notable social status" (*Romans*, 911). Theissen further claims Erastus had "a Greek name" and was "a successful man who rose in the ranks of the local notables, most of whom were of Latin origin" (*Setting*, 83).

134. So Talbert, *Romans*, 339; Theissen, *Social*, 83; de Vos, *Church*, 199–201; Witherington, *Conflict*, 33–34; Dunn, *Romans*, 911; Byrne, *Romans*, 460.

The Social Background of Roman Corinth 121

Consequently, he would have been wealthy and seen as being a potential patron of Paul and the Corinthian congregation, after he was converted to the Christian faith.[135] Moreover, the descriptions describe him as a trustful Christian and co-worker to Paul and associate him with Timothy. Paul sent this man Erastus with Timothy to Macedonia (e.g., Acts 19:22) and the tradition always mentions Erastus in close relation to Timothy (e.g., Rom 16:23; Acts 19:22; 2 Tim 4:20). Clearly, Erastus was a prominent member who supported Paul in the Christian community at Corinth. Yet, Paul never explicitly acknowledges this support in terms of the language of patronage.

Paul also mentions Stephanas of Achaia in 1 Corinthians 1:14–17 where he is named with Crispus and Gaius. In this passage, Paul appears to refer to these three important persons as representatives of each ethnic group: Jews, Romans, and Greeks, while he discusses division and baptism within its wider context of 1 Corinthians 1:13–17. The reason for this is because there were factions among different ethnic groups in the Corinthian congregation. In order to reclaim the Christian community from the grips of factionalism and unite the Christians, Paul emphasizes his authority over the whole congregation regardless of different ethnic origins, by reminding the Corinthians that he himself baptized Crispus, Gaius, and Stephanas. In doing so, Paul claims that though the Corinthian congregation comprises different ethnic groups and social classes, it should be united as the body of Christ unlike the secular clubs and associations at Corinth (1 Cor 12:12–31, esp. v. 27). Therefore, in this particular context the meaning of baptism should be observed in close relation to the problem of schism in the Christian gatherings at Corinth.[136]

Furthermore, in 1 Corinthians 1:16 Paul seems to have almost forgotten to name Stephanas with the other two, and only as an afterthought came to remember himself baptizing Stephanas and his household as well ("I did baptize also the household of Stephanas"). Due to this, the Corinthian audience may well have thought Paul regarded Stephanas as a less important leader than Crispus and Gaius, as the letter was being read publicly to them. This is Paul's rhetorical strategy. It is more likely that Paul intentionally named Stephanas later than Crispus and Gaius or

---

135. He "was probably converted by Paul through contact in the marketplace when Paul was making tents and had to pay fees to Erastus" (Witherington, *Romans*, 400).

136. So also Carter, "Big," 56–58; Pogoloff, *Logos*, 106.

pretended to forget his name in his letter. This is because he knew that more of the Corinthian Christians of high social status followed Crispus and Gaius as leaders more than the lower ranked Stephanas. Paul, however, subtly acknowledges and draws attention to his devotion and dedication to the Corinthian congregation. The function of Stephanas as role model is then clearly and explicitly revealed in 1 Corinthians 16:15-18.

In verse 16:15 Paul mentions the name of Stephanas together with his household. In this verse it is said that at Corinth the household of Stephanas were the first converts to Christianity and that they have committed themselves to serving fellow Christians. From this verse two things are known. One is that Stephanas and his household must have been the first Christians Paul baptized at Corinth (cf. 1 Cor 1:16). The other is that they were seen by Paul as role models for the Corinthian Christian community. Paul says, "I urge you to be subject to such men (the household of Stephanas) and to every fellow worker and laborer (*kopiaō*)" (16:16).[137] This idea is also affirmed in 1 Corinthians 16:17 where Paul speaks of Stephanas with Fortunatus and Achaicus. Here Paul exhibits his excitement because of their visit to the place where he is, where it seems that they all helped support the Pauline mission. That is why in verses 17-18 Paul says that "they supplied what was lacking on your part . . . they refreshed my spirit and yours; therefore acknowledge such men." In this expression, Paul appears to insist on the spiritual/moral leadership of Stephanas rather than affirming that Stephanas was ranked highly on the social scale and wealthy. Furthermore, it is apparent that Stephanas was considered a leader for the Christians of Greek origin, who formed the numerical majority in the Christian *ekklēsia* in Corinth. It is clear, therefore, that Paul names Stephanas twice in 1 Corinthians 16:15-18 not because he encourages the Corinthian Christians "to show a little more respect for . . . Stephanas," as Meeks argues,[138] but because Paul intended a rhetorical effect on the Corinthian Christians, that they should see Stephanas (and his household) as the best example of *ekklēsia*. Keeping these in mind, we now turn to an investigation of members of Roman origin in the Corinthians Christian community.

---

137. Paul uses the Greek words *kopos* and *kopiaō* often in 1 Corinthians, as he refers to Christian workers who labored for the ministry of Jesus (see 15:10, 58; 16:16; cf. 2 Cor 11:23).

138. Meeks, *Urban*, 78.

Romans

Romans had inhabited Corinth about a century before Paul came to the city. Hellenistic Corinth was resurrected as a Roman colony in 44 BCE.[139] Thereafter, the city was repopulated by colonists who came substantially from Rome. Engels claims that "we do not know their numbers but in all likelihood there were not many, perhaps only 3,000."[140] Of them, the majority were freed people, while a small number were Caesar's army veterans and urban poor.[141] As argued earlier, these Roman colonists most likely had experienced the influence of Cicero's rhetoric and eloquence on the Romans of his time, and his political power in the Roman world of the first century BCE. They would have brought Cicero's theories of rhetoric and eloquence with his rhetorical handbooks into the Romanized city of Corinth when they came from Rome.

Due to such colonizing policies, Corinth no longer remained a traditional Hellenistic city but became more of a Romanized city not only in its social, administrative, and political systems but also in its architecture. It became more like Rome, the center of the Roman Empire. Moreover, Latin became the official language in the city of Corinth rather than Greek.[142] This is a significant argument in support of the influence of Cicero's rhetorical legacy on the civic life of the Corinthians in the first century CE. His rhetorical handbooks, which were written in Latin, were considered as a model of rhetoric, wisdom, and eloquence in Greco-Roman educational contexts (see above). As a result, the older Hellenistic cultural heritage was fading, and the original population of the area would have been replaced rapidly by the migrants who came from Rome as well as other Mediterranean cities in the Roman Empire.

The citizens (Latin, *cives*) of Roman Corinth comprised two significant groups. One was the Roman colonists and their descendents, and the other was the *incolae*, non-Roman citizens including native Corinthians. The latter were not allowed to hold office, though the former and some of the latter were granted the right to vote.[143] By the time the colonists came to Corinth, in other Roman colonies it was normal

---

139. Stambaugh and Balch, *Environment*, 157; Litfin, *Paul's*, 141; Kruse, *Corinthians*, 16.

140. Engels, *Corinth*, 67.

141. de Vos, *Church*, 186; Horrell, *Ethos*, 64–66; Engels, *Corinth*, 68.

142. Witherington, *Conflict*, 7.

143. Engels, *Corinth*, 17.

that wealthy freed persons, though they were economically among the elite of a city, could not be elected into civic offices like *decurio* ("local senate," Greek *boule*) because among these colonists there were included a great number of manumitted slaves. Yet in Roman Corinth, such a restriction did not apply because of the need for repopulation.[144] According to Julius Caesar's order, the freed people were granted the exceptional right to hold politically influential positions such as magistrates and senators (*curiales* or *decuriones*) in Roman Corinth. This is because of their wealth and substantial contribution to the economic and commercial prosperity of Corinth and the need to re-establish the colony quickly.[145] During Augustus's reign (31 BCE–14 CE) this freed people class still held a number of important posts in the administration of the city.[146] Augustus, however, revoked their privilege. The freed people were legally banned from holding such socially and politically privileged positions and even civic office. So then "full Roman citizens" took Corinthian magistracies just as was the case in other colonies. Nonetheless, the freed people could hope that "a civic career would be open to their sons."[147] Due to this, at Corinth in the days of Paul, as in other Roman colonies, the freed people were no longer permitted to belong to such a politically and socially powerful group. Yet, they were wealthy and of higher social standing than the *incolae* who were poor and employed by these freed people as artisans, workers, and slaves.[148]

So a significant question still remains unsolved. Who were Corinth's most politically powerful and socially influential citizens in the mid-first century? Who belonged to the group with the highest social status in the entire Corinthian civic society by the time Paul wrote 1 Corinthians? These people were certainly descendents of the full Roman citizens[149] who had migrated to Corinth by the time of Roman colonization. In the first years of the colony the full Roman citizens dominated Corinthian civic society politically and socially. Consequently, by the mid-first century their descendents dominated the civic community of Corinth when

---

144. Horrell, *Ethos*, 66.
145. Ibid., 65.
146. Cook, *Cambridge*, 188–89.
147. Engels, *Corinth*, 67–68.
148. See Wan, *Power*, 21–22.
149. For a detailed explanation of Roman citizenship, see Jeffers, *Greco-Roman*, 198.

the Corinthian Christian community was founded.[150] They would have gained control of the civil life of Corinth, including its social, economic, and political systems, and even its religious festivals. B. Winter supports this argument stating that "the cultural milieu which impacted life in the city of Corinth was *Romanitas* . . . the dominant and transforming cultural influence was Roman."[151]

For example, this group of people were the great benefactors and patrons of the city of Corinth who served the city as unpaid municipal officials, who donated to the city a great amount of money for their elections and constructed many public buildings at their own expense.[152] Moreover, this network made a large contribution to the Isthmian and Caesarean games and the imperial cult, undertook the administration of these religious festivals, and held luxurious banquets.[153] Consequently, the Roman citizens and their descendants would have been among the wealthiest and of the highest social standing, and the most powerful and influential citizens in the Corinthian civic society in the mid-first century. Furthermore, this group of Corinthians in particular would have considered Cicero as a model of patronage and eloquence, and would have imitated the way Cicero had behaved politically and socially in Rome. They, undoubtedly, would have been influenced by the growing legacy of Cicero's theories of rhetoric and eloquence in their civic community.

Nonetheless, at Roman Corinth there were people of Roman and Italian origins who belonged to the group of low social status and working-class citizens like artisans. This is attested by archaeologists examining Roman Corinth. They have discovered "the lamps and terra sigillata" on which Roman and Italian workers left their Latin names, and "the early Ionic and Corinthian column bases and moldings" which reflected Italian architectural traditions.[154] These were not found in any other cities of Roman Greece. Thus, it is possible that they were of Italian origin.[155]

---

150. See Horrell, *Ethos*, 65.

151. Winter, *After*, 22.

152. Shotter states that "the wealthy members of society took on administrative roles; the absence of salaries for such tasks meant that it was only such people who could undertake them. Local officials were usually elected or chosen by the wealthy from their own number" (Shotter, *Caesar*, 60).

153. Engels, *Corinth*, 18, 68.

154. Ibid., 69; cf. for a discovery of a Corinthian lamp, see Borowski, "Lamp," 63–65.

155. Engels, *Corinth*, 69.

First Corinthians and Romans indicate that Paul made converts among the Corinthians of these ethnic origins, though they were proably a minority group in number. He mentions several Latin names in Romans and 1 Corinthians, such as Tertius (who was the writer of the letter to the Romans, Rom 16:22), Gaius, Quartus, Crispus,[156] Fortunatus, and Achaicus (Rom 16: 22–23; 1 Cor 1:14; 16:17). Of them, Gaius seems to have been a prominent member in the Corinthian church and to have had a good relation to the Christian community in Rome because he is named in 1 Corinthians 1:14 as well as Romans 16:23. This means that to both Christian communities Gaius would have been well-known. Further, it is important to note that Paul names him alongside Erastus, the city treasurer (Rom 16:23). In this respect Gaius would have possessed a social status similar to Erastus who was ranked high on the social scale of Roman Corinth because of his profession. In Paul's mind, and later tradition, these two people seem to have been close friends due to their high social status as well as their support of Paul's mission (see Rom 16:23; Acts 19:22; 2 Tim 4:20). Furthermore, Gaius belonged to the class of Roman freed persons whose forefathers had come to Corinth as colonists and had possessed wealth from merchandizing and trading. This is supported by scholars such as Fee, and is to some extent argued by Bruce and Witherington. These scholars also suggest that Gaius in the Pauline epistles be identified with Titus Justus Gaius in Acts 18:7.[157]

Finally, Gaius appears to have been one of the wealthiest members in the Corinthian Christian community. Paul describes him this way, "Gaius . . . is host to me and to the whole church (*laos polus*)" (Rom 16:23, RSV: cf. Acts 18:10). So, it is assumed that he was well-off enough and owned a house large enough to accommodate the whole Corinthian congregation. As such, Gaius would be regarded as a patron who supported and possibly housed Paul at Corinth, just as Crispus the ruler of the synagogue did (Acts 18:8; 1 Cor 1:14). It is natural, therefore, that he would be regarded as a major patron of Paul and his Corinthian congre-

---

156. As seen earlier, Crispus was clearly a Jew and the ruler of the synagogue. But he appears to have had a good friendship with and a similar social status to Gaius from Paul's point of view because Paul names them together in speaking of a few he baptized in Corinth (1 Cor 1:14–16). In this regard, it may be that Gaius possessed a similar social standing to that which Crispus had within the civic community of Corinth.

157. Fee, *Corinthians*, 62; Bruce, *Corinthians*, 34; Witherington, *Conflict*, 102; cf. Meeks, *Urban*, 57.

gation because, just like Crispus, he was baptized by Paul, but it should be noted that Paul never names Gaius as a patron.

Furthermore, members such as Gaius and Erastus in the Corinthian congregation who were of higher social status would have been in contact at banquets and social clubs with the Corinthian elite and the people who possessed full Roman citizenship and were the most politically powerful and socially influential group in the Corinthian civic community. These Christians would have been influenced to some extent by the mentality and social behavior of the Corinthian elite and by the pattern of politics, patronage, and rhetorical conventions Cicero suggested in his rhetorical handbooks.[158] It is also plausible to suggest that they would have brought social-conventions-oriented behavior into the Christian community at Corinth (e.g., 1 Cor 3:18-23; 6:1-10; 8:6-13; 11:17-19, 22). Therefore, these Christians may well have played a major part in the opposition to Paul in the Corinthian congregation.

When Paul stayed at Corinth, this group of Corinthian Christians appears to have offered to support Paul financially, following the social fashion of patron-client bonds in the Greco-Roman world, just as their contemporaries did. But Paul appears to have rejected such offers (cf. 2 Cor 11:7-9). Understandably, this would raise in their minds a sense of opposition to him. Later, this could have developed into tensions between these Christians and Paul (1 Cor 3:3; cf. 2 Cor 12:20).[159] Thus, these higher status members seem to be closely related to the problems Paul addresses in 1 Corinthians, especially the Corinthian slogans, *panta moi exestin* ("all things are lawful for me" [RSV] in 6:12; cf. 10:23) and *pantes gnōsin echomen* ("all of us possess knowledge" [RSV] in 8:1). Consequently, their behavior could have played a critical role in causing the problems of schisms as described in 1 Corinthians 1-4.

Thus, as argued above, the people of Roman origin took politically and socially important positions in the Corinthian civic society by the time Paul founded the Christian *ekklēsia* at Corinth. Of them, the group possessing full Roman citizenship was the most powerful and influential group in the civic society of Roman Corinth. These people were ranked the highest in the social pyramid. Of course, they possessed much higher social status than other ethnic groups such as the Jews and the Greeks,

---

158. Barclay argues similarly ("Thessalonica," 58), but he does not refer specifically to Cicero's influence on them.

159. See Pogoloff, *Logos*, 189-93.

and most of the political power in the Roman city was concentrated on these full Roman citizens. If any among these Corinthians had been converted to the Christian faith, they would have been closely related to the group Paul talks about in 1 Corinthians 1:26 ("wise," "powerful," and "of noble birth" [RSV]).[160] It is probable that such persons would have argued against Paul on the issue of *sophia* (1 Cor 1–4), because the person understood himself or herself as possessing *sophia* which represented the characteristics of people of education and high social status in the first century Greco-Roman world. Such Corinthian Christians may well have opposed and criticized Paul for his challenge to the importance of rhetorical abilities and conventions, and patronal systems (cf. 2 Cor 10:3–4, 9–10; 11:6).[161]

Thus far, the ethnic composition of the Corinthian congregation and the ethnic origin of each member whom Paul names in Romans 16 and 1 Corinthians have been explored. Yet it should be noted that there were many other individuals in the Corinthian church whom we do not mention because we do not have much information about them and so we can not classify their ethnic origins.

Nevertheless, it is proposed that there were three major ethnic groups: Romans, Greeks, and Jews. The members of Greek origin were the largest group in number, and that those of Jewish origin were the second largest. The majority in these two groups were poor and of the socially lower classes, although there were a few wealthy and higher social status members. By contrast, the members of Roman origin were the minority group in number, but many of them possessed wealth and higher social positions. Furthermore, because of their social status and the strong influence of patronal systems, these Roman members influenced other Corinthians not only in the Christian gatherings but also in the social clubs and associations of the wider Corinthian civic community. In this

---

160. But it is worth noting that any scholarly arguments or evidence to support the presence of full Roman citizens among the Corinthian Christians as addressed in 1 Cor, although Erastus was possibly a Roman citizen for his profession. Yet he is not named in 1 Cor but in Rom 16:23. It is argued, therefore, that he was converted to the Christian faith some time later than the time when Paul wrote 1 Cor. Furthermore, it is noted that Paul possessed Roman citizenship according to Acts 22:25–29; 23:27. This helps us grasp the background of why Paul describes himself as the father (*patēr*) of the Corinthian Christians in 1 Corinthians 4:15. In so doing, he may be gently reminding the Christians that in some respects he possesses higher social status than many of them. This will be developed further below.

161. Pogoloff, *Logos*, 113, 173–78, 190–93.

there was the danger that they influenced some of the other Christians to misuse patronal and rhetorical conventions within the Christian community particularly because of the strong culture of "imitation" and "boasting" as argued above. Such persons would be in danger of esteeming *sophia* and rhetorical skills, particularly eloquent speech, more than the gospel message Paul preached (1 Cor 1:18—3:22), and of using their patronage in inappropriate ways (1 Cor 6; 8; 9; 10; 11). This would play a major and critical factor in causing the Corinthian congregation to be divided into factions (1 Cor 1:10—4:21; cf. 11:18–19). Against such divisive influences, Paul subtly emphasizes the better model of the gathering of Stephanas as that which the Corinthians should follow.

Furthermore, it is suggested that the influence of the social pyramid in the wider Corinthian civic community strongly affected leadership roles in the Christian community. This is because the Corinthian Christians who possessed high social status in the broader civic society could easily have dominated leadership roles and assumed that they had the position of patrons of Paul and the congregation. This is attested in the fact that many Corinthian Christians named in Romans 16 and 1 Corinthians such as Crispus, Erastus, Aquila, Priscilla, (and perhaps also Phoebe and Chloe), possessed some economic wealth and belonged to higher classes in the social pyramid. These Christians were prominent members as well as key leaders in the Christian community, although they were the minority group in number (see Rom 16:1–3, 23; 1 Cor 1:11, 14–16). Nonetheless, the majority of the Corinthian Christians were extremely poor and of lower social standing, and may well have been isolated from the mainstream of church life and excluded from leadership positions. This is because their social class may have prevented them from becoming leaders in the Christian community where, rather than the gospel message and Christian teaching, social positions and social hierarchies were regarded as more important due to the strong influence of cultural and social systems such as patron-client relations and rhetorical skills (1 Cor 1:26–28; 2:1–5). It would be argued that this is a reason why in 1 Corinthians Paul is careful about naming these poor and low social-class Christians; although he consciously identified himself with them especially in terms of social status (e.g., 1 Cor 4:10–13, "we hunger . . . we labour, working with our own hands").

Moreover, social stratification seems to have had a significant impact on the behavior of the Corinthian Christians, particularly their attitudes towards economically poor and socially low-ranked fellow Christians. Just as people of high standing ill-treated the poor and low-class people in the wider civic society, so they seem to have discriminated against and humiliated those fellow believers of poverty and low social status in the Christian community (e.g., 1 Cor 11:21–22). Surprisingly, this discrimination and humiliation even took place in relation to the matter of hospitality and the love-feasts in the Christian gatherings. As Murphy-O'Connor describes:

> The mere fact that all the believers could not be accommodated in the triclinium ("dining room") meant that there had to be an overflowing in the atrium ("courtyard"). It became imperative for the host to divide his guests into two categories: the first-class believers were invited into the triclinium while the rest stayed outside. Even a slight knowledge of human nature indicates the criterion used. The host must have been a wealthy member of the community, so he invited into the triclinium his closest friends among the believers, who would have been of the same social class and from whom he might expect the same courtesy on a future occasion. The rest could take their places in the atrium, where conditions were greatly inferior . . . Moreover, the triclinium could be heated, but the hole in the roof of the atrium exposed those sitting there to the cold air coming down from Mount Parnassos . . . which is snow-covered for nine months of the year.[162]

From this description it seems that there was not much difference between the Christian community and the broader civic community at Corinth in the treatment of the poor and lower-ranked members of society. In the civic community, social status was absolute for all aspects of human life. For instance, according to one's social position, each person learns to expect whether to be respected and honored or despised and humiliated. The importance and value of social standing in the wider civic society seems to have remained unchallenged in the Corinthian Christian community.[163] Thus, it may have been that some Christians of wealth and high standing were ill-treating those lower classes in the Christian gatherings, just as they did in social clubs or associations and in their patronal relationships (1 Cor 11:21, 22). It would not be surprising that their behavior was to a large extent influenced by the

---

162. Murphy-O'Connor, *Corinth*, 183–84.

163. As Victor P. Furnish argues (*Theology*, 30–31; cf. Meeks, *Urban*, 51–73; Judge, *Rank*; Clarke, *Leadership*, 23–39.

social phenomenon of social stratification and social hierarchy that was widespread in the life of the Corinthian civic society in the day of Paul. In the next chapter, therefore, a detailed explanation of the problems of factionalism in the Corinthian *ekklēsia* will be provided in the light of Greco-Roman rhetorical conventions and patron-client systems.

IMPLICATIONS FOR THE STUDY OF 1 CORINTHIANS 1–4

First Corinthians 1–4 comprises not only a diversity of rhetorical elements but also a variety of social indicators that reflect the social and cultural environment of Roman Corinth in the mid-first century CE. This Pauline text is thus a reflection of the civic, social, and cultural life of the Corinthians at the time Paul engaged in discussions with them. There are several significant social indicators alluded to in the text: patronal networks and hierarchies, social stratification (1:26–28; 11:17–22), imperial cults (8:1–13; 10:1–22), athletic games (9:24–27), economic prosperity (4:8), and a diversity of people groups and ethnic origins (12:13).

These social indicators shed light, in a broader sense, on the social environment of the Corinthian civic society of the mid-first century. Patronal networks and social hierarchies were especially significant in shaping the social and cultural milieu of Roman Corinth, as were the rhetorical conventions of the day. These social networks reinforced the power of the sophisticated elite in the wider Corinthian society. In a narrower sense, such social indicators show how deeply the mentality and behavior of the Corinthian Christians was influenced by the wider Greco-Roman culture. Such social and cultural conventions were naturally a part of the life of the Corinthian Christian community, but if followed uncritically, could then cause serious problems, as addressed in 1 Corinthians and 1–4. Some of these conventions appear to have had a profound hold on some of the Corinthian Christians of wealth and high social status, so that they took advantage of their social privilege and humiliated other Christians of lower social status (1:26; 11:17–22). This social-conventions-oriented behavior was a major contributor to the conflict and factionalism in the Corinthian Christian community (1:10–13; 3:1–4).[164]

---

164. Cf. just as in Roman Corinth, so in Korean society there is social stratification due to the strong influence of Confucianism. This deeply affects the life of Koreans (see further below).

Furthermore, imperial patronage and imperial and Greco-Roman cults also affected deeply the mentality and conduct of some of the Christians and contributed to the schisms in the Corinthian Christian community. These issues are more explicitly revealed in 1 Corinthians 8:1—10:22 and lie behind the problem of food offered to idols at Corinth. It is my contention that Paul can only tackle these specific issues after he has laid the foundation for a critique of the "wisdom of this world" in 1 Corinthians 1–4. The underlying problem is the relationship of the Gospel (the "wisdom of God") to the "wisdom of the world" as manifested in the cultural assumptions and practices of the day.

4

A Rhetorical Analysis of 1 Corinthians 1–4

THE FOCUS OF OUR rhetorical analysis will be an investigation of the issues of Corinthian wisdom, eloquence, and boasting that Paul addresses in the first four chapters of 1 Corinthians. These were all characteristics of Greco-Roman rhetorical conventions and seem to have influenced the mentality and behavior of the Corinthian believers. We begin with an examination of Corinthian wisdom and eloquence.

CORINTHIAN WISDOM AND ELOQUENCE

It is my contention that the high value accorded to wisdom and eloquence by the Corinthians as indicated in 1 Corinthians 1–4, was grounded in Greco-Roman rhetorical traditions, especially as typified in Cicero's rhetorical handbooks. In arguing this case, it is appropriate to explore the similarities between elements of Greco-Roman rhetorical conventions as exemplified in the language of Cicero and those reflected in Paul's usage (both positively and negatively expressed) in 1 Corinthians 1–4. The questions of Paul and *sophia*, whilst not completely resolved, have been more than adequately handled in recent scholarship.[1] Therefore, I would explore the social implications of rhetorical elitism and their influence on some of the Corinthian Christians as indicated in 1 Corinthians 1–4.

Again, it must be said that I am not arguing for a direct link between Paul and Cicero—that is neither necessary nor possible—but rather for

---

1. See Litfin, *Paul's*, 109–262; Given, *True*, 83–137; Strom, *Reframing*, 180, 190–95.

the appropriateness of using Cicero as the best example of the rhetorical influences shaping the Roman colony of Corinth.

Wisdom appears to be a slogan in the Corinthian Christian community. Some of the Corinthian Christians were enthralled by wisdom and its verbal expression. This is clearly evident in the Pauline language of 1 Corinthians 1–4. Here, Paul uses the Greek word *sophia* and its equivalent *sophos* twenty-six times—far more than anywhere else in his writings (see 1:17, 19 [twice], 20 [twice], 21 [twice], 22, 24, 25, 26, 27, 30; 2:1, 4, 5, 6 [twice], 7, 13; 3:10, 18 [twice], 19 [twice], 20).

He also employs the related phrases *sophia logou* and *logois sophias* three times (1:17; 2:1, 4; cf. *logos sophias* in 12:8). The translation of the phrase *sophia logou* or *logois sophias* varies scholar by scholar: the RSV translates it as "eloquent wisdom" (1:17), "lofty words or wisdom" (2:1), or "plausible words of wisdom" (2:4). The JNT renders it as "mere rhetoric" (1:17), "surpassing eloquence or wisdom" (2:1), or "compelling words of 'wisdom'" (2:4). The NIV reads it as "words of human wisdom" (1:17), "eloquence or superior wisdom" (2:1), or "wise and persuasive words" (2:4). BAGD interprets it as "cleverness in speaking."[2] Thiselton suggests the translation "clever rhetoric" (1:17), "high-sounding rhetoric or a display of cleverness" (2:1), "enticing words" (2:4).[3] Collins proposes the translation "cleverness of speech" (1:17), "rhetoric or wisdom" (2:1), "persuasive words of wisdom" (2:4).[4] Pogoloff describes *sophia logou* as "clever or skilled or educated or rhetorically sophisticated speech."[5] Clearly, there is a wide range of scholarly interpretation of the phrase *sophia logou*. Nonetheless, such translations all indicate that the phrase *sophia logou* is related to rhetoric, which Plato and Aristotle alike defined as "the art of persuasion."[6] Fee also agrees that it is "characterized by rhetoric (perhaps reason or logic)."[7] Nonetheless, the word "eloquence" is used here as the translation of the phrase *sophia logou* and its equivalent *logos* for the following reasons: the word *logos* recorded in the writings of Plato and Aristotle is frequently translated as "speech"

---

2. BAGD, 759; also Pogoloff, *Logos*, 111.
3. Thiselton, *Corinthians*, 146, 208, 218.
4. Collins, *Corinthians*, 85, 118, 119.
5. Pogoloff, *Logos*, 110.
6. See Plato, *Gorgias*, 453–54; Aristotle, *Rhetoric* 1: 1 1355a21; 1355b8–10; 1:2: 1355b27–28).
7. Fee, *Corinthians*, 64.

or "eloquent speech" in English literature.[8] Cicero also frequently uses the word *eloquentia* in his Latin books such as *De Inventione* 2.2.7 and *De Officiis*, 1.37.132. The Latin word *eloquentia* has the same connotation as the Greek word *logos* in Aristotle's language, meaning "eloquent speech" or "eloquence."

Furthermore, Paul contrasts "wisdom of God" (*sophia tou theou*) with "wisdom of the world" (*sophia tou kosmou*) (1:18-25, 2:1-13, 3:18-23). Clearly, Paul describes the "wisdom of God" as Christ crucified (1:23, 24), yet he does not tell us specifically what he means by the "wisdom of the world." Paul does, however, use the words "wisdom of the world" interchangeably with the phrases "human wisdom" (*sophia anthrōpōn*, 2:5, 13; cf. *sophia sarkikos* in 2 Cor 1:12) and "wisdom of this age" (*sophia tou aiōnos*, 2:6).

At a glance, by using such words and phrases, Paul seems to criticize some of the Corinthian Christians who were particularly "wise," "powerful," and "of noble birth," "according to worldly standards" (1:26). They appear to have preferred the wisdom of the world and human wisdom to Christ crucified as the wisdom of God (1:20, 21; 2:6-8, 13; 3:18, 19) in Paul's eyes. Paul accuses them of liking eloquent speech or eloquence more than the gospel message Paul had preached (1:17; 2:1, 4). He charged them with boasting of the wisdom, eloquence, wealth, power, and high social status they possessed in the wider Corinthian civic society rather than Christ Jesus as the wisdom of God (1:29-31; 4:7, 19). Scholars, such as John P. Heil and H. H. Drake Williams III, claim that Paul criticized the Corinthian preference for worldly wisdom through his use and interpretation of early Jewish literature and Old Testament prophets. Williams argues for echoes of Old Testament prophets in 1 Corinthians 1-4, for example, an echo of Isaiah 28-33 in 1 Corinthians 1:18-25, of Jeremiah 9:22-23 in 1 Corinthians 1:26-31, of Zechariah 4:6 in 1 Corinthians 2:3-5, and of Isaiah 64:3 in 1 Corinthians 2:6-11.[9] Similarly, Heil argues that the Pauline language in 1 Corinthians 1:19 is a reflection of his interpretation of Isaiah 29:14b, that in 1 Corinthians 2:9 is of Isaiah 64:3, and that in 3:19b-20 is of Job 5:13a and Psalms 93:11.[10]

If we collect together the implied critique by Paul of those whom he sees as misrepresenting the gospel and perhaps Paul himself, we reach

---

8. See Plato, *Phaedrus* 268; Aristotle, *Rhetoric* 1:2 1358a36-3 1359a29.

9. Williams, *Wisdom*, 47-208.

10. Heil. *Scripture*, 17-36, 53-67, 77-88.

the following conclusions. Some of the Corinthians to whom Paul refers in 1:26 played an influential and leading role in opposing and criticizing Paul at Corinth. They were the same people whom Paul describes as "these arrogant people" in 4:18-19. In such verses, Paul suggests that these Corinthians were not keen for Paul to visit the Corinthian Christians, after he had left the city. Nonetheless, we now have a question still to be answered. What particular points did these "arrogant" Corinthian Christians and Paul argue about? This question should be answered in light of the social and cultural milieu of first century Corinth. Against the background we have described, two points seem to stand out in Paul's mind: 1. Paul devalued their social and cultural understandings of *sophia* and *sophia logou* (e.g., 1 Cor 1:17—3:23; 2 Cor 10:1—11:6). 2. Paul refused to establish "normal" patron-client relationships with them and did not accept their financial patronage (e.g., 1 Cor 9:3-23; 2 Cor 11:7-11; see further below).

The majority of Paul's implied Corinthian opponents possessing wealth and high social status, as argued earlier, were the Roman elite in the Corinthian Christian *ekklēsia*. They would have had frequent contacts with the group of full Roman citizens at *collegia* in the wider civic community. Moreover, after Paul had left Corinth, they would have brought into the Christian community elements of the social and cultural phenomena of the first century Greco-Roman world, including the social and rhetorical understandings of wisdom and eloquence (see above). It is a reasonable assumption, therefore, that some of the Corinthian Christians and Paul's implied Corinthian opponents were influenced to some degree by Greco-Roman rhetorical traditions, as typified by Cicero's legacy of *sapientia* and *eloquentia*.[11]

---

11. The process of mutual influence between individuals and groups within society can be informed by the methods of social psychology. This sort of study includes "how groups affect individual people and how an individual affects a group" and how individuals influence one another in a larger social system and in a given situation (Aronson, *Animal*, 11; similarly David and Myers, *Psychology*, 5-6; Worchel, *Understanding*, 7-8, 10). These findings of social psychology confirm that the Christians in Roman Corinth could not avoid being influenced by their contemporaries and the prevailing social and rhetorical conventions that deeply impacted the mentality and social behavior of the people in the wider society. It is also likely that some of the Corinthian Christians were influenced by Greco-Roman rhetorical conventions in general, and by individuals like Cicero and Aristotle, which is broadly consistent with the findings of social psychology.

For instance, the way that Cicero relates wisdom to wealth and rulers is similar to the attitude that some of the Corinthians and Paul's implied Corinthian opponents had towards wisdom within their Christian community. Paul describes these Corinthians according to worldly standards, as wise, wealthy, powerful, and of noble birth (see 1 Cor 1:26). They continued to express their wealth in the Christian community (e.g., 11:22). Paul argues that they also valued social and worldly understandings of wisdom, especially the wisdom of the rulers of their age (2:6), and eloquence more highly than Christ crucified as the wisdom of God and the gospel message Paul preached (1:18—3:22).

Furthermore, some of the Corinthian Christians praised those people who possessed wisdom and eloquence. They may well have considered wisdom and eloquence as hallmarks of a high level of rhetorical ability and as indicating education, wealth, and high social status (e.g., 1 Cor 1:18–26; 2:1–4; 2 Cor 10:10). At this time, Dio Chrysostom urged people of wealth and high social class to have training in eloquence and to devote themselves to wisdom for their public career and social influence. He states,

> That a man . . . who possesses great wealth and has every opportunity to live in luxury by day and night, should in spite of all this reach out for education also and be eager to acquire training in eloquent speaking . . . seems to me to give proof of an extraordinarily noble soul and not only ambitious, but in very truth devoted to wisdom. You, as it seems to me, are altogether wise in believing that a statesman needs experience and training in public speaking and in eloquence. For it is true that this will prove of very great help toward making him beloved and influential and esteemed instead of being looked down upon . . . The man who intends to have a public career . . . should increase . . . the effectiveness of his oratory . . . Among the foremost historians I place Thucydides . . . for not only is there a rhetorical quality in the narrative portion of his speeches, but he is not without eloquence.[12]

This statement indicates that wisdom and especially eloquence were of importance for people who possessed wealth and high social status and who desired to have influential and powerful positions in their

---

12. Chrysostom, *Discourse*, 18.1, 2, 9, 10. This is quite similar to Cicero's ideas about wisdom and eloquence, and Dio Chrysostom seems to have been influenced by Cicero's legacy. This is further evidence that Cicero's legacy had an ongoing impact on Greek-speaking people in the first century Greco-Roman world.

civic society in the first century CE. It is no wonder, then, that some of the Corinthian Christians of wealth and high social status understood *sophia* and *sophia logou* as social and cultural conventions, insisted on them, and regarded them highly, just as their contemporaries in the wider Corinthian civic society.

The problem such people caused in the Christian communities was, however, that they brought the social and cultural understandings of wisdom and eloquence into the mixed Christian communities. They were shaped more by these understandings than Christ as the wisdom of God and the gospel message. So Paul sharply criticizes these Corinthians' attitude towards *sophia* and *sophia logou* in 1 Corinthians 1–4. He therein appears to argue against them with rhetorical skill and subtlety, even though he claims not to have any himself (see 1 Cor 1:17; 2:1–4). This is particularly evident in Paul's words: "the word of the cross is folly (*mōria*) to those who are perishing" (1:18); "has not God made foolish (*mōrainō*) the wisdom of the world?" (1:20); "the wisdom of this world is folly with God" (3:19).[13] In these verses Paul uses exaggeration and irony to challenge his Corinthian audience to reconsider their understandings of wisdom and their relationship to worldly wisdom. They would not be in the Christian *ekklēsia* if they really thought the cross of Christ was foolish. So these words appear to be an attempt by Paul to sharpen the boundaries between insiders and outsiders—between "Christ-ones" and "worldly-ones":—so that the un-named opponents might reconsider their position.

Furthermore, from Paul's perspective, these Corinthian Christians regarded the Greco-Roman rhetorical legacy of wisdom and eloquence as their cultural pattern rather than the model of Christ and Paul, being under the influence of their contemporaries with whom they had contacts at *collegia* in the wider Corinthian civic society. They boasted (*kauchaomai*) of the wisdom and eloquence they possessed in terms of social and cultural influence (e.g., 1:29; 3:21; 4:7). They urged other Corinthian Christians to imitate (*mimētēs*) in the way that Cicero had boasted (*gloriatur*) about his eloquence and his influence in Roman society, and had urged the Romans of his time to imitate (*imitator*) their ancestors (see below).

---

13. Paul uses the words *mōria* and *mōrainō* frequently. These words occur six times in 1 Corinthians 1–4 (1:18; 20, 21, 23; 2:14; 3:19) out of nine times in the entire New Testament.

Moreover, they underestimated Paul, the founder of the Corinthian Christian community, because he did not follow the elitist patterns and models of the wealthy and because he did not value rhetorical skills in the same way in his preaching of the gospel message (1:17; 2:1–4; 2 Cor 11:6). They, thus, understood him as not possessing rhetorical skills that would compare favorably with those of his contemporary rhetoricians and sophists. In recent Pauline scholarship there is a growing consensus that during his ministry at Corinth Paul did not mimic the rhetorical eloquence and social habits of high Corinthian society, although he employed "accepted rhetorical forms" in his writings, and especially in 1 Corinthians 1–4 ("his letters are weighty and strong," 2 Cor 10:10).[14] That is why, as Fee argues, Paul's preaching appeared to lack "rhetoric and wisdom."[15] Litfin claims that Paul had "pronounced rhetorical deficiencies in his preaching,"[16] and Given also comments that "Paul would not present his gospel rhetorically" for certain reasons.[17] There are three possible reasons for this. The first reason is that Paul did not indeed possess good abilities in speaking. Paul himself confessed that he was unskilled in speaking (2 Cor 11:6). Paul's lack of rhetorical skills in speech is also attested in the Corinthians' words, "his speech (is) of no account" (RSV) or "his speaking amounts to nothing" (NIV) (2 Cor 10:10). Of course, this humble confession by Paul could itself be a rhetorical ploy.

Second, Paul was afraid that if he had preached the gospel with eloquence, he would have distorted the gospel and have distracted the Corinthians from "the real power of the gospel message" whose essence is Christ crucified as the wisdom of God (1 Cor 2:5).[18] Clearly, after Paul's departure there were in Roman Corinth others (perhaps including Apollos) who preached and lived in a way that compromised the gospel Paul had preached (see Acts 18:24–26). They used eloquence in their preaching and mimicked the cultural and rhetorical customs that the contemporary sophists and rhetoricians practiced (see below). They wished to be recognized as competitive teachers who had rhetorical skill and who were supported financially by patrons in the Christian communities. Some of the Corinthian Christians then accepted the distorted

14. Witherington, *Conflict*, 123.
15. Fee, *Corinthians*, 95.
16. Litfin, *Paul's*, 170.
17. Given, *True*, 99 n. 58.
18. Witherington, *Conflict*, 123.

gospel which resulted from the way the opponents lived and preached. That gospel differed from Paul's gospel in which Christ crucified as the wisdom of God was the focus of "boasting" (e.g., 1 Cor 1:31; 2 Cor 10:17; 11: 3-4).

The last reason that can be given for Paul's avoidance (or subversion) of rhetorical prowess is that he deliberately preached the gospel message relying on a "demonstration of the Spirit and power" of God rather than by using human wisdom, eloquence, and persuasive (or enticing) words of wisdom (1 Cor 2:1-9). Consistent with this, Paul also deliberately intended to make the gospel free of charge and free of patronal obligations in his preaching (1 Cor 9:18). This behavior was distinct from other contemporary teachers, sophists, and rhetoricians. In the time of Paul, sophists and rhetoricians advertised themselves as teachers of great ability in rhetorical conventions and earned a living from their patrons. In this manner, they were recognized by people of the city. They even competed among themselves to obtain students and train them in their schools. First-century teachers charged "exceedingly high fees."[19] It was usual that a teacher, on first arriving in a city, advertised himself "by sending out invitations indicating the time and place where he would present his credentials and declaim. At the appointed hour he addressed the gathered assembly."[20] In this address he talked of his academic qualifications and career and of his good character in order to make the audience trust him. Afterwards, he invited the audience to nominate a topic. He then spoke on the topic and demonstrated his rhetorical skills and especially his eloquence.[21]

Unlike those sophists and rhetoricians, and unlike the practices of other apostles (1 Cor 9:3-6), Paul, as a newly arrived teacher in Corinth, intentionally refused to follow such expected procedures. He was not indeed interested in advertising himself and preaching the gospel with overt rhetorical prowess, eloquence, and human-wisdom-oriented

---

19. Winter, *After*, 36. Dio Chrysostom witnessed the atmosphere of competition among sophists in first-century Roman Corinth. He visited the city in between 89-96 CE. He describes that " . . . one could hear crowds of wretched sophists around Poseidon's temple shouting and reviling one another, and their disciples, as they were called, fighting with one another . . . " (Chrysostom, *Discourse* 8.9; also Murphy-O'Connor, *Corinth*, 100).

20. Winter, *After*, 36.

21. Ibid., Favorinus (ca. 80-150 CE) is an example (see Favorinus, *Discourse* 37.9, 22; 37.8; cf. Litfin, *Paul's*, 144).

speech in order to attract the Corinthian citizens. Paul instead addressed the gospel message according to the inspiration and demonstration of the Spirit and power of God (1 Cor 2:4, 10-13, 16), as he himself claimed. He refused to mimic in his preaching the rhetorical and cultural customs and traditions that the contemporary sophists and rhetoricians practiced. He even gave up making use of his right to put a financial claim upon the Corinthian believers in order to make the gospel free of charge in his preaching ("not making full use of my right in the gospel," 9:18). He preached the gospel free of charge to all Corinthians, whether educated or uneducated, whether of high social status or lower class, and of whatever ethnic origin (1 Cor 9:18, 19). If Paul had wanted, as a teacher and an apostle, he could have requested and accepted financial support from the new patrons of the Corinthian Christian community. This was a traditional pattern in Christian communities of Paul's time (1 Cor 9:3-6; "the Lord commended that those who proclaim the gospel should get their living by the gospel" in v. 14). This was also consistent with the social and cultural practices in civic societies within the first century Greco-Roman world (e.g., 1 Cor 9:7, 10-12). Yet Paul did not do so in Corinth (9:12, 15, 18), although he did accept a monetary gift from the poorer Macedonian Christian communities (2 Cor 11:9). Paul's seemingly inconsistent practice contributed in part to causing tensions between his opponents and him, and the problem of conflict and divisions among the members in the Corinthian congregation (1 Cor 3:3; 1:10; 2 Cor 11:10; 12:20).

Regardless of the reasons why Paul did not reinforce cultural expectations in his rhetoric, it appears from his letters to the Corinthians that he disregarded and devalued their tendency to esteem highly wisdom and eloquence. This may be the reason why it appears that Paul did not make any prominent converts among the Roman Corinthians of full Roman citizenship and the highest social classes in Corinthian civic society. Nonetheless, he made several converts among the Roman and Latin Corinthians of the freed people classes.

Furthermore, Paul's behavior seems to have provoked some of the Corinthian Christians who expressed great love for the rhetorical, cultural, and social values of wisdom and eloquence. Because of this, they attacked Paul's rhetorical deficiencies in his preaching and his refusal of patronal relationships and financial support (see further below). This consolidated their opposition to him and even cast doubt on the genuineness of his apostleship (e.g., 1 Cor 9:1-23; 2 Cor 10-13).

Instead, some of these Pauline opponents seem to have preferred Apollos to be their leader in the Christian community because they considered him as having better rhetorical skills, consistent with his Alexandrian origin.[22] Unlike Paul, Apollos apparently was more adept at displaying his rhetorical skills and eloquence in his speech. Luke supports this view of Apollos's eloquence, depicting him as "an eloquent man" (*anēr logios*, Acts 18:24). Those Corinthian Christians who had a favorable impression of Apollos's speech would no doubt have offered Apollos patronage and financial support, which he apparently accepted. This is supported by 1 Corinthian 9:4-6, "Do we not have the right to our food and drink... Or is it only Barnabas and I who have no right to refrain from working for a living?" Clearly Barnabas and Paul worked for a living, yet most of the apostles and Christian teachers Paul knew did not because of the Lord's command that "those who proclaim should get their living by the gospel" (1 Cor 9:14). Apparently, Apollos was included among those Christian teachers and workers who received financial support from some wealthy members of the Corinthian congregation, and who were perhaps among Paul's implied Corinthian opponents.[23] It is quite plausible to suggest that these more wealthy Corinthian Christians were patrons of Apollos, who Paul then (teasingly or in reality) accuses of sloganeering: "I belong to Apollos" (*egō eimi Apollō*). Such behavior would explain Paul's description of the party of Apollos in Corinth, after Paul had left the city (1 Cor 1:12; 3:4). This would also constitute a major factor in causing the Corinthian congregation to split into factions, which were one of the most critical problems in the Corinthian Christian gatherings (1 Cor 1:10-13; 3:1-9; 4:6-7).

CORINTHIAN BOASTING

Some of the Corinthian Christians, as briefly noted earlier, were perceived by Paul to be boasting about their wisdom, eloquence, wealth, power, and high social status in the Corinthian Christian *ekklēsia* (e.g., 1:26, 29-31; 4:7, 19). In 1 Corinthians Paul uses the Greek verb *kauchaomai* six times (1:29, 31 [twice]; 3:21; 4:7; 13:3). The verse 13:3 is included

---

22. See Pogoloff, *Logos*, 181; also Sumney, *Satan*, 76-77.

23. This is supported by Pogoloff (*Logos*, 193) and Hays (*Corinthians*, 147).

here, though this verse is disputed among scholars in terms of text criticism.[24] Paul refers to the other forms *kauchēma* three times (5:6; 9:15, 16) and *kauchēsis* once (15:31). In 2 Corinthians Paul uses these words even more frequently than in 1 Corinthians. The word *kauchaomai* occurs twenty times, *kauchēma* is found three times, and *kauchēsis* also appears six times. As such, Paul frequently uses the word *kauchaomai* and its equivalents in his letters to the Corinthians. It is likely, therefore, that the issue of boasting became critical in the Corinthian Christian community by the time Paul wrote 1 and 2 Corinthians and caused conflict in the Corinthian congregation.[25]

The way Cicero had boasted (*gloriatur*) was, as argued earlier, typical of the way some Corinthians boasted, and is inversely related to Paul's ironic "boasting" (e.g., 1 Cor 1:28; 5:6; 9:15, 16; 15:31; 2 Cor 11:18, 21; 12:1). Cicero's legacy of wisdom and eloquence indicates the prevalence of imitating (*mimeomai*) and boasting (*gloriatur*) in eloquence and political success, to the glory of the ancestors (see above). Paul accuses some of boasting about their wisdom, eloquence, and high social status rather than Christ as the wisdom of God (1 Cor 1:29–31; 3:21). How much Paul himself is using exaggeration and irony to make his point we cannot tell for sure. But we sense his concern that these Corinthian Christians were influenced too heavily by their Roman Corinthian contemporaries with whom they had frequent contacts at clubs and associations in the wider Corinthian civic communities. Bearing this argument in mind, we now investigate the issue of "boasting" within the Pauline text of 1 Corinthian 1–4.

The word *kauchaomai* occurs in 1:29–31 for the first time in 1 Corinthians 1–4. In verse 31 in particular, Paul borrows the biblical teaching about boasting from Jeremiah 9:22–23. Interestingly, this Old Testament passage appears explicitly in 2 Corinthians 10:17. Jeremiah 9:22-23 says,

---

24. Zmijewski, "*Kauchaomai*," 276.

25. For scholarly examinations of boasting in 1 and 2 Corinthians, see Lambrecht, "Boasting," 352–68; Forbes, "Comparison," 1–30; Barrett, "Boasting,ʛ 363–68; Travis, "Boasting, 527–32; Judge, "Boasting," 37–50; Hahn, "Boast," 227–29; Spicg, "*Kauchaomai*," 298–302; Bultmann, "*Kauchaomai*," 645–54. Barrett examines the issue of boasting in the Pauline epistles and especially 1 and 2 Corinthians from psychological and theological perspectives ("Boasting," 363–64). Unlike him, the issue of boasting in 1 Corinthians 1–4 is investigated here in terms of the rhetorical situation of first-century Corinth (see also Forbes, "Comparison," 1; Judge, "Boasting," 47).

Let not the wise boast (Greek. μὴ καυχάσθω ὁ σοφὸς: Heb. אל־יתהלל חכם) in his wisdom (ἐν τῇ σοφίᾳ αὐτοῦ: בחכמתו), and let not the strong boast in his strength or might (ἐν τῇ ἰσχύι αὐτοῦ: בגבורתו), and let not the rich boast in his riches (or wealth) (ἐν τῷ πλούτῳ αὐτοῦ: בעשרו), but he who boasts, let him boast (καυχάσθω ὁ καυχώμενος: יתהלל המתהלל) in this, that he understands and knows that I am the Lord (ἐγώ εἰμι κύριος: אני יהוה).²⁶

In the context of Jeremiah 9:22–23, the words "wisdom" (Hebrew, חכמה), "might" (Heb. גבורה) and "wealth" (Heb. עשר) imply "both distorted individual identity and well being and distorted societal identity and well being."²⁷ Especially the word "might" "refers not only to individual physical strength (Judges 8:2) but also to military and political power (1 Kings 15:23; Isaiah 11:2)."²⁸ In Jeremiah's view, the people were boasting (Heb. תהל) about the wisdom, power, and wealth they possessed and considered these social resources more important than the knowledge of God. From Jeremiah's perspective, their boasting revealed an "anthropocentric" bias and preoccupation.²⁹ Hence, Jeremiah critiques the way they boasted (Jer 9:22). He challenges them to stop boasting of the sources of their social security in terms of wisdom, power, and wealth. Furthermore, he encourages his people to boast of the knowledge of God and base their boasting on "God's faithful character and acts such as steadfast love, justice, and righteousness" which are truly "the source of identity and well being, of security and governance" for them.³⁰ By doing this, Jeremiah challenges his people to move from their anthropocentric boasting about wisdom, might, power, and wealth, to the "theocentric" boasting about the knowledge of God and his steadfast love, justice, and righteousness.³¹ These sorts of themes are evoked in 1 Corinthians 1:26–31 as well.

26. Barrett, "Boasting," 364. G. R. O'Day states, "the heart of Jer 9:22–23 is a teaching about boasting, which has clearly sapiential elements in its vocabulary, theme and form" (O'Day, "Jeremiah," 260). 1 Cor 1:26–31 also, apparently, includes the issue of wisdom. Clearly, Paul uses the Jewish understanding of modesty before God, found in Jeremiah, in order to critique the inappropriate behavior of some of the Corinthian Christians in the Christian communities, so argues Williams (*Wisdom*, 103–32).

27. O'Day, "Jeremiah," 261.

28. Ibid.

29. Ibid.

30. Ibid., 262.

31. Ibid.

In the Pauline passage, the issue of boasting is dealt with in close relation to the social and cultural environment of Roman Corinth in the first century CE. This is evident in that the Pauline language of 1 Corinthians 1–4 includes "wise," "according to worldly standard," "powerful," "noble birth," and "to boast" (vv. 26, 29). Clearly, these Pauline words reflect on the social status and behavior of some of the Corinthian Christians.

Paul perceived them to be boasting about their wisdom, wealth, power, and high social status in the Christian community. Paul's boasting was "a parody of conventional norms" which was "absolutely de rigueur" in the first-century Greco-Roman world and Roman Corinth.[32] Similarly, Forbes argues that Paul's boasting was "a parody of the forms of rhetorical self-advertisement current" in Greco-Roman societies in the first century CE.[33] This culture of boasting is, as has been argued, part of the rhetorical and cultural legacy of Cicero's writings and example. The Corinthians, and particularly Roman Corinthians, would have been influenced by the pattern of "boasting" (*gloriatur*) and "imitation" (*imitator*) prevalent in Greco-Roman rhetoric encouraged by Cicero. Paul's implication that they were boasting about their wisdom, eloquence, wealth, power, and high social status in their Corinthian civic society thus has some substance.[34]

This legacy of boasting is also related more specifically to the tendency towards boasting occurring among sophists and teachers of rhetoric in the sophist movement of the first-century Greco-Roman world and Roman Corinth.[35] Boasting was particularly prevalent in a sophistic and rhetorical educational environment. Teachers competed among themselves to secure a good number of students in their schools

---

32. Judge, "Boasting," 47; similarly, Travis, "Boasting," 520. Scholars interpret the word "boasting" as "self-admiration," "self-praise," "self-glorification," "self-commendation," "self-advertisement," and "self-presentation" (Judge, "Boasting," 47; Travis, "Boasting," 520; Forbes, "Comparison," 1, 7–8).

33. Forbes, however, admits that it is difficult to "specify what these forms might be" (Forbes, "Comparison," 1).

34. This argument is supported by Forbes who claims that "consistent conventions relating to self-praise (or boasting) can be shown to exist from at least 100 BCE (and Cicero's day), through Paul's time, and beyond (the time of Plutarch, and Dio Crysostom)" (Forbes, "Comparison," 8).

35. The sophist movement at Corinth is evidenced by Dio of Prusa (ca. 40–112 CE) and his eighth oration, *Or 8*; "Diogenes" or "On Virtue"; Favorinus (ca. 80–150 CE) and his Corinthian oration (*Or. 37*), and Plutarch of Chaeronea (ca. 50–120 CE) and his work, *Questions Conviviales* (see Winter, *Philo*, 123–40).

and advertized and displayed their rhetorical skills in public assemblies (*ekklēsia*). In so doing, they were recognized publicly and were honored by their students and the wider populace. These popular teachers boasted about their rhetorical abilities.[36] This is also in accord with Cicero describing teachers of rhetoric as boasting about themselves. He states, "The professors and masters of rhetoric . . . boasted before an audience . . . (of) their knowledge of literature and poetry, and the doctrines of natural science."[37] He further says, "anybody (can) boast about . . . his (or her) success . . . You actually make a habit of boasting (*gloriari*) that you did so."[38]

The students, whom the teachers of rhetoric educated, also demonstrated their exclusive loyalty to their teachers and praised their rhetorical abilities. They promoted their teachers' "professional attributes" and "educative prowess."[39] Thus, boasting (or self-praise) was "a prime characteristic of popular teachers" and their followers in the sophistic and rhetorical educational context of Roman Corinth.[40]

In order to critique such conduct, Paul employs several contrasting phrases in 1 Corinthians 1-4: "foolish"-"wise," "weak"-"strong," "low"/"despised"-"noble birth," and "things that are not"-"things that are" (1:18-28). In Paul's perception, some of the Corinthian Christians boasted about their social privilege—wisdom, wealth, power, and high social status—in the Christian *ekklēsia* (1:26). Nonetheless, Paul appears to overturn the boasting and contends that they would not find any favor in the eyes of God by expressing their social privilege in the Christian community. He reminds them of "God's paradoxical election": He elected the foolish, poor, and powerless of the world to shame the wise, wealthy, and powerful (1:27-28).[41] This is evident in the fact that the majority of the Corinthian Christians consisted of "people whom the world scorns" or people who were poorer and of lower social classes (see 1:26; 4:8-13).[42] Paul, therefore, appeals to them to stop boasting about their social privilege before God and in the Christian community (1:29)

---

36. See Winter, *After*, 37.
37. Cicero, *De Oratore*, 3.32.127.
38. Cicero, *Paradoxa Stoicorum*, 1.1.15; 1:4:32.
39. Winter, *After*, 36, 39.
40. Forbes, "Comparison," 8-9.
41. Hays, *Corinthians*, 32.
42. Ibid., 33.

and instead to boast about Christ Jesus who has become "our wisdom, our righteousness and holiness and redemption" (1:30–31).

Moreover, to argue against this group of Corinthian Christians, Paul quotes Isaiah 29:14, "I will destroy the wisdom of the wise, and the cleverness of the clever I will thwart" (1 Cor 1:19). He also states that "the foolishness of God is wiser than humans" (1:25a) and that "God chose what is foolish in the world to shame the wise" (1:27a). In these words Paul contrasts Corinthian wisdom with the wisdom of God. He seems to highlight intrinsic differences of quality between the two kinds of wisdom. The former is "human thought-based" and "cultural conventions-oriented" wisdom, while the latter "divine power-oriented" and "Christ-crucified-oriented" wisdom. He saw that some of the Corinthian Christians valued the former more highly than the latter, and even boasted about themselves because they believed they had such human and culturally oriented wisdom (e.g., 1:29; 3:18; 4:7).

This rhetorically-oriented wisdom, in Paul's eyes, motivated and stimulated some of the Corinthian believers to act arrogantly (1 Cor 4:18) and over-zealously and to engender strife among themselves (3:3a). They behaved in "an immature way" and operated in a worldly (Greco-Roman) fashion, just as the unbelieving contemporary Corinthians with whom they had frequent contacts at banquets and *collegia* in the broader Corinthian civic society (3:3b).[43] Moreover, such behavior and boasting no doubt played a factor in causing schisms in the Corinthian Christian *ekklēsia* (1 Cor 1:10). Paul, therefore, criticized their mentality and conduct and challenged the Corinthian ideals of wisdom (1:20; 2:6).

As a further challenge to this behavior, Paul demonstrates the wisdom that is "Christ-crucified-oriented" wisdom in 1 Corinthians 1–4. This wisdom he describes first as the power of God first for salvation to all who have faith (1:18, 21) and second for the resurrection of the dead (1 Cor 15:12–57). By his power God raised the crucified Christ from the dead as the wisdom of God (1 Cor 15:12–57). This is regarded as the essence of the gospel message Paul preached in Corinth (1 Cor 15:1–4) and as the ground for Paul's boasting (1 Cor 9:15, 16). Preaching the gospel message of Jesus Christ as the wisdom of God, Paul challenges his opponents whether, they too, considered the word of the cross foolish

---

43. Winter, *After*, 41. Winter understands the Corinthian Christians' zeal (*zēlos*) in relation to the attitude of students towards their teachers in first century Roman Corinth, ibid., 39.

(1 Cor 1:18a) and boasted of the social and cultural understandings of wisdom (1 Cor 1:29). Furthermore, Paul challenges them to turn their back on such an inappropriate mentality and behavior ("no human being might boast in the presence of God," 1 Cor 1:29; "let no one boast of people," 1 Cor 3:21), and also urges them to imitate the way he boasts of the gospel of Christ crucified as the wisdom of God (1 Cor 1:30, 31; 3:18; 4:16).

Some of the Corinthian Christians may also have boasted about their high status in the social pyramid and social and patronal connections with those Corinthians who had power and control of the social and political positions in the broader Corinthian civic communities (e.g., 1:26). It appears that they believed that their social privilege would help them find more favor in gaining and playing leadership roles in the Christian *ekklēsia* and the house/temple of God, just as in the wider civic society and so they naturally took control of leadership positions in the Christian communities (e.g., 3:5–15; 4:1, 2). This mentality and behavior can be seen as a result of the heavy influence of cultural and rhetorical conventions together with the social and patronal networks that characterized the civic life of the first century Greco-Roman world.

Paul denounces such thinking and behavior when he says: "the weakness of God is stronger than humans" (1:25); "God chose what is weak in the world to shame the strong" (1:27b); "God chose what is low and despised in the world, even things that are not, to bring to nothing things that are" (1:28). In these expressions, Paul compares the Corinthian Christians' social privilege with their calling from God. In 1 Corinthians 1–4, he appears to have argued that his opponents should see the social status they possessed (1:26) as God's gift (4:7; 7:7) and that the calling they received from God should be considered more important and valuable than their social privilege in the Christian communities (1:26a). That is why Paul argued so strongly that they should stop expressing their social privilege and boasting in the Christian communities (4:7).[44] It is worth noting, however, that nowhere in 1 Corinthians does Paul disregard and devalue their social privilege in itself. Paul criticizes their misconduct and the improper behavior with it, especially their boasting about it (e.g., 5:6). Clearly, he recognized different classes of social status among the Corinthian Christians and encouraged them to remain in the situation in which they were and maintain the social status that they

---

44. Similarly, Collins, *Corinthians*, 109.

had when God called them, whether free or slave (1:26; 7:22). Whatever situation they were in and whatever social status they possessed, that was the will of God (7:23). Paul says, *ekastos en ō eklēthē adelpoi, en toutō menetō para theō* ("Brother and sisters, in whatever state each was called, there let him or her remain with God," 7:24). Hays affirms that "Paul's point is to reassure his readers that they should not be troubled about their present social location and that they should focus their attention on serving God, wherever they stand in the social order."[45] Similarly, Witherington argues, "Paul's advice is not to evaluate oneself by the larger society's values."[46] Winter also affirms,

> Paul did not allow non-Roman Christian free men to sell themselves into slavery as a route to Roman citizenship . . . Aspiring to the status of Roman citizenship, with its attendant financial and social benefits via the route of voluntary slavery, was therefore forbidden.[47]

Nonetheless, some scholars such as Neil Elliott disagree with this argument. Elliott asserts,

> Paul hopes his readers will not be preoccupied with their present circumstances, but he certainly does not absolutize those circumstances themselves as "God's calling." Staying in one's position is not the governing principle in 1 Corinthians 7, or even in 7:21. To the contrary, it makes far better sense to read the verse as Paul's urgent wish not to be misunderstood as encouraging slaves to continue in their state longer than they have to.[48]

However, Paul's language in 7:17–24 does not indicate that Paul encouraged the Corinthian Christians to aspire to higher social status, although this was a social phenomenon in their time. Rather, he encouraged them to stay with their social status, whether slave or free (7:21–24; 12:13) and ethnic identity, whether Jew or Gentile (7:18–20; 12:13). Moreover, Paul succinctly argued that they should consider God's calling (*klēsis*) more valuable than social status and ethnic identity. In this respect, therefore, Paul is ecclesiologically radical and politically conservative.

In Paul's argument, there is no difference, in terms of God's calling, between those Corinthians who possessed high social status and others

45. Hays, *Corinthians*, 126.
46. Witherington, *Conflict*, 184.
47. Winter, *Welfare*, 162.
48. Elliott, *Liberating*, 35.

of lower class; between wise (or educated) and foolish (or uneducated); between socially influential and powerful and powerless; between wealthy and poor; and between free and slave (1 Cor 1:27, 28; 7:20–24). Paul, thus, reminds the Corinthian Christians that they were all "equal" in Christ (3:8). In other words, they were "equally brothers and sisters in Christ regardless of their social situation."[49] They were all "God's fellow workers" (3:9). They were all "servants of Christ and stewards of the mysteries of God" (4:1). He also encouraged them to recognize that they were all people of the Spirit of God, not of flesh (2:14–16; 3:3). They could comprehend the thoughts and wisdom of God through the Spirit only (2:11). Each of them had "his or her own gift from God, one of one kind and one of another" (7:7; also 2:12, 14; 12:4–11, 27–30). Moreover, Paul encouraged them to acknowledge that just as Apollos and Paul himself were called (3:5–9), so they were all called by God to boast of the Lord Jesus Christ as the wisdom of God and the power of God, not of human wisdom or social privilege (1:31; 3:18–21). God made Christ the foundation of their wisdom (*sophia*), "righteousness" (*dikaiosunē*), "sanctification" (*agiasmos*), and "redemption" (*apolutrōsis*) (1:30).

In summary, Paul is convinced that some of the Corinthian Christians valued too highly their social and cultural understandings of wisdom and eloquence and their social privilege in the Christian communities. They further boasted about themselves and their possessions in terms of social and cultural advantage. This boasting was a result of the strong influence of Greco-Roman rhetorical traditions and the legacy of social and patronal networks.

To challenge this thinking, Paul borrows the biblical teaching of boasting from Jeremiah 9:23. He perceived similarities between the biblical situation and his own Corinthian circumstances, and then accommodated the biblical text to the situation of the Corinthian Christians. By doing this, Paul challenged the Corinthian Christians to leave their anthropocentric and social-and-cultural-conventions-oriented boasting and imitate him as one boasting in the Lord Jesus Christ as the wisdom of God. This is theocentric and Christ-centered boasting used for the purposes of cultural transformation and building up the *ekklēsiai*.

---

49. Witherington, *Conflict*, 184.

5

A Social Analysis of 1 Corinthians 1–4

1 CORINTHIANS 1–4 APPEARS to comprise social indicators of first-century Roman Corinth such as social networks, patronage, and social stratification, and it also appears to indicate that these social indicators were uncritically exercised in the Corinthian Christian community and played a critical factor in causing the community to split into factions. Bearing these in mind, we now turn to an analysis of social clubs and associations (*collegia*) that were closely interrelated with these social and patronal networks.

SOCIAL CLUBS AND ASSOCIATIONS (COLLEGIA)[1]

In the first-century Greco-Roman world, social clubs and associations (*collegia*) existed at all levels of society. All people regardless of social status voluntarily organized and joined *collegia*.[2] In these *collegia*, people engaged in various social and religious activities: "a sacrifice to a god, an occasional meal, a drinking party, an exchange of different political views or a confirmation of shared ones."[3]

---

1. A modified version of this section is published in *Horizons in Biblical Theology* (see my "Characteristics of Collegia").

2. See Stambaugh and Balch, *Environment*, 125; Chow, *Patronage*, 66; Jeffers, *Greco-Roman*, 74–76. Slaves could also join these *collegia*, and particularly the funeral *collegia* described further below (see Harrill, *Slaves*, 150; also Rives, *Religion*, 125).

3. Stambaugh and Balch, *Environment*, 124–25. For more details about *collegia*, see Meeks, *Urban*, 77–80; Garnsey and Saller, *Empire*, 156–59; Stambaugh and Balch, *Environment*, 124–26; Chow, "Patronage," 117–20; MacMullen, *Relations*, 75–79.

These private and voluntary *collegia* were closely related to patronal networks because members of wealth and high social-status supported the clubs by making significant financial contributions to dinner parties, banquets, and other social activities. They were patrons of the clubs. In so doing, they took control of the *collegia* and exercised their authority over other members who became their clients. These clients, in return, offered them honor, social assistance, and promises of solidarity and loyalty. In this process, patronal hierarchies were established between some members of wealth and high social status who were patrons and others of lower classes who were clients within these social clubs and associations. This was characteristic of patronal relationships in civic and social communities in the first-century Greco-Roman world including Roman Corinth.[4]

The Corinthian Christians Paul refers to as "wise," "powerful," and "of noble birth" in 1 Corinthians 1:26, would have been part of such *collegia* through which they would have had frequent contacts with non-Christians. They would then have been part of patron-client networks with those people who possessed full Roman citizenship and the highest social status and who had power and control in Corinthian civic society.

In the Greco-Roman world, there were generally three different sorts of *collegia* (often overlapping in function): professional *collegia*, *collegia sodalicia*, and *collegia tenuiorum*. Professional *collegia* comprised businesspersons, merchants, traders, physicians, carpenters, weavers, fullers, bakers, silversmiths, and shippers. This sort of club was closely related to the commercial prosperity of first-century Roman Corinth. People who belonged to these clubs possessed considerable wealth and contributed economic services to the city. Furthermore, they acted as patrons of the city. They supported financially the imperial cults and the Isthmian games. They also built patronal relationships with imperial officials such as the governor of Achaia. By means of these relationships, they were promoted to higher social classes in the Corinthian civic communities.

The *collegia sodalicia* were joined for religious reasons. People gathered together in these clubs usually on a monthly basis, and honored and worshipped gods as their patron deities. In this respect, Christian gatherings and Jewish synagogues in Corinth would have been recognized as similar to these *collegia* by non-Christians and non-Jewish believers. The *collegia tenuiorum* comprised poorer people. The poor organized

---

4. Meeks, *Urban*, 78; Garnsey and Saller, *Empire*, 157; Chow, "Patronage," 119.

these clubs for the primary purpose of funerals and the burial of the dead for members, and they can be seen as "burial societies, guaranteeing a proper burial for their members."[5] In addition, permanent immigrants established their own formal societies and ethnic *collegia*. One of the important activities at these *collegia* was to worship their traditional deities. For instance, "a certain Karpion son of Anoubion dedicated an altar to Sarapis and the emperor Septimius Severus on behalf of the household of Alexandrians, probably a group of resident Alexandrians, in Tomis on the coast of Lower Moesia."[6] It can be said that in the first-century Greco-Roman world many people belonged to one or the other of these *collegia* which were significant in maintaining the social fabric of the day.[7]

It is, however, "not always easy or even appropriate to make sharp divisions between them" because "virtually all associations shared the same basic features."[8] One feature is that every association had its own patron deity that the members worshipped. For example, craftspeople as members of professional *collegia* could worship as their own patron deity "Minerva, the goddess of handicrafts."[9] Another is that all *collegia* were concerned about the deaths of their members. If anyone of its members died, the association organized his or her burial, paid all the expenses, and performed the funeral rite.[10] The third is that many associations emphasized fellowship among their members including festivities and shared meals together on a regular basis. For instance, "the worshippers of Diana and Antinous in Lanuvium had regular group dinners; the regulations specify that the annual *magistri cenarum*, "dinner-masters," were to provide good wine, bread, sardines, tablecloths, hot water, and service."[11]

As such, that the people in Greco-Roman times voluntarily organized and joined *collegia* seems to have been inevitable for their professions or religious practices or socializing purposes in the broader civic communities such as Roman Corinth. On this basis, it is assumed that some of the Corinthian Christians would have continued to maintain their membership in these *collegia* even after conversion to the Christian

---

5. Rives, *Religion*, 125.
6. Ibid., 122–23.
7. See Meeks, *Urban*, 77–80; Stambaugh and Balch, *Environment*, 124–26.
8. Ibid., 122.
9. Ibid., 123
10. Ibid., 125.
11. Ibid.

faith. Furthermore, they may well have regarded their Christian community as either one of the *collegia sodalicia* or *collegia tenuiorum*. This is glimpsed in Paul's description of the Corinthian Christians' eating meat offered to idols (1 Cor 8 and 10) and of their understanding of "baptism for the dead" (1 Cor 15).

Collegia Sodalicia

Some of the Corinthian Christians may well have seen the Corinthian Christian *ekklēsia* as something like the *collegia sodalicia* where people honored and worshipped Roman and Greek gods as their patron deities. This would be, probably, because, as Theissen states, "The . . . Christian communities were comparable to religious clubs according to their objective."[12] Moreover, the possibility of the misconception of the Corinthian Christian community as one of the *collegia sodalicia* is evident in 1 Corinthians 8 and 10. In these chapters, Paul appears to address the problem of the Corinthian Christians' eating food dedicated to idols and their implied idol worship. This is why Paul often employs the Greek word *eidōlon* (idol, 8:4, 7; 10:19; 12:2; cf. 2 Cor 6:16) and its equivalents, *eidōleion* (idol's temple, 8:10), *eidōlothuton* (food sacrificed to idols 8:1, 4, 7, 10; 10:19), *eidōlolatrēs* (idolater, 5:10, 11; 6:9; 10:7) and *eidōlolatria* (idolatry, 10:14). Nevertheless, in both chapters Paul seems to pay more attention to whether the behavior of the "strong" causes wounding to the conscience (*suneidēsis*) of the "weak," than whether eating sacrificial meat is idolatry itself.

In recent Pauline scholarship, however, the interpretation of 1 Corinthians 8 and 10 is controversial and has produced a flood of literature.[13] Thus, it is necessary to provide a brief summary of selected scholarly arguments about these two chapters. P. W. Gooch suggests that though Paul thought the eating of meat sacrificed to idols "permissible for the Christians," Paul's "main concern in 1 Corinthians 8 and 10" is to argue that the Corinthian Christians should "refrain from exercising (their) right" to eat such meat "for the sake of (the) *suneidēsis*" (which

---

12. Theissen, "Structure," 77.

13. See Barrett, "Sacrificed"; Murphy-O'Connor, "Food"; Fee, "*Eidōlothuta*"; Horsley, "Consciousness"; Black, "Weak"; Willis, *Idol*; Gooch, "Consciousness"; and *Dangerous*; Nasuti, "Woes"; Fisk, "Eating"; Meggitt, "Meat"; Yeo, *Interpretation*, 5–14, 76–211; Dawes, "Danger"; Smit, "Disposition"; Sanders, "Paul"; Newton, *Deity*; Cheung, *Idol*; Sumney, "1 Corinthians"; Smith, *Symposium*, 1–172; Fotopoulos, *Offered*.

Gooch argues should not be translated as "moral conscience" but "bad feelings") of the weak.¹⁴ This is because their eating would harm the weak and bring upon them "a painful wound" (1 Cor 8:7–13; 10:28–29).¹⁵ Similarly, D. Newton contends that chapter 8 reveals Paul's strong disapproval of some of the Corinthian believers' participation in temple meals because this eating damaged the weak believers. 10:14–22 confirms this Pauline position.¹⁶

Furthermore, the issue of eating sacrificial meat should be seen from a communal point of view and linked to the theme of *agapē* in chapter 13, which is the basis for Christian behavior. W. L. Willis contends that "there is a fundamental agreement in Paul's arguments" about eating meat in 1 Corinthians 8 and 10.¹⁷ "In 1 Corinthians 8 Paul sets forth four basic arguments: (1) a critique of "rights" (or "freedom," *exousia*, 1 Cor 8:9; 9:4, 5, 6, 12, 18) on the basis of love (*agapē*), (2) a reminder of the necessity of considering the other person, (3) the importance of the communal dimension of Christian faith, and (4) Paul's own conduct as exemplary."¹⁸ Willis further claims that in chapter 10 Paul insists that the Corinthian Christians "must not participate in the (quasi) religious meals of their pagan neighbors held at an idol shrine" for the religious meals were idolatry. This Pauline insistence is based on "the Jewish heritage" that an act of worship is given only to God the Father (8:6).¹⁹

Similarly, D. E. Smith claims that in 1 Corinthians 8 and 10 Paul addresses different meal situations and describes the "meal ethic" as one of "social obligation" which believers should participate in.²⁰ In chapter 8 he describes a believer in "a chance encounter with a brother or sister who is participating at a banquet in a temple dining room" (8:10).²¹ In chapter 10 he pictures a believer who is invited to dine "at the home of an unbeliever" (10:27).²² In both chapters Paul presents the importance of meal ethics at a banquet, which is similarly applied "among brethren

14. Gooch, "Consciousness," 247–48, 251.
15. Ibid., 249.
16. Newton, *Deity*, 312–13.
17. Willis, *Idol*, 113.
18. Ibid.
19. Ibid., 221–22.
20. Smith, *Symposium*, 209, 211.
21. Ibid., 210.
22. Ibid., 211.

at the Christian communal meal."²³ Paul insists that when a believer participates at a banquet or is invited to eat at the home of an unbeliever, the believer creates "friendship" (*philia*) and "communal bonds" with the unbeliever.²⁴ These are comparable to those created among brethren in the Christian community. Especially, this friendship can be understood in the same sense as *agapē* in chapter 13. This *agapē* is "the ethical basis for social obligation at the communal meal."²⁵ Smith further argues that in these chapters, Paul pays more attention to the social obligation a believer has towards a fellow believer or an unbeliever at "a communal meal" than to whether the food offered to idols "has an efficacy."²⁶ Paul acknowledges that such food does not (8:4–6; 10:29–30). Furthermore, Paul insists that the believer's action should not offend the conscience of the fellow believer or that of the unbeliever. It rather has to lead to "upbuilding" (*oikodomē*, 10:23) and be "beneficial" (*sympheron*, 10:33).²⁷

Furthermore, scholars argue that Paul advised the Corinthian believers to abstain from participating in sacrificial meals because it was a sin of idolatry.²⁸ Others understand the issue in an ethical sense. G. D. Fee asserts that in Paul's thought, the eating of food dedicated to idols is forbidden not because it is absolutely idolatry or it is prohibited as law, but because it is "incompatible with life in Christ."²⁹ Murphy-O'Connor argues that to eat meat sacrificed to idols did not diminish the Corinthians' spiritual gifts. In other words, it was not a matter of the sin of idolatry but a moral issue. "Idol meat was morally neutral."³⁰ Similarly, Horsley contends that the issue of the eating of idol-meat was ethical. It was a matter of "relationship between people, not of one's inner consciousness."³¹

None of these scholars, however, explicitly relates the issue of eating meat to the problem of factionalism (*schismata*) in the Corinthian con-

---

23. Ibid., 210.
24. Ibid., 210–11.
25. Ibid., 211.
26. Ibid., 209.
27. Ibid., 210.
28. See Barrett, "Sacrificed," 153; Smit, "Disposition," 490–91; Sanders, "Paul," 81; Dawes, "Danger," 98; Sumney, "1 Corinthians," 333.
29. Fee, "*Eidōlothuta*," 196–97.
30. Murphy-O'Connor, "Food," 298.
31. Horsley, "Consciousness," 589.

gregation (1 Cor 1:10; 11:18–19). It is nonetheless argued that the issue of meat offered to idols is closely related to the schisms in the Corinthian Christian community Paul addresses in 1:10–12, as does Newton, albeit briefly.[32] It is also necessary to separate 1 Corinthians 8:1—10:22 from 10:23—11:1 for Paul addresses different issues in such two different contexts.[33] In the former, Paul deals with the issue of eating food offered to idols in temples and imperial cults. He sees the worship in these locations as idolatry and opposes it because this idolatry led to immorality (see 1 Cor 9:8–14; 10:1–22), just as in the classic Jewish critique of idolatry.

In the latter, however, Paul tackles the issue of eating meat within the context of a domestic cult. The main participants in the household cults were the deceased ancestors and the family members. The living were obligated to venerate (or show respect and honor for) the dead ancestors and make offerings to them at the family home and the gravesite on a regular basis. In so doing, they felt reunited with the dead. For these reasons, the household cult played an important part in maintaining the identity of the family in Greco-Roman world.[34] Paul does not speak out against this domestic cult nor against the eating of meat in that context (see 1 Cor 10:25, 27). So, it is appropriate to investigate these two issues in different contexts. This separation also helps to evaluate these issues from a Korean-Confucian Christian perspective (see further below). In this section, therefore, we pay attention only to the issue of idol worship in temples and imperial cults.

A careful interpretation of the issue of "meat offered to idols" should pay close attention to the words, *eidōlon* (idol, 8:4, 7; 10:19), *daimonion* (demon, 10:20, 21), *theos* (god, 8:5, 6; 10:20), and *kurios* (lord, 8:5, 6; 10:21), and then investigate these words in close relation to the imperial cult and patronage, and the *collegia sodalicia*. In chapters 8 and 10, the words *eidōlon, daimonion, theos,* and *kurios* can be interpreted several ways (except when the words *theos* and *kurios* clearly refer to God the Father [*theos patēr*, 8:6; 10:20 and Lord Jesus Christ [*kurios Iēsous christos*, 8:6; 10:21]). Newton argues that these words can refer to "a physical image or representation," "a false god," or "heroes and emperors."[35] All

32. Newton, *Deity*, 277.
33. So does Winter (*After*, 269–301).
34. See Rives, *Religion*, 117–18; Mikalson, *Ancient*, 133–36; Osiek and Balch, *Families*, 83; E. Ferguson, *Backgrounds*, 168, 170, 176.
35. Newton, *Deity*, 285–86.

these interpretations are plausible in consideration of the social situation of first-century Roman Corinth. The city had numerous temples, shrines, and ritual sites, numbering at least twenty-six.[36]

It is thus plausible to claim that the words, "many gods" (*theoi polloi*) and "many lords" (*kurioi polloi*), of which Paul speaks in 1 Corinthian 8:5, include the emperor whom some of the Corinthian Christians had worshipped and venerated in the imperial cult (1 Cor 8:7). This is supported by Newton. He states, "What does emerge in 8:5 is that Paul refers here to a wide spectrum of beings . . . such as upperworld gods, underworld gods, emperors, heroes, and even divine ancestors to various degrees."[37] The emperor was described as "lord," "savior," "son of a god," and "patron" because of the influence of imperial patronage and the imperial cult. For example, "At the end of his life, (Julius) Caesar (d. 44 BCE) . . . was appointed a god of the Roman state by the Senate," and Augustus was frequently depicted as "a god on earth, or a god-like individual in contemporary poetry and private iconography."[38] Similarly, Winter comments that the people in the Roman Empire "referred to the emperor as Lord."[39]

This notion then helps us understand 1 Corinthians 8:1–13 and 10:1–22 in a wider context. Some of the Corinthian Christians appear to have described themselves as people who possessed knowledge (*gnōsis*) (v. 1). Boasting about their *gnōsis* they conducted themselves arrogantly and acted on their *gnōsis* (vv. 1, 10). In the *gnōsis* that "an idol has no existence" and "there is no God but one" (1 Cor 8:4), they, like their contemporaries in the wider society, continued their membership in *collegia sodalicia*, even after conversion to the new faith in Christ. In such *collegia sodalicia* they associated with those who honored gods as their patron deities and ate meat offered as sacrifices to the deities (8:7, 10; 10:18–20). Perhaps they attended the imperial cult, and dedicated sacrifices to the emperor and called him lord, savior, and god, and implicitly worshipped him as the universal patron (v. 5). Perhaps some also participated in dinner parties and banquets, and ate food sacrificed to deities in the temples and to the emperor in the imperial cult (v. 10).[40]

36. See Witherington, *Testament*, 268–69.
37. Newton, *Deity*, 288.
38. Gradel, *Emperor*, 109–10.
39. Winter, *After*, 285.
40. "Many temples had adjoining dining rooms for cultic meals. Archaeological

They may well have even regarded the Corinthian Christian community as another of the *collegia sodalicia* where they called on the name of the Christian God and the Lord Jesus Christ, worshipped and venerated him as their patron deity, just as they did in other *collegia sodalicia* in the wider civic society (1 Cor 8:4–5).

Furthermore, it is consistent with this inference to suggest that they may well have brought into the Christian community the patronal hierarchical structures that were usually found in the *collegia sodalicia*. From this patronal hierarchical perspective, some of the Corinthian Christians of wealth and high social status would have viewed God as a patron deity ranked at the highest level in the Christian *ekklēsia*. Paul appears to agree, to a certain extent, with this view since he describes God as the Father and Creator through whom all things and people exist (1 Cor 8:6). Seemingly, this affirms that God can be regarded as a patron deity in Christian communities. They then considered themselves as being ranked in the middle and saw themselves as patrons of the Christian community. This thinking seems to have led them to regard Paul's social status lower than theirs. That is why they expected to give Paul, as a client, financial support. Yet he refused to accept their offer (1 Cor 9:12–23). He "avoided such patronage by means of self-support in the workshop."[41] Moreover, they would have viewed the rest of their fellow Christians as ranked at a lower level in the social pyramid of the Christian *ekklēsia*.[42] They appear to have regarded the Lord's Supper as akin to the banquets and dinner parties of the *collegia sodalicia*, and the temples and the imperial cult. There they ate food sacrificed to deities and the emperor (see above). As would have occurred in such dinner parties, so social discrimination against other fellow Christians and especially some members of who were poor and of lower classes at the Lord's Supper (and love-feasts) occurred (see 1 Cor 11:17–22). They did not permit poorer fellow Christians to sit around the same table as they did, but they instead left them to eat outside of the building in the courtyard. These poorer and lower-ranked Christians seemed to have been provided with poorer quality food.[43]

---

evidence indicates that these were common in the area of Corinth" (E. Ferguson, *Backgrounds*, 180).

41. Johnson, "Epistolary," 500 n. 46.
42. See Chow, "Patronage," 119.
43. See Murphy-O'Connor, *Corinth*, 183–84.

Paul, however, criticized these unnamed leaders because, by doing this, they abused the genuine meaning of the Lord's Supper and despised the Christian form of gathering (*ekklēsia tou theou*) where all members should be treated equally as brothers and sisters in Christ regardless of their social class (1 Cor 3:8; 11:22).[44] On the other hand, they affirmed that the God of Jesus is the one true God—and that the idols/emperors were not true Gods (8:4)—therefore, it did not matter in other respects if they participated in banquets and dinner parties in the wider Corinthian society. Paul, however, strongly condemned the social consequences of idol worship in the temples, where attendees and worshippers often behaved immorally especially in terms of sexual licentiousness and prostitution, using the traditional Jewish understanding that idolatry leads to immorality (1 Cor 9:8–12; 10:1–13).[45]

Paul wished to protect the Corinthian Christian *ekklēsia* from such immorality (e.g., 1 Cor 5:9–11). He says, "We must not indulge in immorality" (1 Cor 10:8). For these reasons, Paul critiqued as demonic the patron deities that some members in the Corinthian Christian community implicitly venerated at temples and then encouraged them to stop such worship of idols (1 Cor 10:14).[46] Their conduct further harmed and wounded some Christians who were weak, although they did not necessarily intend or notice this (1 Cor 8:7), resulting in factions in the Christian *ekklēsia* (11:18–19).

Paul suggests, therefore, that they should take care lest their behavior become an obstacle to the weak (1 Cor 8:9), lest it wound the other brothers and sisters' conscience (*suneidēsis*) (1 Cor 8:10), and lest it cause the weak to fall. Moreover, Paul argues that it is a sin against Christ to wound the conscience of the brothers and sisters in the Corinthian congregation (8:7–13) because this partly caused the Corinthian Christians to split into factions (1:10; 11:18–19; 12:25). Furthermore, Paul had a strong emphasis on unity in the Corinthian Christian community as the body of Christ (*sōma christou*) (1 Cor 12:1–31). He also claimed

---

44. See Witherington, *Conflict*, 184.

45. So argue R. E. Ciampa and B. S. Rosner. They state that Paul took "the traditional Jewish approach to dealing with sexual immorality and idolatry" (Ciampa and Rosner, "Structure," 218). In Roman Corinth, sexual liberty played a part both in some religious festivals and in temple precincts (see Witherington, *Conflict*, 13; also Murphy-O'Connor, "Saint," 152).

46. It is important for me to re-interpret the Corinthian attitude towards gods and the imperial cult from my own Korean-Confucian Christian context (see further below).

that the Corinthian Christians should have love (*agapē*) towards one another (1 Cor 8:1; 13:1-13). Particularly in 1 Corinthians 13:13, "so faith, hope, love abide, these three; but the greatest of these is love," Paul values love more highly than faith (*pistis*) and hope (*elpis*).[47] C. Stettler further states,

> By his excursus on love in 1 Corinthians 13 Paul emphasizes that love is the purpose and criterion of spiritual gifts. The gifts are but instruments of love, of the mutual upbuilding of the church. Exercising different spiritual gifts is the specific, individual way in which different Christians serve one another in love.[48]

As such, Paul seems to assert that to have love towards one another is the most necessary and important way to reclaim the Corinthian congregation from the grips of factionalism.

Collegia Tenuiorum

Some of the Corinthian Christians may also have understood the Christian *ekklēsia* to be more of a kind of *collegia tenuiorum*, formed for the purpose of arranging funerals and the appropriate burial of the dead. This argument is supported, to a certain degree, by other scholars. J. B. Rives argues that in Greco-Roman times "Christian groups (were) involved in the burial of their fellows," as their contemporaries were in the wider society.[49] B. Rawson states, "Death, burial and commemoration . . . have a particular role for a religious community . . . In the first century . . . the early Christian community (shared) similarities in commemorative practices and attitudes to family relationships," which took place in voluntary *collegia*.[50] W. A. Meeks proposes that:

> We have no evidence about the funeral practices of Pauline Christians—a silence that in itself would be grounds for doubting a direct identification of the Christian groups with *collegia tenuiorum*—but we can hardly doubt, in the face of . . . the enigmatic reference to "baptism (for) the dead" in 1 Corinthians 15:29, that these groups made appropriate provision for the burial of deceased Christians.[51]

---

47. Similarly, argues Smith (*Symposium*, 211).
48. Stettler, "Command," 46.
49. Rives, *Religion*, 125.
50. Rawson, "Family," 134-35.
51. Meeks, *Urban*, 78.

Witherington also comments that some of the Corinthian Christians would have "viewed the Christian community as a burial society."[52]

Moreover, the consideration of the Corinthian congregation, as analogous to a sort of *collegia tenuiorum*, is glimpsed in 1 Corinthians 15 and particularly in the Pauline description of baptism for (or on behalf of) the dead (*baptisma huper tōn nekron* in 15:29), as Meek argues briefly above. The interpretation of this Pauline phrase is controversial in recent Pauline scholarship. A. C. Thiselton thus says that 1 Corinthians 15:29 is "a notoriously difficult crux," and H. Conzelmann comments that 15:29 is "one of the most hotly disputed passages" in 1 Corinthians.[53] Scholars split into several groups: One group of scholars argues that the Corinthians were baptized for the "sake" of the dead who were unbaptized, to make sure of their reunion with them at the resurrection.[54] Another group asserts that the Corinthians exercised baptism "on account" (or "for the benefit") of the dead to express public allegiance to the deceased patron apostles, through whose testimony they were converted and baptized, and thus to give great honor to them and reward them for their apostolic ministry.[55]

The majority of scholars contend that some of the Corinthian Christians practiced "vicarious (or "proxy") baptism" for the dead in order to help them get through "a difficult transition from this world and the next" and receive "eternal security."[56] "Vicarious baptisms imply, as a corollary, the expectation of resurrection" of the deceased who died, not hearing the gospel.[57] The problem of this contention is that there is no evidence that vicarious (or proxy) baptism for the dead was undertaken in Corinth in the first century CE. This practice was, however, practiced in the second century CE among heretics. This is attested by Chrysostom acknowledging that the Marcionites adopted the practice of vicarious baptism as a custom. "When any Catechumen departs this life . . . if he or she wishes to receive baptism . . . thus they baptize him or her in the stead

---

52. Witherington, *Conflict*, 293 n. 10.
53. Thiselton, *Corinthians*, 1240; Conzelmann, *Corinthians*, 275.
54. Thiselton, *Corinthians*, 1248.
55. Patrick, "Living," 74–76; also White, "Baptized," 498; Murphy-O'Connor, "Baptized," 532–43.
56. DeMaris, "Corinthian," 676; Witherington, *Conflict*, 294; similarly, Conzelmann, *Corinthians*, 275; Morris, *Corinthians*, 214; Winter, *After*, 103–5.
57. Goulder, *Competing*, 189.

of the departed one (Chrys. *Hom. Epist. I ad Cor.* 40.1)."⁵⁸ Some scholars do not explain clearly their positions in this debate.⁵⁹ Nonetheless, we are more concerned to investigate the attitudes towards baptism of the Corinthians in relation to their consideration of the Christian community as analogous to a sort of *collegia tenuiorum* and to explore these attitudes as factors in causing divisions in the Corinthian congregation.

In 1 Corinthians 15:29 Paul asks the Corinthian audience two rhetorical questions: "Now if there is no resurrection, what will those do who are baptized for the dead? If the dead are not raised at all, why are people baptized for them?" (NIV). The rhetorical questions imply that some members of the Corinthian Christian community would have had themselves baptized (or have been baptized) for the dead (*nekroi*).⁶⁰ At the same time, some seem to have denied the resurrection of the dead in some way. Seemingly, this group of Corinthian Christians paid much more attention to the matter of funerals and the burial of the dead than the doctrine of the resurrection of the dead that Paul had taught during his stay at Corinth. This is perhaps because they regarded the Christian gatherings as similar to one of the *collegia tenuiorum* in which they continued to be members. They then thought that the Corinthian Christian community was formed, in a sense, for the purposes of arranging funerals and making adequate provision for the burial of dead Christian members including themselves.⁶¹

Some Corinthian Christians would also have brought into the Christian community some of the cultural and religious assumptions and practices that prevailed in the wider society and particularly in the *collegia tenuiorum*. "Proper burial was so great a concern that clubs (and especially *collegia tenuiorum*) existed to ensure that members were adequately mourned and buried, and these were very popular in imperial Roman society."⁶² The Corinthians, and especially the Greeks and Romans who were preoccupied with the world of the dead, had a strong

58. Conzelmann, *Corinthians*, 275, 276 n. 117.

59. See Hays, *Corinthians*, 267; Bruce, *Corinthians*, 148–49.

60. In 1 Corinthians 15 *nekros* occurs thirteen times; although it is nowhere found in the rest of 1 Corinthians. *Nekros* (dead, lifeless) is used to mean "having never been alive and lacking capacity for life." When it is used for a person, it means "a corpse who is no longer physically alive" (BAGD, 667).

61. Similarly Meeks, *Urban*, 78.

62. DeMaris, "Corinthian," 664; cf. Meeks, *Urban*, 78; Witherington, *Conflict*, 293 n. 10.

sense of obligation toward the deceased. The Romans and Greeks believed that it was their (the living's) obligation (or duty) that in order to help their dead "become integrated in the realm of the dead," they had to bury the dead properly and mourn adequately for them. Afterward, they commemorated the dead by visiting the grave and holding graveside feasts. They believed that "the dead could benefit directly from actions performed on their behalf, particularly at the grave."[63]

In a similar sense, it seems that some Corinthian Christians appear to have understood Christian baptism in this way (1 Cor 15:29). They may well have understood that the baptism of their household included their dead ancestors (*hoi nekroi*)—whether they had believed or not before death[64] because they considered this "baptism for the dead" as an appropriate public expression and extension of their veneration and commemoration toward dead ancestors (or "living spirits"). Performing such an inclusive "baptism for the dead," they would have believed that they fulfilled the obligations and duties which, as living descendants, they had to exercise and that in so doing they were connected and reunited with their dead. This argument agrees with R. E. DeMaris in the sense that the Corinthian believers' attitude to baptism was related to the practices of first-century Corinthian religion in their wider civic society and those in the *collegia tenuiorum* but disagrees with him about "vicarious baptism" for the dead in 1 Corinthians 15:29.[65]

Paul himself speaks of "baptism into Moses" which is, in a sense, similar to such an inclusive and retrospective view of "baptism for the dead," in 1 Corinthians 10:1–13 where he deals with the Israelites who travelled in the wilderness. Nonetheless, this argument may seem forced to some readers because in the biblical text Paul does not in fact employ the word *nekroi* at all. So it is rather likely that in this analogy Paul seems to assume a context in which "living" Israelites were baptized into a "living" Moses. He does not simply describe the story of dead

---

63. DeMaris, "Corinthian," 663–64.

64. In 1 Corinthians 15, the Greek word *nekroi*, with or without the article *hoi*, refers to all the dead and all corpses in the grave who are subject to mortality, rather than only to deceased Christians (see Fee, *Corinthians*, 776). Horsley supports the view that in certain Hellenistic circles . . . the words *hoi nekroi* refer to corpses which are distinctively separated from the soul (mind or spirit) (Horsley, *Corinthians*, 201; cf. Patrick, who regards *hoi nekroi* only as the dead Christians and apostles named in 1 Corinthians 15:5–6 ["Living," 74]).

65. See DeMaris, "Corinthian," 661–82.

Israelites but appears to emphasize the vivid event of the Exodus of the Israelites who were (being) passing through the sea and were (being) travelling in the dessert (vv. 1–5). This is in itself an affirmation that the "dead ancestors" are still seen as "living" (or "alive in Christ") in some real sense (see 1 Cor 10:4).

Paul describes, "Our fathers (or ancestors) were all under the cloud, and all passed through the sea, and all were baptized into Moses in the cloud and in the sea" (1 Cor 10:1–2).[66] Therein, Paul clearly takes as an example his Jewish ancestors who were baptized into Moses as their leader and hero. Paul, thereby, venerates and commemorates the deeds of his Jewish ancestors and Moses. Some Corinthian Christians would probably have identified their view and practice of "baptism for their deceased" with the idea of "baptism into Moses" (1 Cor 10:2), if he had addressed this question regarding the ancestral Israelites to the Corinthian audience during his ministry in Corinth (1 Cor 10:1–13).

By the way, the issue of baptism appears to have been one of the underlying factors that caused the problem of factionalism in the Corinthian congregation. Paul uses the Greek word *baptizō* ten times (1:13, 14, 15, 16 [twice], 17; 10:2; 12:13; 15:29 [twice]), but he uses it nowhere in 2 Corinthians at all. The word occurs only in the literary context where Paul addresses the problem of schisms, except for 10:2 "baptized into Moses." Winter states, "1 Corinthians 1:13–17a suggests that some significance had been attached to the baptisms of those involved in strife and jealousy."[67] Witherington also comments, "1 Corinthians 15 (and esp. 15:29) manifests clear evidence of factionalism. Only some were saying 'There is no resurrection of the dead,'" Others were exercising baptism for the dead.[68] In 1 Corinthians 12, therefore, in order to encourage them to leave the spirit of factionalism, Paul challenges the whole Corinthian congregation, not just a few members, to understand their baptism into one body of Christ by one Spirit. He says, "We were all baptized into one body" (12:13). Paul, in fact, baptized a few members, not the entire congregation, who were representatives of the major ethnic groups—Jews, Romans, and Greeks—during his ministry at Corinth (1 Cor 1:14–16).

66. Interestingly, "the expression 'baptized into Moses' is nowhere to be found in Jewish sources; Paul has coined the phrase on the basis of Christian language" (Hays, *Corinthians*, 160).

67. Winter, *After*, 104.

68. Witherington, *Conflict*, 295 n. 20.

Furthermore, there is a significant distinction between Paul, who saw it as the body of Christ (1 Cor 12:25-27) and the temple of God (1 Cor 3:16-17), and those who saw it as a sort of *collegia tenuiorum*. It is clear, consequently, from the perspective of some in the Christian gatherings of Corinth that they did not see much difference between the *ekklēsiai* and other social *collegia tenuiorum* since they all gathered together on a regular basis for social relationships, talked about funerals and burial of the dead, and occasionally shared meals together (e.g., 1 Cor 11:17-34). One difference to other social *collegia tenuiorum* would have been that the Christians met together more frequently than once a month.[69] Paul also strongly argued that the Christian *ekklēsia* was not just like a *collegia tenuiorum* formed for the purposes of arranging funerals and the appropriate burial of the dead. Rather, it was the body of Christ in which "there (was) no discord" and "the members (had) the same care for one another" (1 Cor 12:25-27). It was the temple of God in which "God's Spirit dwells" (1 Cor 3:16-17). It was also more like a household (*oikos*) where God is the Father. The Corinthian Christians were his children and should call themselves brothers and sisters and have household relationships under God as *paterfamilias* rather than patronal relationships (e.g., 1:16; see further below).

In 1 Corinthians 15:29 some of the Corinthian Christians appear to have denied the resurrection of the dead—and yet it does not necessarily mean that they did not believe in the resurrection of Christ.[70] This is supported by Paul's language in the wider context of 1 Corinthians 15:12-58: "How can some of you say that there is no resurrection of the dead" (1 Cor 15:12), and "some one will ask, 'how are the dead raised? With what kind of body do they come?'" (v. 35).[71] Their denial of the resurrection of the dead is an indication that they were influenced, to some extent, by Greco-Roman religions (paganism) prevailing in the wider Corinthian society. Some Christians of this group probably comprised wealthier and higher-social-status members. They would have

---

69. Associations "may not meet together more than once a month . . . " (MacMullen, *Relations*, 79).

70. See Winter, *After*, 105.

71. Paul poses these rhetorical questions, as confirmed by R. J. Sider who argues that "*pōs* is frequently used to introduce rhetorical questions which challenge or reject an idea" (Sider, "Conception," 429). D. Watson also argues that the section from v. 35 to the end of the chapter is composed of rhetorical pieces (Witherington, *Conflict*, 306), and Schmithals says that "it is seriously to be doubted that people in Corinth posed the questions in v. 35" (Conzelmann, *Corinthians*, 280).

continued strong patron-client bonds with the Corinthian citizens who had power and control of the social and political positions in the wider society. They also conducted the religious festivals such as the Isthmian games and the imperial cult and adhered to Greco-Roman paganism. In doing this, they continued "strong ties to pagan society" and were probably affected, to some degree, by Greco-Roman religious thoughts.[72]

In Greco-Roman paganism people "did not place much stress on a blessed afterlife. (They thus thought that) religion was to be practiced for its present benefits such as health and safety."[73] Yet they believed "in the immortality of the soul/spirit and the cessation of the body's senses at death."[74] In other words, there was no idea in Greco-Roman paganism that the dead would be raised or resurrected in bodily form (*sōma*) after being buried (e.g., 1 Cor 15:35). They considered the body as inferior to the soul/spirit (*pneuma*) in quality. For these reasons, the conceptions of resurrection of the dead and the resurrection body as addressed in 1 Corinthians 15 were completely enigmatic and problematical to people who adhered to such Greco-Roman religious thoughts.[75] This would be a puzzling issue for young Christians who were newly converted from such a Greco-Roman religious background.

Even though they were already converted to the Christian faith, some of the Corinthian Christians still expressed skepticism (or doubt) about Paul's teaching on the resurrection of the dead because they adhered to misconceptions about the resurrection body and had difficulty conceiving of the concept of bodily resurrection as a reality. For them this was a major stumbling block, since a body in their thinking was "synonymous with mortality and corruptibility,"[76] and thus unable to inherit immortality. Rather, it was more acceptable to them that a soul/spirit only is involved with immortality.[77] On the contrary, Paul argues

---

72. Witherington, *Conflict*, 295. These Corinthian Christians did not have to be always the same ones as those who performed "baptism for the dead" probably because of differences of social status, *collegia*, and ethnic origin (similarly Witherington, *Conflict*, 295 n. 20).

73. Witherington, *Conflict*, 293.

74. Winter, *After*, 104.

75. E. Ferguson comments that there was no idea of the resurrection of the dead . . . in most ancient Greco-Roman religions "outside some Jews and the Christians," but the Zoroastrians had a concept of the resurrection of the flesh (*Backgrounds*, 211–49).

76. Witherington, *Conflict*, 306.

77. See Winter, *After*, 104–5; also Witherington, *Conflict*, 307.

strongly that a body will also be involved in the event of the last triumph (1 Cor 15:54), and it shall then be transformed into eternity or immortality (1 Cor 15:52, 53). For Paul, it is clear that eternity or immortality involves both *sōma* and *pneuma*.[78] Thus, there is a significant distinction between Paul and this group of Corinthian Christians in understanding the matter of the resurrection of the dead. These Corinthian Christians were still attached to the idea of Greco-Roman thought and argued for the immortality of a soul/spirit and the mortality of a body. These different understandings about the resurrection of the dead may well have caused tension and conflict between Paul and them.

In 1 Corinthian 15, therefore, Paul appears to critique their skepticism about the resurrection of the dead.[79] In reaction to this skepticism, Paul insists that the Corinthian Christian gatherings are the *ekklēsia* of the God who raised Christ from the dead (1 Cor 15:15). He further challenges the Corinthian Christians to believe in the resurrection of their transformed dead bodies (*nekroi*) as a reality in the future (1 Cor 15:16–18) and preach the death and resurrection of Christ as the essence of the gospel, just as he did during his ministry at Corinth (1 Cor 15:3–11). Paul also encourages them to "be steadfast and immovable, always abounding in the work of the Lord" Jesus Christ (15:58), "the first fruit of those who fall asleep" (15:20).

To sum up, some of the Corinthian Christians (including some who may be termed Paul's Corinthian opponents) were embedded in systems of patronage in their Christian community, just as their contemporary Corinthians were in the social clubs and associations such as the professional *collegia*, *collegia sodalicia*, and *collegia tenuiorum*. Those who possessed wealth and high social standing considered themselves as patrons of the Christian community and other fellow Christians as their clients and those who were poorer and of the lower social classes in particular. In the Christian *ekklēsia* they also assumed the "normal" social stratification and patronal hierarchies among the members and continued to express their high social status and (probably unintentional) discrimination against other fellow Christians of lower social status such as slaves (e.g., 1 Cor 1:26–31; 4:6–7, 8–10; 7:21–23). Apparently, from their point of view, the Christian *ekklēsia* could be seen as analogous to one of the *collegia sodalicia* and *collegia tenuiorum* where patron-client

---

78. Witherington, *Conflict*, 307.
79. See DeMaris, "Corinthian," 678–79; Winter, *After*, 105; Hays, *Corinthians*, 268.

systems played a vital role in interconnecting between patrons and clients of various social levels within the *collegia*.

In reaction to what he sees as improper mentality and behavior, Paul asserts that the Corinthian Christian *ekklēsia* is no less or more than the temple of God (1 Cor 3:16–17) where God the Father is worshiped as the creator, not simply as a patron deity (1 Cor 8:4–6). Paul also refers to the Corinthian congregation as the body of Christ (1 Cor 12:27). Christ crucified and raised is the essential and profound foundation of the Christian *ekklēsia* (1 Cor 1:18–24; 3:11). It is also seen as a faith community where Christ crucified, as the wisdom and power of God and his gospel, is considered core and central (1 Cor 1:18–24). This identity of the *ekklēsia* as temple of God and body of Christ stands over against any identification with Greco-Roman or imperial temples, and the feasting and immorality associated with them. But we have noted that Paul is much more open to, and affirming of, any association with household (and, by implication, ancestral) identities. This will be significant for our further analysis below.

Lastly, Paul stresses that in the Corinthian Christian gatherings there should not be any social stratification, patronal hierarchies, discrimination, or boasting about social privilege among the members (e.g., 1 Cor 1:26, 28, 29; 3:21; 4:6–7; 7:21–22; 11:22). Instead, there must be unity and love in Christ among the members, equal treatment of all members whether of high social status or lower, and a high value placed on the proclamation of the gospel message in which the death and resurrection of Christ is central (1 Cor 1:17, 31; 2:1–5; 3:5–9; 12:25; 13:1–13). We now move on to a closer investigation of the relationship between these patron-client systems and the problem of schisms in the Corinthian congregation (1 Cor 1:10–12).

THE PROBLEM OF SCHISMS

The Party of Paul and the Party of Apollos

It has been observed that in first-century Corinth, as in the wider Greco-Roman world, people of wealth and high social status used patronal systems to (re)produce their power in politics and extend their social influence within society. A person's political power and social influence was measured according to the number of patronal networks and clients they had as a patron. In this social atmosphere, it was shameful if patrons of wealth and high social status did not have a good number of clients,[80] so they naturally desired to establish as many patronal networks as possible. This then caused them to have a spirit of rivalry and competition among themselves, to the extent of using invective and accusations to denounce and reproach one another. Such rhetorical exchanges characterized the civic life of the Greco-Roman world and Roman Corinth in the first century CE.[81]

Some of this spirit of rivalry and competition may well have been brought into the Corinthian congregation by some of the Corinthian Christians. A few possessed wealth and high social status and had frequent contacts with Corinthians of full Roman citizenship and the highest social status at banquets and *collegia* in the wider Corinthian civic communities. They also were affected deeply by the social and cultural tendencies of patronal networks and rhetorical conventions, as typified by Cicero's legacy (see 1 Cor 1:26), as argued earlier.

In order to build their patronal networks, some of the Corinthian Christians of wealth and high social status would have approached and been approached by poorer and lower social-status fellow Christians wishing to become their clients, just as occurred in other social clubs and associations. The majority of the Corinthian Christians were poor and ranked low in the social pyramid.[82] To these poor Christians, patronage was more than a social institution. It was a means of survival in the wider Corinthian civic society in which people were tightly tied by patron-client networks (see above). Because of this, the poor Christians could hardly refuse the wealthy and high social-status Christians' proposals. These wealthy Christians would find it hard not to use their patronal networks to take control of the Christian community and keep it under their authority after Paul had left Corinth. Such social-conventions-oriented behavior would cause serious tensions with Paul and other fellow Christians, tensions which would then develop into schisms (*schismata*) among the members in the Corinthian Christian community (1 Cor 1:11). Yet R. B. Hays claims that "the divisions (*schismata*) at Corinth should not necessarily be understood to be clearly organised parties"

---

80. See Malina and Rohrbaugh, *Synoptic*, 75.
81. See Marshall, *Enmity*, 35–90.
82. Theissen, "Structure," 76–77; as re-affirmed by J. J. Meggitt (*Poverty*, 41–180; "Response," 85–94).

but more likely "inchoate dissentions and arguments brewing" among the members.[83]

It is furthermore argued that from the perspective of patron-client relations and patronal hierarchies there were two major parties in the Christian community after Paul had left Corinth: the party of Paul and that of Apollos (3:4-6; 4:6). Yet, in the Pauline language there are initially four names (Paul, Apollos, Cephas, and Christ) given as the leaders of each party (1 Cor 1:12), and then three (Paul, Apollos, and Cephas) (3:22). The argument of existence of two major parties at Corinth is supported by scholars such as Pogoloff (see above), Witherington, Hays, and Thiselton. Witherington argues that it is doubtful that there was a Christ party in the Corinthian Christian community or that Cephas actually visited the city of Corinth.[84] Hays and Thiselton also have doubts about Peter's presence at Corinth.[85] It is also argued here that the Christ party or the phrase "I belong to Christ" (*christou*, 1:12) was not used by the Corinthians, but that Paul himself added it to draw the Corinthians' attention closer to the topic of Christ crucified and his gospel (1:17-23), and to introduce the issue of baptism that was also related to the divisions at Corinth (1:13b-16). This phrase leads naturally to the following rhetorical questions such as "Is Christ divided?" and "Was Paul crucified for you?" (1:13; RSV). This argument is also supported in 3:23 where Paul distinguishes Christ's group (*christou*) from all other human-oriented groups. In this way Paul emphasizes that the Corinthian Christians as a whole belong only to Christ crucified, the Lord, rather than particular human leaders (3:18-23).[86] Paul insists that in God's temple there must be no divisive parties and no "personal allegiance to particular leaders,"[87] so that no one boasts about humans but about Christ crucified (3:21). Therefore, it is clear that the divisions at Corinth were not created by "clearly defined theological differences" but by personal preferences for particular leaders in the congregation, emulating the patronal networks of the wider society.[88]

83. Hays, *Corinthians*, 22.
84. Witherington, *Conflict*, 83, 87.
85. Hays, *Corinthians*, 22; Thiselton, *Corinthians*, 128.
86. See Mitchell, *Reconciliation*, 83-86; Thiselton, *Corinthians*, 133.
87. Hays, *Corinthians*, 22.
88. Ibid.

Paul names several Corinthian Christians in Romans and 1 Corinthians: Chloe, Crispus, Gaius, Stephanas, Prisca, Aquila, Fortunatus, Achaicus, Phoebe, and Erastus (1 Cor 1:11, 14–16; 16:15–20; Rom 16: 1, 23). All these people appear to have been prominent members of the Corinthian congregation. It is, however, worth noting that Paul omits Phoebe and Erastus in 1 Corinthians, although they were prominent members in the Corinthian community. It is, therefore, supposed that Erastus and Phoebe were later converts than those named in 1 Corinthians or that the two were not directly related to the problem of *schismata* in the Corinthian congregation when Paul wrote 1 Corinthians. Phoebe in particular was a *diakonos* of the Christian community in Cenchreae rather than in Corinth (Rom 16:1). By the way, it does not necessarily mean that all of those named belonged to the Pauline party (1 Cor 1:12; 3:4)—Gaius and Erastus probably did not (see below). Thus, whether these Corinthians actually used the slogan, "I belong to Paul" (1 Cor 1:12; 3:4) is doubtful; but it seems that Paul would be happy to include them in his party (e.g., 1 Cor 4:14–17), at least for the rhetorical effect of their positive public naming as the letter is read to the community.

Thus, Paul appears to have deliberately named these Corinthians and used the naming as part of his rhetorical strategy. He mentions some of the names of Corinthian Christians in 1 Corinthian explicitly to praise their commitment to the ministry of God in Corinth. Paul appreciates, for example, the household of Stephanas devoting themselves to the service of the saints and refreshing his spirit in association with Fortunatus and Achaicus (1 Cor 16:15–18). Paul also expresses his gratitude to Prisca and Aquila for risking their necks for his life (1 Cor 16:19; Rom 16:3–4).

On the other hand, Paul seems to have named some of the Corinthian congregation who argued against him in 1 Corinthians, to win them over, not to judge or blame them (e.g., 1 Cor 1:14). Similarly K. K. Yeo argues that "the best approach for Paul is not to judge, or to praise one party, but to 'talk it over' with them."[89] Yet Paul appears not to have publicly shamed anyone in the congregation but, rather, encourages the whole congregation to leave the inappropriate environment of factionalism and to be united in Christ. Paul says, "I appeal to you, brothers and sisters, by the name of our Lord Jesus Christ, that all of you

---

89. Yeo, "Hermeneutic," 296.

agree and that there be no dissensions (*schismata*) among you but that you be united in the same mind and the same judgment" (1 Cor 1:10).

It is further proposed that the Pauline party would most likely have included a large number of Corinthian Christians who were poor and of lower social classes. Paul explicitly identifies himself with these poorer and lower-status Christians for the sake of the gospel of Christ (1:26–28; 4:8–13).[90] These poorer Christians were the ones at risk of being marginalized in the congregation and humiliated by other fellow Christians who continued to express their wealth and high social status in the Christian community (1 Cor 11:17–22). They are the "weak" (*asthenēs*) of whom Paul speaks in 1 Corinthians 9:22–23, and identifies with in 4:10 ("we are fools for Christ's sake . . . weak . . . [and] in disrepute"). It would not be surprising, therefore, to find a mutual identification between these poorer Christians and Paul.

On the other hand, the party of Apollos may well have included some other Corinthian Christians of wealth and high social status (1 Cor 1:26; 4:8) and poorer Christians who established patron-client bonds with these wealthier ones. It is supposed that Gaius and Erastus were probably among these wealthier Christians. Gaius appears to have been one of the wealthiest members in the Corinthian Christian community because only he is named as having a house big enough to accommodate the whole congregation (Rom 16:23). Poorer and lower social-status Christians were apparently humiliated at the Lord's Supper undertaken in a house like his (e.g., 1 Cor 11: 22), where only the wealthy were able to recline at the table in the triclinium.[91] Erastus was the city treasurer in Corinth (Rom 16:23). His high public office suggests that he was a major magistrate in the local government, socially powerful and ranking highly in the social pyramid of Roman Corinth (see above).

The wealth and high social status that Gaius and Erastus possessed fits well in the argument that some of the Corinthian Christians had frequent contacts with Corinthians who had full Roman citizenship and power and control of the social political positions in the Corinthian civic society. They were influenced heavily by the social and cultural value systems characterized by patronal networks and rhetorical conventions and influenced, to some degree, by Cicero's legacy (see 1 Cor 2:1–5). These Christians rose in social status to higher positions in the

---

90. See Hays, *Corinthians*, 148.
91. See Murphy-O'Connor, *Corinth*, 183–84; Lampe, "Eucharistic," 5–6.

wider Corinthian civic communities by making considerable financial contributions to the city. This was the way to gain honor and prestige in the first-century Greco-Roman world.[92]

In a similar manner, it is argued that by using their money these Christians were able to have leadership positions and naturally exercise control of the Christian community. They effectively became patrons of the Corinthian Christian *ekklēsia*. That is why they no doubt approached Paul and offered to establish patronal relationships with him, also offering him financial support. Nevertheless, Paul refused to accept their financial support (1 Cor 9:12, 15–19) since he was aware of the hidden implications of their monetary gift. He suspected that they wished to put the congregation under their control by using their wealth, social status, and patronal hierarchies (cf. 2 Cor 11:7–11; 12:13–18).

Paul's refusal of their proposal did not make sense to them at all because in Greco-Roman culture all teachers received remuneration from their students.[93] Similarly, "a genuine apostle would accept full payment."[94] Paul himself knew this, as is evident in the fact that he received monetary gifts from the Macedonian Christians (2 Cor 11:9) and that he did not criticize the other apostles and Cephas who accepted financial gifts from Christians (1 Cor 9:3–7).[95] Paul, however, refused to accept the Corinthian Christians' patronage (with the exception of Phoebe [see Rom 16:1–2]) and financial support during his stay at Corinth. He did not build patronal relationships with them (1 Cor 9:15). Sze-Kar Wan argues that the inconsistency in Paul's actions regarding financial gifts caused some of the Corinthian Christians to oppose him.[96]

There are two possible reasons for Paul's refusal of the Corinthians' financial support: first, Paul did not want to put an obstacle and stumbling block in the way of the gospel of Jesus Christ crucified (1 Cor 9:12). He did not want to "burden the Corinthians or take advantage of them in anyway. As their "parent" in Christ, he wanted to give to them rather than receive from them" (2 Cor 11:9; 12:14–18).[97] Second, Paul was aware of the social and cultural tendencies of Roman Corinth and

---

92. Pogoloff, *Logos*, 193.
93. Winter, *After*, 36.
94. Barnett, "Apostle," 49.
95. See Pogoloff, *Logos*, 193; Everts, "Financial," 296.
96. Wan, *Power*, 29.
97. Everts, "Financial," 296.

the mentality and behavior of some of the Corinthian Christians who were influenced deeply by the wider social and cultural value systems. He saw in the Corinthians' offer of financial support that they were affected deeply by the social phenomenon of patron-client systems and social mobility through money. He did not want them to implicate him and take advantage of their patronal networks, thereby enhancing their social privilege in the Christian community. Rather, he reminded them that their social privilege and patronal systems did not ensure leadership positions and give them the right to take control of the Christian *ekklēsia* (1 Cor 1:26-29). Furthermore, Paul appealed to them to make a pure commitment to the gospel of Christ crucified and the Christian mission rather than give high value to worldly wisdom, economic possessions and social status (1 Cor 4:1). He also insisted that the gospel message of Christ crucified, the wisdom and power of God, must be preached to everyone free of charge (1 Cor 9:15-18).

Instead of receiving financial support from the Corinthians, Paul worked as a leatherworker/tentmaker to support himself (see Acts 18:1-3). He recognized that "this sort of menial labor" and "low-status occupation" did not at all fit him as a truly authentic apostle in the light of Greco-Roman culture (1 Cor 9:7).[98] His attitude differed from that of other itinerant Christian teachers and preachers who visited Roman Corinth. They acted like "respectable philosophical teachers" and rhetoricians, and received momentary gifts from wealthy members of the Corinthian Christian community.[99] Nevertheless, Paul did not act like them. He, rather, conducted himself like an uneducated, poor, and low social-status person (e.g., 1 Cor 4:10-12). Hence, it seems that some in the Corinthian *ekklēsia* did not regard Paul as their leader at all. Moreover, they suspected the genuineness of his apostleship. To them "he was not in any true sense an apostle."[100]

Paul argued against their suspicions regarding his apostleship. He defended (*apologeomai*) his apostleship and asked the following rhetorical questions, "Am I not free?" "Am I not an apostle?" "Have I not seen Jesus our Lord?" (1 Cor 9:1). With these rhetorical questions, Paul asserted that he was a free apostle who offered and proclaimed the gospel message to all people free of charge for Christ's sake. He chose to make

98. Hays, *Corinthians*, 147
99. Ibid.
100. Barnet, "Apostle," 49.

no use of the right that "those who proclaim the gospel should get their living by the gospel" (1 Cor 9:12-14). Further, Paul contended that he was a truly authentic apostle because he encountered the risen Christ Jesus the Lord, just as the other apostles and Cephas had (1 Cor 15:5-8; cf. Gal 1:12, 23-24). He had established the Corinthian Christian community based on the gospel of Jesus Christ crucified and resurrected (1 Cor 1:17-18; 15:3-4). Thus, Paul reminds the Corinthians that they are the "seal" of his authentic apostleship (1 Cor 9:2).[101]

It is suggested in 1 Corinthian 9:5-6 that of the apostles and the Christian teachers and preachers who came to Corinth only Barnabas and Paul did not accept monetary gifts from the Corinthians but worked for a living (v. 6). After Paul's departure, it appears that Apollos, an Alexandrian, came to Corinth (Acts 18:24, 27; 19:1). Clearly, Apollos was one of these Christian teachers who accepted financial support from some wealthier members of the Corinthian congregation. Nevertheless, Paul did not criticize him at all.[102] These wealthier Corinthian Christians, who had been refused their offer of patronage by Paul, may well have approached Apollos and suggested supporting him financially. He seems to have accepted their financial support.

In this way, it can be proposed that these wealthier Corinthian Christians established patronal relationships with Apollos, supported him financially, and offered him accommodation. Naturally, they would have preferred Apollos as their Christian teacher and leader to Paul. They were a group that Paul describes as claiming, "I belong to Apollos" (1Cor 1:12). Wealthier Christians like this seem most likely to have been leaders of the Apollos party (1 Cor 1:12; 3:4). The leaders of Apollos's party can thus be seen as the Corinthians who brought patronal hierarchical structures into the Christian community, just as were exercised in other social clubs and associations. They were zealous (*zēlos*) about building patronal networks with other fellow Christians who were poorer and of lower social-status (1 Cor 3:3), and caused striving and quarrelling (*erides*) between themselves and Paul and leaders of the Pauline party (1:10; 3:3).[103] They were the certain people who were "inflated with arrogance ... (and) self-importance" and who did not welcome Paul's subsequent visits to

---

101. Hays, *Corinthians*, 149.

102. See Pogoloff, *Logos*, 193; Hays, *Corinthians*, 147.

103. Mitchell argues that the word *eris* is used frequently in Greek literature referring to political discord or strife and its causes (Mitchell, *Reconciliation*, 81).

Corinth (1 Cor 4:18).[104] They were also some of the people of whom Paul speaks in 1 Corinthians 1:26, referring to themselves as "wise" (*sophoi*), "powerful" (*dynatoi*), and "of noble birth" (*eugeneis*).

As the founder of the Corinthian congregation, Paul critiqued their improper behavior. He strongly argued that the Christian community was not like the social associations and clubs, and should not adopt patronal hierarchical structures. Rather, it was more like a household (*oikos*) where God is the Father. It is important to note that Paul always describes the Christian *ekklēsia* together with the conception of household (*oikos*), like "the household of Stephanas" (*ho oikos Stephavou* in 1 Cor 1:16; cf. 16:15), differing from secular *collegia*. This is further evident in Paul's household language, such as brothers or sisters, children and father in 1 and 2 Corinthians. Like the Christians in Rome and Asia Minor, the Corinthians gathered as an *ekklēsia* in houses (*oikoi*) (Rom 16:5). That is why this Christian community was called an *oikos* community rather than *collegia* (1 Cor 1:16).[105] Paul emphasizes that in the Christian *ekklēsia* as the body of Christ, unlike secular *ekklēsia* and *collegia*, there should be intimate relationships like brothers and sisters and parents and children as a family under the parenthood of God the Father.[106] These relationships differ from the patronal relationships that were widespread in the wider Corinthian civic society.

Nevertheless, that the Corinthian Christians met together in houses (*oikoi*) (1 Cor 16:19) would have caused the factions as addressed in 1 Corinthians 1–4. The Corinthian Christian *ekklēsia* as a whole consisted of several smaller Christian gatherings which took place in different households because of the limitations of space. In general, a single household did not accommodate the whole congregation at the same time, though we note the exception of Romans 16:23 and Gaius's house. Thus, the Corinthian Christians divided themselves into groups and gathered in different homes and places.[107]

Furthermore, Paul adopted household patterns for his Christian communities' basic structure, but with God as the *paterfamilias*.[108] In

---

104. Thiselton, *Corinthians*, 376.
105. See Winter, *After*, 206–11.
106. Joubert, "Managing," 217–18.
107. Jeffers, *Greco-Roman*, 81–82.
108. See Barton, "Sense," 225, 243.

order to understand the conception of household in the first-century Greco-Roman world it is worth noting that, as Jeffers states:

> ... the first century household among the Greeks and Romans was defined in terms of the head of the family. The oldest male in the blood line of the family, was called the *paterfamilias* by the Romans. Every living thing over which he held authority was part of the household: relatives by blood, women who married blood relatives, slaves, former slaves, even livestock.[109]

Furthermore, it can be argued that the definition of first-century Greco-Roman households would have included the "living spirits" of the ancestors that "were a part of family religion in the home."[110] Particularly, the spirit of the family head (Latin, *genius*; Greek, *idios daimon*) was understood as "the ancestral spirit playing the role of a guardian angel or attendant spirit."[111]

In terms of such Greco-Roman household concepts, Paul would describe Christ as the head of every man (1 Cor 11:3) and the head of the Christian community (*ho christos kephalē tēs ekklēsias*) at least in the later Pauline tradition (cf. Eph 1:22; 5:23). This Pauline description would help his Corinthian audience understand his argument that, as the foundation of the Christian community, Christ should have authority over the Christian community and take control of it, no one else, not even Paul, just as the *paterfamilias* in a Greco-Roman household (1 Cor 12:18). Horizontally, however, the Corinthian Christians and Paul should call themselves brothers and sisters and have household relationships under God as *paterfamilias* (e.g., 1:26; 2:1).

For these reasons, Paul apparently distinguished the Corinthian Christian *ekklēsia* from other secular *ekklēsia* and *collegia* that were characterized by patronal hierarchical structures because the Christian *ekklēsia* was based on intimate family relationships under the parenthood of God the Father. In it, therefore, there must be unity among the members who should exercise the love of God the Father and Jesus Christ the Lord (1 Cor 13:1–13).[112] Furthermore, Paul reminded the Corinthian Christians that he was their father in Jesus Christ through the gospel, and they were all his beloved children and offspring. They

---

109. Jeffers, *Greco-Roman*, 82; similarly Rives, *Religion*, 117–22.
110. Witherington, *Conflict*, 293.
111. Ibid., 293 n. 10.
112. See Engberg-Pedersen, "Gospel," 570.

were all equal in his sight and the eyes of God, whether they were of high social status or the lower classes, and whether they were wealthy or poor (1 Cor 3:8). Their social status and economic possessions did not make any difference for them in serving Jesus Christ crucified as the wisdom and power of God. Instead, as servants of God they were all required to exercise stewardship in the work of God (1 Cor 4:1, 2) and love one another as brothers and sisters in Christ (1 Cor 13:13). Last, Paul dares to suggest (ironically!) that he himself is the patron of them all, and urges them to imitate him as their truly spiritual father in Christ (1 Cor 4:15, 16). We now turn to an analysis of patronal systems in relation to Paul's description of the phrase *ho stauros christou* in 1 Corinthians 1–4.

THE CROSS OF CHRIST

Paul deals with the issue of the crucifixion of Christ in the broader context of schisms within 1 Corinthians 1–4. He employs the Greek word *stauros* and its verbal form *stauroō* only in the first two chapters of 1 Corinthians where the words occur six times (1:13, 17, 18, 23; 2:2, 8). Clearly, Paul uses the word "the cross of Christ" (*ho stauros christou*) in order to reclaim the Corinthian Congregation from the grips of factionalism (*schismata*, 1:10–12). On one hand, the word "cross" (*stauros*) is used in opposition to the words "wise" (*sophos*), "powerful" (*dynatos*) and "of noble birth" (*eugenē*) (1 Cor 1:26). These words certainly refer to the Corinthian Christians of the higher social classes. On the other hand, the word *stauros* is associated with the words, "foolish" (*mōros*), "weak" (*astheneō*), "low" (*agenēs*) and "despised" (*exoutheneomenos*) (1 Cor 1:27–28). These words apparently describe the majority of the Corinthian Christians who were poor, uneducated, and of lower social classes.

Using the phrase *ho stauros christou* in 1 Corinthians 1–2, Paul begins his argument that Jesus Christ, as the power of God, abandoned his glory and privilege in heaven and came down upon a cross, which is referred to as the curse of God (1 Cor 2:8; cf. Gal 3:10–14[113]).

---

113. The original text is "Cursed (*kekatēramenos*) by God (*hupo theou*) is every one hung on a tree" (LXX Deut 21:23). Paul must have had particular reasons why he omitted *upo theou* ("by God") after *epikataratos* ("be cursed") and why he referred to the original setting of Deuteronomy 21:23 in the context of a law-curse in relation to the death of Christ. As regards the former, by omitting *hupo theou* Paul intends to highlight "the absolute nature of the curse itself" rather than to avoid a direct saying that "Christ was cursed by God."(Longenecker, *Galatians*, 122). In quoting Deuteronomy 21:23 Paul appears no doubt to consider both its original context and the Jewish understanding

Paul presents Christ crucified as the pattern and example that the Corinthian Christians should follow. The wealthier and higher social-status Corinthians should stop the uncritical expression of their social privilege in the Corinthian Christian *ekklēsia* (1 Cor 1:26–28). Moreover, they should turn their backs on factionalism and bring about an atmosphere of reconciliation in the Christian community that is the temple of God (1 Cor 3:16, 17) and the body of Christ (1 Cor 12:27). They should be "united in the same mind and the same judgment" (1 Cor 1:10).

Paul further appeals to some of the Corinthian Christians of wealth and of high social status and encourages them to imitate him as a pattern. He exercised the message of the cross of Christ in his everyday life, and sacrificed his social status for the sake of the gospel of Christ crucified, identifying with the majority of Corinthian Christians of the lower social classes. He worked with his hands at a trade as a tent cloth maker and supported himself (see 1 Thess 2:9; Acts 18:3). This is attested in the Pauline descriptions in Corinthians 4:8–13: "We are weak" (v. 10). "We are in disrepute" (v. 10). "We labor, working with our own hands" (v. 12). "We are now as the refuse of the world, the offscouring of all things" (v. 13).

Moreover, Paul relates the phrase "the cross of Christ (*ho stauros christou*)" to the power (*dynamis*) of God. He knows that the word (*logos*) of the cross of Christ appears as "folly to those who were perishing" (1 Cor 1:18). It "looks like nonsense to a lost and perishing world" for it had nothing to do with social privilege and social and cultural values of wisdom and eloquence, which they regarded highly.[114] Yet, it is the power of God in Paul's argument (1 Cor 1:18). Christ's crucifixion has the power of forgiveness, salvation, redemption, righteousness, and sanctification for those who believe in Christ crucified as Savior and Lord (1 Cor 1:18, 30).[115] This is the power of God in Christ crucified. God chooses the "foolish," the "weak," the "low," and the "despised" according to worldly and human standards, in order to shame the "wise," the "strong" and the "powerful" in the world and particularly in the Corinthian civic society

---

of the language "hanging on a tree." But, in connection with the death of Christ, Paul considers the latter more important than the former because Paul, in verse 13, sees Christ's death as the redemptive event to free those people who are under the curse of the law, and he also insists that only through the death of Christ can they participate in the blessing of Abraham (vv. 9, 14).

114. Hays, *Corinthians*, 27.

115. See Pickett, *Cross*, 58–84.

(1 Cor 1: 26–28). Therefore, no one boasts about his or her wisdom and social privilege in the presence of God, but boasts of Christ crucified the wisdom of God and the power of God (1 Cor 1:24, 29, 30).

Finally, Paul reminds the Corinthian Christians of the Lord Jesus Christ who died on the cross to reconcile them to God the Father (1 Cor 1:18, 21). The cross of Christ has the power of reconciliation (cf. 2 Cor 5:18–19). Paul believes that the message of the cross of Christ should give a challenge to the Corinthian Christians and reclaim them from the grips of factionalism. They would then be united in the one Spirit and the one body of Christ crucified (1 Cor 1:10; 12:12).

In summary, in 1 Corinthians 1–4 Paul addresses the problem of *schismata* that occurred in the Christian community at Corinth. It has been shown that these two main schisms were closely related to the strong influence of patron-client relations that were so characteristic of the civic society of Roman Corinth in the mid-first century CE. The leaders of the Apollos party were influenced heavily by the social and cultural customs and value systems of the first century Greco-Roman world. Thus, they brought patronal and hierarchical structures into the Christian community and continued to boast about their wealth and high social status. They practiced patronage too uncritically in the Christian *ekklēsia*, just as they did in *collegia*, taking advantage of the Christian community to elevate their social status in the wider Corinthian civic society. Paul, however, sharply criticized their misuse of patronal networks in the Christian community and regarded them as people of the "flesh" (*hōs sarkinois*) and as "babes in Christ" (*hōs nēpiois en christō*; 1 Cor 3:1). Furthermore, he asserted that the Corinthian Christians should relate to one another in terms of *oikos* relationships under God as *paterfamilias*. They should understand themselves as brothers and sisters in Christ crucified rather than as patrons and clients. Therefore, they should leave factionalism and should all be united in one Spirit and the one body of Christ crucified. We now turn to an examination of Paul's rhetorical strategy in response to the Corinthian problems as addressed in 1 Corinthian 1–4.

PAUL'S SUBVERSIVE RHETORICAL RESPONSE TO THE CORINTHIAN PROBLEMS

When Paul heard of reports of such divisive and discriminatory behavior among the Corinthian Christians (1 Cor 1:11), he responded with emotion and even anger (1:10, "I appeal to you"). To Paul, it was unthinkable that in a Christian community seen as "God's temple" (*to naon tou theou* in 3:16–17) and "the body of Christ" (*to sōma christou* in 12:27), some wealthy members of higher social standing humiliated and discriminated against others of lower classes (11:22).

When he stayed at Corinth, Paul claims that he taught them the gospel message of Jesus Christ only (1 Cor 2:2, "I decided to know nothing among you except Jesus Christ crucified"). He did not use his social status. Paul indeed belonged, in some respects, to an upper class. Ronald F. Hock argues that the language of Paul in 1 Corinthians 9:19 ("Therefore, although I am free from all persons, I have enslaved myself to all, in order that I might gain more converts") and 2 Corinthians 11:7 ("Did I commit a sin by demeaning myself, in order that you might be exalted, because I preached God's gospel to you free of charge") confirms his social status.[116] Hock claims that only people of the higher classes could use such language, not people of the lower status.[117] Therefore, it is clear that Paul came from one of the higher social classes. Nevertheless, he worked as a leatherworker (or tentmaker) to support himself financially in order to preach God's gospel free of charge, even though some would regard his work as slavish and demeaning. This was so typical among higher class Greeks and Romans in the Greco-Roman world. For example, Musonius Rufus and Dio Chrysostom alike belonged to the upper classes and were exiled. Both worked with their hands to support themselves during their exile. "Musonius worked on a farm. Dio worked all sorts of menial jobs, such as painting, digging, and drawing water."[118] As such, Hock maintains that the Pauline language referring to his trade in 1 Corinthians 9:19 and 2 Corinthians 11:7 responds more closely to the attitude of higher class people toward the work than that of the lower. Hock's proposal is plausible, but Paul's language in these two verses does not necessarily represent his attitude to work. Rather, it appears to show what the Corinthian Christians may have thought of Paul in terms of his manual work.

For the ministry of God, however, he rather "stepped down the social ladder" and identified with the people of low social status, and worked with his hands at a trade as a tentcloth maker and supported himself (e.g., 1 Thess 2:9, "labor"; Acts 18:3, "leatherworker"). In the time

---

116. Hock, "Tentmaking," 555–64.

117. Ibid.

118. Ibid., 556, 562–64; cf. Cicero described a close relationship between people's social status and their professions in his time (see Cicero, *On Duties*, 1.150–51).

of Paul, the practice of a trade among Jewish men was not uncommon, since it was a Rabbinic ideal to combine Torah and trade. The Jew who devoted himself to the study of Torah also learned and practiced a trade for the sake of his independence. So, many Rabbis practiced a trade.[119] Because of this, Todd D. Still argues for Jewish parallels with Paul's idea of labor in 1 Corinthians 1–4.[120] It nonetheless would be argued that the most important context in which to interpret 1 Corinthians 4:12 and the word "labor" or the phrase "working with our own hands" is the Greco-Roman Corinthian context, in which Paul is stepping down the social ladder to maintain his profession as a leatherworker (Acts 18:3). Paul himself has a robust Jewish view of the value of a trade, but he knows that the Greco-Roman perception of manual work is very different, and he plays on this.[121]

In this sense, Paul appears to describe his sacrificial daily life, and that of his fellow-workers for the ministry of God, in 1 Corinthians 4:8–13, as follows: "we are weak . . . we are disrepute" . . . "we wear ourselves out working with our own hands . . . we are treated as the garbage (*perikatharmata*) of the earth, the off-scouring (*peripsēma*) of the world, to this every day" (1 Cor 4:10–13). The two Greek words *perikatharmata* and *peripsēma* are used synonymously. They refer to "sweeping" or "scraping" or "offscouring," that is to say, what is removed from the floor in the procedure of cleaning, such as "sawdust," "scrapings of any sort," and any dirt from "floor-sweepings."[122] Some scholars further argue that the word *perikatharmata* refers to "cleansings" and "expiations" in the context of a scapegoat in particular.[123]

These words occur nowhere else in the New Testament and the Septuagint, but in Greek literature, in particular, the word *katharmata* or *perikatharmata* was usually employed to mean the "scapegoat" type of sacrificial victim who was thrown out and sacrificed to a god to appease the god.[124] Using these words, Paul seems to remind his Corinthian

119. See Hock, " Tentmaking," 557; *Context*, 21–22; Applebaum, "Economic," 716.

120. Still "Manual," 291–95.

121. Witherington, *Quest*, 90, 128; cf. Theissen, *Social*, 104; Hock, *Context*, 68.

122. Calvin, *Corinthians*, 95; Thiselton, *Corinthians*, 364; Fee, *Corinthians*, 180; Witherington, *Conflict*, 146; Morris, *Corinthians*, 79.

123. Calvin, *Corinthians*, 95; Witherington, *Conflict*, 146; Barrett, *Corinthians*, 112–13.

124. Bruce, *Corinthians*, 51; Barrett, *Corinthians*, 112–13; Calvin, *Corinthians*, 95; Thiselton, *Corinthians*, 364; Fee, *Corinthians*, 180; Witherington, *Conflict*, 146.

leaders of an expiatory rite normally known to the Greeks. A criminal was dedicated to a god, and the criminal was then dragged from corner to corner all over the city. People believed that in so doing, the criminal with himself or herself took away the evil and sins that were lurking in the whole city. The criminal was handed over to a god to appease the god and, thereby, cleansed the rest of the inhabitants completely. The criminal was a scapegoat or sacrificial victim for atonement of the entire city.[125]

In addition, by using these words, Paul borrowed ideas from the Septuagint, especially Proverbs 21:18, "the wicked become a ransom (Hebrew, כֹּפֶר: Greek, περικάθαρμα) for the righteous" (NIV). The Hebrew word כֹּפֶר normally refers to "appease," "make amends," "provide reconciliation or atonement for someone by an offering."[126] In this respect, the Hebrew word is also used in Lamentations 3:45, "you have made us an offscouring and refuse in the midst of the peoples" (KJV), and Isaiah 53:3, "He was despised, he shrank from the sight of persons, tormented and humbled by suffering; we despised him, we held him of no account, a thing from which persons turn away their eyes" (NEB).[127]

Furthermore, it is likely that in this particular context (1 Cor 4:8-13), by employing the two Greek words *perikatharmata* and *peripsēma*, Paul keeps in mind the crucifixion of Jesus Christ and his humiliation on the cross. He also intends to parallel the life of Jesus with the current situation of his colleagues and himself. They have dedicated their whole lives to the work of Christ, although they hunger and thirst and are persecuted and slandered. On the other hand, it seems that in terms of social stratification contrasting with some of the Corinthian Christians who possess high social status (e.g., "wise," "strong" and "honor" in 4: 10), Paul does intentionally empty himself of his social privileges and classify himself with people of much lower status for the work of Christ.

Subsequently, demonstrating his own rhetorical prowess (at least in written form, 2 Cor 10:9-10), Paul turns the tables upside down. He suddenly changes his tone. He now claims the Corinthian Christians as his children and depicts himself as their father—their *paterfamilias* (1 Cor 4:15). In order to help us know how much this depiction would confront

---

125. Calvin, *Corinthians*, 95; Thiselton, *Corinthians*, 364.

126. Holladay, *Lexicon*, 163.

127. See Hanson, "1 Corinthians," 214-15; Hay, *Corinthians*, 73; Calvin, *Corinthians*, 95; Thiselton, *Corinthians*, 364; Fee, *Corinthians*, 180; Morris, *Corinthians*, 79; Barrett, *Corinthians*, 113.

the Corinthians, it is worth noting that in 1 Corinthians as a whole Paul frequently calls them *adelphoi* ("brothers" or "sisters") (e.g., 1:10, 11, 26; 2:1; 3:1; 4:6; 7:24, 29; 10:1; 11:33; 12:1; 14:6, 20, 26, 39; 15:1, 31, 50, 58; 16:15). In 1 Corinthians Paul sees the Corinthians as ranked at the same social standing as his own, but at this time his attitude changes. He depicts the Corinthians as his children and himself as their father only here in 1 Corinthians 4:15; although in 2 Corinthians he also describes them as children (e.g., 6:13; 12:14). With this description, he seems to consider them—"in Christ"—as lower than himself in the social pyramid. In other words, he claims this spiritually high status to admonish his Corinthian opponents and further correct their unjust behavior in ill-treating and humiliating the members of lower social standing within the Corinthian congregation. For rhetorical effect, Paul claims to be the patriarch and patron of them all. In other words, he deflates their hierarchies and challenges patronal systems by pulling rank on his opponents as a "humble father" of them all.

He then appeals to them to imitate him (*mimētai mou*, its verbal form is *mimeomai*) (1 Cor 4:14–16; cf. 11:1).[128] This is Paul's ironic use of imitation. In this passage, Paul uses the word *mimētēs* in close relation to the singular form of *egō* (v. 16). Yet, it is employed with its plural form in 1 Thessalonians 1:6 and 2 Thessalonians 3:7, 9 and is also used with the word *theos* in Ephesians 5:1 and with the phrase *tōn ekklēsiōn tou theou* in 1 Thessalonians 2:14. In so doing, Paul claims that the Corinthian Christians should not imitate any other teachers or leaders in the congregation but him. Some of these leaders may well have been influenced to some extent by the way the Corinthian elite of full Roman citizenship imitated the way Cicero had boasted of the glories of rhetoric. These leaders would also have been influenced to a certain degree by the way Cicero had encouraged the Romans to imitate their ancestors, as recorded in his rhetorical handbooks (see above). In a similar manner, these leaders may well have obliged some Corinthian Christians of lower social status to imitate them as a model of wisdom and eloquence in the Corinthian Christian community. Paul, however,

128. The Greek word *mimētēs* and its verbal form *mimeomai* occurs seven times in 1 Corinthians (4:16; 11:1) and also in the deuteron-Pauline literature (1 Thess 1:6; 2:14; 2 Thess 3:7, 9; Eph 5:1). In Greco-Roman culture the word *mimētēs* meant "bringing to expression, representation, and portrayal. It implies the notion of transfer of character or personality from one person to another, e.g., from parents to children, from teacher to pupil, and from God to human beings" (Sanders, "Imitating," 358).

reacts against their behavior. In the imperative tone, Paul differentiates himself from these leaders. He was the founder of the Christian community at Corinth. Depicting himself as their father, he claims an even higher social status—albeit ironically, and "in Christ" (1 Cor 4:15). He, however, sacrificed his social status for the sake of the mission of Christ, even though his life was full of hardship and sufferings (1 Cor 14:11–13), similar to that of Christ. Paul appeals to the Corinthian Christians to imitate the way he lived out the humility and suffering of Christ for the sake of the gospel of Christ crucified, rather than the way his opponents boasted about their wealth and high social status.

Furthermore, for a better understanding of 1 Corinthians 4:16, it is important to note that in conjunction with the preceding passage (4:9–13), Paul urges the Corinthians to be aware of his suffering for Christ's sake. He parallels it with the suffering of Jesus Christ crucified. Clearly, he appeals to them to imitate his sacrificial life as a servant of Christ (vv. 8–13) and his prioritizing of the proclamation of the gospel of Jesus Christ crucified in his ministry (e.g., 1 Cor 1:18–25).[129] He also warns them against allowing their behavior to be influenced uncritically by the social and rhetorical customs and value systems of the wider civic society. By saying that *parakalō . . . humas, mimētai mou ginesthe* ("I appeal to you to become imitators of me"), therefore, Paul claims that in the Corinthian Christian community as the body of Christ (e.g., 1 Cor 12) there must be no humiliation nor discrimination nor social hierarchy, but there should be a spirit of sacrifice and love among the members for Christ's sake (1 Cor 13).

Paul uses household language to describe the relationship between the Corinthians and himself. I argue that Paul uses here the phrases *tekna mou agapēta* ("my beloved children" [RSV]) and *murious paidagōgous* ("countless guides" [RSV]) in order to describe, from a mischievous rhetorical perspective, the Corinthian Christians as ranked lower in the social pyramid than himself, claiming to be ("in Christ") one of their few "fathers" (*patēr*; 1 Cor 5:15).[130] He briefly claims this high social position in contrast to his usual attitude of identifying himself with people of

---

129. See ibid., 359.

130. In the Greco-Roman culture of Paul's day, the relationship between a father and his children was seen as "the relationship of authority and subordination . . . Roman fathers had extraordinary power over their children . . . " (Stambaugh and Balch, *Environment*, 123–24). "The father maintained power over his adult sons until his death" (Jeffers, *Greco-Roman*, 81–82).

lower classes (1 Cor 4:8–13) for the purpose of his argument.[131] Paul now pokes fun at their patriarchal hierarchies. Here is a huge irony. Paul claims to be the patriarch in order to attack the patriarchs.

Paul here uses the word "father" (*patēr*) metaphorically in order to identify himself as one of the few "fathers" in the Corinthian Congregation. He refers to the *murious paidagōgous* ("many guides") in order to relativize the authority of others claiming to have teaching authority. The Greek word *paidagōgos* occurs three times in the New Testament as a whole. Interestingly, it is found only in Paul's epistles and appears once in 1 Corinthians 4:15 and twice in Galatians 3:24–5 where he uses the word in a metaphorical sense referring to the Torah.[132] In ancient Greco-Roman culture the Greek word *paidagōgos* referred to a servile class in the social pyramid. The *paidagōgos* supervised, escorted, protected, guided and accompanied a child aged from six or seven to twelve according to the master's instruction, when the child went to school and came back from it. Hence, in Paul's time the *paidagōgos* was not seen as teacher, as such, but as "caretaker" and "trusted slave."[133] Therefore, it can be understood that referring to himself as a *patēr* and the other leaders as *paidagōgous*, Paul seems to reclaim his authority as the founder of the whole Corinthian congregation ("my beloved children" in 4:14) and, at the same time, to remind the Corinthians that the other leaders were *paidagōgous* who acted within his instructions. This is because he intends to correct some of the Corinthians who misunderstood that these leaders, and teachers such as Apollos, possessed higher social status and better rhetorical skills and eloquence than Paul (e.g., 1 Cor 1:26; 2:4; cf. 2 Cor 11:6). That is why, rather than Paul, they claimed Apollos as their leader because of the strong influence of the social and rhetorical milieu of first-century Corinth ("according to worldly standards" in 1 Cor 1:26; cf. 3:4).

This is one of the substantial causes of divisions within the Corinthian congregation (1 Cor 1:10). In order to reclaim the Corinthians from the spirit of factionalism, therefore, Paul claims in this passage that he is the spiritual father (*patēr*) of the Corinthian Christians, by reminding them that he can claim higher social status than them in Christ, if they wish to

---

131. See Martin, *Body*, 66.

132. Witherington, *Grace*, 262–67.

133. Martin, *Body*, 66; similarly argued by Thiselton, *Corinthians*, 370; Hay, *Corinthians*, 73; Fee, *Corinthians*, 185; Morris, *Corinthians*, 80; Barrett, *Corinthians*, 115.

play such games. Paul further wished to remind them of their unity as a household and the body of Christ (*to sōma christou*; 1 Cor 12:12–31)[134] rather than simply as an *ekklēsia*. This idea is similar to Trevor J. Burke's argument. He argues that in an effort to "prevent further divisions, Paul at a strategic point in the letter (chapters 1–4) employs the father-child metaphor in order to unite the Corinthians under himself as their common *patēr*. As the founder-father of the community, Paul expects his children to heed his position, submit to his authority, follow his example, obey his instructions, and be aware of his love for them."[135] So it is clear that Paul used the father-child metaphor in order to reclaim the Corinthians from the atmosphere of factionalism that was strongly influenced by hierarchical systems in the wider civic society of first-century Corinth. Yet, it is argued that Paul's rhetorical use of irony made this argument and drove his point home. Paul was not establishing a spiritual patriarchy in order to replace biological patriarchy, but was ironically undermining patriarchy altogether. Such an understanding ought to be taken into account to grasp the problem of *schismata* and the nature of *sophia* that Paul addresses in the first four chapters of 1 Corinthians.

---

134. The Greek word *sōma* is one of the most important words in understanding the problematic issues in 1 Corinthians (Ellis, "Sōma," 133; Dunn, *Theology*, 70–73; Gundry, *Sōma*; Martin, *Body*, 125–28, 194–97). It appears forty-six times in 1 Corinthians as a whole. It has at least four possible meanings as follows: first, it simply means "a living body of a human being" in 5:3; 12:12, 15, 16, 17; 15:44. Second, it means a body of a "plant and seed structure" in 15:35. Third, it means "a unified group of people" in 10:17. Lastly, it means the Christian *ekklēsia* as "the body of Christ" in chapter 12 (BAGD, 983–84). The word *sōma* here refers to the first one and the third one, the Christian gatherings as the living body of Christ.

135. Burke, "Father," 95–113.

6

Summary of the Rhetorical and Social Analysis of 1 Corinthians 1–4

IN THE PREVIOUS CHAPTERS I reconstructed the social and rhetorical environment of 1 Corinthians 1–4. This leads us to the conclusion that this Pauline text critically engages the consequences of an uncritical use of Greco-Roman rhetorical conventions and social and patronal networks that was evident in the improper mentality and behavior of some in the Christian community. The language of 1 Corinthians 1–4 also reflects the social and ethnic composition of the Corinthian congregation and argues for mutuality in diversity.

The "not many" among the Corinthian Christians to whom Paul refers in 1 Corinthians 1:26–29 seems to have been closely related to the people Paul later addresses as "these arrogant people" (4:18–19), and it appears that these arrogant Corinthians were not keen for Paul to re-visit the Corinthian Christian *ekklēsia*. The evidence given indicates that these Corinthian Christians were among the elite in the Corinthian congregation and possessed wealth, power, and high social status in the wider civic community. They would have had frequent contacts with the group of full Roman citizens in the *collegia* of the wider society. Moreover, after Paul's departure, they continued to practice in the Christian community elements of the social and cultural phenomena of the wider Corinthian civic society in the first century CE, including, especially, the social and rhetorical understandings of wisdom and eloquence and hierarchical patronal systems.

Paul draws distinctive contrasts between the wisdom of God and that of the world in 1 Corinthians 1–4 (e.g., 1:18–25; 2:6–7), wherein he appears to highlight intrinsic distinctions of quality between the two sorts of wisdom. Paul seems to refer to the wisdom of the world as a human-thought-based and cultural-conventions-oriented wisdom that dominated the thinking of some in the Corinthian Christian community. Their understandings of wisdom are consistent with the Greco-Roman rhetorical traditions, as typified by Cicero's legacy of wisdom and eloquence, which affected the mentality and social behavior of the Corinthians in the wider civic community in the time of Paul (1:19; 2:6). Contrasting with this cultural-conventions-oriented wisdom, Paul presents the wisdom of God as the "foolish" yet powerful wisdom of Christ crucified. This sort of wisdom has a power that saves and transforms people who believe in Jesus Christ (1:21, 24; 2:7).

Paul seems to think that some of the Corinthian Christians not only valued the cultural-conventions-oriented wisdom more highly than Jesus Christ crucified as the wisdom of God, but even boasted about themselves as having such human-based wisdom (e.g., 1:29; 3:18; 4:7). To argue against this inappropriate conduct of boasting, Paul borrows the biblical teaching of boasting from Jeremiah 9:23. In so doing, Paul challenged the Corinthian Christians to leave their anthropocentric and social and cultural-conventions-oriented boasting and imitate him as one boasting in the Lord Jesus Christ as the wisdom of God. This is a theocentric and Christ-centered "boasting" used by Paul for the purposes of cultural transformation and building up the *ekklēsiai*.

In the previous chapter, the preference for cultural-conventions-originated wisdom among some Corinthians and Paul's reaction to it will be evaluated from a Korean-Confucian Christian context, where some Korean Christians adhere to "Korean-Confucianism-oriented' wisdom and express its social implications in the Christian communities.[1]

Furthermore, in the previous chapter, the problem of the *schismata* Paul addresses in 1 Corinthians 1:10 and 11:18 was investigated in close relation to patronal networks and *collegia*, which were significant influences on the social fabric of the Corinthians, whether believers or non-believers. This investigation led us to the argument that some of

---

1. Strom initiates a dialogue between the issues of rhetoric and the Corinthians' attitude to it, as addressed by Paul in 1 Cor, and an Australian context (see Strom, *Reframing*, 190–95, 225–30). This is what I am also attempting in my Korean context, though on a less philosophical and more social level.

the Corinthian Christians continued the uncritical practice of patronage and continued to express patronal hierarchies in the Christian *ekklēsia*, just as they did in the *collegia*. They boasted about their social privilege in the Christian community and used their patronal connections with the Corinthian elite to take control of the leadership within the *ekklēsia*. They built patronal relationships with their fellow Christians who were poorer and of lower social classes and effectively discriminated against them (11:22). Moreover, they took advantage of the Christian community to build political power and social influence and to aspire to higher positions in the wider Corinthian civic society (1 Cor 9:1–18).

Such Corinthian believers appear to have regarded the Corinthian Christian *ekklēsia* as more of a sort of *collegia* where patron-client systems played a vital role in interconnecting between patrons and clients of various social levels within the *collegia*. Two consequences of this are proposed. First, in 1 Corinthians 8:1–10:22 Paul seems to argue against some of the Corinthian Christians who described themselves as people who possessed knowledge and boasted of it (8:1). In so doing, such Corinthian Christians seem to have justified their behavior of participating in dinner parties and eating food sacrificed to deities in the temples and to the emperor in the imperial cult. There, they effectively participated in sacrifices to the emperor and affirmed him as lord, savior, and god, and implicitly worshipped him as the universal patron (8:5, 10). One reason why they behaved this way is, as I have argued, that they continued their membership in *collegia sodalicia*, where they effectively worshipped gods as their patron deities and ate meat offered as sacrifices to the deities, even after conversion to the Christian faith (8:7, 10; 10:18–20). They may have even considered the Corinthian Christian community as another of the *collegia sodalicia*, where they called on the name of the Christian God and the Lord Jesus Christ, and worshipped and venerated him as their patron deity (1 Cor 8:4–5). Furthermore, eating meat offered to deities in the temples and to the emperor in the imperial cult carried the danger that it would wound the conscience of some weak Christians, although they might not necessarily intend or notice this (1 Cor 8:7).

Paul argues, however, that it is a sin against Christ to wound the conscience of the brothers and sisters in the Corinthian congregation (1 Cor 8:7–13). They should take care lest their behavior become an obstacle to the weak (1 Cor 8:9), and cause the weak to fall (1 Cor 8:10, 13). Moreover, Paul defined their behavior as idolatry and exhorted them to stop worshipping idols in the temples and the imperial cult (1 Cor 10:14). He also used the traditional Jewish understanding that idolatry leads to immorality in order to condemn the social consequences of idol worship in the temples (1 Cor 9:8–12; 10:1–13), where attendees and worshippers could become involved in sexual licentiousness (1 Cor 6:12–20; 7:1–40).[2] Paul wanted to prevent the Corinthian Christians from practicing such immorality (e.g., 1 Cor 5:9–11). These points will help re-interpret the Corinthian attitude to Greco-Roman gods and the imperial cult and Paul's response to it from a Korean-Confucian Christian context, where Korean Christians were compelled to worship a Japanese emperor during Japanese imperialism in Korea from 1910 to 1945, and where many Koreans engage in household veneration of ancestors.

Furthermore, some Corinthian Christians may well have seen the Christian *ekklēsia* as more of a sort of *collegia tenuiorum*, formed for the purposes of arranging funerals and the appropriate burial of the dead. This argument is supported by the first rhetorical question in 1 Corinthian 15:29, which implies that some of the Corinthian Christians engaged in a baptism on behalf of the dead in the Christian community. They may well have understood their "household baptism" (1 Cor 1:16) as including an appropriate public expression of their veneration and commemoration toward dead ancestors (or "living spirits"). Practicing this sort of inclusive baptism, they would have believed themselves to be fulfilling the obligations that they, as living descendants, had to exercise to be connected and reunited with their dead. Such an interpretation accords with the reason why the Corinthians in the wider society formed *collegia tenuiorum*. It suggests that the provision of an appropriate burial for the dead, and ongoing recognition of them, was regarded as one of the duties which, as living descendants, the Corinthians had to practice towards their dead ancestors. In so doing, they expressed veneration for the dead. It is concluded, therefore, that some Corinthian Christians regarded the Christian *ekklēsia* as another sort of *collegia tenuiorum* in

---

2. Scholars argue that in Roman Corinth sexual liberty played a part both in some religious festivals and in temple precincts (see Witherington, *Conflict*, 13; Murphy-O'Connor, "Saint," 152). Such sexual licentiousness in the wider civic community would no doubt influence the conduct of some of the Corinthian Christians. That is why Paul addresses the problems of sexual immorality in 1 Cor 6:12–20 and of marriage in 1 Cor 7:1–40 (Murphy-O'Connor, "Slogan," 391–96; Braxton, *Tyranny*, 9–34; Deming, *Celibacy*; Watson, "Reviews on Deming," 97–99). To justify their indecent sexual conduct, some Corinthians claimed, "All things are lawful for me" (1 Cor 6:12).

Summary of the Rhetorical and Social Analysis of 1 Corinthians 1–4   193

which people were interconnected by patronal networks even after death, and this is glimpsed in their understanding of baptism on behalf of the dead (1 Cor 15:29).

Nonetheless, as the founder of the Corinthian congregation—and even "patron" or "father" on another level—Paul criticized the misuse of patronal networks in the Christian community. Yet he does not criticize the public expression of commemoration towards dead ancestors in 1 Corinthians (see further below). Paul, instead, strongly argued that the Christian community should not be understood as a social association or club (*collegia*), and should not reinforce patronal hierarchical structures. Rather, Paul uses the language of the household (*oikos*) where God is the only *paterfamilias*. For Paul, the *ekklēsia* should be established in intimate family relationships under the parenthood of God the Father. In it, therefore, there must be unity among the members who should exercise the love of God the Father and Jesus Christ the Lord (1 Cor 13:1–13). The implicit Pauline acceptance of the Corinthian expression of veneration towards dead ancestors has profound implications for a Korean-Confucian Christian context in which ancestor veneration (*jesa* in Korean) is controversial among Korean Christians today (see further below).

It has also been claimed that underneath the factions named by Paul (which were most likely exaggerated for rhetorical effect), lay the party of Paul and that of Apollos (3:4–6; 4:6). The Pauline party would most likely have included a large number of Corinthian Christians who were poor and of lower social classes. Paul explicitly identifies himself with these poorer and lower-status Christians for the sake of the gospel of Christ (1:26–28; 4:8–13). These poorer Christians were the ones at risk of being marginalized in the congregation and humiliated by other fellow Christians who continued to express their wealth and high social status in the Christian community (1 Cor 11:17–22).

On the other hand, the party of Apollos may well have included some other Corinthian Christians of wealth and high social status—such as Gaius and Erastus, perhaps (1 Cor 1:26; 4:8; Rom 16:23)—together with Christians who established patron-client bonds with these wealthier ones. The wealth and high social status that wealthier Corinthian Christians possessed supports the argument that some of the Corinthian Christians had frequent contacts with Corinthians who had full Roman citizenship and power, and control of the social political positions in the Corinthian civic society. They were therefore heavily influenced by the social and cultural value systems characterized by patronal networks and rhetorical conventions (1 Cor 2:1—5:9).

It is highly likely that such Christians would assume that Paul would establish patronal relationships with them, and so they naturally would have offered him financial support and hospitality. Nevertheless, Paul refused to accept their financial support (1 Cor 9:12, 15-19). He was aware of the complications of the hidden intentions behind their monetary gift. He no doubt realized the danger that they would thereby keep the congregation under their control by using their wealth, social status, and patronal hierarchies (cf. 2 Cor 11:7-11; 12:13-18) in that way. So instead of receiving financial support from them, Paul insisted on working as a leatherworker/tentmaker to support himself (see Acts 18:1-3). Whereas he recognized that this kind of menial work did not really establish him as a truly authentic apostle in the eyes of Greco-Roman culture (1 Cor 9:7), he insisted that it embodied the ethics of the way of Jesus Christ.

It seems, however, that these wealthier Corinthian Christians established normal patronal relationships with Apollos, supported him financially, and offered him accommodation. Naturally, then, they appreciated the ministry of Apollos as their Christian teacher and leader in preference to Paul. Paul even goes so far as to describe them as claiming, "I belong to Apollos" (*egō eimi Apollō*, 1 Cor 1:12). Wealthier Christians like this seem most likely to have been leaders and patrons of the Apollos party (1 Cor 1:12; 3:4).

Paul's subversive use of rhetoric would have challenged some of the Corinthian Christians of wealth and of high social status and encouraged them to imitate him as a pattern. He exercised the message of the cross of Christ in his everyday life. He voluntarily relinquished the privileges of his social status for the sake of the gospel of Christ crucified, and identified with the majority of Corinthian Christians of the lower social classes. He also reminds the Corinthian Christians of the Lord Jesus Christ who died on the cross to reconcile them to God the Father (1 Cor 1:18, 21). The cross of Christ has the power of reconciliation (12:12). Paul believed that the message of the cross of Christ should challenge the Corinthian Christians, transform their understanding of true wisdom, and reclaim them from the grips of factionalism. They would then be united in the one Spirit and one body of Christ crucified (1 Cor 1:10; 12:12).

Summary of the Rhetorical and Social Analysis of 1 Corinthians 1–4   195

Ethnicity and social class were two further critical factors which caused the schisms in the Christian community (e.g., 1 Cor 1:10–11). Among the diversity of ethnic groups there would have been tensions and conflicts that contributed to the factions in the congregation. That is why in the passage where Paul deals with the issue of baptism in close relation to the problem of schism (1 Cor 1:10–17), he mentions explicitly the three prominent leaders Crispus, Gaius, and Stephanas. This is because each of them represents the three major ethnic groups: Jews, Romans, and Greeks (vv. 14, 16). Paul's careful and deliberate naming of Stephanas (1 Cor 1:16; 16:15, 17) appears to have the rhetorical effect of establishing him—as a representative of the poorer Greek majority—as a role model of service to the whole community (1 Cor 16:15–17).

In response to these conflicts, however, Paul insists on unity among the diversity of ethnic groups within the Corinthian Christian community. This is revealed in 1 Corinthians 12:12–13 where Paul encourages them to be united as one body of Christ who transcends ethnic and cultural barriers and distinctions (v. 12). He also appeals to them to be "baptized into one body" by one Spirit and to "drink of one Spirit" (v. 13). With these words, Paul seems to challenge them to leave the unhelpful behavior of factionalism and not to claim any ethnic superiority and privilege in the Christian community. Instead, they are to be inspired by the Holy Spirit who brings them together as the body of Christ from different ethnic backgrounds, and they then are to reconcile and embrace one another and share the spirit of household and kinship in Jesus Christ. Yet this does not mean that the Corinthian Christians should give up their ethnic identities and cultural customs. Paul, rather, appears to encourage them to keep their racial and cultural heritage within the Christian community (1 Cor 7:17–24).[3] This Pauline message will be explored again in the following chapter, where the problem caused by Corinthian ethnic diversity, and Paul's reaction to it, will be re-read from a Korean-Confucian Christian context. This context is under the influence of the spirit of *danil minjok* that literally means one nation and also

---

3. Braxton however argues that in 1 Cor 7:17–24 Paul responds to the Corinthian Christians who raised the issues of the circumcised/uncircumcised and slave/free because these issues caused the problem of schisms among the members in the Corinthian congregation (see Braxton, *Tyranny*, 9–154). Nonetheless, it appears more appropriate that these two illustrations are understood as examples of the confusion over appropriate boundary markers between the Corinthian Christians and the wider Corinthian community.

refers to a homogeneous race. This spirit continues to affect the mentality and social conduct of Korean Christians in some way today, and will be critically evaluated in the next chapter.

Furthermore, the Pauline language of 1 Corinthians 1:26–28 appears to reflect the wide range of social status to which the Corinthian Christians belonged. In the social pyramid of first-century Roman Corinth, some few members belonged to the higher classes and the vast majority to the lower classes. These social differences (and distinctions) between the Corinthian Christians may well have influenced the allocation of leadership positions in the Christian community. The Corinthian Christians who possessed high social status in the broader civic society could easily have dominated leadership roles and assumed the position of patrons of Paul and the congregation. This would leave the majority of the Corinthian Christians, who were extremely poor and of lower social standing, isolated from the mainstream of church life and excluded from leadership positions—not to mention the best food at the love-feasts (1 Cor 11:22–23). Their social class prevented them from becoming leaders in the Christian community because rather than the gospel message and Christian teaching, social positions and hierarchies and gifts of eloquence and tongues (1 Cor 12:8, 10) were regarded as more important.

To correct such unjust behavior, Paul, as the "father" of the whole congregation, ironically claims to be the patriarch and patron of them all (1 Cor 4:15). Paul here uses the word "father" metaphorically in order to distinguish himself from nearly all the other leaders in the Corinthian congregation. He refers to most of them as the "countless guides" in order to show to the Corinthians that these leaders may in God's eyes be ranked lower than himself (1 Cor 4:15). Paul then appeals to them to imitate him (1 Cor 4:16). This is Paul's ironic use of imitation and boasting. In so doing, Paul undermines those Corinthian Christians who imitated other teachers and leaders in the congregation. He reacts against their behavior. In the imperative tone (e.g., 1 Cor 4:16), Paul differentiates himself from these leaders. As the founder of the Christian community at Corinth, he depicts himself as their father and as possessing high social status according to the values of another "Empire." He, however, forsakes this social status for the sake of the mission of Christ, even though his life was full of hardship and sufferings (1 Cor 14:11–13) similar to that of Christ. Paul appeals to the Corinthian Christians to imitate the way he lived out the humility and suffering of Christ for the sake of the gospel of Christ crucified rather than the way some of the Corinthians boasted about their wealth and high social status.

This social analysis of the Corinthian behavior caused by social stratification and Paul's reaction to it will now be evaluated, together with the other issues already raised, from a Korean-Confucian Christian context. In this context, some Christians who are poor and uneducated are excluded from leadership positions such as the eldership (*jangro* in Korean) and isolated from the decision-making groups in the church. It will be argued that this reflects the Confucian over-emphasis on wisdom, education, and knowledge, and its social consequences.

So the analysis above has highlighted these different factors and their contributions to the problem that Paul addresses in 1 Corinthians and particularly chapters 1–4. Each of these factors played a critical part in dividing the Corinthian Christian *ekklēsia* into groups. We now turn to an evaluation of the rhetorical and social analysis of 1 Corinthian 1–4 from a Korean-Confucian Christian context, where there are also tensions and divisions between believers over the understanding of true wisdom and its social implications.

7

Cross-Cultural Hermeneutics of 1 Corinthians 1–4 for Korean-Confucian Christians Today

THUS FAR, THE RHETORICAL and social situation of Roman Corinth in the first century and the social and ethnic makeup of the Corinthian church have been analyzed. This analysis enabled a re-evaluation of Paul's response to the problems in the Corinthian *ekklēsia*. The results of these investigations are now evaluated from a Korean-Confucian Christian context for contemporary Korean readers. In this process, the beginnings of a dialogue takes place between the issues concerning Paul and the Corinthian Christians in the first century and those concerning Korean Christians and their cultural heritage in the twenty-first century.[1] Furthermore, there is the promise of biblical insight into the social and cultural issues that Korean-Confucian Christians face in their daily lives today, not in the simplistic expectation that some acultural (or meta-cultural) biblical truth will tell Koreans what to do, but in the hope that a closer understanding of the "Gospel process" in Corinth will suggest new possibilities for the Korean church. Many analogies can helpfully be drawn and intersections explored between the issues addressed by Paul in 1 Corinthians and the issues facing contemporary

---

1. In principle, the issues addressed in this chapter cover all Korean Christians, whether Catholics or Protestants. Nonetheless, some of the issues tackled in the work, for example, "Shinto Shrine Worship" and "Ancestor Veneration," are no longer controversial in Korean Catholicism today, but still remain controversial in Korean Protestantism (see below). The issues of Confucian wisdom traditions and the spirit of *danil minjok* are both equally related to Korean Catholicism and Protestantism.

Korean Christians. There are many directions these engagements could take; but, first, Korean wisdom and its social consequences—education and social standing—in Korean-Confucian society will be the focus.

WISDOM AND ITS SOCIAL MANIFESTATIONS IN A KOREAN-CONFUCIAN CONTEXT AND T'OEGYE AS AN EXAMPLE OF WISDOM

Just as our investigations of Corinthian *sophia* involved an analysis of its social manifestations—patronal hierarchies and social stratification—so, too, will any explanation of wisdom traditions from another cultural perspective. This process requires an appreciation of the social and cultural expressions of wisdom in society, together with an engagement with the biblical perspectives and processes. It is appropriate, therefore, that I, as a Korean-Confucian Christian, should attempt to read and interpret from the perspective of my own Korean-Confucian context the Corinthians' expressions of *sophia* and the Pauline critique of them as indicated in 1 Corinthians 1–4.

It will be explored that the Corinthians in the Greco-Roman world of the first century CE and the Koreans in the Confucian context of the sixteenth century and today have analogous attitudes towards wisdom and its social manifestations. Unlike the Corinthians in the first-century Greco-Roman world, however, Koreans do not emphasize the importance of eloquence (or eloquent speech) and relate it to social privilege. They consider written documents and exams more important than oral ones. In Korean society, in order to elevate one's social status and take leadership positions, one should obtain good marks in the exams that the Korean government provides or those of the giant private companies, e.g., Hyundai, LG, and Samsung. Most of these exams comprise written exams, not oral ones. Hence, I neither employ a rhetorical method in this chapter nor include an investigation of Corinthian eloquence, as such, from a Korean-Confucian context. Nonetheless, a cultural phenomenon of imitation, which seems to be like Greco-Roman understandings of imitation, appears in Korean mentality and social behavior. Yet, this sort of imitation does not require an oral and rhetorical foundation. It is fundamental to the Korean "one nation," "one people," self-understanding (conformity). This will be developed below.

Ancient philosophers and thinkers such as Plato, Aristotle, Cicero, and Seneca the younger valued wisdom (*sophia* and *sapientia*) and children of wisdom highly. Because of their legacies and influences, Paul accuses the Corinthians of valuing human wisdom and its social consequences more highly than Christ as the wisdom of God. So, also in Korean society of our time, wisdom (*jeehye/sulgi*) is highly regarded, which is evident in many current social phenomena.[2]

Philippe Thiébault expresses the high value of wisdom in Korean society when he asserts that "Korean thinkers, assimilating first classical Confucianism and enriching it with Neo-Confucianism, have taken seriously external and internal fulfillment, 'wisdom (*jeehye/sulgi*) inside, kinship outside.'"[3] This statement indicates that there is close relationship between wisdom traditions, Neo-Confucianism, and social kinship patterns in Korean society. In other words, Neo-Confucianism has had, and continues to have, a deep impact on the shaping of wisdom traditions and society in Korea. Of all the Korean Neo-Confucian scholars, T'oegye (1501–1570), and his Confucian ideas of wisdom, is the most significant for understanding how these factors still shape the social fabric of Korean Christianity today.[4]

Since Confucianism was first introduced into the Korean peninsula thousands of years ago, it has greatly influenced Korean culture, including social relations, family structure, education, philosophy, religion, and the political and economic systems.[5] There is no aspect of Korean culture that Confucianism has not influenced in some way. Thus, it is said that "Korean culture has grown and flourished as a Confucian one,"

---

2. This is suggested even by the great number of Korean women who have had *jeehye* and *sulgi* as their first names. In other societies and cultures, such a phenomenon might well occur too, such as the use of Sophia in English culture, but it is particularly notable in Korea.

3. Thiébault, "Self," 27. "Neo-Confucianism" is called "Chu His Learning" and was founded in the twelfth century in China. This is a developed form of Confucianism that originated with Confucius (Kong Fuzi, 552–479 BCE) in China (see Raguin, "Confucianism," 1).

4. For more details on T'oegye's wisdom, see Appendix 2 further below.

5. On the date it first entered Korea, there is no unanimous agreement in Korean Confucian scholarship (see Choung, et. al., *Philosophy*, 1–25). The possible date is given as between 4 BCE and 1 CE (Hwang, *Hanguk*, 14). But it is clear that Confucianism was first introduced into the Korean peninsula before the three kingdoms were established (*Koguryo*, *Paekche*, and *Silla*). In the fourth century, Confucianism began to influence the patterns of political and social order in the kingdoms. For instance, in 372 a Confucian educational academy reportedly was established in the kingdom of *Koguryo* and then in *Paekche* and *Silla* (see Nahm, *Panorama*, 21; Wagner, et al., *Old*, 37; Deuchler, *Transformation*, 14; Jung, *Ukyoyihae*, 3).

and that after the fifteenth century, the mainstream of Korean culture was "rooted in the soil of Confucianism and, moreover, contemporary Korean society remains within the boundary of Confucian influence."[6]

Confucianism has several distinctive characteristics that have made a strong impact upon Korean mentality and social behavior. It plays the most influential role in composing ethical and moral standards for Koreans. Regardless of religion, all Koreans have grown up and lived within the influence of Confucian moral and ethical teachings, because Confucianism serves to "uphold the moral character of the individual" and "promote moral order in society."[7] This is well expressed in the Five Principles (or Morals) of the Great Declaration of Ethics (*oh reun*). The first principle is *bu ja yu chin*, meaning that there is love between parents and children, which mostly emphasizes filial piety. The second one is *gun sin yu ui*, meaning that there is a right relationship between an emperor and his people, which emphasizes social justice. The third one is *bu bu yu buyl*, meaning that there is mutuality between a husband and a wife, which emphasizes role and duty in a family. The fourth one is *jang yu yu suh*, meaning that there is order between elderly people and young people, which emphasizes respect towards elderly people. The last one is *bung u yu shin*, meaning that there is trust between friends, which emphasizes reliance in social relationships.[8]

The teachings of the Five Principles, to a certain extent, are in accordance with the "household codes" in the New Testament (e.g., Col 3:18—4:1; Eph 5:21—6:9).[9] On this basis, it is clear that there is a similarity between the teachings of Christianity and those of Confucianism

---

6. Keum, *Confucianism*, iii, 49–51. By the time the *Choson* dynasty (1393–1910) was established, Neo-Confucianism was treated as "the official ideology of the new state because a number of Confucians played a leading role in founding the dynasty. Later on, Confucianism began to take a more influential position in the whole area of human life in the Korean peninsula" (Keum, *Confucianism*, 37–49). In spite of this, it is true that Shamanism, Buddhism, Taoism, *Tonghak* ("Eastern Learning") or *Ch'ondogyo* and other indigenous traditions, as well as Confucianism, all are part of Korean culture (see Kim, *Shamanism*, xiv, 26–27, 66, 98–99, 149, 189–91; Lee, *Formation*, 97–101, 106, 115). So they all should be considered important in providing Korean cultural identity. But Confucianism appears to influence the whole area of Korean life in general more than the others and appears to be the major shaper of Korean cultural identity.

7. Keum, *Confucianism*, 33.

8. See Jung, *Ukyoyihae*, 214–15.

9. Towner, "Households," 417–19. In these passages, there are teachings about wives/husbands, children/ parents, and slaves/masters. Interestingly, these codes are taken from Hellenistic philosophy and social ethics, ibid.

when it comes to basic moral and ethical issues. Although the household codes appear in the deuteron-Pauline literature, there are also connections with the Hellenistic vice and virtue lists which appear in the earlier Pauline epistles (e.g., Gal 5:19–25).

T'OEGYE AS AN EXAMPLE OF WISDOM

Confucianism also has a strong impact on the philosophical perceptions of humanity (*insung*) and wisdom in Korean society. In Korean Confucian thought, and especially T'oegye's philosophical ideas, it is believed that all humans are innately good because they trust in a god as the ultimate being who resides in human nature and who is very close to human beings.[10] Yi I (Yulgok; 1536–1584), a Confucian thinker, states, "people have an original good nature, in which there are no distinctions of past and present, wisdom and foolishness."[11] Similarly, T'oegye referred to wisdom as a part of human nature, or Four Beginnings, comprising benevolence, righteousness, propriety, and wisdom. He understood human nature as perfectly good, certainly analogous to Mencius's (Mengzi, 371–289 BCE) argument about "the ultimate justification" of human nature.[12] According to T'oegye, it is said that the Four Beginnings are endowed by Heaven (*T'ien*, Nature) and regarded as "innate, moral characteristics" of the fundamentally perfect goodness of human nature or as "the four roots of moral goodness inherent in human nature."[13] In other words, T'oegye thought that wisdom, as part of the Four Beginnings, is imparted by Heaven (or Nature). Furthermore, T'oegye emphasized a close relationship between wisdom and becoming a sage. Wisdom is the most necessary element for a person to become a sage (*hyunin* or *sungingoonja*). In T'oegye's mind, it was his ultimate purpose of study (or learning) that he would obtain wisdom and become a sage, just like Confucius and Mencius. Hence, it is clear that T'oegye gave a high value to the wisdom required for becoming a sage.[14]

10. Keum, *Confucianism*, 34.

11. Thiébault, "Yulgok," 72; cf. Xunzi (ca. 310– ca. 211 BCE), who argues that human beings are sinful and evil because in human life there is always jealousy, hatred, quarrel, homicide, and lewdness (see Yao, *Confucianism*, 79; also Jung, *Ukyoyihae*, 99–101, 113–14).

12. Wei-ming, "T'oegye's," 263.

13. Chung, *Neo-Confucianism*, 40, 51; Wei-ming, "T'oegye's," 264; Hwang, "Neo-Confucian," 231.

14. Cho, *Sunghak*, 20–42.

Nonetheless, T'oegye's perceptions of wisdom also contrast with some biblical understandings of wisdom. Paul says in Romans 3:9b–11a, "... all people ... are controlled by sin ... There is no one righteous, not even one. No one understands." In the wider biblical text of 3:9–11a in Romans, Paul talks about the advantage of the Jews; for example, they are "entrusted with the oracles of God" (3:2b). He acknowledges that the advantage which the Jews have is "great and important in every respect," but at the same time he reminds all that "there is at least one respect in which (they have) no advantage—(they are) no less sinful before God."[15] In Romans 3:9b–11a, however, Paul affirms that the Jewish advantage does not grant the Jews any soteriological benefit in that all people, whether Jews or Gentiles, are alike "under the power of sin ... None is righteous ..." (3:9b–10a). This understanding appears to challenge T'oegye's assertion that a human being has an intrinsically good nature, although this comparison seems forced because these two figures did not come out of the same context of faith and philosophy. Paul refers to the issue of sin in Romans 3:9b–11a in terms of his Christian belief, while T'oegye insists on the innately good nature of human beings in terms of his philosophical understanding of human beings and their moral (or ethical) tendencies.

On the other hand, Paul states in 1 Corinthians that, "Jesus Christ (is) the wisdom of God" (1:24), "... He (Jesus Christ) has become wisdom for us from God" (1:30), and "... your (Corinthians') trust should not rest on human wisdom but on God's power (Jesus Christ)" (2:5). These words are in some agreement to T'oegye's contention that wisdom comes from Heaven (or Nature) and a person becomes a sage by obtaining wisdom.

An even stronger influence of Confucianism is found in Korean educational systems. In Korean society these three—the possession of wisdom, high education, and high social standing—are considered synonymous. This is due to the substantial impact of the Korean Confucian point of view regarding education, and the high value given to wisdom. Confucianism has fundamentally influenced both school and home education. In school education, Confucian ideas make a decisive impact upon its aims, its method, and its curriculum. Based on such a Confucian conception, Koreans cultivate their character and personality through education.[16]

15. Cranfield, *Romans*, 65.
16. Keum, *Confucianism*, 33.

It may be argued, however, that Confucianism has also negatively affected Korean education in that it places undue emphasis on the reputation of a person, their family, and their social achievements. This means it is tempting for Koreans to praise and welcome only the wise and educated people—the elite. It is considered natural in Korean society that the uneducated and the powerless are isolated from society; and the educated, wise, and ruling elites take the powerful and authoritative positions.[17]

Last, a Korean-Confucian understanding of social stratification affects social hierarchies in Korean society, in which there were four distinctive social classes established, especially in the *Choson* dynasty.[18] These are as follows: the higher classes (*yangban* and *sonbi*), the middle class (*jungyin*), the lower class (*sangmin*, which literally means "commoners"), and the lowest class (*chonmin*). These four social classes no longer exist in Korean law today. The legal category of social classes seems to have disappeared from Korean society during the time between the Japanese colonization (1910–1945) and Korean War (1950–1953). Nevertheless, in Korean mentality these classic divisions continue. These divisions instead turn both to racism towards foreigners and to *sonbi sasang*, which refers to Confucian elitism. Some Koreans see foreigners, who have different skin colors and mixed blood, as lower than themselves on the social scale (see below).

Both *yangban* and *sonbi* referred to those people who were well-educated and elite. They were the highest social class. The Korean word *yangban* literally means "two divisions." It describes "Korea's elite and aristocratic class" and "the two types of government officials, the civil and the military."[19] This *yangban* class not only took all the high ranking government positions, but they also owned "all land other than that owned by the royal family, the government and the Buddhist temples."[20] The *sonbi* refers to a learned Confucian scholar who did not desire a government post. He instead had more interest in self-improvement and knowledge and in teaching Confucian philosophy and ideology. He might not be

---

17. Lee, *Jeuntong*, 175.

18. This *Choson* dynasty was the last kingdom in Korean history. At the time of the *Choson* dynasty Confucian philosophy and customs were widespread all over the Korean peninsula. Confucianism, thus, was highly valued in the civic life of Koreans. This *Choson* dynasty was ended by the invasion by Japan in 1910 (see Park, *Wangjo*, 120–70).

19. Kalton, *Diagrams*, 220 n. 15.

20. Kim, *Arts*, 23.

wealthy but still belonged to the elite and high social class, as the *yangban* did, because of his knowledge of Confucianism.[21] In addition, it can be said that there was a slight difference between *yangban* and *sonbi*. All *sonbi* should become *yangban*, while all *yangban* did not belong to the group of *sonbi*. T'eogye was a *sonbi*, not just a *yangban*, because he dedicated his life to studying how to improve Korean society by Confucian philosophy and to practice Confucian thoughts as a political ideology.

The middle class *jungyin* were skilled people such as physicians, accountants, meteorological observers, court painters, interpreters, secretaries, and people who were involved in trading and who were often wealthy. They were not, however, legally allowed to elevate their social status through their wealth, unlike these wealthy Corinthians who could rise in status through their money because of patronage systems. At the lowest level in Korean society were the *sangmin* and *chonmin*. Farmers and craftspeople belonged to the *sangmin*, while slaves and actors to the *chonmin*. Both the *sangmin* and *chonmin*, alike, were uneducated and usually poor.[22]

In Korean society today, there is still a widespread Confucian tendency. This is called *sonbi sasang* or *sonbi* syndrome or *sonbi-ism*.[23] In Korean-Confucian society, rather than the *yangban*, the *sonbi* are most respected because of their commitment to study and education. That is why this feature is called *sonbi sasang* rather than *yangban sasang*. This *sonbi sasang* emerges from the Confucian over-emphasis on educated and elite people such as the *yangban* and *sonbi*. It has been part of the Korean mentality for hundreds of years since the *Choson* dynasty. In the twenty-first century, *sonbi sasang* is attested in both tendencies: Koreans give high respect to scholars; university and college professors; and people of higher education and knowledge. They also highly value wisdom (*jeehye/sulgi*), and regard the educated as people of wisdom and as having leadership capacities in politics.

Two occurrences support this argument. One occurrence was in December 2007 when several candidates (e.g., Keun-Mo Jung, Hoi-Chang Lee, Dong-Young Jung, Guk-Hyun Moon, and Myong-Bak Yi) for the election of the Korean presidency were former university professors, CEOs of giant private companies, and graduates from the the

21. National Museum of Korea, *Neo-Confucianism*, 10.
22. Kim, *Arts*, 23.
23. The Korean word *sasang* means "thought."

top university in Korea (Seoul National University). The other occurrence, most recently in Korea, was the creation of a new phrase, *shin jee shik yin*, that literally means "people of new knowledge." This phrase is used, particularly, to praise and honor Koreans who invent and pioneer something new in relation to Information Technology. This phrase is closely related to the rapid development of the Information Technology industry in Korea in the twenty-first century.

Consequently, in Korean Confucian society, the uneducated and ignorant (people of *sangmin* and *chonmin* origins) tend to be ignored and despised and also isolated and marginalized from the mainstream of society. In this regard, there are similarities between the behavior of some of the Corinthian Christians who were influenced by the social and cultural systems of first-century Roman Corinth, such as rhetorical conventions and patronal networks, and that of some Koreans who are affected by Confucian teachings. They both appear to over-emphasize education, knowledge, and social standing.

Moreover, the *sonbi* syndrome, to some extent, affects Protestant Korean churches, where it causes a problem of discrimination. Some members of higher education, wealth, and high social positions take leadership positions in Korean Christian communities; whereas, others who are uneducated and poor are excluded from those leadership positions. This is similar to the Corinthian Christian Community in Paul's day. Some Corinthian Christians of wealth and higher social status seem to have despised their fellow Christians of lower classes (e.g., 1 Cor 11:22).

In Korean Protestantism there are traditionally three different offices: pastor or minister (*moksa*), elder (*jangro* for man, *kwonsa* for woman), and deacon(ness) (*jipsa*).[24] Some Korean Christians often understand these offices in the light of social and hierarchical structures and view the elder (*jangro*) as having a higher position than the deacon (*jipsa*) in the church. They also relate the office of elder to a high position in the wider civic society.[25] In Korean-Confucian Christian society, the office of elder does not only indicate a leadership position in the church but also refers to wealth and high social status. It often happens that in order to become an elder, a person needs to be well educated, wealthy, or have a high social position in the wider civic society. He has to be

---

24. Cf. in 1 Timothy 3:1–13 where there are two offices described: *episkopos* (v.1; cf. Titus 1:7) and *diakonos* (v.8).

25. See Han, "Multicultural," 124–26.

wealthy enough to contribute a large amount of money to the church he is ordained with. In spite of this, he would willingly become an elder because the office of elder helps him rise in status and obtain honor and a better reputation in the wider society.[26]

Nevertheless, the office of deacon is not closely related to social status in the Korean-Confucian Christian context. In becoming a deacon or deaconess, there is not much difference between a Christian who possesses wealth and high social status and another who is poor and uneducated. Furthermore, women are not entitled to be elders (*jangro*) but *kwonsa* in most Protestant Korean churches in Korea and overseas, which tend not to share leadership roles with women. This *kwonsa* does not technically refer to a leadership position in the church but rather to a helping and assistant role. In this respect, there is not much difference between *kwonsa* and female *jipsa* (deaconess). They do not have an upfront role in leadership and the decision-making process. Their duty and responsibility is to help and support pastors and (male) elders to do ministry and conduct services and accompany them while visiting homes and hospitals. It is also their responsibility to prepare meals for the whole congregation and oversee food distribution on Sundays. Most Korean churches, whether in Korea or overseas, have a lunch meal together after the morning service as a Christian tradition (11 am or 12 noon). Yet, it is reported that a Protestant Korean church in Sydney, Australia, has most recently appointed two *kwonsa*s as elders. This church made a significant step forward in terms of challenging other Korean churches that hesitate to appoint female elders in its leadership office.

This Korean Christian (Protestant) attitude is similar to the behavior of some of the Christians who possessed wealth and high social status at Roman Corinth. They suggested that Paul should accept patron-client relations and accept financial gifts. They, thereby, wished to take leadership roles and put the Christian community under their control (2 Cor 11:7–11)

On the other hand, the Corinthian Christians who were poor and belonged to the lower classes were humiliated and discriminated against in the Christian community. They were, of course, excluded from

---

26. It is worth noting that "to most people today, a primacy of honor doubtless suggests a status of eminence and a role of leadership that is purely ceremonial: a mark of public recognition without practical rights or duties, much like honorable citizenship, an honorary fellowship in a college, or an honorary degree . . ." (Daley, "Position," 529–30).

leadership positions and the Lord's Supper (1 Cor 11:22). Similarly, in Protestant Korean churches some Christians who are poor and uneducated are excluded from leadership positions, such as the eldership, and isolated from the decision-making group in the church.[27] This reflects the Confucian over-emphasis on wisdom, education, and knowledge. It also reflects the undue Confucian emphasis on the fame and reputation of a person; their family; their social achievements; and the *sonbi* syndrome prevailing in the wider Korean Confucian society.

Nevertheless, Paul's message in 1 Corinthians challenges such assumptions and social-conventions-oriented conduct. Paul argues that no one should boast about his or her social privilege—wisdom, high education, wealth, power, and high social status—in a Christian community (1:26), since no one can find any favor in the eyes of God by expressing such social privilege. This serves to remind Korean Christians of God's paradoxical election: He elected the foolish, poor, and powerless of the world to shame the wise, wealthy, and powerful (1:27–28). Paul also emphasizes that each Christian has his or her gift(s) given from God and should use the gifts in serving the body of Christ rather than his or her social privilege (12:1–19). All Christians, whether educated or uneducated, whether wealthy or poor, or whether of higher social status or lower standing, are equally called by God according to their gifts. They then serve the body of Christ as God's fellow workers (1 Cor 3:5–9) to build up the community in love.

Furthermore, Paul's challenge to the Corinthians reverberates through the ages for Korean Christians to boast about "Christ-crucified-originated" wisdom in Christian churches rather than "human thought-based" and "cultural-conventions-oriented" wisdom. Or in other words, there is a challenge here for Korean Christians who have uncritically adopted "Korean-Confucianism-oriented" wisdom. Paul describes this "Christ-crucified-oriented" wisdom as the power of God; first: for salvation to all who have faith (1:18, 21), and second: for the resurrection of the dead (1 Cor 15:12–57). By his power, God raised Christ from the dead as the wisdom of God, who had died on the cross (1 Cor 15:12–57). This should be regarded as the essence of the gospel message that Korean Christians preach in the Christian churches (1 Cor 15:1–4) and

---

27. We here have to remind ourselves that Jesus welcomed the poor and the marginalized (e.g., Luke 4:18). We should also be aware of James's warning about partiality in the Christian communities (James 2:1–9).

as the ground for their boasting (9:15, 16). Preaching the gospel message of Jesus Christ as the wisdom of God, Paul also challenges Korean Christians to stop boasting of the Confucian understandings of wisdom and social achievement (1:29). Furthermore, Paul urges us to imitate the way he boasts of the gospel of Christ crucified as the wisdom of God (1:30, 31; 3:18; 4:16). Christ Jesus has become "our wisdom, our righteousness and holiness and redemption" (1:30–31). We now turn to a further social manifestation of wisdom thought: an investigation of the imperial cult of first-century Roman Corinth from a Korean-Confucian Christian context.

SHINTO SHRINE WORSHIP

The imperial cult, sometimes involving emperor worship, was active by the time Paul established the Christian *ekklēsia* at Roman Corinth.[28] At the imperial cult, the Corinthians worshipped and venerated not only deceased emperors but also the reigning one, and even living members of the imperial family. Some of the Corinthian Christians were apparently involved in this practice (1 Cor 8:1–6). These practices then caused problems in the Corinthian Christian community, especially as regards the issues of idol worship (1 Cor 10:1–22) and food dedicated to idols (8:1–13), and the resulting affirmation of the inscribed patronal networks from the Emperor down. Given this, Paul's response to this imperial cult will be explored in the light of Japanese imperialism in Korea from 1910 to 1945 and Shinto Shrine worship (*sin sa cham bae* in Korean), where a Japanese emperor is worshipped.[29]

In the early half of the twentieth century, Korea was colonized by Japan. On the twenty-ninth day of August in 1910 it was publicly announced all over the Korean peninsula that Korea had been annexed by Japan.[30] Since then, thousands of Korean Christians were involved

---

28. Paul does not directly address the issue of imperial cults anywhere in 1 Corinthians, although he explicitly deals with that of "meat offered to idols" in chapters 8 and 10. However, this issue seems to be implied in both chapters (see Horsely, "Empire," 72–102).

29. K. K. Yeo provides a cross-cultural reading on the issue of food offered to idols, addressed in 1 Cor 8 and 10 from a Chinese-Confucian Christian perspective and particularly that of ancestral "worship." (see Yeo, *Interpretation*, 15–49, 212–22). Yet he does not separate 1 Cor 8:1—10:22 from 10:23—11:1, although Paul clearly addresses different issues in these two different contexts (see above).

30. Institute of Korean Church, *Kidokyoeui*, 309.

in resistance and independence movements against Japan. The following two events are important to mention in this context: the "105 Men Incident" (or the "Christian Conspiracy Case") in 1911 and "the March First (*Samil* in Korean) Independence Movement" in 1919. In these two independence movements, Christians played a substantial role in leadership and hundreds of Christians were then persecuted and executed by Japanese colonizers. In particular, the 105 Men Incident is seen as the Japanese colonizers' most significant persecution of Christians in Korean church history. In 1907 a political party called *Shin Min Hoe* (the New People's Party) was organized. Many Christian leaders were actively involved in the party, although it was secular. They were arrested on "charges of conspiracy for the assassination of Governor General Terauci in 1910. This incident was called 'the 105 men Incident'" because 105 Christian leaders were imprisoned.[31] Besides this, there were a large number of Christians including Protestants and Catholics involved in national independence movements, although Western missionaries opposed their involvement.[32] Furthermore, in the March First Independence Movement more than half of the leaders were Christians. "On the first day of March, 1919, the leaders of resistance movements against Japanese colonial rule issued their declaration of independence which was read at a public park in Seoul, triggering nationwide demonstrations demanding national independence."[33] There were thirty-three leaders of which seventeen were Christians. This independence movement incurred further persecution of many Christian leaders. It is claimed, however, that this movement has become "the outstanding example and symbol for nationalist aspiration and one of the sources for indigenous and Minjung theology."[34]

After the March First movement, the Japanese colonial government compelled Koreans to change their family names to a Japanese form and use Japanese language in all public schools and churches. Moreover, this colonial government forced all Koreans, and particularly Christians, to attend Shinto shrines and worship the Japanese emperor.[35] It was in 1935 that Shinto shrine worship was thoroughly and compulsorily forced on

---

31. England, *Asian*, 505.
32. Ibid.; Institute of Korean Church, *Kidokyoeui*, 308.
33. England, *Asian*, 505.
34. Ibid.; Min, *Kidokyohoisa*, 307.
35. England, *Asian*, 506.

all Christians. This even applied to Western missionaries in the Korean peninsula. Nonetheless, Korean Christian leaders and Western missionaries strongly opposed to this Shinto shrine worship defining it "as interference with religious belief."[36]

At that time, the most outstanding resistance against Shinto shrine worship took place in Pyongyang (which is now the capital of North Korea) because this city had the largest Christian population. It was thus called the "Jerusalem of Korea."[37] In this city there were two American missionaries, G. S. McCune and V. L. Snook, who were both principals of Christian schools. The Japanese local government in Pyongyang forced them, as representatives of Christian schools, to pay respect to Shinto shrines. The Japanese government threatened to close the schools and make them leave the Korean peninsula, unless they practiced Shinto shrine worship. Nevertheless, they refused to participate in the Shinto shrine worship according to their consciences, whereupon they were removed by force from their principalships and expelled to America. From then on, the Japanese colonial government more thoroughly compelled all Korean Christians to give respect to Shinto shrines.[38]

Choo Ki Chul, senior pastor of the San Jung Hyun Presbyterian Church in Pyongyang, claimed that Shinto shrine worship was idol worship according to the Ten Commandments, especially the first two (Exodus 20:1-6).[39] He was then imprisoned for seven years and martyred in 1944, a year before Korean independence took place. Afterward, because of their refusal to participate in veneration of Shinto shrines, more than 2000 Christians all over the Korean peninsula were arrested. Of them, fifty were executed in prison. About two hundred churches were also forced to close down by the Japanese authorities.[40]

Meanwhile, some Korean Christians and some Western missionaries began to assert that Shinto shrine worship should be seen as a political act rather than a religious one. In other words, it could be seen to mean

36. Ibid.
37. Min, *Kidokyohoisa*, 426.
38. Ibid.
39. "You shall have no other god to set against me. You shall not make a carved image for yourself nor the likeness of any thing in the heaven above, or on the earth below, or the waters under the earth. You shall not bow down to them or worship them . . ." (vv. 3-5a).
40. England, *Asian*, 506.

nothing other than an expression of patriotism, allegiance, and loyalty to the state and the Japanese ruling emperor. They, accordingly, claimed that it should not be seen as a matter of idol worship from a Christian perspective but merely as an observation of the law of the state. They further argued that even if paying respect to Shinto shrines might be idol worship from a Christian point of view, there was no point refusing Shinto shrine worship and risking many Christians being martyred and hundreds of churches shut down. Roman Catholics in Korea had taken a similar position because in 1936 the pope allowed Korean Catholics, as well as Japanese Catholics, to worship the emperor and give respect to Shinto shrines.[41]

Consequently, there were diverse arguments about Shinto shrine worship among Christians and their leaders. Some agreed to show veneration and homage to Shinto shrines, whereas the others refused. Such actions caused divisions in the Christian communities in Korea. For example,

> In Busan the Christian churches disputed Shinto Shrine worship. People of the party of Rev Kil Chang Kim argued for it, while the others opposed it . . . Rev Jae Hwa Choi who had been involved in independence movements . . . didn't offer veneration to Shinto shrines . . . He preserved his Christian faith.[42]

In summary, during the Japanese imperialist invasion of Korea, Shinto shrine worship was used as a symbol of "Japanese imperial rule."[43] It further became a critical factor in causing severe persecution and divisions in the Christian churches all over the Korean peninsula. It is interesting to observe that with regard to the issue of emperor worship there are similarities and analogies between the Christian context of Roman Corinth in the first century and that of Korea in the early twentieth century. Just as there was social pressure for the Corinthian Christians in the day of Paul to worship and venerate the Roman emperor and the imperial family members due to the imperial cult and imperial patronage (1 Cor 8:1–13; 10:1–30), so Korean Christians during Japanese imperialism were forced to worship the Japanese emperor and pay respect to Shinto shrines.

---

41. Min, *Kidokyohoisa*, 427.
42. Park, *BusanJin*, 183. This is my own translation from the Korean script.
43. England, *Asian*, 506.

It is also true that in these two extremely different social contexts the worship of emperors was alike, seen as idolatry from some Christian viewpoints (1 Cor 8:5) but not from others. This is related to the Ten Commandments in Exodus 20:1–6 (1 Cor 10:1–22). In both contexts many of the Christians thus refused to worship emperors (1 Cor 10:14). The issue of emperor worship later turned to the problem of factionalism in both the Corinthian and Korean Christian communities (1 Cor 1: 10; 8:7–13). In the Korean churches, as an act of respect for the state, some agreed to the demands of the Japanese emperor, while others refused because it was idolatry. Similarly, in the Corinthian Christian community some members accepted their act of worshipping the Roman emperor as part of the social system of the imperial cult and imperial patronage. They also accepted the eating of meat offered to idols with the slogans "all things are lawful" (1 Cor 10:23) and "no idol is real" (1 Cor 8:4), whereas others rejected it (1 Cor 8:1–13).

In 1 Corinthians 8, however, Paul neither supports nor blames their behavior directly; although he appears to have strongly commanded them not to be idolaters and stop idol worship in the temple in 1 Corinthians 10 (vv. 6, 14). In other words, he does not speak of whether it is a sin against Christ for some of the Corinthian Christians implicitly to worship the Roman emperor and to eat food sacrificed to idols—which are only "so-called Gods" (1 Cor 8:4–6). Rather, he suggests that they should take care lest their behavior become an obstacle to the weak (*tois asthenesin*) (1 Cor 8:9), lest it wound the other brothers and sisters' conscience (*suneidēsis*) (1 Cor 8:10), and lest it cause the weak to fall. Paul further argues that it is a sin against Christ to wound the conscience of the brothers and sisters in the Corinthian congregation (8:7–13) because this partly caused the Corinthian Christians to split (*schismata*) (1:10; 11:18–19; 12:25).

In this respect, it is argued that Paul seemed more concerned about the problem of factions in the Corinthian congregation than the issues of emperor worship and food dedicated to idols themselves; although these issues apparently helped to cause the factions among the Corinthians. He does strongly condemn the social consequences of idol worship in the temples—using the traditional Jewish understandings that idolatry leads to immorality (1 Cor 10:1–22)—but his overall focus is always on the implications for the *ekklēsia*. Thus, Paul had a strong emphasis on unity in the Corinthian Christian community as the *sōma christou*

(1 Cor 12:1–31). He also claimed that the Corinthian Christians should have *agapē* towards one another (1 Cor 8:1; 13:1–13). Particularly in 1 Corinthians 13:13, "so faith, hope, love abide, these three; but the greatest of these is love," Paul highly values *agapē* more than *pistis* and *elpis*.[44] He seems to assert that to have love towards one another is the most necessary and important way to reclaim the Corinthian congregation from the grips of factionalism.

This Pauline message should help contemporary Korean Christians to re-evaluate Shinto shrine worship during Japanese imperialism in the early twentieth century. Many Korean Christians tend to criticize and blame some forefathers who participated in the veneration of Shinto shrines and view them as compromising their Christian faith with the world and committing idolatry against God. These Koreans further criticize the forefathers for betraying the Christian faith and saving their own lives. That is why many Koreans highly value those other forefathers who refused to pay respect to Shinto shrines and were persecuted for preserving their Christian faith. They should, however, consider the important Pauline message of unity and love in Christian communities before they judge whether the Shinto shrine worship that their forefathers performed was idolatry. In 1 Corinthians 8–13 Paul clearly emphasizes the unity of the body of Christ and the reconciliation of the saints, and takes a remarkably relaxed attitude to "indirect involvement" in idol-meat through the meat markets and neighborhood meals. These are not issues to be judgmental about or to split the church over (1 Cor 10:31—11:1).

ANCESTOR VENERATION

Korean Christians tend to use the phrase "ancestor 'worship'" in order to help English-speaking readers understand better the practice of Korean ancestral rites, but I prefer to use the phrase "ancestor 'veneration'" or "ancestor 'commemoration'" because it more accurately reflects the idea of ancestral rituals in a Korean-Confucian Christian context.

Surrounding the issue of emperor worship, there lies a deeper connection to household cults and ancestral veneration, in both Corinth and Korea. The domestic cults were popular among Greeks and Romans in the first-century Greco-Roman world. Jews in the first century CE

---

44. Smith argues similarly *Symposium*, 211.

also commemorated their ancestors in various ways. For example, Paul expressed great respect and reverence towards Abraham because of his faith in God (see Rom 4:1–25; Gal 3:6–9). Nevertheless, this Jewish veneration towards their ancestors was unlike the Greek and Roman domestic cult.

According to Rives, "the main objects of (the) household cult were, on the one hand, the household gods, and, on the other, the family dead."[45] Greeks and Romans commonly erected household shrines (*lararium*) or altars in their houses. Therein the people placed images or paintings of household spirits, and those of heroes and ancestors. They offered them animals and vegetables as a sacrifice on a regular basis.[46] Rives states further:

> Civic officials had an interest in upholding and even regulating the traditional (Greek and Roman) forms of domestic cult. A candidate for public office in Athens, for example was traditionally asked whether he had family tombs . . . In Rome Cicero regarded it as an essential part of an ideal city-state that heirs be required to maintain family cults (*On Laws* 2.48), and the *pontifices*, one of the chief groups of public priests, did exercise some authority in matters of household cult such as burial law and the inheritance of religious duties.[47]

In Greco-Roman times all members in the household participated in the domestic cult. They got together on a daily basis and invoked their household "living spirit" and dead ancestors (family members) to protect them. As they performed ancestral rites and venerated their deceased ancestors, they understood that they were closely connected with their deceased ancestors. In other words, this ancestor veneration functioned as uniting in fellowship between the living and dead members of a family. The cult (veneration) of the deceased helped to "maintain the identity of the family over time."[48] This household cult and especially the veneration of the dead can be compared to ancestor veneration in a Korean Confucian context. As the domestic cult was a significant part

---

45. Rives, *Religion*, 117; see also Mikalson, *Ancient*, 133–37; E. Ferguson, *Backgrounds*, 166–68.

46. Rives, *Religion*, 119. The offering of a sacrifice was followed by a dinner party (See E. Ferguson, *Backgrounds*, 168, 170, 176; also Mikalson, *Ancient*, 135).

47. Rives, *Religion*, 121.

48. Rives, *Religion*, 118; see also Osiek and Balch, *Families*, 83; Mikalson, *Ancient*, 133–36.

of Greco-Roman culture, so ancestor veneration is an integral part of Korean Confucian society in our time.

Roman (and Greek) domestic worship is glimpsed in 1 Corinthians 10:23—11:1 where it appears that Corinthian Christians would have been invited by their unbelieving contemporaries to private dinner parties and feasts (1 Cor 10:27). The food (or meat) that they ate at the dinner may well have been offered as a sacrifice at a domestic cult (or ancestor veneration) before being served. In Greco-Roman times, when people had meals in their houses, they first dedicated a small portion of food to domestic deities and deceased heroes and ancestors, and then began to eat. This was a domestic, religious, and dietary custom in the Greco-Roman world in the first century CE.[49] There is no doubt, therefore, that this custom took place in Roman and Greek homes in first-century Corinth. This is affirmed in 1 Corinthians 10:28, where Paul confirms that a host may say, "this (meat) has been offered in sacrifice."

Paul suggests that if Corinthian Christians were invited to such a private dinner and were disposed to go, they should go and eat "whatever is set before (them) without raising any question on the ground of conscience" (v. 27). He further commands, "whether you eat or drink, or whatever you do, do all to the glory of God" (v. 31). In 1 Corinthians 10: 27–29 it is clear that Paul allowed them to go, when they were invited to such a private meal, because he agreed that the Corinthian Christians had a right or freedom (*exousia*) to do whatever they liked to do ("all things are lawful," 1 Cor 10:23). Yet, he imposed conditions upon it: Their behavior should have to be "helpful" not for "their own good," but for "the good of (their) neighbor(s)" and for the advantage of many people (1 Cor 10:23, 24, 33). Their conduct should "build up" the *ekklēsia* of God and please all people in the Christian community (10:32). Their behavior should "give no offence to" any brother and sister in the house of God (10:32). They should also do all things for the glory of God (*doxa theou*, 10:31). If they did not follow such conditions, they should not go to such a private feast and eat food offered as a sacrifice to idols (1 Cor 10: 28, 29). Paul appears to have made these conditions with the Corinthians because he needed to take proper precautions to prevent their behavior from wounding the conscience of weak Christians (10:29). Moreover, he wished their conduct not to cause the problem of tension and schisms in the Corinthian Christian gatherings (1 Cor 11:18–19).

49. See E. Ferguson, *Backgrounds*, 166–68.

We now turn to evaluate the issue of eating meat offered as a sacrifice at the domestic cult (or ancestor veneration) from a Korean-Confucian Christian context, particularly ancestor veneration (or ancestral rites or ancestor rituals, *jesa* or *jo sang soong bae* in Korean).⁵⁰ As argued, some of the Corinthian Christians who ate food dedicated to idols caused the wounding of the consciences of weak Christians and the problem of tensions and divisions in the Corinthian Christian gatherings (1 Cor 8:1–13; 10:23–33; 11:17–22). Similarly, insofar as ancestor veneration is seen as "idol worship" in Korean Christian homes, there are still tensions between those who perform ancestor veneration and others who do not; those who are "passive participants" and those who will have nothing to do with it.

Ancestor veneration has been part of the life of Korean Confucian society for a long time. It is an essential and integral part of Korean Confucian life and culture.⁵¹ T'oegye put a strong emphasis on ancestral veneration in Korean Confucian society and thoroughly committed himself to practicing it. He also argued that Koreans should serve deceased ancestors in the same way they serve livings elders. So, it is important in Korean culture to have an attitude of faithfulness, veneration, and reverence towards deceased ancestors in the rite of ancestor veneration.⁵²

Martina Deuchler states that in Confucianism, ancestor veneration is seen as "the most filial act a son could perform for his parents," but notes that daughters cannot join this ritual in most homes.⁵³ Yet, there is an exception now that a daughter who is the only child in her family is allowed to participate in the ritual. If a son (or daughter) fails to perform ancestral rites, this is "taken as evidence of insufficient filial piety," and he is punished by custom. For instance, "his living elders disqualify him from conducting services for them after they die," and he can be "excluded from a place in the ancestral shrine because an unfilial son cannot eat sacrificial food with his father."⁵⁴ This son is also blamed as *bae eun mang duk han jasik* (which literally means a son who loses gratitude from his

50. As do Hays and Newton, briefly (see Hays, *Corinthians*, 143; Newton, *Deity*, 397), yet this will be developed in more detail than they do. For ancestral rituals in a Korean-Confucian Christian context, see also Lee, *Ancestor*, and Moltmann, "Respect," 13–26, esp. 16 n. 2.

51. Keum, *Confucianism*, 33.

52. See Yoon, "T'oegye," 7–17, esp. 11.

53. Deuchler, *Transformation*, 176.

54. Ibid.

parents) by his relatives and neighbors. Many Koreans also believe that through this ritual activity they not only express respect and veneration towards their deceased parents and ancestors but also strengthen bonds with their relatives who participate in it. This is because ancestral rituals take place from time to time in the context of family reunions.[55] Koreans perform ancestral rituals on special occasions such as the days the deceased ancestors died, New Year's Day (January first), and Full Moon Day (August fifteenth) in the Korean lunar calendar.

Nevertheless, in Christian circles, ancestor veneration has been contentious for centuries since Christianity was first introduced to Korea in the late eighteenth century for Catholics (1784) and the late nineteenth century for Protestants (1884).[56] Most Korean Protestants regard ancestor veneration as (heretical) idolatry due to the following superstitious characteristics of ancestor veneration.[57] In the rite of ancestor veneration Koreans "offer something in return for the benefits received from (a deceased ancestor) and keep (his or her) memories alive."[58] Thus, they prepare the particular food as a sacrifice that their deceased ancestor loved to eat while alive, and prostrate themselves before the photo of a dead ancestor or the tablet which bears the name of a deceased person. Moreover, some Koreans believe that during the ancestral ritual the spirit of a dead ancestor visits the ritual site and eats the sacrificial food. In return, the spirit then blesses and guides the living descendents, and protects their household from evil and misfortune.[59]

Notwithstanding, it is argued that such superstitious characteristics are not the pure form of Korean-Confucian ancestor veneration, but they are mixed with superstitious ingredients of indigenous folk cults, such as shamanistic cults, in Korea. A shamanistic rite (*gut* in Korean) is a different form of ancestral veneration in Korean society. A shaman (*mudang* in Korean) conducts this shamanic cult, just like a Protestant pastor or Catholic priest at the Christian worship service. The *mudang* plays a mediating role in helping people communicate with their de-

---

55. Ibid.

56. England, *Asian*, 481, 491.

57. In Korean Protestantism, the main churches belonging to the "evangelical" circle are Baptist, Evangelical holiness church, Presbyterian, Methodist, Church of Christ, Assembly of God, and the Salvation Army.

58. Chung, *Encounter*, 17.

59. Ibid.

ceased ancestors who emerge as spirits. As Kim describes, at this shamanic ritual "many offerings such as food, wine, fruits and clothes, (are) arranged to please the spirits (of ancestors), and the shaman dance(s) and sing(s). (The ritual is) held at night because spirits were not very active during the daytime."[60] The shamanic ritual (*gut*) includes practices of healing and exorcism to expel evil spirits, similar to those described in the Gospels (e.g., Matthew 8:1–17, 29–34; 9:8; John 4:43–54; 5:1–9).[61]

This shamanistic ritual is primarily conducted to worship and appease ancestral spirits. These spirits are believed to have supernatural power to heal the sick and provide happiness, prosperity, fortune, protection from evil, and so on. The shamanistic rite is mostly practiced by those (uneducated) Koreans who live in rural areas today.[62] However, shamanism is:

> not recognized officially as a religion . . . (although it is) the oldest religion . . . (and) remains the most prevalent form of religiosity in Korea . . . (This is because) in (post) modern Korea, numerous challenges toward shamanism have all become serious threats to its continued existence . . . Most educated Koreans are embarrassed if shamanism becomes a topic of conversation. They are quick to deny that shamanism has had anything to do with decent folk, and even quicker to terminate the discussion by proclaiming that it is no longer a part of Korean life.[63]

Thus, most Koreans, whether Christians or not, devalue Korean shamanism as animism and superstition rather than value it as an integral part of Korean traditional religious practices.

Nevertheless, such superstitious elements in ancestral veneration, whether at Confucian or shamanistic ritual sites, need careful analysis before being accepted by Christians. For example, when participants describe the food prepared for ancestor veneration as a sacrifice offered to a dead ancestor, and they believe the spirit of the deceased protects their household from evil and misfortune, it is clear that something more than respect for ancestors is the motivating force. These elements appear to contradict Paul's argument that all things, including protection from evil, come from God the Father (1 Cor 8:6), and his command

60. Kim, *Shamanism*, 37–38.
61. Ibid., 37–38.
62. See Ro, "Communicating," 216–17.
63. Moon, "Dream," 238–40.

that the Corinthian Christians not offer sacrifices to a *daimonion*, but to God (1 Cor 10:20). The primary and major purpose of traditional ancestor veneration is to express filial piety to dead ancestors and to honor their memory; a practice Paul does not even draw attention to, though it was certainly present in all the homes of non-believers. In this process, Korean Protestants can come to see ancestor veneration as an integral part of Korean traditional customs rather than as idolatry.[64]

These Korean Protestants should also consider that such ancestral veneration is not equated with the Christian understanding of the worship service (*yeh bae* in Korean) in which Christians give their exclusive devotion to God. Rather, the ancestor ritual comprises the conception of reverence and veneration towards deceased ancestors—an affirmation of the whole household of God.

In the service of ancestral veneration, the first son of a dead ancestor holds a cup of Korean traditional rice wine with both hands and moves it around over the table on which incense burns. He repeats this a few times. This is an act of opening the ritual and inviting the spirit of the deceased to the ritual site. The rest of the male participants then make a deep bow before the photo of the deceased ancestor. They kneel, and place one hand by the other and then put them together on the floor, and bow the head deeply down on top of the hands. They repeat this deep bow a few times. The photo is placed at the center of the back row on the table on which food is arranged in rows and a brazen bowl full of white rice is placed, in the middle of which a brazen spoon is turned upward. This means to invite the sprit to the meal table, use the spoon, and eat the food. Afterwards, the food is served to all participants to eat. At this meal, they strengthen bonds with one another. Sons and daughters are all welcome to the meal.

Nevertheless, in Protestant Korean churches it is believed that when in the service of the ancestral ritual and the people bow down a few times before the pictures or statues of their deceased ancestors, it is definitely idolatrous worship that is taking place. Most Korean Protestants understand that from a biblical perspective, this is clearly seen as idol worship, because Exodus 20:4–5 says, "You shall not make for yourself an idol (Hebrew, פֶסֶל: Greek, εἴδωλον) in the form of anything in heaven above

---

64. Similarly, L. K. Lo argues in a Chinese Confucian context that "the mixed superstitious element in the present ancestral veneration (has to be) criticized, but the original meaning of filial piety (should be) confirmed" (Lo, "Chinese," 133: cf. Yao, *Confucianism*, 199–204.

or on the earth beneath or in the waters below. You shall not bow down to them or worship them . . . " (NIV).[65]

It is argued, however, that this understanding is taken out of its biblical context. In the context of Exodus 20:4-5, the Hebrew word פֶסֶל means an "idol of stone, clay, wood, and metal" (cf. 2 King 21:7).[66] The word פֶסֶל appears to be closely related to the Hebrew words כֶסֶף אֱלֹהֵי ("gods of silver") and אֱלֹהֵי זָהָב ("gods of gold"), which are further in verse 23 within the same chapter. Hence, it can be argued that the Hebrew word פֶסֶל ("idol") in Exodus 20:4-5 refers to a statue or idol made of silver (כֶסֶף) and gold (זָהָב), which the Israelites substituted for the God who brought them up out of Egypt, and then worshipped as their god. Exodus 32:1-8 makes clear their idolatrous behavior. Verse 8 reads, "They . . . made themselves an idol cast in the shape of a calf. They bowed down to it and sacrificed to it." This is clearly idolatry and contravenes the commandment, "You shall not bow down to and worship (anything like) a carved image in the heavens above, or on the earth below, or in the waters under the earth" (Exod 20:5; NEB).

Yet, it can be argued that this Scripture does not address the issue of ancestral veneration, as such. The word פֶסֶל ("idol") in Exodus 20:4-5 does not mean to include their deceased ancestors—Abraham and Jacob—as those whom the Israelites worshiped as idols. Moreover, the broader context of Exodus 20:1-23 does not indicate that ancestor veneration is idolatry, such that believers should ban themselves from practicing it in their homes. Furthermore, Paul does not refer to Exodus 20:4-5 and challenge the Corinthian Christians to stop ancestral rites in homes in 1 Corinthians 10:23—11:1, where he appears to tackle the issue of domestic ancestor veneration. On the contrary, Paul reminds the Corinthian audience of the idolatrous conduct of the Israelites in the wilderness (e.g., Exodus chs. 13, 14, 16, 17, 32; Num. chs. 11, 14, 16, 20, 21, 25) within 1 Corinthians 10:1-10 as part of the wider context of 8.1—10:22. Therein, he deals with the problem of some of the Corinthian Christians' idol worship in the context of temples and imperial cults. Paul further takes a direct quotation from Exodus 32:6 (see above), and in 1 Corinthians 10:7, and warns against their improper behavior. He then

65. This is based on my experience. Most of the Korean pastors and laypeople I have seen in Protestant Korean churches agree with this argument, including myself until I discovered a new understanding of ancestor veneration in 1 Cor 10:23—11:1 (see below).

66. Holladay, *Lexicon*, 294.

commands them, "Do not be idolaters as some of them (the Israelites) were"; as it is written, "the people sat down to eat and drink and rose up to dance" (1 Cor 10:7), and "shun the worship of idols" (10:14). In this way, Paul has distinctively different arguments between the issue of idol worship in temples and imperial cults, and the ancestor veneration occurring in domestic contexts (see below).

Early Korean Catholics, and especially the Franciscans, also strictly prohibited converts from practicing ancestor veneration because they defined it as idolatry.[67] Rome confirmed this definition and stopped Korean Catholics from practicing it, although it was an integral part of Korean Confucian culture. As a result, in the 1800s, particularly in 1801, 1839, and 1866–1871, many Korean Catholics were severely persecuted by the Confucian government called the *Choson* or *Yi* Dynasty. Catholicism was condemned as "a heterodoxy that rejected Confucian ethics, loyalty to the king and the state, and the virtue of filial piety."[68] Korean Catholic scholars thus describe the first 100 years of Korean Catholicism as "a history of bloody persecution."[69] It is interesting, nonetheless, that in recent times Korean Catholics are now allowed to perform ancestral rites in their homes without affecting their Catholic faith. They no longer define these practices as idolatry.

For Korean Protestants, however, ancestor veneration is still controversial. It is a critical factor in causing trouble and divisions in some Korean Christian families due to disagreement about it between some members who see ancestor veneration as idolatry and others who regard it as an act of filial piety toward their deceased ancestors. The trouble becomes even worse in a home where a husband and the first in his family are non-Christian but his wife is Christian. The wife attempts to prohibit the performing of ancestral rituals in her home because she sees it as idolatry from her Christian point of view. On the other hand, her husband and son know that through this ritual activity they perform the most filial act, as a son for their deceased parents. This example is based on my experiences not only in my home but also in the churches I have ministered in for more than ten years. Interestingly, Korean Christians who live as migrants in foreign countries such as Australia and America have the same problem, as regards to ancestor rituals, as other Korean

---

67. Kidokgyo Yeunguhoe, *Kidokgyoeui*, 76–80.
68. England, *Asian*, 481, 483.
69. Ibid., 481.

Christians who live in Korea. It is apparent that ancestor veneration is an essential element of Koran Confucian culture. This ancestor veneration has a great impact on the life of all Koreans including Christians wherever they live.

Some Protestant Christians feel distant and isolated from their non-Christian relatives and neighbors who perform ancestor rituals as evidence of their filial piety. Some Christians instead perform *chu do yeh bae* (which means "memorial service"), which is a modified form of ancestral veneration (*jesa*) undertaken in the light of Christian worship. This *chu do yeh bae* comprises prayers, hymns, Scripture readings, and a short sermon and benediction by a minister. It is then followed by a communal meal that strengthens bonds with family members and participants.[70] By substituting ancestral veneration for *chu do ye bae*, these Christians "feel they can now legitimately fulfill the fifth commandment to honor father and mother" (e.g., Exod 20:12).[71] This is, however, seen as an insufficient filial act by their relatives who are non-Christians and prefer traditional forms of ancestor veneration. Therefore, many Protestant Christians are caught in a dilemma between *jesa* and *chu do yeh bae*.

Furthermore, part of the ritual custom of ancestor veneration persists even in daily life, especially in "the daily etiquette of greeting and conversation."[72] For instance, in the greeting custom, in order to show respect and veneration young people always bow once before elderly people on the street, at home, or in church. Young people make a low bow with the upper body. They may shake hands with the elderly only when the latter first asks them to do so. Otherwise, they might be accused of being impolite or rude or uneducated. In conversation and discussion, especially in classes, students must not disagree with or criticize teachers at any time because of the idea that teachers are always respected by students and the latter always obey the former.[73] This respect for "the living elders" transmutes at their death into great reverence for the ancestors in general.

70. See Newton, *Deity*, 397.
71. Ibid.
72. Keum, *Confucianism*, 34.
73. "Teachers commonly control their students with both legitimated authority and Confucian ethical values, which are somewhat analogous to those between parents and offspring. Students believe that they are indebted to their teachers for the benefits bestowed, just as daughters and sons are indebted to their parents." (Lee, "Higher," 1–11).

Today, some Protestants are still greatly troubled due to their refusal to perform ancestor veneration. The refusal is viewed as evidence of insufficient filial piety in Korean Confucian society, but most Korean Protestants see ancestor veneration as idolatry because they consider it as an act of worship or a religious act towards someone/something else than the Christian God. This view has been deeply rooted in (conservative) Korean Protestant tradition for decades. Moreover, (conservative) Korean Protestants express a decisively negative attitude towards any type of ancestor veneration. They do not like even to give value to it as an integral part of Korean-Confucian life, and they separate themselves from it completely. They do not allow anyone to perform ancestral rites in their houses at all. They refuse to accept invitations to participate in a ritual of ancestor veneration that their non-Christian relatives host. They refuse to bow down a few times before the photo of a deceased ancestor or eat food prepared for the dead ancestor, even if they are unintentionally among participants of the ritual. This is also my own experience with my family, relatives, Christian friends, and ministers in Korea. I behaved exactly like the Korean Protestants described above at my father's funeral two decades ago. As the first son, I refused to bow down before his tomb. I did this for my mother who, as a devoted Christian, did not want me to do so. She was proud of me because I had gone to a bible college and became a minister. So, she believed it was her responsibility to protect her son from committing idolatry by bowing down before his dead father. My refusal, however, embarrassed my relatives and the rest of the non-Christians at the funeral. They were all angry at my behavior; it did not make sense to them at all. I was, from their traditional Confucian point of view, *bae eub mang duk han ja sik* (which literally means a son who loses gratitude from his parents). But I was a devoted and faithful Christian son from my mother's traditional (conservative) Korean-Protestant point of view.

In 1 Corinthians 10:23—11:1, however, Paul appears not to support such obviously (conservative) Korean-Protestant thoughts, and instead commands the Corinthian believers to stop such a (religiously) exclusive attitude towards ancestral veneration. In 10:25–27 Paul seems to have given a challenge both to the "strong" and "weak" Corinthian Christians (cf. 4:10; 8:9–10; 9:22), as he did in 7:17–24.[74] The former ate (or would

---

74. Cf. J. P. Heil states, "with strong emphasis on 'all' (*pan*) Paul commands not just part of his audience—either the so called strong or weak—but everyone in his audience" (Heil, *Scripture*, 165). His argument is helpful ,for there may well have been some Corinthian Christians who were identified neither as the "strong" nor the "weak."

eat) food offered as a sacrifice at a private dinner alongside, or following after domestic cultic performance. The latter felt (or would feel) their conscience wounded by the "strong" Christians' behavior.[75] In 10:27 Paul appears to have challenged the "weak" Christians to go to private dinner feasts and "eat whatever (was) set before them without raising any question on the ground of (their) conscience," if they were invited by their unbelieving contemporaries and were disposed to go. In 10:28–29 he also seems to have commanded the "strong" Christians, if necessary, not to eat food dedicated as a sacrifice at domestic cults and to consider the conscience of the "weak" Christians if they raised a critical question about the food the "strong" ate because their conscience was hurt by it (8:7–11). Yet, it is not clear whether they would in fact raise the question or not—it remains a hypothetical possibility that Paul considers.

Nonetheless, it is important to note that Paul does not blame either the behavior of the "strong" or that of the "weak" at all in 1 Corinthians 10:25—11:1, even though he had expressed a decisively determined attitude towards the worship of idols earlier ("shun the worship of idols," 1 Cor 10:14). He does not judge it as an act of idolatry that the "strong" Christians went to private dinner parties and ate food offered as a sacrifice at the domestic cults (and most probably including the rite of ancestor veneration).[76] Rather, Paul commands them to consider as primary the conscience of other fellow Christians and then decide whether or not to exercise their right (*exousia*) to eat food offered in sacrifice (10:28–29).

At this point, we have a crucial question unsolved: Why does Paul here challenge both the "strong" and "weak" Corinthian Christians? This is because the issue of eating food offered in sacrifice, to some extent, caused—or at least was a symptom of—the problem of *schismata* among the members in the Corinthian Christian community (11:18–19). In 1 Corinthians 10:23–33, therefore, it is Paul's major concern that every Corinthian Christian, whether "weak" or "strong," should use his or her

---

75. See Hays, *Corinthians*, 174. In the previous passages Paul blamed the "strong" Christians' inappropriate conduct and challenged them to stop it on behalf of the "weak" ones (see 1:26–29; 4:8–13; 5:6–13; 6:12; 7:36; 8:1–6; 9:22; 10:14, 23).

76. A. T. Cheung and J. P. Heil correctly argue that at dinner parties "in private homes . . . there is no necessary or presumptive connection between food and idolatry . . . This kind of meal is unlike . . . temple meals [in which *eidōlothuta* are most probably served] . . . Paul's advice in this case . . . [is that they] simply eat; it is not necessary [for them] to know the nature of the food" (Cheung, *Idol*, 157; Heil, *Scripture*, 167 n. 19).

right (or liberty) for building up the *ekklēsia* of God (vv. 23, 32)[77] for "the good" and "advantage" of other fellow Christians, not for his or her own good and advantage (v. 24, 33); for the sake of the conscience of fellow brothers and sisters in Christ (vv. 28-29); for the glory of God (v. 32) and the sake of the gospel (cf. 9:23); and for salvation of other people (v. 33; 9:22). In other words, Paul insisted that all Corinthian Christians should use their *exousia* to build up unity in the Christian community rather than to allow judging to cause *schismata* in it. Furthermore, Paul encouraged every Corinthian Christian to imitate the way he behaved as a servant of Christ crucified (11:1): He made himself a slave to all in order to win more of slaves for Christ (9:19) and became "weak" to the "weak" in order to win the "weak" (9:22).

This Pauline message provides a challenge to (conservative) Korean Protestants to re-evaluate ancestral veneration in their Korean Confucian context. (Conservative) Korean Protestants tend to judge ancestral veneration from the perspective of Korean-Protestant traditional interpretations of it and to reject it as idol worship. They see it as a religious act or an act of worship in which participants are believed to give exclusive devotion to the spirits of deceased ancestors. (Conservative) Korean Protestants tend not to consider it as an essential and integral part of Korean traditional customs and as akin to the daily etiquette of greeting and conversation in which younger people pay respect to older ones.[78] Korean Protestants might be encouraged to regard ancestor veneration

---

77. In 1 Corinthians (8:1; 10:23; 14:3) the phrase "to build up'" is "paralleled to encouragement and consolation . . . Paul uses the language of ["to build up"] in connection with everyday situations like the tensions between the strong and the weak, and the problem of food offered to idols (8:1—10:22) and (the issue of household cults (10:23—11:1))" (Stettler, "Command," 45; words in brackets are mine).

"For Paul [the words 'to build up"] should characterize . . . Christian behavior in a general way: benefiting others (6:12; 10:23; 12:7; 14:6) and seeking the good of others (10:24) . . . [The phrase "to build up"] is further characterized by serving one another, carrying one another's burdens and pleasing one another, not oneself. Finally, according to 1 Cor 8:1 [the phrase "to build up"] is synonymous to love: love builds up (similarly Eph 4:16). Therefore for Paul building one another up is synonymous with serving one another in love," ibid., 45-46; words in brackets are mine.

78. Mark Brett correctly states, "wherever veneration of ancestors is constitutive of culture, the way in which these practices are absorbed into Christian faith will present complex theological issues . . . (But) they will need to be considered carefully within the affected communities, without one side claiming superiority over the other" (Brett, "Ancestral").

as a practice of commemorating the word and deed of their deceased ancestors and expressing veneration and respect towards them.

Lung-Kwong Lo argues a similar position in the Chinese Confucian context, since a similar controversy on ancestral veneration occurs in Chinese Christianity. Lo suggests that Chinese ancestral veneration has to be viewed from "the perspective of gospel and cultures" rather than "gospel and religions."[79] Furthermore, K. K. Yeo defines the practice of ancestor veneration as an act of filial piety that the Chinese are culturally encouraged to perform towards their deceased ancestors, and states, "to advise the Chinese not to practice ancestor veneration . . . is implicitly advising them not to be Chinese, not to love their parents, not practice love, etc."[80]

Even Western theologians are beginning to see the relevance of this argument to their culture. J. Moltmann encourages his Western readers to open their consciousness and acknowledge the presence of their deceased ancestors in their consciences and memories. He argues that the things that happen to a father or mother impact the conscience and lives of his or her children; for example, "the sins of the fathers burden the conscience of their children. The blessings of the ancestors fulfill the lives of their offspring."[81] He further states, "in modern Western countries (people) need a new culture of memory in order no longer to live (their) days as individuals, but rather to look beyond those days."[82]

These scholars' arguments would challenge (conservative) Korean Protestants to be freed to explore another way to assimilate their Christian faith into their Korean-Confucian tradition and culture rather than separate the former from the latter. We do not have to think that they commit a sin of compromising their faith in God with paganism and heresy. Furthermore, we need to have a less judgmental attitude towards Korean Confucianism and ancestor veneration in order to build up Korean Confucian traditions and customs within our Christian faith or the other way around. Yet, this has to be done as long as it does not damage and distort the gospel message. Moreover, before we devalue ancestor veneration as idolatry and express an exclusive attitude towards it and to non-Christians performing it, we would do well to consider the

---

79. Lo, "Chinese," 134, 136.
80. Yeo, "Interpretation," 309.
81. Moltmann, "Respect," 22–23.
82. Ibid., 21.

important Pauline message of unity among members in the Christian family and communities. Thereby, Korean Christians may be encouraged to use our *exousia* to give no offence to anyone around us but to build up Christian homes and communities, not to seek our own benefit but that of others, and to further the transforming presence of Christ's presence both within the *ekklēsia* and thereby, ultimately, in the wider community as well (1 Cor 10:24-33).

MONOETHNIC COMMUNITY[83]

The ethnic composition of the Christian *ekklēsia* at Roman Corinth has been necessarily examined from the perspective of diverse ethnic communities because the Corinthian congregation no doubt reflected the wider multicultural and multiethnic community. It consisted of people of different ethnic origins (1 Cor 1:11, 22, 23; 12:12; 16:12-19; cf. Acts 18:1-28; Rom 16 1-3, 23). This is simply a reflection of the ethnic and cultural makeup of the wider civic society at Roman Corinth in the first century. As seen earlier, in the time of Paul at Corinth there was a diversity of ethnic migrant communities including the Romans, Jews, and Greeks who came from all over the Roman Empire.

Such ethnic diversity of the people in first-century Roman Corinth can be paralleled with the cultural and ethnic makeup of Australia's population in our time. A large number of ethnic immigrants have come to Australia from all over the world. They have lived together in Australia in an increasingly multicultural society. For example, in Melbourne and the State of Victoria people from over 140 nations live and a total of 151 languages are spoken.[84] In 1973 the term "multiculturalism" was first introduced into Australia. In 1977 multiculturalism was recommended as a public policy describing Australia as a multicultural society.[85] Meanwhile, all of them have also continued in their own distinctive ethnic groups: an English community, an Italian, a Chinese, a Korean, an American, an Australian born, and so on, and have been bearing their own cultural backgrounds and practicing their customs and celebrating their traditional festivals.

---

83. A modified version of this section is published. See my "1 Corinthians 12:12-13."

84. Online: http://www.monash.edu/international/australia/.

85. For a detailed explanation of Australia's multicultural policy, see online: http://www.immi.gov.au/facts/06evolution.htm.

Furthermore, the demographic make-up of Australia in the next fifteen years is foretold,

> In his latest set of projections, based on migration trends of the past 10 years, Charles Price has estimated that in the year 2025, people of Anglo-Celtic background will make up 62 percent, and people of other European origins 15 percent of the total population; that is, a total of 77 percent will be of European background. People of Asian background will make up 16 percent of the total population. Among the Asians, the Chinese will be the largest ethnic group at 7 percent. Four percent of the population will be of Middle Eastern (including Lebanese, Turkish, and Egyptian) origins and 2 percent of Aboriginal and Torres Strait Islander background.[86]

Responding to this multiculturalism, many Australian churches have a vision to become multi-cultural communities comprising a diversity of small ethnic groups. Each group intermingles with other ethnic groups in the wider church community, but the church highly values and encourages each member to practice their own customs and traditions and to observe their own cultural festivals. This is based on my previous pastoral experience at Oakleigh Baptist church in Victoria, Australia, a few years ago. During my ministry, the church was a multicultural, multinational and multilingual community where people spoke three different languages (English, Korean, and French) in Sunday services.[87]

Korea, however, differs from Roman Corinth in the first century and Australia in our time in terms of its ethnic and cultural formation. Roman Corinth and Australia are alike as multicultural and multiethnic societies, whereas Korea is a monocultural and monoethnic one. For 5,000 years of history, Korea has carefully kept its race, language, and culture homogeneous, although it was invaded and occupied several times by the neighboring countries China and Japan. Consequently, the Koreans are described as a uniquely homogeneous ethnic group with their own language, culture, and customs. They are "purely of one common blood origin."[88]

---

86. Online: http://www.aph.gov.au/Library/Pubs/rn/1996-97/97rn19.htm.

87. For this type of ministry, see Anderson, *Multicultural*, 137–60; Garces-Foley, *Crossing*, 79–102, 139–50.

88. Choi, "Review of *Gender*," (online: http://koreaweb.ws/ks/ksr/ksr02-03.htm); Lee, "National," 9; cf. Pai and Tangherlini, *Nationalism*.

Many Koreans are proud of their racial purity and even claim it to be an integral part of their national identity. This is drawn from the strong influence of the spirit of *danil minjok* (which literally means one nation and also refers to a homogeneous race or a pureblooded nation) that originated from the myth of *Dan goon*, the founder of *han minjok* (the Korean nation). This spirit has passed on to Koreans from generation to generation for several thousands of years and has deeply penetrated into the Korean mentality. Thus, it has played a vital and significant role in forming and shaping Korean culture, just as Confucianism has (see above). It helped bring the Koreans together as one nation and promote a unity among them to resist Japanese imperialism in the early twentieth century.[89] Furthermore, the spirit of *danil minjok* helps both North and South Koreans find something culturally and historically in common between them and makes it easier to dialogue for unification. Just as with Confucianism, so this spirit of *danil minjok* is an essential part of the national identity for both countries beyond the differences of political ideology.[90]

On the other hand, the spirit of *danil minjok* has also had a critical and negative impact upon the Korean mentality in that some racism (*injong chabyl*) exists. Many Koreans over-emphasize the importance of their racial purity and the role of the spirit of *danil minjok* in shaping Korean national identity. This causes them to have exclusive attitudes towards people of different races and different skin colors. It can encourage Koreans to have racist ideologies and to consider their own nation superior to others. This racist ideology is also manifested in the policy of the South Korean government. Its constitution prohibits Koreans from possessing dual citizenship. For example, a Korean who lives in a foreign country such as Australia and gains citizenship there is forced to surrender their Korean citizenship.[91]

Many Koreans understand this racism in a way that is analogous to social class. They view themselves as ranking higher than other nations, who have different skin colors and mixed blood. In other words,

---

89. Choi, "Review of *Gender*," 1.

90. Cf. Ryu, *North*; Breen, *Koreans*, 246–47. This argument cannot be developed further here.

91. Yet, it is noted that the current Myong-Bak Yi government has submitted a proposal to the Korean parliament early 2010. An important part of the proposal is to amend Korean constitution to allow limited Koreans to possess dual citizenship (see Hong Ki Hye Jun, online: http://www.pressian.com/article/article.asp?article_num=60100413143453).

they regard themselves as *yangban* (which refers to the highest class) and other nations as *sangmin* (which literally means common people) or *chonmin* (which literally means people of lowest class). This sort of racism lies at the bottom of Korean mentality because of the strong influence of the spirit of *danil minjok*. Similarly, commentators such as Michael Breen claim that Korean people are too "nationalistic and have a racist obsession with their blood."[92] It appears, therefore, that many foreigners who live in Korea feel discriminated and rejected by Koreans in general.[93]

Further, many Koreans, whose mentality has been strongly influenced by the spirit of *danil minjok* and whose race is homogeneous, would not be able to empathize with those people who have mixed blood, mixed culture, and mixed ethnic origins. Because of these reasons, many Koreans would tend to avoid people of such mixed cultural backgrounds. Some of them have a very strong exclusive, and even hostile, attitude towards other Koreans who marry spouses of different ethnic origins. They consciously exclude such Koreans from the mainstream of Korean society.

Furthermore, the spirit of *danil minjok* causes, to some extent, diasporal Koreans, particularly those of the first migrant generation hesitate to make intimate relationships and intermingle with people of different ethnic and cultural origins in multicultural and multiethnic societies such as Australia and America. Of course, these Koreans may bond much more closely and encourage the formation of their own ethnic and cultural community where they might, without hindrance, practice their own customs and observe their traditional festivals within the wider multicultural society. Yet, no doubt the spirit of *danil minjok* troubles some Koreans in the building up of close relationships and friendships and interweaving with people who come from different nations and different linguistic, cultural, and ethnic backgrounds. Moreover, the spirit of *danil minjok* leads diasporal Koreans to form their own exclusive ethnic communities that are isolated socially and culturally from other ethnic communities within the wider multicultural society and even from the host society. They have no close link with other ethnic communities. They rather tend to establish a small Korean community that has more intimate contacts with their home country than the country and society

92. Breen, *Koreans*, 28.
93. Ibid.

where they reside at the present time. Furthermore, Korean migrant churches tend to keep their own monocultural tradition and to have exclusive attitudes towards people of different ethnic origins in a wider multicultural society.[94] D. A. Carson thus criticizes this exclusiveness of Korean migrant churches in America.[95]

Therefore, it is argued that the spirit of *danil minjok* has led, to some extent, to improper behavior among some Koreans. It also causes some Koreans to have exclusive attitudes towards, and discriminate against, people of different ethnic, linguistic, and cultural backgrounds. This ethnocentric behavior appears to be similar to that of some of the Corinthian Christians in the day of Paul. They possessed wealth and high status and tended to have exclusive attitudes towards the others of low status. These tendencies developed into divisions among the members in the Corinthian Christian community (1 Cor 11:18-19; 12:25). In reaction to this inappropriate attitude, Paul insists that they should all be united in one spirit regardless of different races and different social classes. This is attested in his words, "For just as the body is one and has many members, and all the members of the body, though many, are one body, so it is with Christ. For by one Spirit we were all baptized into one body—Jews or Greek, slaves or free—and all were made to drink of one Spirit" (1 Cor 12:12-13). In these words, Paul appears to have encouraged the Corinthian Christian community to transcend ethnic, gender, and social boundaries and to be open and welcoming to people of different ethnic origins and different social classes.[96] This idea is also clearly exhibited in Galatians 3:28 (cf. Col 3:11) where Paul says, "there is neither Jew nor Greek . . . neither slave nor free . . . neither male nor female; for you are all one in Christ Jesus." For a better understanding of Paul's broader idea of openness and inclusiveness toward people of different ethnic, gender, and social backgrounds in his epistles, these texts including Galatians 3:28 need to be carefully examined, since they address the same issues of ethnic and cultural identity.

In recent Pauline scholarship, the interpretation of Galatians 3:28 is controversial. John M. G. Barclay claims that in Galatians 3:28 Paul argues that in the Christian community, the gospel and love of Christ should be emphasized more than any particular ethnic cultural traditions, and

---

94. See Moon, "Dream," 233-34; Han, "Multicultural," 114-35.
95. Carson, *Love*, 95.
96. See Park, *Either*, 55; also Chia, "Review on Yee," 210.

that the commitment to Christ enables Christians to encompass simultaneously diverse cultural particularities. This is because the gospel of Christ creates a new community where ethnic and cultural barriers are broken down among its members and variant cultural traditions can be practiced. A particular culture such as the Jewish one should not be "absolutized or allowed to gain hegemony" in this new community.[97] This, however, does not mean Jewish Christians were pressured to abandon observance of their cultural customs such as circumcision, Sabbath, and dietary laws.[98] In agreement with Barclay's analysis, it is argued that, in the same way, Paul's teachings in 1 Corinthians do not require Koreans to deny their entire cultural heritage in favor of "Western Christianity."

In opposition to this view, however, Daniel Boyarin states that Galatians 3:28 shows the Pauline idea of "a non-differentiated, non-hierarchical humanity," whereby Paul sought to eradicate human difference as expressed in terms of ethnicity, hierarchy, and gender.[99] He instead claimed a "universal humanity" and coerced a sameness that neglects cultural differences and ethnicity.[100] In this way, according to Boyarin, Paul disregarded and devalued human cultural particularities, especially those of the Jews. Thereby, Paul devalued the genealogy of the Jews and the significance of circumcision in Jewish ethnicity, which was "the very symbol of genealogy."[101] Further evidence of this is that Paul allegorized and spiritualized literal and physical circumcision and described it as a spiritual experience in Christ.[102]

Such a program of "ethnic cleansing" in the name of Paul's gospel is evident in some aspects of the Western Christian mission to Korea. As stated above, for example, from their Western Christian perspective, early Christian missionaries to Korea devalued the significance of ancestral veneration in Korean culture and regarded it as idolatry. Yet it plays an essential part in shaping Korean-Confucian cultural identity.[103]

Philip F. Esler, in some agreement with Boyarin, asserts that "an ethnic ascription is one which classifies persons in terms of their basic,

97. Barclay, "Multiculturalism," 211.
98. See ibid.; also *Mediterranean*, 385.
99. Boyarin, *Radical*, 8.
100. Ibid., 7–8, 95, 215, 257.
101. Ibid., 8, 120.
102. Ibid., 80, 144–45.
103. See Hangook Kidokgyo, *Kidokgyoeui*, 76–80.

most general identity . . . determined by their origin and background."[104] The Jews in the Christian community of Galatia ascribed to themselves "the status of an ethnic group by reference to their descent from their glorious ancestors Abraham (and Sarah)."[105] This Jewish ascription motivated the Jews to maintain their ethnic identity and to defend the boundaries which separated them from the Gentiles. According to Esler, Paul however opposed them and redefined Abraham's descendants as only those who believed in Jesus Christ as Savior, rather than the Jews. "Mixed Jewish-Gentile table fellowship" seriously attacked such Jewish identity boundaries.[106] So the Jews and strict Jewish-Christians banned the Gentiles from participating in table fellowship with them. As a result, in the Christian community of Galatia there were inter-group conflicts between some Jewish believers and the Gentile believers.[107] Esler sees it as inevitable that a new "ethnos"—that of the "Christians"—will eventually replace all ethnic differences.

This sort of understanding leads some Korean Christians (as it did some Western missionaries beforehand) to believe that all Christians, regardless of their different ethnic origins, will end up as members of the same universal culture, as it were, a "Kingdom-of-God" culture—a culture which often just reflects the "invisible" dominant culture rather than a transforming "Christian" multiculture. Therein, no one claims his or her own ethnic cultural particularity but instead embraces a general universal Christian "ethnos" and culture as his or her new ethnic cultural identity. In so doing, some Korean Christians put more emphasis on engagement in "the task of participation in God's own work of establishing his reign in the world" than on considering the expression and practice of their own assumed ethnic cultural customs in wider multicultural societies such as Australia and America.[108] It is a reflection of this, for example, that Korea is the world's second largest country today in terms of engagement in Christian world-missions and sending Christian missionaries overseas.[109]

---

104. Esler, "Boundaries," 222.
105. Ibid.
106. Ibid., 225.
107. Ibid., 228–30.
108. Moon, "Dream," 247.

109. "The Korea World Missions Association has released recently some statistics on the Korean mission. The number of Korean missionaries as of February 2006 is

Some Korean Christians (including myself, formerly) believe that conversion to the Christian faith challenges us to stop expressing our own Korean-Confucian cultural identity and leave it behind, and instead accept a brand new Christian (church) culture or a "Kingdom-of-God" culture. We consider the former secular and are opposed to the latter. We also think that the two cultures should not coexist in a church and that every church all around the world, no matter where it is located, should neglect the cultural particularity of its immediate context and have the same Christian and "Kingdom-of-God" culture.

There is, however, a question unsolved: is that the whole point that Paul addresses in Galatians 3:28 as well as 1 Corinthians 12:13? In these texts Paul appears not to argue that ethnic, cultural, social, and gender distinctions (differentiations) should be removed from his communities (1 Cor 7:17–24; Gal 2:15; cf. Col 3:22). Rather, he encourages Christians to maintain their racial (cultural) particularities and social status ("Every one should remain in the state in which he or she was called," 1 Cor 7:20) and be transformed/renewed from within. Paul, for example, argues that Gentile-believers (the uncircumcised) in Corinth did not need to become like Jewish-believers (the circumcised). Paul says, "Was any one at the time of his call uncircumcised? Let him not seek circumcision" (1 Cor 7:18). He also maintains that Christ-believing slaves "did not cease to be slaves" except (and significantly so) in the eyes of God and the *ekklēsia* (1 Cor 7:21–22; cf. Col 3:22).[110]

Nonetheless, as Dunn claims, in Galatians 3:28 Paul is saying that these factors, "as distinctions, marking racial, social and gender differentiation, which were thought to indicate or imply relative worth or value or privileged status before God, . . . no longer have that significance" in Christian communities.[111] In other words, no particular ethnic people such as the Jews find any privileged favor in the eyes of God or benefit, by observance of their cultural customs, to become justified and reckoned righteous before God. Instead, all, regardless of whether they are Jews or Gentiles, are justified by (or through) faith in and of Jesus Christ (Gal 2:16–17). Yet Paul does not suggest that the Jewish believers should ban practicing their cultural traditions in the Christian community. He,

---

14,086 in 180 countries (about 19,000 according to non-official counts)" (online: http://www.international.ucla.edu/korea/events/showevent.asp?eventid=5347).

110. Dunn, *Galatians*, 207; similarly Witherington, *Grace*, 278.

111. Dunn, *Galatians*, 207.

rather, appears to have encouraged them (not proselytes) to exercise their traditional customs and maintain Jewish identity as long as these Jewish customs were not seen as a means for justification in Christ (Gal 2:15–21; cf. Rom 3:1–2).

Furthermore, it appears that Paul recognized the existence of ethnic (cultural), social, and sexual barriers among the members in the Galatian Christian community. He thus commanded all the Galatian believers to be united in Jesus Christ who transcends such racial, social, and gender distinctions.[112] Paul states, "... you are all one in Christ Jesus" (Gal 3:28). As Dunn states:

> In which case the character of the "oneness" becomes clear: not as a leveling and abolishing of all racial, social or gender differences, but as an integration of just such differences into a common participation "in Christ," wherein they enhance (rather than detract from) the unity of the body, and enrich the mutual interdependence and service of its members. In other words, it is a oneness, because such differences cease to be a barrier and cause of pride or regret or embarrassment, and become rather a means to display the diverse richness of God's creation and grace, both in the acceptance of the "all" and in the gifting of each.[113]

In a similar sense, Paul insists on unity in diversity among the social and racial factions of the Corinthian Christians in 1 Corinthians 12:12–13. He admonished them to be united as one body of Christ (v. 12) and "bonded together by the Spirit" (v. 13), since their ethnic (cultural) and social differentiation caused *schismata* in the Christian community (1 Cor 1:10; 11:18–19).[114] In other words, Paul encouraged them to leave the improper conduct of factionalism and transcend their racial, cultural, and social barriers. They should then embrace one another as brothers and sisters in Christ, no matter what race and no matter what social class they belonged to.

This distinctive Pauline message presents a challenge to Korean Christians who have ethnocentric tendencies, to develop inclusive attitudes towards people of different races and different ethnic origins. This is also an encouragement to (re)build Christian communities to be more multicultural and welcoming of all people, regardless of different ethnic

---

112. See Witherington, *Grace*, 278.
113. Dunn, *Galatians*, 208.
114. Hays, *Corinthians*, 214.

and social backgrounds. This reflects Paul's ecclesiological vision. He was an advocator of Christian communities that comprise a diversity of ethnic/cultural, social/economic, age and gender distinctions, but which maintain harmony and unity among followers of Jesus (1 Cor 12:12–14; Gal 3:28).

Conclusion

Throughout the work, 1 Corinthians 1–4 has been investigated in terms of social and rhetorical approaches for two reasons. One is that these methods have provided the most helpful understandings to the background of the Corinthian Christian behavior that Paul addresses. The other is that these methods (especially the rhetorical perspectives) have helped us re-read Corinthian conduct and Paul's reaction to it from within a Korean-Confucian Christian context. We have thus attempted a cross-cultural conversation between two extremely different horizons, the first-century Corinthian Christian situation and the twenty-first century Korean-Confucian Christian context. In this cross-cultural conversation, four parties—Paul, his Corinthian audience, myself, and my readers (twenty-first century Korean Christians)—were invited to a dialogue table. These four parties talked to each other and asked each other different questions and supplied different answers.

At the outset, in chapter 1, a wide range of scholarly hypotheses about the identification of Paul's Corinthian opponents as implied in 1 Corinthians were dealt with. Those of Winter and Pogoloff motivated us to reconstruct the social and cultural situation of 1 Corinthians 1–4 in terms of rhetorical and social perspectives. Winter in particular explores analogies between the behavior of some Corinthian Christians of wealth and high social status and sophistic tendencies in the wider society. These tendencies include student–teacher relationships, patron–client bonds, a spirit of competitiveness and rivalry, the preference for rhetorical abilities, and the high value given to wisdom and eloquence. Such behavior appears to have been heavily influenced by the social and cultural conventions of first-century Roman Corinth, and to have played a crucial factor in causing divisions in the Corinthian Christian community, as evident in 1 Corinthians 1–4.

Yet Pogoloff, in a similar way to P. W. Gooch, argues that Paul did not reject Greco-Roman rhetorical traditions as such, but rather the behavior of his Corinthian opponents who expressed uncritically the cultural and social values of wisdom and eloquence in the Christian community. This argument has challenged us to see that no Christian can be free from the impact of the cultural and social practices that predominate in the life of the society where he or she was born and lives. To demonstrate this, Paul uses rhetorical patterns and skills in writing 1 Corinthians 1–4, in order to argue against the uncritical absorption of human wisdom. Hence, we do not have to see, in a completely negative way, the contribution of Korean-Confucian traditions and customs to the formation of Korean-Christian faith. Korean-Confucianism has had a profound influence upon the lives of Koreans today, regardless of their religious persuasion. Nonetheless, we need to develop more critical reflection on the Korean-Confucian influences shaping Korean Christian traditions that are in danger of distorting the biblical processes and message, and especially that of Paul in 1 Corinthians 1–4.

In chapter 2, the rhetorical sensibilities of Roman Corinth in the time of Paul were reconstructed. Greco-Roman rhetorical traditions, and especially Cicero's rhetorical legacy, would have had a major role in determining the social behavior of the Corinthians in the mid-first century CE. Hence, Cicero's rhetorical handbooks were used as the principal guide to define 1 Corinthians 1–4 as a rhetorical discourse. It was thereby demonstrated that the Pauline text comprises the characteristics of both deliberative and epideictic rhetoric and that there are specific similarities between Cicero's rhetorical handbooks and the Pauline language of 1 Corinthians 1–4 in terms of their use of the words, "boasting" and "imitate." Yet these words are closely related to the Corinthian Christian preference for social and worldly understandings of wisdom and eloquence as described in 1 Corinthians 1–4. In other words, Paul both uses and critiques Greco-Roman rhetorical patterns and their social legacy.

In chapter 3, the deep impact of patronage on the civic life of the Corinthians in the time of Paul was explored. The Corinthian people, regardless of social status, were interconnected as patron and clients by patronal systems that had an adverse effect on the communal life of the gathered followers of Jesus. The majority of these Corinthian Christians were poor and of low social status, for whom patronage was a means of survival in the wider Corinthian civic society. Because of this, the poor Christians could hardly refuse the patronal proposals of fellow Christians of wealth and high social status. On the other hand, to wealthy and high social-class Christians, patronage would be understood as a means of extending and reproducing their social influence in the Christian community. It would also be natural for these wealthy Christians to use their patronal networks to take control of the Christian community and keep it under their authority. Consequently, this patronage-based behavior in the Christian community appears to have caused tensions with Paul as indicated in 1 Corinthians, especially chapter 9.

By using their money and social prestige, some of the wealthy and high social-class Christians appear to have assumed they would have leadership positions and become patrons of the Corinthian Christian *ekklēsia*. They then assumed that they would establish patronal relationships with Paul and offered him financial support. Nevertheless, Paul refused to accept their financial support (1 Cor 9:12, 15–19). In their offer of monetary gifts, he saw that they were strongly influenced by the social phenomenon of patronal systems and social control through money and status. He did not want them to implicate him and take advantage of their patronal networks and continue to exercise their social privilege in the Christian community. Rather, he reminded them that their social privilege and patronal hierarchical systems did not ensure leadership positions and give them the right to take control of the Christian *ekklēsia* (1 Cor 1:26–29). Paul further challenged them to make a pure commitment to the gospel of Christ crucified, which he preached to everyone free of charge (1 Cor 9:15–18).

In the next part of chapter 3, the social environment of Roman Corinth in the day of Paul was investigated. The city was crowded with a great number of inhabitants and a wide range of people groups who migrated and visited from all over the Roman Empire. Paul made a number of Corinthian converts in such social circumstances. Hence, the Pauline community at Corinth was made up of a diversity of social and ethnic backgrounds, though there were three major ethnic groups: Greeks, Jews, and Romans. The members of Greek origin were the largest group in number, and those of Jewish origin were the second largest (see 1 Cor 1:22; 12:13). Most of these two groups were poor and of the socially lower classes, although there were a few wealthy and high social status members. By contrast, the members of Roman origin were the minority group in number, but many of them possessed wealth and higher social positions.

In the last part of chapter 3, the social and ethnic distinctions among the Corinthian Christians were explored. These distinctions seem to have also been a cause of conflicts in the Christian community (1 Cor 1:10–12; 11:18–19). In response to these conflicts, Paul reminds the Corinthians that he himself baptized Crispus, Gaius, and Stephanas, who were the key leaders of each ethnic group (1 Cor 1:14–16). In so doing, Paul argues that though the Corinthian congregation comprised different ethnic groups and social classes, it should be united as the body of Christ (1 Cor 12:12–31). Furthermore, Paul seems to have deliberately named Stephanas, together with Crispus and Gaius, as an afterthought of special note (1:14–16). Paul would have known that more prominent members of the Corinthian congregation followed Crispus and Gaius as leaders than Stephanas because of their higher social status. Paul, however, draws attention to the dedication to the Christian community of the household of Stephanas again, just before the completion of 1 Corinthians (16:15–18). This would be part of Paul's rhetorical strategy. He appears to have presented Stephanas (and his household) as the best example of the whole congregation to follow in terms of Christian ethics, leadership, and dedication to the Christian mission in Corinth.

In chapter 4, it was exhibited that Paul criticizes the behavior of the Corinthian Christians in misusing Greco-Roman rhetorical conventions and patronal systems in the Christian community. The frequently occurring phrase *sophia logou* refers to the cultural-conventions-oriented wisdom and eloquence that some Corinthian Christians of wealth and high social status valued more highly than Jesus Christ crucified and the gospel message which Paul preached in Corinth (1:18–25). They also boasted about themselves as possessing such human-based wisdom and rhetorical skills and even encouraged fellow Christians of lower social class to imitate them. This is reflected to some extent in Paul's ironic use of "boasting" and "imitator" (1 Cor 1:29–31; 4:16). Paul deliberately uses these two words, and also refers to himself as the "father" of them, for rhetorical effect in 1 Corinthians 1–4 (1:29; 3:18; 4:7, 15). In so doing, he subverted the social- and cultural-conventions-rooted thinking and behavior expressed in the Christian community. Paul demonstrates Christ crucified as the wisdom of God and gives the highest value to him (1

Cor 1:24). He further challenges the Christians to boast of Jesus Christ as the Lord (1:31) and imitate the humility and sacrifice he exercised as a servant of God (4:8–13, 16).

In chapter 5, it was hypothesized that some Corinthians would have considered the Christian community as similar to a kind of *collegia*, *collegia tenuiorum*, and *collegia sodalicia* where patronage commonly operated to interconnect patrons and clients of a diversity of social levels within the social associations. This group of wealthy Corinthian Christians continued to assume the validity of hierarchical patronal systems and boasted about their social privilege and prestige in the Christian *ekklēsia*. To challenge them to leave behind such behavior, Paul differentiates the fundamental structure of the Corinthian congregation from that of such *collegia*. Contrasting with the latter, he describes the former as an *oikos* community where God is the only *paterfamilias* and all the members are interconnected as brothers and sisters in Christ and share the love of God the Father and Jesus Christ the Lord (1 Cor 13:1–13).

Nevertheless, though Paul is critical of some aspects of Greco-Roman social and cultural conventions; he himself makes use of such conventions and persuasive rhetorical strategies, even briefly claiming to be a *paterfamilias* of the community (1 Cor 4:15) in order to effect change. In so doing, he does not devalue the Corinthian Christians' ethnic particularities and traditional customs (especially those of the Jews) (see 1 Cor 1:26; 7:17–24). He does argue against a particular ethnic group claiming superiority over the other (1 Cor 12:13) because these social, cultural, and ethnic elements played a major role in dividing the Corinthian Christians into factions (1 Cor 1:10; 3:3; 11:18–19). To reclaim them from the grips of factionalism, Paul presents Jesus Christ as the one who transcends social, cultural, and racial boundaries and encourages the Christians to exercise unity and harmony in Christ as one body (12:12–13).

The attitude Paul expressed towards Greco-Roman social and cultural elements that characterized the social fabric and civic life of first-century Roman Corinth, motivates us to see the value of Korean-Confucian cultural traditions and customs where we were born and have lived. These traditions and customs have heavily influenced, and deeply penetrated, the lives of Korean people for hundreds of years. Hence, it is impossible to speak of Korean culture without referring to Korean Confucianism. The mixed Pauline attitude toward Greco-Roman culture provides significant analogies and insights for us in attempting to re-read 1 Corinthians from our own cultural perspective.

In chapter 7, following chapter 6 where a summary of the rhetorical and social analysis was provided, the reconstruction of the social and rhetorical background of the Corinthian behavior and Paul's response to it as addressed in 1 Corinthians was evaluated from a Korean-Confucian Christian context. In so doing, a cross-cultural dialogue between the two polarizing social and cultural contexts, that of the mid–first century Roman Corinth and that of twenty-first century Korea, was attempted. Analogies, intersections, and differences in these two contexts were also explored. In this intercultural dialogue, a collective methodology of historical, social (sociological), philosophical, and contextual approaches was employed, rather than the same methods—social and rhetorical approaches—as used for the reconstruction of the social and rhetorical environment of 1 Corinthians 1–4. In particular, the rhetorical perspective is not so helpful for the investigation of the Confucian situation of Korean society. The civic society of first-century Roman Corinth was influenced by Greco-Roman social and cultural conventions such as rhetorical and patronal elitism. Korean society, in contrast, does not place much importance on eloquence as such. Koreans instead consider written documents more important than eloquent speech. It is commonly understood in Korean society that to gain higher social status and take leadership positions, one should obtain good marks in the written—not oral—exams that the Korean government provides or those of the giant private companies.

Nevertheless, historical analysis was used to examine the history of Korean Confucianism, especially as exemplified in the life of T'oegye, and to study Confucian understandings of wisdom. In a social (sociological) sense, we have explored how Korean Confucianism has influenced to a large extent the structural formation of Korean society (e.g., social, educational, family, political, and religious structures) and the shaping of a Korean worldview, mentality, and social behavior was explored. On this basis, we have attempted to re-read some of Paul's critique of Greco-Roman culture within Korean-Confucian culture, with the following insights.

Korean-Confucian-rooted wisdom (as exemplified by T'oegye's legacy) deeply penetrates the life of Korean churches and Christian communities. Some Korean Christians insist on the importance of social achievements and boast of their social prestige in the Christian communities due to the strong influence of Korean Confucianism and its emphasis on wisdom, education, knowledge, and the reputation of person and family. Hence, some Korean Christians who are wealthy, educated, and of high social status easily dominate leadership positions in the church, while poor and uneducated Christians are marginalized from decision-making groups. In reaction to this, however, I have presented Paul as arguing that no one should boast about his or her social privilege—wisdom, high education, wealth, power, and high social status—but about Jesus Christ crucified as the wisdom of God in Christian communities (1 Cor 1:26–29).

Korean Christians were compelled to attend Shinto shrine worship by the Japanese government during Japanese imperialism in the early twentieth century. Some Christians regarded it as idol worship, while others understood it as an act of demonstrating respect to a Japanese emperor. This caused divisions among members in the Christian communities at that time, and even affects many Korean Christians today, who tend to blame those forefathers who expressed veneration to Shinto shrines, and judge them as compromising their Christian faith with the world and committing idolatry against God. In response to this issue, we have suggested the primacy of Paul's argument that it is, rather, a sin to damage the conscience of another by our deeds and words, causing the Christian community to split, and that one should take care lest our behavior wound the conscience of another and lest it cause the person to fall (1 Cor 8:9–10).

Ancestral ritual continues to be a controversial issue in Korean Christian (Protestant) homes today. In some Christian homes the issue of ancestor veneration causes divisions among family members. Some express a critical attitude towards ancestral commemoration and see it as idolatry, and others view it as a filial act whereby they venerate and commemorate the deeds and words of the dead. In response to this crucial issue, we have encouraged those Korean Christians who define ancestor veneration as idolatry, based on Exodus 20:4–5 and its wider context (20:1–23), to reconsider their understanding of the Scripture that, in fact, does not address the issue of ancestral veneration. The Hebrew word פסל ('idol') in such biblical verses does not mean to include their dead ancestors—such as Abraham and Jacob—as those whom the people of

Israel worshiped as idols. It can be concluded, therefore, that their understanding is taken out of its biblical context.

Moreover, Paul does not refer to Exodus 20:4-5 in 1 Corinthians 10:23—11:1, where he seems to address the issue of eating food at domestic dinner parties in the context of household cults and most probably ancestral veneration (10:27). Paul, here, appears not to challenge the Corinthian believers to remove the performance of household (and ancestral) rites from their homes. This is clearly a different attitude from that which he expressed in the preceding verses (10:1-22) as part of the broader context (1 Cor 8:1—10:22). In these texts, Paul does argue against some Corinthian Christians who appear to have acted on their superior knowledge and participated in dinner feasts taking place in the context of the worship of gods and emperors in temples and involving imperial cults. These dinner feasts commonly included sexual immorality (e.g., 1 Cor 5:1-13; 6:12-20). They thus behaved idolatrously from Paul's point of view (8:1-5), in a way similar to that of the Israelites in the wilderness (see 1 Cor 10:5-11; also Exodus chs. 13-17, 32; Numbers chs. 11, 14, 16, 20, 21, 25). To correct such idolatrous conduct, Paul takes a direct quotation from Exodus 32:6 and commands them, in an imperative tone, "Do not be idolaters as some of them (the Israelites) were; as it is written, "the people sat down to eat and drink and rose up to dance" (1 Cor 10:7), and "shun the worship of idols" (10:14). As such, we have arrived at the conclusion that in 1 Corinthians 10:23—11:1, Paul appears neither to have regarded ancestor veneration as idolatry nor challenged the Corinthian Christians to stop themselves from performing it in their homes. Rather, he seems to have introduced Moses, his deceased ancestor, as a hero and encouraged them to venerate and commemorate the deeds of his Jewish ancestors who had been "baptized into Moses" (1 Cor 10:1-4). This, also, may well be the key to understanding Paul's apparent acceptance of the practice of "baptism for the dead" (1 Cor 15:29), whereby whole households were baptized into Christ, including their ancestors.

In spite of this, many Korean Christians tend to disregard the value of ancestral veneration in Korean culture and express a critical and judgmental attitude towards it. This attitude hurts other Christians who perform it as a filial act to the dead, and further causes conflicts and divisions in the church and Christian home. In response to such attitudes, I have presented Paul as arguing that a Christian should use his or her *exousia* to build up unity and harmony in the church and Christian home rather than cause divisions in it (1 Cor 10:23, 32). Christians are called to exercise it for the advantage of fellow Christians, not for their own (10: 24, 33), for the glory of God (10:32), and for salvation of other people (10:33; 9:22). I have also encouraged Korean Christians to have a less judgmental attitude towards ancestor veneration. Thus, they should not consider it as idolatry but as an integral part of Korean-Confucian traditional customs and thereby build up Korean cultural customs within our Christian faith.

Nonetheless, the performance of ancestral veneration appears to consist of superstitious characteristics: participants may believe that the spirit of the dead protects their household from evil and misfortune, if they please the spirit through the ancestral rites. This superstitious element may be equated with the Christian understanding of worship by which Christians pray to God to protect their families from the harm of the Devil. Such elements incorporated into ancestral veneration would seem to be against Paul's argument in 1 Corinthians 8 that all things, including protection from evil, come from God the Father (v. 6). Christians should critically examine these sorts of superstitious ingredients in ancestral veneration before performing it in their Christian homes.

Lastly, the problem caused by the ethnic diversity among the Corinthian Christians and Paul's response to it was evaluated from a Korean-Confucian Christian context. Most Koreans have been deeply impacted by the spirit of *danil minjok* and over-emphasize the homogeneous aspect of national identity. Consequently, they tend to have an exclusive attitude towards people of different races, different skin colors, and mixed blood. This tendency further penetrates the life of Korean Christians in Korea and diaspora Korean Christians overseas, especially those of the first generation migrants. Some of these diaspora Korean Christians have difficulty building close relationships with people of different ethnic origins and different language backgrounds in multicultural societies, such as America and Australia. Many migrant Korean churches in such countries tend to be monoethnic (and monocultural) and not to welcome as members those Christians who come from different ethnic backgrounds and speak different languages. In response to Korean Christians of such ethnocentric tendencies, I have underscored the Pauline message of 1 Corinthians 12:12–13 (and Galatians 3:28). In these verses Paul does not claim that the Corinthian Christians should give up expressing their own ethnic and cultural particularities in the Christian communities. He instead refers to Jesus Christ as the agent who transcends ethnic, social, and gender distinctions (1 Cor 12:13; cf. Gal 3:28) in order to reclaim the Corinthian Christian community from the spirit of factionalism (1 Cor 1:10–12; 11:18–19). He further encourages them to break through their racial differences (and boundaries), embrace one another as sisters and brothers in Christ, and be united into one body by one Spirit (1 Cor 12:13).

As above, I have attempted a cross-cultural (or intercultural) dialogue between the two polarizing social and cultural contexts and critically evaluated the Pauline message of 1 Corinthians and chapters 1–4 from a Korean-Confucian Christian context. This sort of biblical hermeneutics encourages contemporary readers who practice the Christian faith in the context of multiculturalism (e.g., America and Australia) to value their own cultural traditions and respectfully study them. The readers can then interpret these traditions critically in terms of the biblical (Pauline) message that comes out of the early Christians' encounter between the Gospel and their social and cultural contexts. In so doing, the readers can find clues for a dialogue between Christianity and other cultures, analogous to the dialogue between the insights of this rhetorical and social analysis of 1 Corinthian 1–4 and the Korean-Confucian Christian context today.

Appendix 1

Cicero: Rhetorical Theories

CICERO SPENT HIS ADULTHOOD in the last decades (106–43 BCE) of the Roman Republic (509–31 BCE). His life reflected and represented that of the people of power and high social status in the Rome of his day. Cicero was one of the most powerful and influential men in the civic society of Rome in the first century BCE. As Plutarch (ca. 45–120 CE) states: "He had the greatest power in the state."[1] He goes on to describe Cicero's status; "Cicero's power in the city (or Rome) reached its greatest height at this time, and since he could do what he pleased . . . (Octavianus) Caesar sent messengers to Cicero begging and urging him to . . . manage affairs as he himself thought best."[2]

Dio Cassius supports this. He highlights in his *Roman History* Cicero's political career and his power by the time Julius Caesar was assassinated (March 44 BCE). When Rome was politically chaotic, he took control in the senate and united the members of the senate and protected it from factionalism. The senators valued and followed all of Cicero's advice. Cassius says, "Cicero, whose advice they (the senators) actually followed . . ."[3]

---

1. Plutarch, *Cicero*, 24.1; also 40.1; 43.1.
2. Plutarch, *Cicero*, 45.4–6.
3. Dio Cassius, *Roman History*, 44.22.

As a contemporary of Julius Caesar and Pompey, Cicero began his political career as a magistrate or *Quaestore* in 75 BCE. He then took several different positions: senator (74 BCE), *Curle Aedile* (69 BCE), *Praetor Urbanus* (66 BCE), consul (63 BCE), *Augur* (53 BCE), and proconsul of Cilicia (51–50 BCE). He was then in exile and retired from public service before the death of Julius Caesar in 44 BCE.[4]

Cicero was a significant figure in the history of Roman politics and rhetoric. Moreover, it seems impossible to speak of Roman history without dealing with him. Thus, Quayle states,

> Whatever estimate you may retain concerning Cicero, you cannot leave him out of the history of Rome . . . you cannot write a history of Rome and leave Marcus Tullius Cicero out . . . He was not the greatest man in his day, but he was the most versatile man in Rome. I take it he was the greatest man produced, save Julius Caesar only, who was a Hercules. All other men only reached to this Hercules's belt.[5]

For these reasons, the Romans of his time and the next generations were greatly influenced by Cicero and his theory of rhetoric and eloquence. An example from Plutarch illustrates this point. "I (Plutarch) learn that (Octavianus) Caesar . . . paid a visit to one of his daughter's sons; and the boy . . . had in his hands a book of Cicero . . . Caesar took the book (from him) and read a great part of it as he stood . . . then gave it back to the youth, saying: 'a learned man, my child, a learned man and a lover of his country.'"[6] Furthermore, many Romans in the first and second century CE, who spoke either Latin or Greek, were inspired by Cicero. In other words, he still lived on in the spirit of Roman and Greco-Roman culture and became an icon of Greco-Roman rhetoric in the first-century Roman world. This is clearly evidenced in Plutarch's language, "his (Cicero's) fame for oratory abides to this day."[7] In addi-

---

4. See Cicero, *Post Reditum in Senatu*, 21; *Epistularum ad Atticum*, 1.4; *Epistulae ad Familiares*, 15.4.8–10; 16.11.3; 16.12.5; Josephus, *Jewish Antiquities*, 14.66; Strabo, *Geography*, 10.2.13; Plutarch, *Cicero*, 8.1; see also Cowell, *Cicero*, 1–2, 165–269; Broughton, *Magistrates*, 97–357. In addition, W. A. Quayle names the places Cicero visited: Athens, Rhodes, Samos, Ephesus, Galatia, Antioch (in Syria), Laodicea, Cappadocia, Parthia, Phrigia, Lycaonia, Iconium, Cilicia, Tarsus, Asia, and Pamphylia (Quayle, "Cicero," 709–10).

5. Ibid.

6. Plutarch, *Cicero*, 49.5.

7. Ibid., 2.5.

tion, Cicero appears frequently in such Greek and Latin writings of the first and second century CE as Tacitus's (ca. 55–120 CE) *Dialogue de Oratoribus*, Suetonius's (ca. 75–140 CE) *De Rhetoribus*, and Dio Cassius's (ca. 150 CE–ca. 235 CE) *Roman History*. It is appropriate, therefore, to use Cicero and his rhetorical theories as a model of Greco-Roman rhetorical patterns in the first-century Roman colony of Corinth.

Cicero describes the importance of Greece and Athens for his study of rhetoric. He says, "Greece, which has ever claimed the leading part in eloquence, and of Athens, that discoverer of all learning, where the supreme power of oratory was both invented and perfected . . . "[8] In addition, Ferguson claims that "in Athens on a foreign tour he attended the lectures of Antiochus of Ascalon (an Academic) and Zeno of Sidon (an Epicurean), and in Rhodes he became intimate with Posidonius (a Stoic)."[9] Cicero includes their names in his *Academica* 1.10.38; 2.6.16–20; 2.24.75.

Cicero seems to have been bilingual and able to speak both Latin and Greek with versatility. When he was young, he was already familiar with Greek culture and language.[10] Thus, he managed to speak Greek, and used Greek words frequently in his writings (see *De Oratore*, 1.2.9; 3.28.110; *Epistulae ad Familliares*, 13.15.1–2; *De Fato*, 1.1). He translated Plato's *Protagoras* and *Timaeus* into Latin in 45 BCE.[11] Plutarch states that Cicero "made it his business to compose and translate (Greek) philosophical dialogues, and to render into Latin the several terms of dialectics and natural philosophy."[12]

In agreement with Aristotle,[13] Cicero claims that there are three different types of oratory or rhetorical discourse—deliberative (*deliberativo*),

8. Cicero, *De Oratore*, 1.4.13.
9. E. Ferguson, *Backgrounds*, 357.
10. See Gveritt, *Cicero*, 164.
11. Grant, *Cicero*, 356.
12. Plutarch, *Cicero*, 40.1.

13. The characteristics of Aristotle's three genres of oratory may be summarized in this way: An orator or author uses a deliberative rhetoric when she or he intends to persuade his or her hearers to take some action in the future. This sort of speech is either "exhortation" or "dissuasion." Its primary concern is to promote the beneficial or advantageous. The orator employs a judicial oratory when she or he is seeking to urge the audience to make a judgment about events that occurred in the past. This judicial speech is either "prosecution" or "defense." Its central issue is justice. An author or speaker uses epideictic oratory when she or he wants to persuade hearers to reaffirm or take hold of some viewpoint in the present, while the author celebrates or denounces some people

epideictic (or demonstrative, *demonstrativo*), and judicial (or forensic, *iudiciali*). Nonetheless, Cicero's description of these oratorical types is slightly different from Aristotle.

Epideictic (or demonstrative) discourse is present-situation-oriented oratory. It is used when an orator praises and censures a person. This sort of speech has to do with what is honorable about the person. Epideictic speech deals with the person's attributes: mind, body, and external circumstances.[14] The virtue of mind comprises wisdom, justice, courage, and temperance. The virtue of body consists of health, beauty, strength, and speed. And the external circumstances are public office, money, connections by marriage, high birth, friends, country, and power. In speaking of these virtues and circumstances, an orator praises and censures his subject and also his audience and promotes honorable attitudes within the audience. In summary, epideictic speech focuses on issues of honor.[15]

Deliberative rhetoric is future-oriented discourse. It is commonly employed in political debates. Using this class of speech, an orator expresses his or her opinion on a political subject.[16] Cicero argues that deliberative oratory is delivered to "retain, increase, or acquire some advantage" and some honor, "or on the other hand to throw off, lessen, or avoid some disadvantage" or dishonor.[17] Cicero further states, "in the

---

or some quality. This kind of speech is "praise" or "encomium" or "blame" or "invective." The central concern is what is honorable (Aristotle, *Rhetoric*, 1:3 1358b8–28; see also Kennedy, *Interpretation*, 19; Fiorenza, "Rhetorical," 390–91). These rhetorical genres also appear in Cicero's description of rhetoric, but with some further developments. Aristotle's attitude towards rhetoric differed from that of Plato. Aristotle insisted on the usefulness of rhetoric, though, similar to Plato, he defines rhetoric as "the faculty of discovering the possible means of persuasion in reference to any subject whatever" and "a counterpart of dialectic" (Aristotle, *Rhetoric*, 1.1.1; 1.1.14; also *Rhetoric*, 1: 1 1355a21; 1355b8–10; 1:2: 1355b27–28).

According to Aristotle, there are three modes of proof or three methods of effecting persuasion: the first kind depends on the personal character of the speaker (*ethos*); the second on putting the audience into a certain frame of mind (*pathos*); the third on the proof, or apparent proof, provided by the words of the speech itself (*logos*) (Aristotle, *Rhetoric*, 1:2: 1358a1–21; see also Litfin, *Paul's*, 80). Cicero includes these three modes in his rhetorical handbooks (see *Orator*, 21.71; *De Oratore*, 1.5; *De Inventione*, 1.14.20; 1.50.92–93; see also DiCicco, *Ethos*, 41–50).

14. Cicero, *De Inventione*, 2.59.177.
15. Ibid., 2.59.177; 2.51.156.
16. Ibid., 2.4.13.
17. Ibid., 2.5.18.

deliberative type ... Aristotle accepts advantage as the end, but I prefer both honor and advantage"[18] This is evidence that Cicero's definition of rhetoric is slightly different from Aristotle and that he developed his theory of rhetoric further on the basis of Aristotle's theory of rhetoric.

Cicero also argues that in using deliberative oratory, an orator seeks in his or her audience the following things:[19] The first thing has to do with something honorable (*honesta*) that attracts the audience not by any prospect of gain but by its natural merit and its own worth. Belonging to this category are virtue, knowledge, and truth.[20] The second has to do with something advantageous that draws an audience's attention not because of its own worth and intrinsic goodness but because of some profit and advantage that is derived from it. Money belongs to this class.[21] The last thing is sought by uniting qualities of honor and advantage, such as a good reputation, friendship, rank, glory, and influence. Cicero describes,

> Friendship is a desire to do good to someone simply for the benefit of the person whom one loves, with a requital of the feeling on his or her part. Rank is the possession of a distinguished office which merits respect, honor, and reverence. Glory consists in a person's having a widespread reputation accompanied by praise. Influence is a fullness of power, dignity, or resources of some sort.[22]

These have to do with something that "entices people and leads them on, and also holds out to them a prospect of some advantage to induce them to seek it more eagerly."[23] In summary, in the deliberative speech, honor and advantage are the qualities to be sought, while baseness, disadvantage, and dishonor to be avoided.[24]

Forensic or judicial speech is used in courts of law. This type of speech includes accusation and defense. Its inquiry is towards what is just.[25] Forms of argumentation which fit forensic rhetoric are "conjec-

18. Ibid., 2.51.156.

19. Ibid., 2.52.157.

20. See ibid. The virtue here refers to virtues of mind such as wisdom, justice, courage, and temperance. They themselves are honorable, ibid., 2.53.159.

21. See ibid., 2.52.157.

22. Ibid., 2.55.166.

23. Ibid., 2.52.157.

24. Ibid., 2.52.158.

25. See ibid., 2.4.12.

tural issues (or issue of fact)," "inference," "definition," "transfer," "comparison," "retort of the accusation," "shifting the charge," "confession and avoidance," "plea for pardon," and "reward and punishment."[26] Cicero, however, comments that many of the topics and principles of forensic rhetoric are not clearly distinct from those of epideictic and deliberative orations.[27] Here is an example: "from the principles of advantage and honor he may show how inexpedient and base is the course of conduct which the opponents say we were or are bound to follow, and how advantageous and honorable is our act or request."[28]

Cicero provides a brief description of the function of parts of the art of rhetoric.[29]

> Invention (*inventio*) is the discovery of valid or seemingly valid arguments (*argumenta*) to render one's cause plausible. Arrangement (*dispositio*) is the distribution of arguments thus discovered in the proper order. Expression (*elocutio*) is the fitting of the proper language to the invented matter. Memory (*memoria*) is the firm mental grasp of matter and words. Delivery (*pronuntiatio*) is the control of voice and body in a manner suitable to the dignity of the subject matter and the style.[30]

Finally, in his *Topica* Cicero demonstrates how to invent arguments.[31] Some arguments are drawn from the following: Conjugation (which means words of the same family, for example, wise, wisely, wisdom), similarity (or analogy), difference, contraries, corollaries, antecedents, consequents, and contradictions. Others are derived from efficient causes, effects, comparison with events of greater, lesser, or equal importance, etc.[32]

---

26. Ibid., 2.4.14—2.51.155. Here Cicero provides a great number of examples for each argumentative form.

27. Ibid., 2.4.13; 2.51.155–56.

28. Ibid., 2.47.141.

29. "The material of the art of rhetoric seems to me to be that which . . . Aristotle approved," ibid., 1.7.9. This is another evidence of Cicero's development of his theory of rhetoric based on Aristotle's theory.

30. Ibid.

31. This *Topica* was written in 44 BCE and was inspired by Aristotle's writings (see Cicero, *Topica*, 1.1–2).

32. For detailed explanations of each element, see Cicero, *Topica* 3.13; 3.11—7.31.

Appendix 2

T'oegye: Life and Wisdom

WE NOW TURN TO a brief examination of the life of T'oegye. Without tackling the philosophy of the prominent Confucian scholar Yi Hwang, whose honorific name is T'oegye, it would not be possible to discuss Korean Confucianism and Confucian wisdom, just as it is not reasonable to talk about Reformation theology without dealing with Calvinism and the theology of Calvin. In order to help understand the value and importance of Yi T'oegye in the history of Korean Confucianism and philosophy, we continue this comparison with John Calvin and his Reformation theology. They were contemporaries in the sixteenth century, John Calvin (1509–1564) in Europe and Yi T'oegye (1501–1570) in East Asia, though they had such different backgrounds in religion, thought, and philosophy. Calvin was one of the key originators of Reformation theology, and his theology and theological perspective has deeply affected many Christian scholars throughout Christian history until today. In a similar sense, Yi T'oegye is esteemed in terms of a Korean context. Due to such interesting connections between the two, in fact, some Korean Christians have recently attempted comparative studies between T'oegye's philosophy, especially the thought of *Kyung*, referring to "reverence," and Calvin's theology, especially his Christology and the Christian idea of reverence for God.[1] Consequently,

1. See Yi, "Kyung"; Choi, "Kyung-Idea"; Heo, "Tien."

the importance of Yi T'oegye in the history of Korean Confucianism and philosophy deserves comparison with that of John Calvin in the history of Christianity and Reformation theology in particular.

There is no question that Yi T'oegye was one of the most respected and honorable *sonbi*s in Korean history and a *yangban* of integrity. He was also the most distinguished scholar of Korean Neo-Confucianism and the pioneer contributing to "the establishment of a golden age" in Korean Neo-Confucianism; his philosophy and thought has profoundly influenced Koreans until today.[2] It is no exaggeration, therefore, to claim that the name of T'oegye itself represents Korean (Neo-)Confucianism as a whole. Yi Ik, a seventeenth century Confucian scholar, said that what T'eogye was in Korea was the same as what Confucius was in China.[3] There were thousands of Confucian scholars in Korean history. Yet none of them is compared with T'oegye in terms of his influence on Korean mentality and national cultural traditions and contribution to the development of Korean Neo-Confucianism. Due to this, T'oegye is one of the most frequent topics explored in Korean Confucianism and philosophy today. For instance, a great number of postgraduate students have recently written their doctoral dissertations on T'oegye's thought and philosophy. Many universities have academic institutes of T'oegye studies which have constantly conducted a number of annual conferences on T'oegye and have published thousands of articles regarding T'oegye. Furthermore, beyond the Korean peninsula, conferences and significant studies on T'oegye have recently been occurring in other countries such as Japan, China, America, and European countries, including Germany. Furthermore, the universities which focus on T'oegye are Dankuk University, Gunkook University, Kyungbook University, and Andong University. In addition, there are several journals published whose titles borrow his name, such as *T'oegye-hak-bo* (Journal of T'oegye Studies), *T'oegye-hak* (T'oegye Studies), *T'oegye-hak-yungu* (Research of T'oegye Studies), *T'oegye-hak-non-chong* (Collection of Journal of T'oegye Studies), and *T'oegye-hak-gwa-hankook-moonhwa* (T'oegye studies and Korean Culture). At the government level there was an exhibition on Neo-Confucianism in the *Choson* dynasty in November 2003, which was conducted by the Department of Archaeology and the

---

2. Ryūtarō, "Differences," 243; see also Yao, *Confucianism*, 118–20.

3. Kim, *T'oegye*, 18.

National Museum of Korea. There I witnessed firsthand the important position T'oegye takes in Korean Confucianism.

To focus our attention on T'oegye's contribution to the development of Korean Neo-Confucianism, we should observe his life at the time he first entered a Confucian academy.[4] At the age of twenty-two in 1523,[5] with the purpose of disciplining himself in the Confucian way of learning, T'oegye entered the Confucian Academy, Songgyun'gwan. During this time he experienced the deep effect of the purge of 1519. It caused students to be disinterested, to lack concentration on study, and to leave the academy. He oftentimes heard from his fellow students that there was no point in studying hard. Yet T'oegye was still absorbed in reading and study, facing the wall, so that he was "made an object of mockery."[6] T'oegye then obtained the book *Simgyong* (Classics of the Mind-and-Heart) which became the most important book in establishing his Confucian thought systematically. He used to read it in the early morning every day until his death.[7]

In 1534, the twenty-ninth year of King Chungjong, T'oegye passed the national examination, which led to an official career, and began to enter government service. For fifteen years he served in office with four kings (Chungjong [1506–1544], Injong [1544–1545], Myongjong [1545–1567], Sonjo [1567–1608]). During their reigns, they highly valued T'oegye's study and personality, and all of these kings fervently desired

---

4. On the twenty-fifth of November in 1501 Yi Hwang was born the youngest of seven brothers and a sister in a modest *yangban* family in the village of Ongye, located near Andong in modern Kyungsan Bukdo, about 200 kilometers southwest of Seoul. He is known worldwide by his honorific name, T'oegye, which was taken from the small village which used to be called *T'ogye*, near his birthplace, where he spent the last two decades of his life fully devoted to study, writing, and teaching (Kalton, *Diagrams*, 14–15).

5. The year 1523 was just four years after the purge of *Gimyo* in 1519. Briefly, this was a purge of the literati, the enthusiastic Confucian scholar- officials, whose head was Cho Kwangjo who entered office first in 1515. They attempted a political and social reform with an ethical and political ideology of Neo-Confucianism, with the assistance of King Chungjong. But soon after the king tired of their uncompromising reform, which they pushed too far and too fast, and he purged Cho Kwangjo and his group in 1519. At that time the movement which Cho Kwangjo and his group led was "a center of attention and hopes," especially for young (Confucian) students including T'oegye. This purge seriously affected all the intellectuals, including the students in Songgyun'gwan (Kalton, *Diagrams*, 12–14; Park, *Wangjo*, 178–94).

6. Kalton, *Diagrams*, 16; Yun, *Hwang*, 72–73.

7. Ryu "T'oegye'eui," 276.

him to become their assistant, teacher, and advisor.⁸ He was appointed to the ministries that were generally concerned with "drafting royal documents, compiling dynastic history, or composing documents addressed to the Ming court" (that was the Chinese kingdom), which provided opportunities for him to utilize his "scholarly and literary talents."⁹

Besides such ministries, he was appointed to other high-ranking government positions, but he politely refused to accept the positions. Rather, he seriously desired to retire from public service due to his ill health. He also had some other reasons for retiring, such as his own experience of the effect of the literati purges of the Neo-Confucian scholar-officials (which occurred in 1498, 1504, 1519, and 1545), his non-interest in political power, and his lifelong desire to immerse himself in the Neo-Confucian fashion of study and self-cultivation, and writing and teaching.¹⁰ During the period of government service, T'oegye was gradually becoming known to the government and the people. He built a high reputation as a "conscientious official" and a "man of integrity" and became famed as the master of Chu Hsi' Learning (so-called Neo-Confucianism, founded in the twelfth century in China) and as a poet.¹¹

When he was forty-nine years old in 1549, his yearning for retirement from public life finally came to a reality. He went to T'ogye (which was renamed T'oegye later) near his birth place where he fully devoted himself to learning, and he wrote and taught his disciples, as well. During the retirement period of twenty-one years, T'oegye was visited by the brilliant young Confucian student, Yi Yulgok (1536–1584), in 1558. Soon after, this meeting led to a disciple/teacher relationship between them for thirteen years until T'oegye's death. This was historically significant because, later, Yulgok's disciples formed "the school of the primacy of *ki* (material force) (*Chukip'a*)," whereas T'oegye's followers became "the school of the primacy of *li* (principle) (*Chulip'a*)."¹² These were the two divergent parties representing Korean Neo-Confucianism as a whole. Soon after the encounter with Yulgok, for seven years from early 1559 to late 1566, T'oegye carried on the debate of the "Four-Seven thesis" (*sachillon*) with the young scholar Ki Taesung (Kobong,

8. Park, *Choson*, 178–220.
9. Kalton, *Diagrams*, 16.
10. See Chung, *Neo-Confucianism*, 24–25.
11. Kalton, *Diagrams*, 15–16.
12. Chung, *Neo-Confucianism*, 24-32; see also Ryu, *T'oegye*, 161.

1529–1592). This became recorded as the first free scholarly debate and a genuine philosophical debate between a master and a disciple (a free debate between the two was abnormal in a Korean Confucian context then, and even still today) in the whole history of Korean Confucianism. In this debate, T'oegye discussed psychology (emotions or feelings) and anthropology (human nature). Moreover, this debate symbolizes "a major landmark of philosophical sophistication in the tradition of East Asian Confucianism."[13]

In 1568, King Sunjo called him again and appointed him to a position as a teacher of the King. At this time, T'oegye wrote *Sunghak sipdo* (the Ten Diagrams of the Learning of the Sages), the greatest work of his entire thought and philosophy, with his comments on Chu His' Learning.[14] T'oegye attributed it to the king, and the king then ordered a big screen to be made with the work on it and it surrounded his throne so that he could read it every day. Of all his writings, this is the most important work to understanding T'oegye's Confucian thought, which has been deeply affecting Korean Confucian wisdom ever since. On the eighth of December in 1570 T'oegye died.[15] After T'oegye, a great number of scholars were influenced by his Neo-Confucian thought. There were more than 300 disciples who carried on his Confucian philosophy from the sixteenth century to the eighteenth century, such as Yu Sungryong, Ki Taesung, Yi Dukhong, Yi Yulgok, Cho Mok, Yi Jae, Yi Ik, and Yi Hangro.[16]

13. Hwang, "Cultivation," 217–34; see also Wei-ming, "Perception," 261–81; Chung, *Neo-Confucianism*, 25.

14. Additionally, a list of T'oegye's writings is as follows: *Ch'unmyung tosul* (Diagrammatic Explanation of the Mandate of Heaven) in 1553, *Kyemong chunui* (Problems Regarding the Study of Changes) in 1557, *Chujasu churyo* (Essentials of Master Chu's Correspondence) and *Chasung nok* (Record for Self-Reflection) in 1558, *Songge Wun Myung ihak t'ongnok* (Comprehensive Records of the School of Principle in the Sung, Yüan, and ming Periods) in 1559, Three "Four-Seven Letters" in 1559–1566, *Paeksa Sigyo Chunsumnok ch'ojun insu kihu* (Postscript to a Conveyed Copy of Ch'en Hsien-Chang's *Instructions through Poetry* and Wang Yang-ming's *Instruction for Practical Living*), and *Chunsumnok nonbyun* (Critique of Wang Yang-ming's *Instruction for Practical Living*), and *Heoam sunsaeng haengjang* (Biographical Account of Master Chu His) in 1566, *Yukcho so* (Six-Article Memorial) in 1568, *Sasu haeui* (A Commentary on the Four Books) in 1569, *Samgyung haeui* (Commentary on the Three Classics) and *Sim mu ch'eyong pyun* (Critique on the Saying "the Mind Does Not Have Substance and Function"), and *Pi iki wi ilmul pyunchŭng* (Treatise on the Saying That "*I* and *Ki* Are Not One") are not dated (Chung, *Neo-Confucianism*, 199–203).

15. Ryu, "T'oegye," 286–90; Kim, "Hwang," 160–61.

16. Kyungsang buk'do, *T'oegyehak*.

Throughout T'oegye's whole life, his most striking contribution to Korean history, especially the history of Korean Confucianism, was his contextualization or localization into a Korean soil *Chungjuhak* (the Ch'eng-Chu school) and *Chujahak* (the Chu Hsi School) of Chinese Neo-Confucianism.[17] In other words, he shaped a new creative form of Neo-Confucianism which was most relevant to the Korean spirit or culture. It was so called *Choson Sunglihak* (the school [*hak*] of human nature [*sung*] and principle [*li* or *i*]) or Korean Neo-Confucianism. T'oegye theoretically systemized Choson Sunglihak in terms of ontology, epistemology, anthropology, and ethics. Moreover, his idea of the *i* or *li* (principle) and *ki* (material force) dualism profoundly influenced his contemporaries and his disciples who formed the school of the primacy of *li* (*Chulip'a*) later. Such a dualistic tendency appears in his "Four-Seven thesis" and involves the good–evil opposition.[18] Accordingly, it is appropriate to say that since T'oegye there has truly been established in the Korean peninsula an authentic Korean Confucianism that clearly differs from Confucianism in China.

T'oegye, therefore, takes the most prominent position in Korean Confucianism and culture. There is no doubt that he still lives on in the spirit of Korean culture and has become an icon of Korean Confucianism today. It can be said, therefore, that Korean Confucian wisdom is grounded in T'oegye's Confucian philosophical thought, so that it is even called, "T'oegye-ism."

Prior to the study of T'oegye's idea of wisdom, it is helpful to briefly describe a Confucian understanding of wisdom in general, for T'oegye developed his idea of wisdom in accordance with the Confucian tradition. In a Confucian tradition, wisdom (*jeehye/sulgi*) is interchangeably used with "knowledge" (*jee shik*) in general and it, in a broader sense, refers to "knowledge" and "to know." In Chinese characters the word *jee* (wisdom) is composed of the word *jee* (knowledge) and the word *il*

---

17. This school was a Chinese Neo-Confucianism legacy, which was primarily formulated in association with the Sung Chinese philosophers, Ch'eng I (1033–1107) and Chu Hsi (1130–1200). In other words, it is described as *Sungnihak* or *Hsing-li hsüeh* referring to the school (*hak*) of human nature (*sung*) and principle (*li* or *ni* in a Korean pronunciation) which came to and dominated the Korean peninsula in the Choson dynasty (1393–1910). Due to T'oegye's influence, it was introduced into Japan (Chung, *Neo-Confucianism*, xiii).

18. His Four–Seven thesis will not be tackled here (for detail see Chung, *Neo-Confucianism*, 53–118; Yoon, *T'oegye*, 31).

(day), as it stands, and used in a verbal sense it means "to be wise" and "to know." In this regard, it can be interpreted that a human being can obtain wisdom in the course of accumulating (or piling up) knowledge or learning every day.[19]

The Korean Confucian scholar, Jang-Tae Keum sees wisdom and knowledge (*jeesik*) in the same way. In order to tackle the problem of knowledge in Confucianism, he replaces wisdom for knowledge. Here, for wisdom he substitutes knowledge as one of the Four Beginnings. The rest are "benevolence" (*in*), "righteousness" (*eui*), and "propriety" (*ye*).[20] Likewise, in Confucianism both wisdom and knowledge are interchangeably used or have an interdependent relationship.

In a narrower sense, however, wisdom in Confucianism specifically refers to the attempt to distinguish between what is right and what is wrong in terms of a moral or ethical perspective. In short, wisdom refers to a virtue of discernment between the right and the wrong. Mencius especially understood wisdom in a close relation with benevolence (*in*) and righteousness (*eui*), which are moral standards or principles. He, in a strict way, narrowed wisdom down only to the knowledge which could be compatible with benevolence and righteousness. In other words, for him wisdom is knowledge—to know what is right morally, what is benevolent, and what is righteous. He further claimed that a person who does not have wisdom—which is the sense of discernment between right and wrong—is not able to be human.[21] As seen above, in Confucianism wisdom refers to knowledge in a broad sense, but more interestingly it is seen in terms of a moral or ethical perspective, as sense or ability to distinguish what is right from what is wrong. It seems clear, therefore, that in Confucianism wisdom is closely related to moral or ethical behavior. Such an idea was surely carried on by T'oegye.

T'oegye's perception of wisdom (*jeehye*) is certainly shown in his Four-Seven thesis. This Four-Seven topic was originated by Mencius (Mengzi, 371–289 BCE) in the *Book of Mencius* and Confucius (Kong Fuzi, 552–479 BCE) in the *Book of Rites*.[22] According to T'oegye, it is

19. Jung, *Ukyoyihae*, 209.
20. Keum, "Uhake," 243.
21. See Jung, *Ukyoyihae*, 210; Chun, *Meng'ja*, 110–11.
22. See Hwang, "Cultivation," 223. It was Kwon Kun (Yangch'on, 1352–1409) who was the first Neo-Confucian scholar speaking of the four-seven topic in Korea (Chung, *Neo-Confucianism*, 13).

argued that the Four Beginnings (S'adan)—such as benevolence (or humanity), righteousness, propriety, and wisdom—are assigned to human nature (sung) and refer to "the issuance of principle" (li or i); and the Seven Feelings (or Emotions)—representing pleasure, anger, sorrow, fear, love, hatred, and desire—are assigned to "the mind-and-heart (sim)" and refer to "the issuance of material force" (ki).[23]

As seen above, T'oegye regarded wisdom as part of the Four Beginnings, or human nature. If so, in order to grasp T'oegye's conception of wisdom it is proper to see what he discussed about human nature (sung) or the Four Beginnings (S'adan). In so doing, it is noteworthy that T'oegye's perception of the Four Beginnings was deeply influenced by Mencius's idea of human nature. T'oegye's consideration of human nature as being perfectly good certainly accorded with Mencius's insistence upon "the ultimate justification" of human nature.[24] According to Mencius, it is said that the Four Beginnings (or human nature) are imparted or endowed by Heaven (T'ien, Nature) and thus intrinsically good.[25] And also in the Mencius doctrine it is an interesting point that the Four Beginnings are regarded as "innate, moral characteristics" of the fundamentally perfect goodness of human nature or, similarly, as "the four roots of moral goodness inherent in human nature," or "indications of the human potential for moral self-cultivation."[26] So it is an integral part of Mencius's perception of human nature that the Four Beginnings described as moral qualities are essentially good, because they are imparted by Heaven (T'ien). On this basis, it is clear that Mencius regarded the Four Beginnings (or human nature) as the roots and sources of morality. In other words, it can be said that wisdom as part of the Four Beginnings should be seen in an intimate relationship with a moral or ethical sense. This idea deeply influenced T'oegye's perception of the Four Beginnings (or human nature), especially his idea of wisdom.

Besides Mencius, T'oegye's understanding of the Four Beginnings (or human nature) was directly or indirectly influenced by Chu Hsi and Chung Chiun (Ch'uman, 1509–1561) in Ch'unmyungdo (Diagram of

23. Chung, *Neo-Confucianism*, 13; Hwang, "Cultivation," 223; Yoon, "Identification," 228; Kalton, *Diagrams*, 137.

24. Wei-ming, "Perception," 263.

25. Ibid., 263–64.

26. Chung, *Neo-Confucianism*, 40, 51; similarly Wei-ming, "Perception," 264; Hwang, "Cultivation," 231.

Heaven's Imperative). Like them, T'oegye interpreted human nature in the theory of principle (*li*) and material force (*ki*). It is T'oegye's claim that the Four Beginnings as "inborn moral qualities" are purely good.[27] This is because they originate with, or are initiated and dominated by *li* ([heavenly] principle). This principle, in a metaphysical sense, is the Supreme Ultimate (*Tae'geuk*) and the origin of goodness or goodness itself.[28] As seen earlier, T'oegye's perception of the Four Beginnings does not differ from Mencius's. Accordingly, in T'oegye it seems that wisdom is purely good, because it is initiated by the Supreme Ultimate, and that this wisdom should be seen in a close connection with a moral or ethical sense, just as in Mencius. This is certainly attested in T'oegye's emphasis on the close relationship between wisdom and becoming a sage.

Wisdom plays the most significant role in becoming a sage (*hyun'in*, in a similar sense, *sung'in* or *gun'ja*). In T'oegye's mind it was the ultimate purpose (or eventual goal) of study or learning that he would become a sage by virtue of wisdom like Confucius (Kong Fuzi) or Mencius (Mengzi). In T'oegye, thus, it was understood that obtaining wisdom or to be wise and becoming a sage had the same connotation. Accordingly, it is clear that T'oegye highly valued wisdom as part of human virtue in an anthropological perspective in his Confucian thought.[29] This has strongly influenced Korean Confucian wisdom in our time.

---

27. Wei-ming, "Perception," 269.
28. See ibid.; Hwang, "Cultivation," 226; Yoon, *T'oegye*, 37–38, 45.
29. Cho, *Sunghaksipdo*, 20–42.

Bibliography

Adams, Edward, and David G. Horrell, eds. *Christianity at Corinth: the Quest for the Pauline Church*. Louisville; London: Westminster John Knox, 2004.
Adewuya, J. Ayodeji. "Revising 1 Corinthians 11:27–34: Paul's Discussion of the Lord's Supper and African Meals." *JSNT* 30 (2007) 95–112.
Aitchison, Ronnie. *The Ministry of A Deacon*. Peterborough: Epworth, 2003.
Alexander, Loveday. "Paul and the Hellenistic Schools: the Evidence of Galen." In *Paul in His Hellenistic Context*, edited by Troels Engberg-Pedersen. 60–83. Edinburgh: T. & T. Clark, 1994.
Allison, Dale C., Jr. "Critical Notes: Peter and Cephas: One and the Same." *JBL* 111 (1992) 489–95.
Anderson, David A. *Multicultural Ministry: Finding your Church's Unique Rhythm*. Grand Rapids: Zondervan, 2004.
Anderson, R. Dean. *Ancient Rhetorical Theory and Paul*. Bondgenotenlaan: Peeters, 1999.
Applebaum, Shimon. "The Social and Economic Status of the Jews in the Diaspora." In *The Jewish People in the First Century: Historical Geography, Political History, Social, Cultural, and Religious Life, and Institutions*, edited by S. Safrai & M. Stern. 701–27. Assen; Amsterdam: Van Gorcum, 1976.
Aristotle. *Art of Rhetoric*. Translated by J. H. Freese. The Loeb Classic Library. London: Williams Heinemann; Cambridge: Harvard University Press, 1971.
———. *Rhetoric*. In *The Complete Works of Aristotle: the Revised Oxford Translation*. Translated by W. Rhys Roberts and edited by Jonathan Barnes. 2nd vol. Princeton: Princeton University Press, 1984.
Aronson, Elliot. *The Social Animal*. Translated by Ja-sook Gu et al. Seoul: Tam'gudang, 2002.
Australia's multicultural policy. No page. Online: http://www.immi.gov.au/facts/06evolution.htm
Bailey, Kenneth E. "Recovering the Poetic Structure of 1 Cor 1:17—2:12: a Study in Text and Commentary." *NovT* 17 (1975) 265–96.
———. "The Structure of 1 Corinthians and Paul's Theological Method With Special Reference to 4:17." *NovT* 25 (1983) 152–81.
Baird, William. "Book Reviews: *Wisdom and Spirit: An Investigation of 1 Corinthians 1:18—3:20. Against the Background of Jewish Sapiential Traditions in the Greco-Roman Period* by James A. Davis." *JBL* 106 (1987) 149–51.

———. "'One against the Other': Intra-Church Conflict in 1 Corinthians." In *The Conversation Continues: Studies in Paul and John in Honour of J. Louis Martyn*, edited by R. T. Fortna and B. R. Gaventa. 116-36. Nashville: Abingdon, 1990.

Balch, David L. "1 Cor 7:32-35 and Stoic Debates about Marriage, Anxiety, and Distraction." *JBL* 102 (1983) 429-39.

Banks, Robert J. *Paul's Idea of Community: the Early House Churches in their Cultural Setting*. Peabody: Hendrickson, revised, 1994.

Barclay, John M. G. *Jews in the Mediterranean Diaspora: From Alexander to Trajan (323 BCE-117 CE)*. Edinburgh: T. & T. Clark, 1996.

———. "'Neither Jew nor Greek': Multiculturalism and the New Perspective on Paul." In *Ethnicity and the Bible*, edited by Mark G. Brett. 197-214. Brill; Boston: Leiden, 2002.

———. *Obeying the Truth: A Study of Paul's Ethics in Galatians*. Edinburgh: T. & T. Clark, 1988.

———. "Thessalonica and Corinth: Social Contrasts in Pauline Christianity." *JSNT* 47 (1992) 49-74.

Barnett, P. W. "Apostle." In *Dictionary of Paul and His Letters*, edited by G. F. Hawthorne, R. P. Martin, and D. G. Reid. 45-51. Illinois; Leicester: InterVarsity, 1993.

———. "Opposition in Corinth." *JSNT* 22 (1984) 3-17.

Barrett, C. K. *A Commentary on the Epistle to the Romans*. New York: Harper & Row, 1962.

———. "Boasting (*kauchasthai, ktl.*) in the Pauline Epistles." In *L'Apôtre Paul. Personnalité, Style et Conception du Ministère*, edited by A. Vanhoye. 363-68. BETL 73. Leuven: Leuven University Press; Uitgeverij: Peeters, 1986.

———. *The First Epistle to the Corinthians*. BNTC. London: Adam & Charles Black, 1968.

———. "Things Sacrificed to Idols." *NTS* 11 (1964-65) 138-53.

Barton, Stephen C. "Paul's Sense of Place: An Anthropological Approach to Community Formation in Corinth." *NTS* 32 (1986) 225-46.

Baur, Ferdinand Christian. "Die Christuspartei in der korinthischen Gemeinde, der Gegensatz des paulinischen und petrinischen Christentums in der ältesten Kirche, der Apostel Petrus in Rom." *TZfT* (1831) 61-206.

———. "The Epistles to the Corinthians." In *Paul the Apostle of Jesus Christ, His Life and Work, His Epistle and His Doctrine: A Contribution to a Critical History of Primitive Christianity*. Translated by Eduard Zeller. 258-307. vol. 1. 2nd ed. London: Williams & Norgate, 1876.

Berger, K. "Zur Diskussion über die Herkunft von 1 Kor. 2:9." *NTS* 24 (1978) 270-83.

Betz, H. D. "The Problem of Rhetoric and Theology according to the Apostle Paul." In *'Apôtre Paul. Personnalité, Style et Conception du Ministère*, edited by A Vanhoye. 16-48. BETL 73. Leuven: Leuven University Press; Uitgeverij: Peeters, 1986.

———. *Galatians: A Commentary on Paul's Letter to the Churches in Galatia*. Hermeneia. Philadelphia: Fortress, 1979.

Bieringer, Reimund, ed. *The Corinthian Correspondence*. Leuven: Peeters, 1996.

Black, David A. "A Note on 'the Weak' in 1 Corinthians 9:22." *Biblica* 64 (1983) 240-42.

Blattenberger, David E., III. *Rethinking 1 Corinthians 11:2-16 through Archaeological and Moral-Rhetorical Analysis*. Lewiston: Edwin Mellen, 1997.

Boatwright, Mary T. "Theatres in the Roman Empires." *BA* 53 (1990) 184-92.

Borchert, Gerald L. *Assurance and Warning*. Nashville: Broadman, 1987.

Borowski, Oded. "A Corinthian Lamp at Tell Halif." *BASOR* 227 (1977) 63-65.

Boyarin, Daniel. *A Radical Jew: Paul and the Politics of Identity*. Berkeley: University of California Press, 1994.

Branick, Vincent P. "Source and Redaction Analysis of 1 Corinthians 1–3." *JBL* 101 (1982) 251–69.
Braund, David. "Function and Dysfunction: Personal Patronage in Roman Imperialism." In *Patronage in Ancient Society*, edited by A. Wallace-Hadrill. 137–52. London; New York: Routledge, 1989.
Braxton, Brad Ronnell. *The Tyranny of Resolution: 1 Corinthians 7:17–24*. SBLDS 181. Atlanta: Society of Biblical Literature, 2000.
Breen, Michael. *The Koreans: Who They Are, What They Want, Where Their Future Lies*. New York: St. Martin's, 1998.
Brett, Mark. "Ancestral Religion in Postcolonial Perspective." Paper presented at International SBL 2005, Singapore. Forthcoming in *Biblical Interpretation*.
———. ed. *Ethnicity and the Bible*. Brill; Boston: Leiden, 2002.
Broneer, Oscar. "The Apostle Paul and the Isthmian Games." *BA* 25 (1962) 2–31.
———. "Paul and the Pagan Cults at Isthmia." *HTR* 64 (1971) 169–87.
Brooks, James A. and Carlton L. Winbery. *Syntax of New Testament Greek*. Lanham; London: University Press of America, 1979. Revised, 1988.
Broughton, T. Robert S. *The Magistrates of the Roman Republic: 99 BCE–31 BCE*. vol. 2. Chico: Scholars, 1984.
Brown, Alexandra R. *The Cross and Human Transformation: Paul's Apocalyptic Word in 1 Corinthians*. Minneapolis: Fortress, 1995.
Bruce, F. F. *I & II Corinthians*. NCenBC. Grand Rapids: Eerdmans, 1971.
———. *The Epistle to the Galatians*. NIGTC. Exeter: Paternoster; Grand Rapids: Eerdmans, 1982.
Bullmore, Michael A. *St. Paul's Theology of Rhetorical Style: An Examination of 1 Corinthians 2:1–5 in the Light of First Century Greco-Roman Rhetorical Culture*. San Francisco: International Scholars, 1995.
Bultmann, Rudolph K. "Kauchaomai, Kauchēma, Kauchēsis, Egkauchaomai, Katakauchaomai." In *Theological Dictionary of the New Testament*, edited by Gerhard Kittel. Translated by Geoffrey W. Bromiley. 645–54. vol. 3. Grand Rapids: Eerdmans, 1965.
Burke, Trevor J. "Paul's Role as 'Father' to his Corinthian 'Children' in Socio-Historical Context (1 Corinthians 4:14–21)." In *Paul and the Corinthians: Studies on a Community in Conflict: Essays in Honor of Margaret Thrall*, edited by Trevor J. Burke & J. K. Elliot. 95–113. Leiden: Brill, 2003.
Burov, V. G. "The Chinese Philosophical Tradition and Lee T'eogye's Teaching." In *T'oegye'hak yeungunonjeung, je 9 kwon: Seoyangeui T'oegyeyeungu* (Studies on T'oegye, vol. 9: studies on T'oegye in Western world), edited by Whi-chil Song & Gooy-Hyun Shin. 49–56. Dae-gu: Kyung-Book University T'oegye Institute, 1997.
Byrne, Brendan. "Ministry and Maturity in 1 Corinthians 3." *ABR* 35 (1987) 83–87.
———. *Romans*. Sacra Pagina Series 6. Collegeville: the Liturgical Press, 1996.
Calvin, John. *1 Corinthians*. Calvin's New Testament Commentaries, edited by D. W. Torrance and T. F. Torrance. Translated by John W. Fraser. Grand Rapids: Eerdmans; Carlisle: Paternoster, 1996.
Campbell, Douglas A. *The Rhetoric of Righteousness in Romans 3:21–26*. JSNTS 65. Sheffield: Sheffield Academic, 1992.
Carr, Wesley. "The Rules of this Age—1 Corinthians 11: 6–8." *NTS* 23 (1977) 20–35.
Carson, D. A. *The Cross and Christianity Ministry: An Exposition of Passages from 1 Corinthians*. Grand Rapids: Baker; InterVarsity, 1993.
———. *Love in Hard Places*. Wheaton: Crossway, 2002.

———. *Showing the Spirit: A Theological Exposition of 1 Corinthians 12–14*. Grand Rapids: Baker, 1987.

———, Peter T. O'Brien, and Mark A. Seifrid. *Justification and Variegated Nomism, Volume II: The Paradoxes of Paul*. Tübingen: Morh Siebeck; Grand Rapids: Baker Academic, 2004.

Carter, Timothy L. "'Big Men' in Corinth." *JSNT* 66 (1997) 45–71.

Chester, Stephen J. *Conversion at Corinth: Perspective on Conversion in Paul's Theology and the Corinthian Church*. London; New York: T. & T. Clark, 2003.

———. "Divine Madness? Speaking in Tongues in 1 Cor 14:23." *JSNT* 27 (2005) 417–46.

Cheu, Hock-Tong, ed. *Confucianism in Chinese Culture*. Selangor Darul Ehsan: Pelanduk, 2000.

Cheung, Alex T. *Idol Food in Corinth: Jewish Background and Pauline Legacy*. JSNTSup 176. Sheffield: Sheffield Academic, 1999.

Chia, Samuel. "Book Review on Yee, Tet-Lim N.'s *Jews, Gentiles, and Ethnic Reconciliation: Paul's Jewish Identity and Ephesians*. Cambridge; NY: Cambridge University Press, 2005." *Sino-Christian Studies: An International Journal of Bible, Theology & Philosophy* 1 (2006) 199–202.

Cho, Nam-Kook, trans. *Sunghak sipdo* (the Ten Diagrams of the Learning of the Sages). Seoul: Kyoyoukkwahak'sa, 1986.

Choi, Hyaeweol. "Review of *Gender, Ethnicity, Market Forces, and College Choices: Observations of Ethnic Chinese in Korea*, Sheena Choi (2001)," *Korean Studies Review* 2002. No page. Online: http://koreaweb.ws/ks/ksr/ksr02-03.htm.

Choi, Il-Gwang. *The Comparative Study of the Kyung-Idea of T'oegye and the Christian Reverence Thought*. MA diss., The Korea Catholic University, 1996.

Choung, Haechang, et al. *Confucian Philosophy in Korea*. Seongnam: the Academy of Korean Studies, 1996.

Chow, John K. *Patronage and Power: A Study of Social Networks in Corinth*. Sheffield: JSOT, 1992.

———. "Patronage in Roman Corinth." In *Paul and Empire: Religion and Power in Roman Imperial Society*, edited by Richard A. Horsley. 104–25. Harrisburg: Trinity International, 1997.

Chun, Il-Whan, ed. *Meng'ja; Jungchichulhak* (the Book of Mencius; Political Philosophy). Seoul: Jayoomoon'go, 1998.

Chung, Chai-Sik. *Korea: the Encounter between the Gospel and Neo-Confucian Culture*. Gospel and Cultures Pamphlet 16. Geneva: WCC, 1997.

Chung, Edward Y. J. *The Korean Neo-Confucianism of Yi T'oegye and Yi Yulgok: A Reappraisal of the 'Four-Seven Thesis' and Its Practical Implications for Self-Cultivation*. New York: State University of New York Press, 1995.

Ciampa, Roy E., and Brian S. Rosner. "The Structure and Argument of 1 Corinthians: A Biblical/Jewish Approach." *NTS* 52 (2006) 205–18.

Cicero. *Academica; De Natura Deorum*. Translated by H. Rackham. The Loeb Classic Library. Cambridge: Harvard University Press; London: William Heinemann, 1967.

———. *De Inventione; De Optimo Genere Oratorum; Topica*. Translated by H. M. Hubbell. The Loeb Classic Library. London: Williams Heinemann; Cambridge: Harvard University Press, 1968.

———. *De Officiis*. Translated by Walter Miller. The Loeb Classic Library. London: William Heinemann; Cambridge: Harvard University Press, 1968.

———. *De Officiis (On Duties)*. Translated by M. T. Griffin and E. M. Atkins. Cambridge; New York; Port Chester; Melbourne; Sydney: Cambridge University Press, 1991.

———. *De Optimo Genere Oratorum; De Inventione: Topica*. Translated by H. M. Hubbell. The Loeb Classic Library. London: William Heinemann; Cambridge: Harvard University Press, 1960.

———. *De Oratore I–II*. Translated by E. W. Sutton and H. Rackham. The Loeb Classic Library. Cambridge: London: Harvard University Press, 1967.

———. *De Oratore III; De Fato; Paradoxa Stoicorum; De Partitione Oratoria*. Translated by H. Rackham. The Loeb Classic Library. Cambridge: London: Harvard University Press, 1997.

———. *Epistulae ad Familiares*. Translated by W. Glynn Williams. The Loeb Classic Library, London: Williams Heinemann; Cambridge: Harvard University Press, 1965.

———. *Epistulae ad Quintum Fratrem*. Translated by W. G. Williams. The Loeb Classical Library. Cambridge: Harvard University Press, 1989.

———. *Epistularum ad Atticum*. Translated by E. O. Winsted. The Loeb Classic Library. London: Williams Heinemann; Cambridge: Harvard University Press, 1962.

———. *In Catilinam, Pro Murena, Pro Sulla, Pro Flacco*. Translated by Louis E. Lord. The Loeb Classic Library. London: William Heinemann; Cambridge: Harvard University Press, 1967.

———. *Orator; Brutus*. Translated by G. L. Hencrickson and H. M. Hubbell. The Loeb Classic Library. London: William Heinemann; Cambridge: Harvard University Press, 1971.

———. *Philippica*. Translated by Walter C. A. Ker. The Loeb Classic Library. London: William Heinemann; Cambridge: Harvard University Press, 1969.

———. *Post Reditum in Senatu*. Translated by N. H. Watts. The Loeb Classic Library. London: William Heinemann; Cambridge: Harvard University Press, 1965.

Clarke, Andrew D. "Another Corinthian Erastus Inscription." *TynBul* 42 (1991) 146–51.

———. *Secular and Christian Leadership in Corinth: A Socio-Historical And Exegetical Study of 1 Corinthians 1–6*. Leiden: Brill, 1993. Paternoster: Milton Keynes, revised, 2006.

Classen, Carl Joachim. *Rhetorical Criticism of the New Testament*. Boston; Leiden: Brill, 2002.

Collins, Raymond F. *First Corinthians*. Sacra Pagina Series 7. Collegeville: the Liturgical Press, 1999.

Conzelmann, Hans. *1 Corinthians: A commentary on the First Epistle to the Corinthians*. Translated by James W. Leith. Philadelphia: Fortress, 1975.

Cook, S. A., et al., eds. *The Cambridge Ancient History: the Augustan Empire, 44 BCE–CE 70*. vol x. Cambridge: The University Press, 1934.

Corley, Jeremy. "The Pauline Authorship of 1 Corinthians 13." *CBQ* 66 (2004) 256–74.

Cosgrove, Charles H., Herold Weiss, and K. K. Yeo, *Cross-Cultural Paul: Journeys to Others, Journeys to Ourselves*. Grand Rapids: Eerdmans, 2005.

Cowell, F. R. *Cicero and the Roman Republic*. Harmondsworth: Penguin, 1962.

Crafton, Jeffrey A. *The Agency of the Apostle: A Dramatic Analysis of Paul's Response to Conflict in 2 Corinthians*. Sheffield: JSOT, 1991.

Cranfield, C. E. B. *A Critical and Exegetical Commentary on the Epistle to the Romans*. vol. 2. Edinburgh: T. & T. Clark, 1979.

Crocker, Cornelia Cyss. *Reading 1 Corinthians in the Twenty-First Century*. New York; London: T. & T. Clark, 2004.

Dahl, N. A. "Paul and the Church at Corinth according to 1 Cor 1:10—4:21." In *Christian History and Interpretation*, edited by W. R. Farmer, C. F. D. Moule and R. R. Niebuhr. 313–35. Cambridge: Cambridge University Press, 1967.

Daley, Brian E. "Position and Patronage in the Early Church: the Original Meaning of 'Primacy of Honour.'" *JTS* 44 (1993) 529–53.
Das, A. Andrew. *Paul, the Law, and the Covenant*. Peabody: Hendrickson, 2001.
———. *Romans: a Short Commentary*. Grand Rapids: Eerdmans, 1985.
Datiri, Dachollom. "1 Corinthians." In *African Bible Commentary*, edited by Tokunboh Adeyemo. 1377–98. Grand Rapids: Zondervan; Nairobi: WorldAlive, 2006.
David, S. P., and G. Myers. *Social Psychology*. 7th ed. New York: McGraw Hill, 2002.
Davis, James A. *Wisdom and Spirit: An Investigation of 1 Corinthians 1:18—3:20 Against the Background of Jewish Sapiential Translations in the Greco-Roman Period*. Lanham; New York; London: University Press of America, 1984.
Dawes, Gregory W. "But If You Can Gain Your Freedom (1 Corinthians 7:17–24)." *CBQ* 52 (1990) 681–97.
———. "The Danger of Idolatry: First Corinthians 8:7–13." *CBQ* 58 (1996) 82–98.
de Bary, Wm. Theodore and JaHyun Kim Haboush, eds. *The Rise of Neo-Confucianism in Korea*. New York: Columbia University Press, 1985.
De Boer, Martinus. "The Composition of 1 Corinthians." *NTS* 40 (1994) 229–45.
DeMaris, Richard E. "Book Reviews on *Urban Religion in Roman Corinth: Interdisciplinary Approaches*. Edited by Daniel N. Schowalter and Steven J. Friesen. HTS 53. Cambridge: Harvard University Press, 2005." *JBL* 125 (2006) 614–17.
———. "Corinth, the First City of Greece: An Urban History of late Antique Cult and Religion." *JBL* 121 (2002) 769–73.
———. "Corinthian Religion and Baptism for the Dead (1 Corinthians 15:29): Insights from Archaeology and Anthropology." *JBL* 114 (1995) 661–82.
Deming, Will. *Paul on Marriage and Celibacy: The Hellenistic Background of 1 Corinthians 7*. Grand Rapids: Eerdmans, 2004.
Demographic Composition of Melbourne and the State of Victoria. No page. Online: http://www.monash.edu/international/australia/
de Silva, David. *Honour, Patronage, Kinship and Purity: Unlocking New Testament Culture*. Downers Grove: InterVarsity, 2000.
Deuchler, Martina. *The Confucian Transformation of Korea: A Study of Society and Ideology*. Massachusetts: Harvard University Press, 1992.
de Vos, Craig Steven. *Church and Community Conflicts: The Relationships of the Thessalonian, Corinthian, and Philippian Churches with their Wider Civic Communities*. SBLDS 168. Atlanta: Scholars, 1999.
———. "Once a Slave, Always a Slave? Slavery, Manumission and Relational Patterns in Paul's Letter to Philemon." *JSNT* 82 (2001) 89–105.
———. "Stepmothers, Concubines and the Case of *PORNEIA* in 1 Corinthians 5." *NTS* 44 (1998) 104–44.
De Witt, Norman. *St. Paul and Epicurus*. Minneapolis: University of Minneapolis Press, 1954.
Dicicco, Mario M. *Paul's Use of ETHOS, PATHOS, and LOGOS in 2 Corinthians 10–13*. Lewiston: Mellen Biblical Press, 1995.
Dio Cassius. *The Roman History*. Translated by E. Cary. The Loeb Classic Library. London: William Heinemann; Cambridge: Harvard University Press, 1969.
Dio Chrysostom. *Discourse*. Translated by H. Lamar Crosby. The Loeb Classic Library. London: William Heinemann; Cambridge: Harvard University Press, 1962.
Dodd, Brian J. "Paul's Paradigmatic 'I' and 1 Corinthians 6.12." *JSNT* 59 (1995) 39–58.
Donaldson, Terence L. *Paul and the Gentiles: Remapping the Apostle's Convictional World*. Minneapolis: Fortress, 1997.

Downing, F. Gerald. "Review on Robert S. Dutch's *the Educated Elite in 1 Corinthians: Education and Community Conflict in Greco-Roman Context*." *JSNT Booklist 2006* 28 (2006), 90.
Dunn, James D. G. *1 Corinthians*. Sheffield: Sheffield Academic, 1995.
———. *The Epistle to the Galatians*. BNTC. London: Hendrickson, 1993. Revised, 2002.
———. *Romans 9-16*. WBC. vol. 38B. Dallas: Word, 1998.
———. *The Theology of Paul the Apostle*. Grand Rapids: Eerdmans, 1998.
Dutch, Robert S. *The Educated Elite in 1 Corinthians: Education and Community Conflict in Graeco-Roman Context*. JSNTS 271. London; New York: T. & T. Clark, 2005.
Edwards, Thomas Charles. *A Commentary on the First Epistle to the Corinthians*. 4th ed. London: Hodder & Stoughton, 1903.
Elliot, John H. "Patronage and Clientage." In *The Social Sciences and New Testament Interpretation*, edited by Richard L. Rohrbaugh. 144-56. Peabody: Hendrickson, 1996.
Elliott, Neil. *Liberating Paul: the Justice of God and the Politics of the Apostle*. Maryknoll: Orbis, 1994. 5th print, 2001.
Ellis, E. Earle. "Soma in First Corinthians." *Interpretation* 44 (1990) 132-43.
———. "'Spiritual' Gifts in the Pauline Community." *NTS* 20 (1974) 128-44.
———. "Traditions in 1 Corinthians." *NTS* 32 (1986) 481-502.
Endsjø, Dag Øistein. "Immortal Bodies, Before Christ: Bodily Continuity in Ancient Greece and 1 Corinthians." *JSNT* 30 (2008) 417-36.
Engberg-Pedersen, T. "The Gospel and Social Practice according to 1 Corinthians." *NTS* 33 (1987) 557-84.
Engels, Donald. *Roman Corinth: An Alternative Model for the Classical City*. Chicago; London: the University of Chicago Press, 1990.
England, John C., Jose Kuttianimattathil sdb, John Mansford Prior svd, Lily A. Quintos rc, David Suh Kwang-sun, and Janice Wicheri, eds. *Asian Christian Theologies: A Research Guide to Author, Movements, Sources*. vol 3. Northeast Asia. Delhi: ISPCK; Quezon City: Claretian; Maryknoll: Orbis, 2004.
Erickson, Anderson. *Traditions as Rhetorical Proof: Pauline Argumentation in 1 Corinthians*. Stockholm: Almqvist and Wilsell International, 1998.
Everts, J. M. "Financial Support." In *Dictionary of Paul and His Letters*, edited by G. F. Hawthorne, R. P. Martin and D. G. Reid. 295-300. Illinois; Leicester: InterVarsity, 1993.
Fee, Gordon D. "*Eidōlothuta* Once Again: An Interpretation of 1 Corinthians 8-10." *Biblica* 61 (1980) 172-97.
———. *The First Epistle to the Corinthians*. NICNT. Grand Rapids: Eerdmans, 1987.
———. "Toward a Theology of 1 Corinthians." In *Pauline Theology 2: 1 & 2 Corinthians*, edited by David M. Hay. Minneapolis: Fortress, 1993.
Ferguson, Everett. *Backgrounds of Early Christianity*. Grand Rapids: Eerdmans, 1987.
Ferguson, S. B., et al. *New Dictionary of Theology*. Leicester: InterVarsity, 1991.
Fiore, Benjamin. "'Convert Allusion' in 1 Corinthians 1-4." *CBQ* 47 (1985) 85-102.
———. *The Function of Personal Example in the Socratic and Pastoral Epistles*. Rome: Biblical Institute, 1986.
Fiorenza, Elisabeth Schüssler. *In Memory of Her: A Feminist Theological Reconstruction of Christian Origins*. New York: Crossroad, 1983.
———. "Missionaries, Apostles, Co-workers: Romans 16 and the Reconstruction of Women's Early Christian History." In *Feminist Theology: A Reader*, edited by Ann Loades. 57-71. London: SPCK, 1990

———. "Rhetorical Situation and Historical Reconstruction in 1 Corinthians." *NTS* 33 (1987) 386–403.

Fishburne, Charles W. "1 Corinthians III. 10–15 and the Testament of Abraham." *NTS* 17 (1961) 109–15.

Fisk, Bruce N. "Eating Meat Offered to Idols: Corinthian Behavior and Pauline Response in 1 Corinthians 8–10 (A Response to Gordon Fee)." *Trinity Journal* 10 (1989) 49–70.

Fitzgerald, John T. *Cracks in an Earthen Vessel: An Examination of the Catalogues of Hardships in the Corinthian Correspondence*. Atlanta: Scholars, 1988.

Flemming, Dean. *Contextualization in the New Testament: Patterns for Theology and Mission*. Leicester: Apollos, 2005.

Forbes, Christopher. "Comparison, Self-Praise and Irony: Paul's Boasting and the Conventions of Hellenistic Rhetoric." *NTS* 32 (1986) 1–30.

Fotopoulos, John. *Food Offered to Idols in Roman Corinth: A Social-Rhetorical Reconstruction of 1 Corinthians 8:1—11:1*. Tübingen: Mohr Siebeck, 2003.

Francis, J. "'As Babes in Christ'—Some proposals regarding 1 Corinthians 3:1–3." *JSNT* 7 (1980) 41–60.

Frid, Bo. "The Enigmatic *ALLA* in 1 Corinthians 2:9." *NTS* 31 (1985) 603–11.

Funk, Robert W. *Language, Hermeneutics, and Word of God*. New York: Harper & Row, 1966.

Furnish, Victor Paul. "Corinth in Paul's Time: What Can Archaeology Tell Us?" *BAR* 14 (1988) 14–27.

———. "Paul and the Corinthians: The Letters, the Challenges of Ministry, the Gospel." *Interpretation* 52 (1998) 229–45.

———. "Theology in 1 Corinthians." In *Pauline Theology 2: 1 & 2 Corinthians*, edited by David M. Hay. 59–89. Minneapolis: Fortress, 1993.

———. *The Theology of the First Letter to the Corinthians*. Cambridge: Cambridge University Press, 1999.

Garces-Foley, Kathleen, *Crossing the Ethnic Divide: the Multiethnic Church on a Mission*. New York: Oxford University Press, 2007.

Garlington, Don. "Role Reversal and Paul's Use of Scripture in Galatians 3:10–13." *JSNT* 65 (1997) 85–121.

Garnsey, Peter and Richard Saller. "Patronal Power Relations." In *Paul and Empire: Religion and Power in Roman Imperial Society*, edited by Richard A. Horsley. 96–103. Harrisburg: Trinity International, 1997.

———. *The Roman Empire: Economy, Society and Culture*. London: Duckworth, 1987.

Gaventa, B. R. "Mother's Milk and Ministry in 1 Corinthians 3." In *Theology and Ethics in Paul and His Interpreters*, edited by E. H. Lovering Jr. and Jerry L. Sumney. 101–13. Nashville: Abingdon, 1996.

Georgi, Dieter. *The Opponents of Paul in Second Corinthians*. Philadelphia: Fortress; Edinburgh: T. & T. Clark, 1986.

Gill, David W. J. "Erastus the Aedile." *TynBul* 40 (1989) 293–301.

Gillihan, Yonder Moynihan. "Jewish Laws on Illicit Marriage, the Defilement of Offspring, and the Holiness of the Temple: a New Halakic Interpretation of 1 Corinthians 7:14." *JBL* (2002) 711–44.

Given, Mark D. "Containing Cunning in 1 Corinthians 1–4." No page. Online: http://course.smsu.edu/mdg421f/Containing%20Cunning.htm.

———. *Paul's True Rhetoric: Ambiguity, Cunning, and Deception in Greece and Rome*. Harrisburg: Trinity International, 2001.

Glancy, Jennifer A. *Slavery in Early Christianity*. Minneapolis: Fortress, 2006.

Gooch, Paul W. "'Consciousness' in 1 Corinthians 8 and 10." *NTS* 33 (1987) 244–54.

———. *Dangerous Food: 1 Corinthians 8–10 in its Context*. Waterloo: Wilfrid Laurier University Press, 1993.

———. *Partial Knowledge: Philosophical Studies in Paul*. Notre Dame: University of Notre Dame Press, 1987.

Gothel, Ingerborg. "On the Description of Confucianism and the Doctrine of Yi Hwang in the 1st Euro-linguistic Publication about Korea." In *T'oegye'hak yeungunonjeung, je 9 kwon: Seoyangeui T'oegyeyeungu* (Studies on T'oegye, vol 9: studies on T'oegye in the Western world), edited by Whi-chil Song and Gooy-Hyun Shin. 41–47. Dae-gu: Kyung-Book University T'oegye Institute, 1997.

Goulder, Michael D. *Paul and the Competing Mission in Corinth*. Peabody: Hendrickson, 2001.

———. "*Sophia* in 1 Corinthians." *NTS* 37 (1991) 516–34.

Gradel, Ittai. *Emperor Worship and Roman Religion*. Oxford Classic Monographs. Oxford: Clarendon, 2002.

Grant, Michael, trans. *Cicero and the Good Life*. London: Penguin, 1971.

Grant, Robert M. *Paul in the Roman World and the Conflict of Corinth*. Louisville; London; Leiden: Westminster John Knox, 2001.

Grindheim, Sigurd. "Book Reviews on Yeo, K. K. (Khok–Khng), Charles H. Cosgrove and Herald Weiss' *Cross-Cultural Paul: Journeys to Others, Journeys to Ourselves*. Grand Rapids: Eerdmans, 2005." *RBL* 8 (2006). No page. Online: http://www.bookreviews.org/pdf/4983_5237.pdf.

———. "Wisdom for the Perfect: Paul's Challenge to the Corinthian Church (1 Corinthians 2:6–16)." *JBL* 121 (2002) 689–709.

Grosheide, F. W. *Commentary on the First Epistle to the Corinthians: The English Text with Introduction, Exposition and Notes*. Grand Rapids: Eerdmans, 1979.

Gruden, Wayne A. *The Gift of Prophecy in 1 Corinthians*. Lantlan; New York; London: University Press of America, 1982.

Guenther, H. O. "Gnosticism in Corinth?" In *Origins and Method: Towards a New Understanding of Judaism and Christianity*, edited by B. H. McLean. 44–81. JSNTSup 86. Sheffield: Sheffield Academic, 1993.

Gundry, Robert H. *Soma in Biblical Theology with Emphasis on Pauline Anthropology*. Cambridge: Cambridge University Press, 1976.

Gunther, John J. *St. Paul's Opponents and their Background: A Study of Apocalyptic and Sectarian Teachings*. NovTSup 35. Leiden: Brill, 1973.

Gveritt, Anthony. *Cicero: the Life and Times of Rome's Greatest Politician*. New York: Random House Trade Paperbacks, 2003.

Hafemann, S. J. "Corinthians, Letters to the." In *Dictionary of Paul and His Letters*, edited by G. F. Hawthorne, R. P. Martin and D. G. Reid. 164–79. Illinois; Leicester: InterVarsity Press, 1993.

Hahn, H. C. "Boast." In *The New International Dictionary of New Testament Theology*, edited by Colin Brown. vol 1. 227–29. Grand Rapids: Zondervan; Exter: Paternoster, 1975.

Hall, David R. "A Disguise for the Wise: METASCHEMATISMOS in 1 Corinthians 4:6." *NTS* 40 (1994) 143–49.

Han, Deouk-Wung. *T'oegye simrihak: sungkeuk mik sahoi simrihak chupgeun* (T'oegye Psychology: A Characteristic and Social Psychological Approach). Seoul: Sunggyunkwan University Press, 1994.

Han, Gil-Soo. "Korean Christianity in Multicultural Australia: Is It Dialogical or Segregating Koreans?" In *Studies in World Christianity*, edited by Alistair Kee. 114–35. vol 10. Edinburgh: Edinburgh University Press, 2004.

Hanges, James. "1 Corinthians 4:6 and the Possibility of Written Bylaws in the Corinthian Church." *JBL* 117 (1998) 275–98.

Hangook Kidokgyo Yeunguhoe. *Hangook Kidokgyoeui Yeuksa* (A History of the Korean Christianity). vol 1. Seoul: Kidokgyomoonsa, 1991.

Hanson, A. "1 Corinthians 4:13b and Lamentations 3:45." *ExpT* 93 (1982) 214–15.

Harrill, J. Albert. *Slaves in the New Testament: Literary, Social, and Moral Dimensions*. Minneapolis: Fortress, 2006.

Hays, Richard B. "The Conversion of the Imagination: Scripture and Eschatology in 1 Corinthians." *NTS* 45 (1999) 391–412.

———. *First Corinthians*. IBC. Louisville: John Knox, 1997.

Heil, John Paul. *The Rhetorical Role of Scripture in 1 Corinthians*. Atlanta: Society of Biblical Literature, 2005.

Hendrix, Holland. "Benefactor/Patron Networks in the Urban Environment: Evidence from Thessalonica." *Semeia* 56 (1991) 39–58.

Heo, Do-Kyung. *A Comparative Study of Tien and God: Centred on Confucianism and Christianity*. MA diss., WonKwang University, 1996.

Héring, Jean. *The First Epistle of Saint Paul to the Corinthians*. Translated by A. W. Heathcote and P. J. Allcock. London: Epworth, 1962.

Herms, Ronald. "'Being Saved without Honor': A Conceptual Link between 1 Corinthians 3 and 1 *Enoch* 50?" *JSNT* 29 (2006) 187–210.

Hester, J. David (Amador). "Re-Reading 2 Corinthians: A Rhetorical Approach." In *Rhetorical Argumentation in Biblical Texts: Essays from the Lund 2000 Conference*, edited by Anders Eriksson, Thomas H. Olbricht, and Walter Übelacker. 276–95. Harrisburg: Trinity International, 2002.

Hiigel, John L. *Leadership in 1 Corinthians: A Case Study in Paul's Ecclesiology*. Lewiston; Queenston; Lampeter: Edwin Mellen, 2003.

Hock, Ronald F. "Paul's Tentmaking and the Problem of his Social Class." *JBL* 97 (1978) 555–64.

———. *The Social Context of Pauline Ministry: Tentmaking and Apostleship*. Philadelphia: Fortress, 1980.

Hofius, Otfried. "Das Zitat 1 Kor 2.9 und das koptische Testament des Jakob," *ZNW* 66 (1975) 140–42.

Holladay, William L., ed. *A Concise Hebrew and Aramaic Lexicon of the Old Testament: Based on the First, Second, and Third Editions of the Koehler-Baumgartner Lexicon in Veteris Testamenti libros*. Grand Rapids: Eerdmans, 1971.

Hollander, Harm W. "The Testing by Fire of the Buildings' Works: 1 Corinthians 3. 10–15." *NTS* (1994) 89–104.

Hooker, Morna D. "'Beyond the Things Which are Written': An Examination of 1 Cor. IV. 6." *NTS* 10 (1963–64) 128–30.

Horrell, David G. *The Social Ethos of the Corinthian Correspondence: Interests and Ideology from 1 Corinthians to 1 Clement*. Edinburgh: T. & T. Clark, 1996.

Horsley, Richard A. *1 Corinthians*. ANTC. Nashville: Abingdon, 1998.

———. "Consciousness and Freedom among the Corinthians: 1 Corinthians 8–10." *CBQ* 40 (1978) 574–89.

———. "Gnosis in Corinth: 1 Corinthians 8:1–6," *NTS* 27 (1981) 32–51.

———. ed. *Paul and Empire: Religion and Power in Roman Imperial Society*. Harrisburg: Trinity International, 1997.

———. "Introduction." In *Paul and the Roman Imperial Order*, edited by Richard A. Horsley. 1–23. Harrisburg: Trinity International, 2004.

———. "Pneumatikos vs. Psychikos Distinctions of Spirituality Status among the Corinthians." *JSNT* 69 (1976) 269–88.

———. "Rhetoric and Empire—and 1 Corinthians." In *Paul and Politics: EKKLESIA, ISRAEL, Imperium, Interpretation: Essays in Honor of Krister Stendahl*, edited by Richard A. Horsley. 72–102. Harrisburg: Trinity International, 2000.

———. *Wisdom and Spiritual Transcendence at Corinth: Studies in First Corinthians*. Eugene, Oregon: Cascade, 2008.

———. "Wisdom of Word and Words of Wisdom in Corinth." *CBQ* 39 (1977) 224–39.

Howard, George. *Paul: Crisis in Galatia: A Study in Early Christian Theology*. London: Cambridge University Press, 1979.

Hubbell, Harry Mortimer. *The Influences of Isocrates on Cicero, Dionysius and Aristides*. New Haven: Yale University Press, 1913.

Hultgren, Stephen. "The Origin of Paul's Doctrine of the Two Adams in 1 Corinthians 15:45–49." *JSNT* 25 (2003) 343–70.

Hurd, John Coolidge. *The Origin of 1 Corinthians*. London: SPCK, 1965.

Hutchinson, Mark. "The Anatomy of Misunderstanding: Readings and Consequences for the Home Australian Korean Churches." *Australasian Pentecostal Studies* 10 (2006/7) 49–72.

Hwang, Ey-Dong. *Hanguk U-Hak SaSang (Korean Confucianism)*. Seoul: Seo Kang, 1995.

Hwang, Joon-Yon. "Neo-Confucian Scholars of the Choson Dynasty and the Problems of Spiritual Cultivation in Case of the 'Four-Seven Debate.'" *Dongyang chulhak yeungu* (Studies of Oriental Philosophy) 25 (2001) 217–34.

Institute of Korean Church History Studies. *Hangook Kidokyoeui Yeoksa I* (A History of Korean Church). vol 1. 16th Century–1918. Seoul: Christian Literature, 1989.

Jang, Wang-Sik. "Yukyo'e chowuljaneun yikneunga?" (Is there a Supernatural Being in Confucianism?) *Sinhak'kwa segye* (Theology and World) 45 (2002) 390–418.

Jang, Yip-Moon. *T'oegye chulhak yipmoon* (Introduction to T'oegye's Philosophy). Seoul: T'oegyehak yeunguwon chul'panbu, 1990.

Jeffers, James S. *The Greco-Roman World of the New Testament Era: Exploring the Background of Early Christianity*. Downers Grove: InterVarity, 1999.

———. "Slaves of God: The impact of the Cult of the Roman Emperor on Paul's Use of the Language of Power Relations." *FeH* 34 (2002) 123–39.

Johnson, Lee A. "Paul's Epistolary Presence in Corinth: A New Look at Robert W. Funk's *Apostolic Parousia*." *CBQ* 68 (2006) 481–501.

Johnson, Terry and Christopher Dandeker. "Patronage: Relation and System." In *Patronage in Ancient Society*, edited by A. Wallace-Hadrill. 219–42. London; New York: Routledge, 1989.

Josephus. *Jewish Antiquities*. Translated by Ralph Marcus. London: William Heinemann; Cambridge: Harvard University Press, 1966.

Joubert, Stephan J. "Managing the Household: Paul as *paterfamilias* of the Christian Household group in Corinth." In *Modeling Early Christianity: Social-Scientific Studies of the New Testament in its Context*, edited by Philip F. Esler. 213–23. London; New York: Routledge, 1995.

Judge, E. A. "Paul's Boasting in Relation to Contemporary Professional Practice." *ABR* 16 (1968) 37–50.

———. *Rank and Status in the World of the Caesars and St. Paul*. Christchurch: University of Canterbury Press, 1982.
Jun, Hong Ki Hye. No page. Online: http://www.pressian.com/article/article.asp?article num=60100413143453.
Jung, Hwang-Myung. *Chuja simsungron'eui T'oegye chulhakjeok chungae* (Chuhee's Theory of Mind in T'oegye's Philosophy). PhD diss., Daejeon University, 2001.
Jung, Jin-Il. *Ukyoyihae* (Understanding of Confucianism). Seoul: Hyoung-Sear, 2000.
Kalton, Michael C., trans. and ed. *To Become a Sage: The Ten Diagrams on Sage Learning by Yi T'oegye*. New York: Columbia University, 1988.
———. "T'oegyewha 21segyheemang (T'oegye and Hope of the Twenty First Century)." *T'oegye hakbo* 110 (2001) 13–32.
Käsemann, Ernst. *Commentary on Romans*. Translated by Geoffery W. Bromiley. Grand Rapids: Eerdmans, 1980.
Keener, Craig S. *1–2 Corinthians*. NCamBC. Cambridge; New York: Cambridge University Press, 2005.
Kennedy, George A. *Classic Rhetoric and its Christian and Secular Tradition from Ancient to Modern Times*. 2nd ed. Chapel Hill; London: the University of North Carolina Press, 1999.
———. *New Testament Interpretation through Rhetorical Criticism*. Chapel Hill; London: the University of North Carolina Press, 1984.
Keum, Jang-Tae. *Confucianism and Korean Thoughts, Korean Studies Series 10*. Seoul: Jimoondang, 2000.
———. *T'oegye hakpaeui sasang I* (Thoughts of T'oegye's Scholars I). Seoul: Gypmoondang, 1996.
———. *T'oegye hakpaeui sasang II* (Thoughts of T'oegye's Scholars II). Seoul: Gypmoondang, 2001.
———. "Uhak'e ituseo jee'eui moonjae (The Problem of Knowledge in Confucianism)." *Sungdae nonmoonjip* 19 (1974) 227–46.
———. "Yugyo'e yikk'suseo jee'eui munjae (Matter of knowledge in Confucianism)." *Sung-Dae nonmun'jyp* (Collection of Sunggyun'kwan University Essays) 19 (1974) 227–46.
Kijne, J. J. "We, Us and Our in I and II Corinthians." *NovT* 8 (1966) 171–79.
Kim, Chang-Dong. "T'oegye Yi Hwang." *Gongkoon* 194 (1985) 151–61.
Kim, Chewon and Won-Yong Kim. *The Arts of Korea: Ceramics, Sculpture, Gold, Bronze, and Lacquer*. London: Thames and Hudson, 1966.
Kim, Chong-ho. *Korean Shamanism: the Cultural Paradox*. Aldershot; Burlington: Ashgate, 2003.
Kim, Ji-Chul. *SongseoJuseok Korindojeonseo* (Commentary on 1 Corinthians). Seoul: Daehan Kidokkyo Seosoe, 1999.
Kim, Johann. D. *God, Israel, and Gentiles: Rhetoric and Situation in Romans 9–11*. SBLDS 176. Atlanta: Society of Biblical Literature, 2000.
Kim, Jong-Seok. *T'oegye simhak yeungu* (A Study on T'oegye's Thought of Mind). PhD diss., Young-Nam University, 1996.
Kim, Jong-suk. *T'oegye hakeui Ihae* (Understanding of T'eogye Studies). Seoul: Il Song Media, 2001.
Kim, Kwang-Su. *Baulseoshin Dasiykki: Korindojeonseo* (Re-reading of the Pauline Epistles: 1 Corinthians). Seoul: EunSung Chu'l pansa, 1999.
Kim, Seung-Hyun. *T'oegye Kyunghak yeungu* (A Study on T'oegye's Thought of Reverence). PhD diss., Chuen-Book University, 2000.

Kim, Seyoon. *Paul and the New Perspective: Second Thoughts on the Origin of Paul's Gospel.* Grand Rapids: Eerdmans, 2002.

Kim, Shi-Gyun. *T'oegye yoonrihak'e kwanhan yeungu* (A Study on T'oegye's Ethics). PhD diss., Do-A University, 1991.

Kim, Yong-Ok. *Korindojeonseo* (Commentary on 1 Corinthians). Seoul: Daehan Kidokkyo Seosoe, 1961.

Klutz, Todd E. "Re-Reading 1 Corinthians after *Rethinking 'Gnosticism'*." *JSNT* 26 (2003) 193–216.

The Korea World Missions Association. No page. Online: http://www.international.ucla.edu/korea/events/showevent.asp?eventid=5347.

Kruse, Colin. *2 Corinthians.* TNTC. Leicester: InterVarsity, 1987. Reprint, 2002.

Kuck, David W. *Judgment and Community Conflict: Paul's Use of Apocalyptic Judgment Language in 1 Corinthians 3:5—4:5.* Leiden: Brill, 1992.

Kwok, Pui-lan, *Postcolonial Imagination and Feminist Theology.* Louisville: Westminster John Knox, 2005.

Kwon, Oh-Bong. *T'oegye'eui yildaegi: Gaeul'haneul baleundal'cherum* (T'oegye's life: like a bright moon in the Autumn Sky). Seoul: Gyoyuk'sa, 2001.

Kwon, Oh-Young. "1 Corinthians 12:12–13: An Ethnic Analysis and its Evaluation from a Korean-Ethnocentric (*danil minjok*) Christian Context." In *Mapping and Engaging the Bible in Asian Cultures: Congress of the Society of Asian Biblical Studies 2008 Seoul Conference,* edited by Yeong Mee Lee and Yoon Jong Yoo. 123–39. Seoul: Christian Literature Society of Korea, 2009.

———. "A Critical Review of Recent Scholarship on the Pauline Opposition and the Nature of its Wisdom (*sophia*) in 1 Corinthians 1–4." *Currents in Biblical Research* 8 (2010) 386-427.

———. "Discovering the Characteristics of Collegia—Collegia Sodalicia and Collegia Tenuiorum in 1 Corinthians 8, 10 and 15." *Horizons in Biblical Theology* (2010) forthcoming.

Kyungsang bukdo. *T'oegyehak yeungu* (T'oegye Studies). vols 8–10, 15, 16–21. Daegu: Hankok Chulpan' sa, 1995.

Lambrecht, Jan. "Paul's Boasting about the Corinthians: A Study of 2 Cor 8:24—9:5." *NovT* 40 (1998) 352–68.

Lamp, Jeffrey S. *First Corinthians 1–4 in Light of Jewish Wisdom Traditions: Christ, Wisdom, and Spirituality.* Lewiston; Queenston; Lampeter: Edwin Mellen, 2000.

Lampe, Peter. "The Corinthian Eucharistic Dinner Party: Exegesis of a Cultural Context." *Affirmation* 4 (1991) 1–15.

———. "The Roman Christians of Romans 16." In *The Roman Debate,* edited by Karl P. Donfried. 216–30. 2nd ed. Peabody: Hendrickson, 1997.

Lanci, John R. *A New Temple for Corinth: Rhetorical and Archaeological Approaches to Pauline Imagery.* New York: Lang, 1997.

Lautenschlager, von Markus. "Abschied vom Disputierer Zur Bedeutung von *Suzētētēs* in 1 Kor 1.20." *ZNW* 83 (1992) 276–85.

Lee, Hun-Goo. *Hanguk Jeuntong Jongkyo hanguk kyohoi* (Korean Traditional Religions and Korean Church). Seoul: Gloria, 1995.

Lee, Jeong-Kyu. "Confucian Thought Affecting Leadership and Organizational Culture of Korea Higher Education." *Radical Pedagogy* 3 (2001). No page. Online: http://radicalpedigogy.icaap.org/content/issue3_3/5-lee.html.

Lee, Jung-Young, ed. *Ancestor Worship and Christianity in Korea.* Lewiston; New York: Mellen, 1998.

Lee, Michelle V. *Paul, the Stoics, and the Body of Christ*. SNTSMS 137. New York: Cambridge University Press, 2006.

Lee, Sang-Syub. *T'oegyeeui Kyung Sasang gwa Calvineui Christo Jungshim Sasang Beegyo* (Comparative Studies between T'oegye's thought of reverence and the Christology of Calvin). MA diss., Hanil Presbyterian University, 2000.

Lee, Sang Taek. *Religion and Social Formation in Korea: Minjung and Millenarianism*. Berlin; New York: Mouton de Gruyter, 1996.

Lee, Young-Ho. "National Identity in the Korean 'I' Consciousness." *Korea Journal* (1978) 1–12.

Legault, André. "Beyond the Things Which are Written (1 Cor. 4:6)." *NTS* 18 (1972) 227–31.

Lim, Timothy H. "'Not in Persuasive Words of Wisdom, but in the Demonstration of the Spirit and Power.'" *NovT* 29 (1987) 137–49.

Litfin, Duane. *St. Paul's Theology of Proclamation: 1 Corinthians 1–4 and Greco-Roman Rhetoric*. SNTSMS 79. Cambridge; New York: Cambridge University Press, 1994.

Lo, Lung-Kwong. "Paul's Gospel to the Gentiles and its Implications for Christian Mission to Chinese." In *Text and Task: Scripture and Mission*, edited by Michael Parsons. 121–39. Carlisle: Paternoster, 2005.

Longenecker, Richard N. *Galatians*. WBC. vol. 41. Dallas: Word, 1990.

Lüdemann, Gerd. *Opposition to Paul in Jewish Christianity*. Translated by M. Eugene Boring. Minneapolis: Fortress, 1989.

MacMullen, Ramsay. *Roman Social Relations 50 BCE to CE 284*. New Haven & London: Yale University Press, 1974.

Malherbe, Abraham J. "The Beasts at Ephesus." *JBL* 87 (1968) 71–80.

———. *Social Aspects of Early Christianity*. Baton Rouge: Louisiana State University Press, 1977.

Malina, Bruce and Richard L. Rohrbaugh. *Social Science Commentary on the Synoptic Gospels*. Minneapolis: Fortress, 1992.

Marshall, Peter. *Enmity in Corinth: Social Conventions in Paul's Relations with the Corinthians*. Tübingen: J. C. B. Mohr (Paul Siebeck), 1987.

Martin, Dale B. *The Corinthian Body*. New Haven; London: Yale University Press, 1995.

———. "Review Essay: Justin, J Meggett, *Paul, Poverty and Survival*." *JSNT* 84 (2001) 51–64.

———. *Slavery as Salvation: the Metaphor of Slavery in the Pauline Christianity*. New Haven; London: Yale University Press, 1990.

Martin, Ralph P. *1, 2 Corinthians*. Word Biblical Themes. Dallas: Word, 1988.

Massey, Preston T. "The Meaning of *Katakaluptō* and *Kata Kephalēs Echōn* in 1 Corinthians 11:2–16." *NTS* 53 (2007) 502–23.

Matera, Frank J. *Galatians*. Sacra Pagina Series 9. Collegeville: the Liturgical Press, 1992.

May, Alistair Scott. *The Body for the Lord: Sex and Identity in 1 Corinthians 5–7*. London; NY: T. & T. Clark, 2004.

Mearns, Christopher L. "Early Eschatological Development in Paul: the Evidence of 1 Corinthians." *JSNT* 22 (1984) 19–35.

Meeks, W. A. *The First Urban Christians: The Social World of the Apostle Paul*. New Haven; London: Yale University Press, 1983.

———. *The Moral World of the First Christians*. London: SPCK, 1987.

Meggitt, Justin J. "Meat Consumption and Social Conflict in Corinth." *JTS* 45 (1994) 137–41.

———. *Paul, Poverty and Survival*. Edinburgh: T. & T. Clark, 1998.

———. "Response to Martin and Theissen." *JSNT* 84 (2001) 85–94.
Mikalson, Jon D. *Ancient Greek Religion*. Malden; Oxford; Carlton: Blackwell, 2005.
Miller, Gene. "*Archontōn tou aiōnos*—A new look at 1 Corinthians 2:6–8." *JBL* 91 (1972) 522–28.
Min, Kyong-Bae. *Hangook Kidokyohoisa* (A History of Korean Church). Seoul: Daehan Kidokyo Ch'ulpansa, 1991.
Mitchell, Alan J. "Rich and Poor in the Courts of Corinth: Litigiousness and Status in 1 Corinthians 6:1–11." *NTS* 39 (1993) 562–86.
Mitchell, Margaret M. "Concerning (*Peri De* in 1 Corinthians." *NovT* 31 (1989) 229–56.
———. *Paul and the Rhetoric of Reconciliation: An Exegetical Investigation of the Language and Composition of 1 Corinthians*. Louisville; Westminster: John Knox, 1989.
Moffatt, James. *The First Epistle of Paul to the Corinthians*. MNTC. 2nd ed. London: Hodder & Stoughton, 1951.
Moffet, Samuel Hugh. *A History of Christianity in Asia*. vol II. 1500–1900. Maryknoll: Orbis, 2005.
Moltmann, Jürgen. "Ancestor Respect and the Hope of Resurrection." *Sino-Christian Studies: An International Journal of Bible, Theology & Philosophy* 1 (2006) 13–26.
Moon, Tae-Ju. "The Korean American Dream and the Blessings of Hananim (God)." In *the Global God: Multicultural Evangelical Views of God*, edited by Aída Besançon Spencer and William David Spencer. 231–47. Grand Rapids: Baker, 1998.
Morgan, G. Campbell. *The Corinthian Letters of Paul: An Exposition of 1 and 2 Corinthians*. New York; London; Edinburgh: Fleming H. Revell Company, 1946.
Morris, Leon. *1 Corinthians*. TNTC. 2nd ed. Grand Rapids: Eerdmans, 1999.
Munck, J. *Paul and the Salvation of Mankind*. Atlanta: John Knox; London: SCM, 1959.
Munro, W. "Interpolation in the Epistles: Weighing Probability." *NTS* 36 (1990) 436–37.
Murphy-O'Connor, Jerome. *1 Corinthians*. New Testament Message. Wilmington, DE: Michael Glazier, 1979.
———. "'Baptised for the Dead' (1 Cor., XV, 29): A Corinthian Slogan?" *RB* 88 (1981) 532–43.
———. "The Corinth that Saint Paul Saw." *BA* 47 (1984) 147–59.
———. "Corinthian Slogan in 1 Cor 6:12–20." *CBQ* 40 (1978) 391–96.
———. "Food and Spiritual Gifts in 1 Cor 8:8." *CBQ* 41 (1979) 292–98.
———. "Interpolation in 1 Corinthians." *CBQ* 48 (1986) 81–94.
———. "Paul and Gallio." *JBL* 112 (1993) 315–17.
———. *St. Paul's Corinth: Texts and Archaeology*. 3rd ed. Collegeville: the Liturgical Press, 2002.
———. *The Theology of the Second Letter to the Corinthians*. Cambridge: Cambridge University Press, 1991.
Myers, G., and S. P. David. *Social Psychology*. 7th ed. New York: McGraw Hill, 2002.
Myrou, Augustine. "Sosthenes: the Former Crispus (?)" *GOTR* 44 (1999) 207–12.
Nahm, Andrew C. *A Panorama of 5000 Years: Korean History*. New Jersey: Hollym International, 1988.
Nasuti, Harry P. "The Woes of the Prophets and the Rights of the Apostle: The Internal Dynamics of 1 Corinthians 9." *CBQ* 50 (1988) 246–64.
National Museum of Korea. *A World of the Neo-Confucianism in Choson Dynasty*. Seoul: National Museum of Korea, 2003.
Neufeld, Dietmar. "Acts of Admonition and Rebuke: A Speech Act Approach to 1 Corinthians 6:1–11." *BI* 8 (2000) 375–99.

Newsome, James D. *Greek, Roman, and Jew: Currents of Culture and Belief in the New Testament World*. Philadelphia: Trinity Press International, 1992.

Newton, Derek. *Deity and Diet: the Dilemma of Sacrificial Food at Corinth*. JSNTS 169. Sheffield: Sheffield Academic, 1998.

Neyrey, Jerome H., ed. *The Social World of Luke-Acts: Models for Interpretation*. Peabody: Hendrickson, 1991.

O'Brien, Peter T., D. A. Carson, and Mark A. Seifrid. *Justification and Variegated Nomism, Volume II: The Paradoxes of Paul*. Tübingen: Morh Siebeck; Grand Rapids: Baker Academic, 2004.

O'Day, Gail R. "Jeremiah 9:22–23 and 1 Corinthians 1:26–31. A Study in Intertextuality." *JBL* 109 (1990) 259–67.

Olbricht, Thomas H. and Jerry L. Sumney, eds. *Paul and Pathos*. SBL Symposium Series 16. Atlanta: Society of Biblical Literature, 2001.

Oropeza, B. J. "Apostasy in the Wilderness: Paul's Message to the Corinthians in a State of Eschatological Liminality." *JSNT* 75 (1999) 69–86.

———. *Paul and Apostasy: Eschatology, Perseverance, and Falling Away in the Corinthian Congregation*. Tübingen: J. C. B. Mohr (Paul Siebeck), 2000.

Orr, William F. and James Arthur Walter. *1 Corinthians*. The Anchor Bible 32. Garden City: Doubleday, 1976.

Osiek, Carolyn and David L. Balch. *Families in the New Testament World: Households and House Churches*. Louisville: Westminster John Knox, 1997.

Pagels, Elaine. *The Gnostic Paul: Gnostic Exegesis of the Pauline Letters*. Philadelphia: Fortress, 1975.

Pai, Hyung Il and Timothy R. Tangherlini, eds. *Nationalism and the Construction of Korean Identity*. Berkeley: Institute of East Asian Studies, University of California, 1998.

Park, Eung Chun. *Either Jew or Gentile: Paul's Unfolding Theology of Inclusivity*. Louisville; London: Westminster John Knox, 2003.

Park, Hyo-Saeng. *BusanJin Church Centennial History 1891–1991*. Busan: BusanJin Church Press, 1991.

Park, Ik-Su. *Nuga guayen cham grisdoyin inga: Korindojeonseo* (Who are Christians really?: 1 Corinthians). Seoul: Daehan Kidokkyo Seosoe, 2002. No page. Online: http://sydneybookland.com/detail.php?code=1482.

Park, Young-Gyu. *Choson Wangjo Shillok* (Veritable Records of the Choson Dynasty). Seoul: Deul neuk, 1996.

Patrick, James E. "Living Rewards for Dead Apostles: 'Baptized for the Dead' in 1 Corinthians 15:29." *NTS* 52 (2006) 71–85.

Pausanias. *Guide to Greece: Central Greece*. Translated by Peter Levi. Harmondsworth; NY; Ringwood; Markham; Auckland: Penguin, 1985.

Pearson, Birger. "Hellenistic–Jewish Wisdom Speculation and Paul." In *Aspects of Wisdom in Judaism and Early Christianity*, edited by R. L. Wilken. 43–66. Notre Dame; London: University of Notre Dame Press, 1975. 43–66.

———. *The PNEUMATIKOS–PSYCHIKOS Terminology in 1 Corinthians: A Study in the Theology of the Corinthian Opponents of Paul and its Relation to Gnosticism*. SBLDS 12. Missoula: Scholars, 1973.

Peel, Malcolm L. and Jan Zandee. "'The Teachings of Silvanus' from the Library of Nag Hammadi (CG VII: 84, 15–118, 7)." *NovT* 14 (1972) 294–311.

Penna, Romano. "The Gospel as 'Power of God' according to 1 Corinthians 1:18–25." In *Paul the Apostle: A Theological and Exegetical Study*. Translated by Thomas P. Wahl. 169–80. vol 1. Collegeville: the Liturgical Press, 1996.

Perkins, Pheme. *Gnosticism and the New Testament*. Minneapolis: Fortress, 1993.

Peterson, Brian K. *Eloquence and the Proclamation of the Gospel in Corinth*. Atlanta: Scholars, 1998.

Philo. *De Virtutibus Prima Pars, Quod Est De Legatione Ad Gaium*. In *The Works of Philo: Complete and Unabridged*. Translated by C. D. Younge. Peabody: Hendrickson, 1993.

Pickett, Raymond. *The Cross in Corinth: The Social Significance of the Death of Jesus*. Sheffield: Sheffield Academic, 1997.

Piper, John. *The Future of Justification: A Response to N. T. Wright*. Wheaton: Crossway, 2007.

Plank, Karl A. *Paul and the Irony of Affliction*. Atlanta: Scholars, 1987.

Plato. *Gorgias, Phaedrus, Symposium, Sophist, Statesman, Protagoras, Meno, Apology, Phaedo*. In *The Dialogue of Plato*, edited by B. Jowett. vols. 1–4. 2nd ed. Oxford: Clarendon, M DCCC LXXV.

Plummer, Robert L. "Imitation of Paul and the Church's Missionary Role in 1 Corinthians." *JETS* 44 (2001) 219–35.

Plutarch. *Comparison of Demosthenes and Cicero*. Translated by Bernadotte Perrin. The Loeb Classic Library. London: William Heinemann; Cambridge: Harvard University Press, 1971.

———. "The Life of Cicero." In *Selected Lives from the Lives of the Noble Grecians and Romans*, Edited by Paul Turner. 69–103. Fontwell: Century, 1963.

———. *Plutarch's Lives: Cicero*. Translated by Bernadotte Perrin. The Loeb Classic Library. London: William Heinemann; Cambridge: Harvard University Press, 1971.

Pogoloff, Stephen M. *Logos and Sophia: The Rhetorical Situation of 1 Corinthians*. Atlanta: Scholars, 1992.

Porter, Stanley E., ed. *Handbook of Classical Rhetorical in the Hellenistic Period 330 BCE–400 CE*. Leiden; NY; Köln: Brill, 1997.

———, and Dennis L. Stamps, eds. *The Rhetorical Interpretation of Scripture: Essays from the 1996 Malibu Conference*. JSNTS 180. Sheffield: Sheffield Academic, 1999.

Price, Charles. No page. Online: http://www.aph.gov.au/Library/Pubs/rn/1996-97/97rn19.htm.

Quast, Kevin. *Reading the Corinthian Correspondence: An Introduction*. New York: Paulist, 1994.

Quayle, William Alfred. "Cicero and Paul." *Methodist Review* 89 (1907) 709–19.

Quintilian. *Institutio Oratoria*. Translated by H. E. Butler. The Loeb Classic Library. London: William Heinemann; Cambridge: Harvard University Press, 1968.

Rawson, Berly. "The Roman Family in Recent Research: State of the Question." *BI* 11 (2003) 119–38.

Reale, Giovanni. *The Concept of First Philosophy and the Unity of the Metaphysics of Aristotle*. Translated by John R. Catan. Albany: State University of New York Press, 1980.

Richards, J. R. "Romans and 1 Corinthians: Their Chronological Relationship and Comparative Dates." *NTS* 13 (1966–67) 14–30.

Richardson, Peter. "Judaism and Christianity in Corinth After Paul: Text and Material Evidence." In *Pauline Conversations in Context: Essays in Honour of Calvin J Roetzel*, edited by Janice Capel Anderson, Philip Sellew, and Claudia Setzer. 42–66. London: Sheffield Academic, 2002.

Rives, James B. *Religion in the Roman Empire*. Malden; Oxford; Carlton: Blackwell, 2007.
Ro, Bong Rin. "Communicating the Biblical Concept of God to Koreans." In *the Global God: Multicultural Evangelical View of God*, edited by Aída BesanÇon Spencer and Wiliam David Spencer. 207-30. Grand Rapids: Baker, 1998.
Robbins, Vernon K. "Argumentative Textures in Socio-Rhetoric Interpretation." In *Rhetorical Argumentation in Biblical Texts: Essays from the Lund 2000 Conference*, edited by Anders Eriksson, Thomas H. Olbricht, and Walter Übelacker. 27-65. Harrisburg: Trinity International, 2002.
Robertson, Archibald, and Alfred Plummer. *The First Epistle of St Paul to the Corinthians*. ICC. 2nd ed. Edinburgh: T. & T. Clark, 1958.
Rohrbaugh, Richard L., ed. *The Social Sciences and New Testament Interpretation*. Peabody: Hendrickson, 1996.
Rosner, Brian S. *Paul, Scripture, and Ethics: A Study of 1 Corinthians 5–7*. Grand Rapids: Baker, 1994.
Ross, J. M. "Not Above What is Written: A Note on 1 Cor 4:6." *ExpT* 82 (1971) 215-17.
Rothaus, Richard M. *Corinth: The First City of Greece. An Urban History of Late Antique Cult and Religion*. Leiden: Brill, 2000.
Ryeu, Sung-Yeul. *T'oegye'eui sunggun'e kwanhan yeungu: sunghaksypdo'reul jungsimeuro* (A Study on the T'oegye's Theory of Sage King: with Special Emphasis on the Ten Diagrams in Sage Learning). PhD diss., Dankook University, 1995.
Ryu, Hun. *Study of North Korea*. Seoul: Research Institute of International and External Affairs, 1968.
Ryu, Myoung-Jong. "T'oegye'eui sam (shang ae)" (Life of T'oegye). *T'oegyehak nonchong* 7 (2001) 273-90.
———. *T'oegye'hakeui chulhak segye* (World of T'oegye's Philosophy). Busan: Shejong Chul'pansa, 2000.
Saller, Richard. "Patronage and Friendship in Early Imperial Rome: Drawing the Distinction." In *Patronage in Ancient Society*, edited by A. Wallace-Hadrill. 49-62. London; New York: Routledge, 1989.
———.*Personal Patronage under the Early Empire*. Cambridge: Cambridge University Press, 1982.
Sanders, Boykin. "Imitating Paul: 1 Cor 4:16." *HTR* 74 (1981) 353-63.
Sanders, Jack T. "Paul Between Jews and Gentiles in Corinth." *JSNT* 65 (1997) 67-83.
Sänger, Dieter. "Die *Dunatoi* in 1 Kor 1.26." *ZNW* 76 (1985) 285-91.
Schmithals, Walter. *Gnosticism in Corinth: An Investigation of the Letters to the Corinthians*. Translated by John C. Steely. Nashville: Abington, 1971.
———. *Paul and the Gnostics*. Translated by John C. Steely. Nashville: Abington, 1972.
Schowalter, Daniel N. and Steven J. Friesen, eds. *Urban Religion in Roman Corinth: Interdisciplinary Approaches*. Cambridge: Harvard University Press, 2005.
Schreiner, Thomas R. *Romans*. BECNT. Grand Rapids: Baker, 1998.
Schweitzer, Albert. *The Mysticism of Paul the Apostle*. London: A. & C. Black, 1931.
Scroggs, Robin. *Christology in Paul and John*. Philadelphia: Fortress, 1988.
———. "Paul: Sophia and Pneumatikos." *NTS* 14 (1967-68) 33-55.
Seifrid, Mark A., D. A. Carson, and Peter T. O'Brien. *Justification and Variegated Nomism, Volume II: The Paradoxes of Paul*. Tübingen: Morh Siebeck; Grand Rapids: Baker Academic, 2004.
Sellin, Gerhard. "Das 'Geheimnis' der Weisheit und das Rätsel der 'Christuspartei' (zu 1 Kor 1-4)." *ZNW* 73 (1982) 69-96.

Seneca the Younger. *De Consolatione, De Tranquillitate Animi, De Brevitate Vitae, De Constantia Sapientis*. Translated by John W. Basore. The Loeb Classic Library. London: William Heinemann; Cambridge: Harvard University Press, 1970.

———. *De Constantia Sapientis*. Translated by J. W. Basore. The Loeb Classic Library. London: William Heinemann; Cambridge; Massachusetts: Harvard University Press, 1963.

———. *Epistulae*. Translated by Richard M. Gummere. The Loeb Classic Library. London: William Heinemann; Cambridge: Harvard University Press, 1962.

———. *Epistulae Morales*. Translated by Richard M. Gummere. vols. I–II, The Loeb Classic Library. London: William Heinemann; Cambridge: Harvard University Press, 1920. Reprint, 1972.

Seo, Yong-Hwa. *T'oegye'eui yinganhak yeungu* (A Study on the T' oegye Perspective of the Human). PhD diss., Keun-Kook University, 1990.

Shotter, David. *Augustus Caesar*. London; New York: Routledge, 1991.

Sider, Ronald J. "The Pauline Conception of the Resurrection Body in 1 Cor. 15:35-54." *NTS* (1975) 428-39.

Slingerland, Dixon. "Acts 18:1–18, the Gallio Inscription, and the Absolute Pauline Chronology." *JBL* 110 (1991) 439-49.

Smit, Joop F. M. "Epideictic Rhetoric in Paul's First Letter to the Corinthians 1–4." No page. Online: http://arachnid.pepperdine.edu/eolbricht/heidelberg/smit.pdf.

———. "The Rhetorical Disposition of First Corinthians 8:7–9:27." *CBQ* 59 (1997) 476-91.

———. "'What is Apollos? What is Paul?' in Search for the Coherence of First Corinthians 1:10—4:21." *NovT* 44 (2002) 231-51.

Smith, Dennis E. *From Symposium to Eucharist: The Banquet in the Early Christian World*. Minneapolis: Fortress, 2003.

Smith, Robert W. *The Art of Rhetoric in Alexandria: Its Theory and Practice in the Ancient World*. The Hague: Martinus Nijhoff, 1974.

Soards, Mario L. *1 Corinthians*. NIBC. Peabody: Hendrickson, 1999.

Song, Sung-Jin. "Yulgokeui shinyoohakjeuk yinganronkwa sinhakeok mannam (Encounter between Yulgok's Doctrine of the Human in Neo-Confucianism and Theology)." *Sinhak'kwa segye* (Theology and World) 45 (2002) 141-61.

Sparks, H. F. D. "1 Kor 2.9 a Quotation from the Coptic Testament of Jacob?" *ZNW* 67 (1976) 269-76.

Spicg, Ceslas. "*Kauchaomai, Kauchēēma, Kauchēēsis*." In *Theological Lexicon of the New Testament*. Translated by James D. Ernest. 298-302. vol 2. Peabody: Hendrickson, 1994.

Stambaugh, John E. and David L. Balch. *The New Testament in Its Social Environment*. Edited by Wayne A. Meeks. Philadelphia: Westminster, 1986.

Stern, Menahen, trans. *Greek and Latin Authors on Jews and Judaism: From Herodotus to Plutarch*. vol 1. Jerusalem: the Israel Academy of Sciences and Humanities, 1976.

Stettler, Christian. "The 'Command of the Lord' in 1 Cor 14:37—A Saying of Jesus?" *Biblica* 87 (2006) 42-51.

Still, Todd D. "Did Paul Loathe Manual Labour? Revising the Work of Ronald F. Hock on the Apostle's Tentmaking and Social Class." *JBL* 125 (2006) 781-95.

Strabo. *Geography*. In *Selections from Strabo*. Translated by H. F. Tozer. Oxford: Clarendon, 1893.

———. *Geography*. Translated by H. L. Jones. London: William Heinemann; Cambridge: Harvard University Press, 1961.

Strom, Mark. *Reframing Paul: Conversations in Grace and Community*. Downers Grove: InterVarsity, 2000.

Strugnell, John. "A Plea for Conjectural Emendation in the New Testament with a Coda on 1 Cor 4:6." *CBQ* 36 (1974) 543–58.

Suetonius. *De Rhetoribus*. Translated by J. C. Rolfe. The Loeb Classic Library. London: William Heinemann; Cambridge: Harvard University Press, 1970.

Sugirtharajah, R. S. *The Bible and the Third World: Precolonial, Colonial and Postcolonial Encounters*. Cambridge: Cambridge University Press, 2001.

Suh, Kwang-Sun, et al. *Minjung Theology: People as the Subject of History*. London: Zed; New York: Orbis; Singapore: Christian Conference of Asia, 1981.

Sumney, Jerry L. "Critical Note: The Place of 1 Corinthians 9:24–27 in Paul's Argument." *JBL* 119 (2000) 329–33.

———. *Identifying Paul's Opponents: the Question of Method in 2 Corinthians*. Sheffield: JSOT, 1990.

———. *'Servants of Satan,' 'False Brothers' and Other Opponents of Paul*. Sheffield: Sheffield Academic Press, 1999.

Swearingen C. Jan. "The Tongues of Men: Understanding Greek Rhetorical Sources for Paul's Letters to the Romans and 1 Corinthians." In *Rhetorical Argumentation in Biblical Texts: Essays from the Lund 2000 Conference*, edited by Anders Eriksson, Thomas H. Olbricht, and Walter Übelacker. 232–42. Harrisburg: Trinity International. 2002.

Tacitus. *Dialogue de Oratoribus*. Translated by W. Peterson and revised by M. Winterbottom. The Loeb Classic Library. London: William Heinemann; Cambridge: Harvard University Press, 1970.

Talbert, Charles H. *Reading Corinthians: A Literary and Theological Commentary on 1 & 2 Corinthians*. New York: Crossroad, 1987.

———. *Romans*. Macon: Smith & Helwys, 2002.

Tayler, C. C. W., ed. *From the Beginning to Plato*. London; New York: Routledge, 1997.

Terry, Ralph Bruce. *A Discourse Analysis of 1 Corinthians*. 1995. No page. Online: http://bible.ovc.edu/terry/dissertation.

Theissen, Gerd. *Psychological Aspects of Pauline Theology*. Philadelphia: Fortress, 1987.

———. "Social Conflicts in the Corinthian Community: Further Remarks on J. J. Meggitt, *Paul, Poverty and Survival*." *JSNT* 85 (2003) 371–91.

———. *Social Reality and Early Christians: Theology, Ethics, and the World of the New Testament*. Minneapolis: Fortress, 1992.

———. *The Social Setting of Pauline Christianity: Essay on Corinth*. Philadelphia: Fortress, 1982; Edinburgh: T. & T. Clark, 1990.

———. "The Social Structure of Pauline Communities: Some Critical Remarks on J. J. Meggitt, *Paul, Poverty and Survival*." *JSNT* 84 (2001) 65–84.

Thiébault, Philippe. "Exploring the Confucian Self: A Critique and Reinterpretation," *Transactions* 73 (1998) 11–40.

———. "Yi I, Yulgok (1536-1584), A Path to Maturation and Fulfilment: Poetry, Philosophy, and Wisdom." *Transactions* 74 (1999) 59–85.

Thiselton, Anthony C. *The First Epistle to the Corinthians*. NIGTC. Grand Rapids; Cambridge: Eerdmans; Carlisle: Paternoster, 2000.

———. "The Meaning of *Sarx* in 1 Corinthians 5:5: A Fresh Approach in the Light of Logical and Sematic Factors." *SJT* xxvi (1973) 204–27.

———. "Realized Eschatology at Corinth." *NTS* 24 (1978) 510–26.

Thomas, Donald F. *The Deacon in a Changing Church*. Valley Forge: Judson, 1969.

Thrall, Margaret E. "The Initial Attraction of Paul's Mission in Corinth and of the Church He Founded There." In *Paul, Luke and the Greco-Roman World: Essays in Honor of Alexander J. M. Wedderburn*, edited by Alf Christophersen, Carsten Claussen, Jörg Frey, and Bruce Longenecker. 58–73. London: Sheffield Academic, 2002.

Tibbs, Clint. *Religious Experience of the Pneuma*. Tübingen: Mohr Siebeck, 2007.

———. "The Spirit (World) and the (Holy) Spirits among the Earliest Christians: 1 Corinthians 12 and 14 as a Test Case." *CBQ* 70 (2008) 313–30.

Tomlin, Graham. "Christians and Epicureans in Corinthians." *JSNT* 68 (1997) 51–72.

———. *Foolishness and Wisdom: The Theology of the Cross in Paul, Luther, and Pascal*. Texas: Exter University, 1996.

Torkki, Juhana. *The Dramatic Account of Paul's Encounter with Philosophy. An Analysis of Acts 17:16–34 with Regard to Contemporary Philosophical Debates*. Helsinki: University of Helsinki, 2004. 1–216. Online: http://ethesis.helsinki.fi/julkaisut/teo/ekseg/vk/torkki/.

Towner, P. H. "Gnosis and Realized Eschatology in Ephesus of the Pastoral Epistles and the Corinthian Enthusiasm." *JSNT* 31 (1987) 95–124.

———. "Households and Household Codes." In *Dictionary of Paul and His Letters*, edited by G. F. Hawthorne, R. P. Martin and D. G. Reid. 417–19. Illinois; Leicester: Inter-Varsity, 1993.

Tranquillus, Gaius Suetonius. *The Twelve Caesars*. Translated by Robert Graves and introduced by Michael Grant. London: Penguin, 1979.

Travis, S. H. "Paul's Boasting in 2 Corinthians 10–12." In *Studia Evangelica*, edited by Elizabeth A. Livingstone. 527–32. vol 6. Papers presented to the Fourth International Congress on New Testament Studies held at Oxford, 1969. Berlin: Akademic-Verlag, 1973.

Tyler, Ronald D. "First Corinthians 4:6 and Hellenistic Pedagogy." *CBQ* 60 (1998) 97–103.

von Nordheim, Eckhard. "Das Zitat des Paulus in 1 Kor 2.9 und seine Beziehung zum-koptischen Testament Jakobs." *ZNW* 65 (1974) 112–20.

Vos, J. S. "Der METASCHEMATISMOS in 1 Kor 4.6." *ZNW* 86 (1995) 154–72.

Voss, Florian. *Das Wort vom Kreuz und die menschliche Vernunft: Ein Untersuchung zur Soteriologie des 1. Korintherbriefes*. Göttingen: Vandenhoeck & Ruprecht, 2002.

Wagner, Edward W. "Mikook'e yisseusueui T'oegye'hak yeungueu jeunmang" (Preview of the Study of T'oegye in America). In *T'oegye'hak yeungunonjeung, je 9 kwon: Seoyangeui T'oegyeyeungu* (Studies on T'oegye, vol. 9: studies on T'oegye in the Western World), edited by Whi-chil Song and Gooy-Hyun Shin. 35–39. Dae-gu: Kyung-Book University T'oegye Institute, 1997.

Wagner, Edward W., et al. *Korea Old and New A History*. Cambridge: Harvard University Press, 1990.

Wagner, Ross J. "'Not beyond the things which are written': A call to Boast only in the Lord (1 Cor 4.6)." *NTS* 44 (1998) 279–87.

Walker, William O., Jr. "1 Corinthians 2.6–16: A Non-Pauline Interpretation?" *JSNT* 47 (1992) 75–94.

———. "The Burden of Proof in Identifying Interpolations in the Pauline Letters." *NTS* 33 (1987) 611–12.

——— "Textual-Critical Evidence for Interpolations in the Letters of Paul." *CBQ* 50 (1988) 622–31.

Wallace-Hadrill, A., ed. *Patronage in Ancient Society*. London; New York: Routledge, 1989.

———. "Patronage in Roman Society: from Republic to Empire." In *Patronage in Ancient Society*, edited by Wallace-Hadrill. 63–87. London; New York: Routledge, 1989.

Walton, Steven. "Rhetorical Criticism: An Introduction." *Themelios* 21 (1996) 4–9.

Wan, Sze-Kar. *Power in Weakness: Conflict and Rhetoric in Paul's Second Letter to the Corinthians*. Harrisburg: Trinity International, 2000.

Wanamaker, Charles A. "A Rhetoric of Power: Ideology and 1 Corinthians 1–4." In *Paul and the Corinthians: Studies on a Community in Conflict: Essays in Honor of Margaret Thrall*, edited by Trevor J. Burke and J. Keith Elliott. 115–37. Leiden: Brill, 2003.

Waters, Guy Prentiss. *Justification and the New Perspectives on Paul: A Review and Response*. Phillipsburg: P. & R., 2004.

Watson, Duane F. "Paul's Boasting in 2 Corinthians 10–13 as Defence of His Honor: A Socio-Rhetorical Analysis." In *Rhetorical Argumentation in Biblical Texts: Essays from the Lund 2000 Conference*, edited by Anders Eriksson, Thomas H. Olbricht, and Walter Übelacker. 260–75. Harrisburg: Trinity International, 2002.

Watson, Francis, *Paul, Judaism, and the Gentiles: Beyond the New Perspective*. Grand Rapids: Eerdmans, 2007.

Watson, Nigel. "Book Reviews on Will Deming's *Paul on Marriage and Celibacy: The Hellenistic Background of 1 Corinthians 7*." *Pacifica* 19 (2006) 97–99.

———. *The First Epistle to the Corinthians*. Epworth Commentary. London: Epworth, 1992.

Welborn, Laurence L. "A Conciliatory Principle in 1 Cor. 4:6." *NovT* 29 (1987) 320–46.

———. "*Mōros genesthō*: Paul's Appropriation of the Role of the Fool in 1 Corinthians 1–4." *BI* 10 (2002) 421–35.

———. "On the Discord in Corinth: 1 Corinthians 1-4 and Ancient Politics." *JBL* 106 (1987) 85–111.

———. *Paul, the Fool of Christ: A Study of 1 Corinthians 1–4 in the Comic-Philosophic Tradition*. London; New York: T. & T. Clark, 2005.

———. *Politics and Rhetoric in the Corinthian Epistles*. Macon: Mercer University Press, 1997.

Wenham, J. W. *The Elements of New Testament Greek*. Cambridge: Cambridge University Press, 1965. Reprint, 1999.

White, Joel R. "'Baptized on Account of the Dead': the Meaning of 1 Corinthians 15:29 in its Context." *JBL* 116 (1997) 487–99.

Widmann, Martin. "1 Kor 2. 6–16: Ein Einspruch gegen Paulus." *ZNW* 70 (1979) 44–53.

Wilckens, U. *Weisheit und Torheit: Ein esegetisch-religionsgeschichtliche Untersuchung zu 1 Kor 1 und 2*. Tübingen: Morh Siebeck, 1959.

Williams, H. H. Drake, III. *The Wisdom of the Wise: The Presence and Function of Scripture within 1 Cor 1:18—3:23*. Leiden; Boston; Köln: Brill, 2001.

Williams, Michael Allen. *Rethinking 'Gnosticism': An Argument for Dismantling a Dubious Category*. Princeton: Princeton University Press, 1996.

Williams, P. J., Andrew D. Clarke, Peter M. Head, and David Instone-Brewer, eds. *The New Testament in its First Century Setting: Essays on Context and Background in Honor of B. W. Winter on his 65th Birthday*. Grand Rapids: Eerdmans, 2004.

Willis, Wendell Lee. *Idol Meat in Corinth: The Pauline Argument in 1 Corinthians 8 and 10*. SBLDS 68. Chico: Scholars, 1985.

Wilson, R. McL. *Gnosis and the New Testament*. Philadelphia: Fortress, 1968.

———. "How Gnostic were the Corinthians?" *NTS* 19 (1972) 65–74.

Winter, Bruce W. *After Paul left Corinth: the Influence of Secular Ethics and Social Change*. Grand Rapids: Eerdmans, 2001.

———. "Civil Litigation in Secular Corinth and the Church: the Forensic Background to 1 Corinthians 6:1–8." *NTS* 37 (1991) 559–72.

———. "Gallio's Ruling on the Legal Status of Early Christianity (Acts 18:14–15)." *TynBul* 50 (1999) 213–24.
———. "Is Paul among the Sophists?" *RTR* 53 (1994) 28–38.
———. *Philo and Paul among the Sophists: Alexandrian and Corinthian Responses to a Julio-Claudian Movement*. 2nd ed. Grand Rapids: Eerdmans, 2002.
———. *Seek the Welfare of the City: Christians as Benefactors and Citizens*. Grand Rapids: Eerdmans; Carlisle: Paternoster, 1994.
Wire, Antoinette Clark. *The Corinthian Women Prophets: A Reconstruction through Paul's Rhetoric*. Minneapolis: Fortress, 1990.
Wisse, F. W. "Textual Limits to Redactional Theory in the Pauline Corpus." In *Gospel Origin and Christian Beginners: in Honor of James M. Robinson*, edited by J. E. Goehring et al. 167–78. Forum Fascicles 1. Sonoma; CA: Polebridge, 1990.
Witherington, Ben, III. *Conflict & Community in Corinth: A Socio-Rhetorical Commentary on 1 and 2 Corinthians*. Grand Rapids; Eerdmans; Carlisle: Paternoster, 1995.
———. *Grace in Galatia: A Commentary on Paul's Letter to the Galatians*. Grand Rapids: Eerdmans, 1998.
———. *New Testament History: A Narrative Account*. Carlisle: Paternoster; Grand Rapids: Baker Academic, 2001.
———. *The Paul Quest: the Renewed Search for the Jew of Tarsus*. Downers Grove; Leicester: InterVarsity, 1998.
———, with Darlene Hyatt. *Paul's Letter to the Romans: A Socio-Rhetorical Commentary*. Grand Rapids: Eerdmans, 2004.
Wong, E. K. C. "The Deradicalisation of Jesus' Ethical Sayings in 1 Corinthians." *NTS* 48 (2002) 181–94.
Woo, Jinseong. "Reading the Bible from a Social Location: A Response." In *Character Ethics and the New Testament: Moral Dimensions of Scripture*, edited by Robert L. Brawley. 169–76. Louisville; London: Westminster John Knox, 2007.
Worchel, Stephen, et al. *Understanding Social Psychology*. 5th ed. Pacific Grove: Brooks; Cole, 1991.
Wright, N. T. *Justification: God's Plan and Paul's Vision*. London: SPCK, 2009.
———. *Paul: Fresh Perspectives*. London: SPCK, 2005.
Wright, Richard A. "Book Reviews on Michelle V. Lee, *Paul, the Stoics, and the Body of Christ*. SNTSMS 137. New York: Cambridge University Press, 2006." *RBL* 9 (2007). No page. Online: http://www.bookreviews.org/bookdetail.asp?TitleId=5596.
Wuellner, Wilhelm. "The Function of Rhetorical Question in 1 Corinthians." In *L'Apôtre Paul. Personnalité, Style et Conception du Ministère*, edited by A Vanhoye. 46–77. BETL 73. Leuven: Leuven University Press; Uitgeverij: Peeters, 1986.
———. "Haggadic Homily Genre in 1 Corinthians 1–3." *JBL* 89 (1970) 199–204.
———. "Where is Rhetorical Criticism Taking Us?" *CBQ* 49 (1987) 448–63.
Yamauchi, Edwin M. "Pre-Christian Gnosticism, the New Testament and Nag Hammadi in Recent Debate." *Themelios* 10 (1984) 22–27.
———. "Gnosis, Gnosticism." In *Dictionary of Paul and His Letters*, edited by G. F. Hawthorne, R. P. Martin, and D .G. Reid. 350–54. Illinois; Leicester: InterVarsity, 1993.
Yao, Xinzhong. *An Introduction to Confucianism*. Cambridge: Cambridge University Press, 2000.
Yeo, K. K. "The Rhetorical Hermeneutic of 1 Corinthians 8 and Chinese Ancestor Worship." *BI* 2 (1994) 294–311.
———. *Rhetorical Interpretation in 1 Corinthians 8 and 10: A Formal Analysis with Preliminary Suggestions for a Chinese, Cross-Cultural Hermeneutic*. Leiden: Brill, 1995.

Yi, Whang. *Kookyek T'oegyejip* (Collections of T'oegye in Korean). Seoul: Kwangmeung yinshaikongsa, 1968.

Yoon, Deuk-Jae. *T'oegye kyoyook sasang yeongu* (A Study on T'oegye's Thought of Education). PhD diss., Keun-Kook University, 1998.

Yoon, Jong-Sun. "T'oegye eseo jongyojek Kyonghyang (T'oegye's Religious Tendency)." *T'oegye hakbo* 72 (1991) 7–17.

Yoon, Sa-soon, trans. *T'oegye sunjip* (Collection of T'oegye). Seoul: Hyunam'sa, 1993.

———. "T'oegye's Identification of 'To Be' and 'Ought': T'oegye's Theory of Value." In *The Rise of Neo-Confucianism in Korea*, edited by Wm. Theodore de Bary and JaHyun Kim Haboush. 223–42. New York: Columbia University Press, 1985.

Young, Brad H. *Paul the Jewish Theologian: A Pharisee among Christians, Jews, and Gentiles.* Peabody: Hendrickson, 1997. 5th print, 2006.

Yun, Chongun. *T'oegye Yi Hwang uhddekkye salatnonga?* (How did T'oegye Yi Hwang Live?). Seoul: Nuhrymtuh, 2003.

Zmijewski, J. "*Kauchaomai.*" In *Exegetical Dictionary of the New Testament.* 276–79. vol 2. Grand Rapids: Eerdmans, 1981.

Scripture Index

OLD TESTAMENT

Genesis

2:7	31, 32

Exodus

13–17	245
13	221
14	221
16	221
17	221
20:1–6	211, 213
20:1–23	221, 224
20:4–5	220, 221, 244, 245
20:5	221
20:12	223
32	221, 245
32:1–8	221
32:6	221, 245

Numbers

11	221, 245
14	221, 245
16	221, 245
20	221, 245
21	221, 245
25	221, 245

Deuteronomy

21:23	179 n. 113

Judges

8:2	144

1 Kings

15:23	144

Job

5:13a	135

Psalms

93:11	135

Proverbs

1:2–7	35
21:18	184

Isaiah

11:2	144
28:33	135
29:14	147
29:14b	135
53:3	184
64:3	135

Scripture Index

Jeremiah

9:22	144
9:22–23	135, 143, 144
9:23	150, 190

Lamentations

3:45	184

Daniel

7:18	18

Zechariah

4:6	135

NEW TESTAMENT

Matthew

8:1–17	219
8:29–34	219
9:8	219

Luke

4:18	208 n. 27

John

4:43–54	219
5:1–9	219

Acts

13:4	108
13:7	108
17:16–34	10 n. 21, 74
17:34	108
18	112 n. 102
18:1	96, 98
18:1–3	113, 175, 194
18:1–28	105, 228
18:2	100, 112, 113, 119
18:3	99, 113, 180, 182, 183
18:4	98, 101, 112
18:5	98
18:5–6	112, 114
18:5–7	115
18:7	112, 126
18:8	112, 112 n. 103, 113, 126
18:8–17	42
18:10	126
18:11	96, 98
18:12	108
18:12–17	97 n. 33
18:17	112
18:24	114, 142, 176
18:24–26	38, 139
18:24–28	114
18:24—19:1	114
18:26	113
18:27	176
19:1	176
19:21	114
19:22	119, 121, 126
22:25–29	128 n. 160

Romans

1:1–13	79
1:7	2
1:15	79
3:1–2	236
3:2b	203
3:9–11a	203
3:9b–10a	203
3:9b–11a	203
3:21–26	79
4:1–25	215
9–11	5
15:14—16:27	79
16	128
16:1	99, 100, 116, 117, 119, 172
16:1–2	73, 116, 174
16:1–3	95 n. 29, 105, 112, 119, 129, 228
16:2	118, 119
16:3	100, 112, 113, 119
16:3–4	172

Scripture Index

16:3–5	113
16:5	177
16:23	105, 108–10, 116, 119–21, 172
16:22	126
16:22–23	126
16:23	126, 128 n. 160, 173, 177, 193, 228

1 Corinthians

1:1–13	12
1:2–3	2
1:5	29
1:7	17
1:10	41, 45, 173, 182, 213
1:10–12	1, 37
1:10–13a	79
1:10–13	96
1:10—4:21	32
1:11	45, 116
1:12	39, 81, 105, 114, 171
1:12–17	40
1:13	179
1:13b–25	79
1:14	126
1:14–16	1, 53, 129, 172
1:14–17	121
1:16	116, 177
1:17	1, 36, 134
1:17–18	42
1:17—2:16	1
1:17–25	30
1:18	36, 180
1:18–24	5, 20
1:18–25	82, 104, 135
1:18–28	146
1:18—3:20	33
1:18—3:22	12
1:19	17
1:20	59
1:21	32, 59, 181
1:22–24	1, 47, 228
1:22–25	112
1:23	23, 36, 105, 106
1:23–25	43
1:24	36, 105, 203
1:26	3, 12, 36, 128, 152, 177
1:26–28	1, 2, 51, 98, 106, 109, 208
1:26–31	20, 79, 135, 144
1:26–29	189
1:28	11
1:29	3, 11, 87, 142, 148
1:30	203
1:30–31	209
1:31	3, 11, 87, 140, 142
2:1–5	30, 48, 49
2:2	23, 179, 182
2:3–5	135
2:4	1, 134
2:5	139, 203
2:6	15, 30, 31, 59
2:6–8	15
2:6–11	135
2:6–16	79
2:9	15, 135
2:10	15
2:10b–14	15
2:12–13	34
2:13	35
2:13–14	31
2:14–15	15
2:16	15
3:1	32, 80
3:1–3	81
3:1–4	96
3:1–9	1
3:1–17	40, 79
3:3	30, 45, 48, 81, 147, 176
3:4	37, 39, 48
3:4–5	40
3:4–6	171
3:4–9	52
3:5	117
3:5–8	81
3:5–9	41
3:8	82, 119
3:9	150

1 Corinthians (continued)

3:10–17	39
3:12–14	23
3:16–17	39
3:18–20	1, 17
3:18–23	80, 127, 135
3:19	59, 138
3:19b–20	135
3:20	134
3:21	84, 142
3:21–23	1, 48
3:22	37, 40, 52, 171
3:22–23	40
4:1	11, 49
4:1–7	81
4:1–21	79
4:2	22
4:3	3, 11
4:3–5	17
4:6	40, 48, 52, 114, 171
4:7	142
4:8	18, 20
4:8–9	81
4:8–13	1, 17, 146, 180, 183, 184
4:10	17, 30, 173
4:12	183
4:14	80
4:14–21	1
4:14–16	80
4:15	185, 187
4:16	1, 11, 87, 186
4:18–19	136, 189
5:1–12	1
5:1–13	7
5:3	20
5:3–4	80
5:6	11, 83, 143
5:10	154
6:1–11	1
6:1–8	83
6:7	20
6:11	7
6:12	127
6:12–20	7, 16
7:1–40	1
7:17–24	149, 235
7:18–19	44, 112
7:21–22	235
8–13	214
8:1–6	209
8:1—10:22	1, 12, 157
8:1–13	16, 25, 158, 213
8:4	154, 213
8:4–5	104
8:5	158
8:7–12	83
8:7–30	213
8:10	155
9:1	175
9:1–27	12
9:1–23	84
9:3	83
9:3–7	174
9:3–23	136
9:4–6	142
9:5–6	176
9:15–16	11
9:18	140
9:19	27, 182, 226
9:19–23	27
9:22–23	173
10:1–22	209
10:7	154
10:14–33	16
10:19	154
10:20	106, 220
10:23	127, 213
10:22–33	225
10:23–30	53
10:23—11:1	1, 157, 216, 221, 224
10:32–33	27
10:33	156
11:1	3, 11, 87
11:2–16	7
11:3	178
11:17–19	12
11:17–22	112
11:17–33	16

11:18–19	232	1:12	59, 84, 135
11:21–22	16	1:13–17	20
11:22	12, 81, 208	3:1–2	95 n. 29
11:17–34	1, 98	5:18–19	181
11:18	1	6:13	185
11:18–19	81, 96	6:16	154
11:18–22	51	7:11	83
12	74	10–11	43
12:1–31	214	10:1—11:6	136
12:1–19	208	10:1—11:33	84
12:1—14:40	1	10:1—13:10	83
12:3	22	10:3–4	128
12:8	59	10:9–10	128, 184
12:12	105, 181, 228	10–13	78, 142
12:12–13	232, 236	10:10	48, 84, 137, 139
12:12–31	81	10:13–18	84
12:13	105, 106, 109, 112, 235	10:17	140, 143
12:25	232	11:3–4	140
13	186	11:6	84, 128, 139, 187
13:1–13	214	11:7	182
13:2	29	11:7–11	84, 136, 174, 194, 207
13:3	87, 142	11:7–9	127
13:8	29	11:9	141, 174
13:13	161	11:10	141
14:6	29	11:18	11, 83, 87, 143
15:1–58	1, 16	11:21	11, 83, 87, 143
15:1–10	43	11:23	122 n. 137
15:25–27	166	11:26	106
15:29	12, 161–64, 166	11:30	83
15:31	11, 87	12:1	11, 83, 87, 143
15:35	167	12:11–14	84
15:44–47	31	12:13–18	174, 194
15:44–54	32, 38	12:14	185
16:1–2	53	12:14–18	174
16:8	96	12:20	45, 127, 141
16:12	52		
16:12–19	105, 228	*Galatians*	
16:15	99, 122, 177	1:6—3:7	79
16:15–20	172	1:12	176
16:17	122	1:23–24	176
16:19	113	2:1–10	43
		2:15	235
2 Corinthians		2:15–21	236
1:1–2	2	2:16–17	235

Galatians (continued)

3:6–9	215
3:10–14	179
3:24–25	187
3:28	232, 233, 235–37
4:8–11	79
5:19–25	202

Ephesians

1:22	178
4:16	226 n. 77
5:1	185
5:21—6:9	201
5:23	178

Colossians

3:11	232
3:18—4:1	201
3:22	235

1 Thessalonians

1:6	185
2:9	180, 182
2:14	185

2 Thessalonians

3:7	185
3:9	185

1 Timothy

3:1–13	206 n. 24

2 Timothy

4:20	119–21, 126

Titus

1:7	206 n. 24

Philemon

1–16	109
1–21	95 n. 29

Hebrews

3:1	79

James

2:1–9	208 n. 27

Author Index

Adams, Edward, 14 n. 2
Aitchison, Ronnie, 117
Allison, Dale C., 40 n. 98
Anderson, David A., 229 n. 87
Anderson, R. Dean, 2 n. 1
Applebaum, Shimon, 183 n. 119
Aristotle, 11, 26, 61, 62, 64, 65, 68, 134–36, 199, 251–54
Aronson, Elliot, 136 n. 11

Baird, William, 34 n. 79
Balch, David L., 91 n. 9, 92, 93 n. 16, 101 n. 54, 107 n. 78, 111 n. 96, 120, 120, 123 n. 139, 151 n. 1, 157, 186, 215
Banks, Robert J., 110
Barclay, John M. G., 22 n. 30, 46 n. 112, 116 n. 114, 127 n. 158, 232, 233
Barnett, P. W., 43 n. 112, 174 n. 94
Barrett, C. K., 21, 44 n. 116, 96 n. 33, 117 n. 116, 143 n. 25, 144 n. 26, 154 n. 13, 156 n. 28, 183 n. 123, 184 n. 127, 187 n. 133
Barton, Stephen C., 177 n. 108
Baur, Ferdinand Christian, 14, 38, 40, 41
Betz, Hans Dieter, 43 n. 123, 78, 79
Boatwright, Mary T., 100 n. 49
Borowski, Oded, 125 n. 154
Boyarin, Daniel, 233

Braund, David, 94 n. 21, 95 n. 29
Braxton, Brad Ronnell, 192 n. 2, 195 n. 3
Breen, Michael, 230 n. 90, 231
Brett, Mark, 226 n. 78
Broneer, Oscar, 100 n. 50, 101
Broughton, T. Robert S., 250 n. 4
Brown, Alexandra R., 15
Bruce, F. F., 14, 21, 78, 96 n. 33, 126, 163 n. 59, 183 n. 124
Bultmann, Rudolph K., 16 n. 9, 143 n. 25
Burke, Trevor J., 118
Byrne, Brendan, viii, ix, 117, 120 n. 134

Calvin, John, 183 n. 122, 184 n. 125, 255, 256
Campbell, Douglas A., 79
Carr, Wesley, 24 n. 42, 38, 42
Carson, D. A., 22 n. 30, 232
Carter, Timothy L., 121 n. 136
Chester, Stephen J., 24, 37, 38, 46
Cheung, Alex T., 154 n. 13, 225 n. 76
Chia, Samuel, 232 n. 96
Chow, John K., 38 n. 94, 46, 89 n. 1, 90 n. 4, 91 n. 8, 92 n. 12, 93 n. 20, 94 n. 24, 95 n. 25, 151 n. 2, 152 n. 4, 159 n. 42

Author Index

Chung, Chai-Sik, 218 n. 58
Chung, Edward Y. J., 202 n. 13, 258 n. 10, 259 n. 14, 160 n. 17, 261 n. 22, 262 n. 23
Ciampa, Roy E., 160 n. 45
Clarke, Andrew D., 46 n. 122, 120, 130 n. 163
Classen, Carl Joachim, 2 n. 1
Collins, Raymond F., 134, 148 n. 44
Conzelmann, Hans, 14, 21, 96 n. 33, 162, 166 n. 71
Corley, Jeremy, 60, 81
Cranfield, C. E. B., 118, 203 n. 15
Crocker, Cornelia Cyss, 19 n. 24

Dahl, N. A., 14, 16
Daley, Brian E., 207 n. 26
Das, A. Andrew, 22 n. 30
Datiri, Dachollom, 6
Dawes, Gregory W., 154 n. 13, 156 n. 28
DeMaris, Richard E., 162 n. 56, 163 n. 62, 164, 168 n. 79
Deuchler, Martina, 200 n. 5, 217
de Vos, Craig Steven, 28, 46 n. 122, 92 n. 14, 97 n. 38, 101, 102, 105 n. 72, 106 n. 76, 110, 120, 123 n. 121
Dicicco, Mario M., 2 n. 1, 78 n. 103, 252 n. 13
Dio Cassius, 69, 74 n. 85, 93 n. 20, 97 n. 34, 249, 251
Dio Chrysostom, 97 n. 37, 98 n. 41, 99 n. 45, 100 n. 48, 137, 140 n. 19, 162, 182
Donaldson, Terence L., 22 n. 30
Dunn, James D. G., 22 n. 30, 44 n. 118, 79, 117, 118 n. 127, 120 n. 133, 188 n. 134, 235, 236
Dutch, Robert S., 10 n. 21, 46 n. 112

Elliot, John H., 90 n. 7, 94 n. 20
Elliott, Neil, 149
Ellis, E. Earle, 188 n. 134
Engberg-Pedersen, T., 46 n. 122, 178 n. 112

Engels, Donald, 96 n. 32, 97, 99, 102, 106 n. 76, 112 n. 100, 114 n. 109, 116 n. 114, 123–25
Erickson, Anderson, 2 n. 1, 10 n. 21

Fee, Gordon D., 24 n. 42, 44 n. 116, 96 n. 33, 113 n. 107, 116 n. 114, 126, 134, 139, 154, 156, 164 n. 64, 183
Ferguson, Everett, 22 n. 32, 77 n. 99, 98 n. 41, 102 n. 58, 103 n. 64, 157 n. 34, 159 n. 40, 167 n. 75, 215 n. 45, 251
Ferguson, S. B., 22 n. 32
Fiorenza, Elisabeth Schüssler, 45 n. 120, 80 n. 112, 117, 118, 252 n. 13
Fisk, Bruce N., 154 n. 13
Flemming, Dean, 4 n. 5, 89
Forbes, Christopher, 143 n. 25, 145, 146 n. 40
Fotopoulos, John, 154 n. 14
Furnish, Victor Paul, 130 n. 163

Garces-Foley, Kathleen, 229 n. 87
Garnsey, Peter, 91 n. 10, 94 n. 21, 95 n. 27, 96 n. 30, 151 n. 3, 152 n. 4
Georgi, Dieter, 14, 21
Gillihan, Yonder M., 38, 42, 43
Given, Mark D., 46 n. 123, 47, 77, 133 n. 1, 139
Glancy, Jennifer A., 7
Gooch, Paul W., 57, 154, 155, 239
Goulder, Michael D., 14, 38, 40–44, 162 n. 57
Gradel, Ittai, 158 n. 38
Grant, Michael, 251 n. 11
Grindheim, Sigurd, 6, 45 n. 120, 46 n. 123
Gundry, Robert H., 188 n. 134
Gveritt, Anthony, 251 n. 10

Hahn, H. C., 143 n. 25
Hanson, A., 184 n. 127
Hays, Richard B., 14, 20, 44 n. 117, 46 n. 122, 96 n. 33, 99 n. 42, 142 n.

23, 149, 163 n. 59, 165 n. 66, 168 n. 79, 170, 171, 176 n. 102, 217 n. 50, 225 n. 75
Heil, John Paul, 15, 135, 224 n. 74, 225 n. 76
Herms, Ronald, 15
Hester, J. David (Amador), 80 n. 112
Hiigel, John L., 14, 16
Hock, Ronald F., 182, 183 n. 119
Horrell, David G., 14 n. 2, 46, 47, 97 n. 34, 113 n. 107, 120, 123 n. 141, 125 n. 150
Horsley, Richard A., 14, 31, 34–38, 96 n. 30, 154 n. 13, 156, 164 n. 64
Hurd, John Coolidge, 15, 16 n. 9

Jeffers, James S., 186 n. 130, 91, 95 n. 26, 124 n. 149, 151 n. 2, 177 n. 107, 178, 186 n. 130
Johnson, Lee A., 80 n. 111, 159 n. 41
Johnson, Terry, 90 n. 7
Josephus, 250 n. 4
Joubert, Stephan J., 177 n. 106
Judge, E. A., 109 n. 91, 130 n. 163, 143 n. 25, 145 n. 32

Kalton, Michael C., 204 n. 19, 257 n. 4, 258 n. 9, 262 n. 23
Käsemann, Ernst, 16 n. 9, 117 n. 116
Kennedy, George A., 2 n. 1, 60 n. 1, 64 n. 27, 76 n. 94, 80 n. 112, 252 n. 13
Keum, Jang-Tae, 201–3, 217 n. 51, 223 n. 72, 261
Kim, Seyoon, 22 n. 30
Klutz, Todd E., 14, 21, 23, 25–30
Kruse, Colin, 123 n. 139

Lambrecht, Jan, 143 n. 25
Lampe, Peter, 98 n. 40, 113 n. 107, 173 n. 91
Lanci, John R., 46 n. 123, 80 n. 112
Lee, Michelle V., 74
Lim, Timothy H., 14, 46 n. 123

Litfin, Duane, 2 n. 1, 10 n. 21, 11 n. 22, 14, 46 n. 123, 60 n. 1, 63 n. 22, 73 n. 84, 80 n. 112, 123 n. 139, 133 n. 1, 139, 140 n. 21, 252 n. 13
Lo, Lung-Kwong, 227
Longenecker, Richard N., 79, 179 n. 113
Lüdemann, Gerd, 14, 38–40

MacMullen, Ramsay, 107 n. 78, 151 n. 3, 166 n. 69
Malina, Bruce, 90 n. 7, 91 n. 10, 94 n. 24, 170 n. 80
Marshall, Peter, 14, 24, 46, 95 n. 28, 170 n. 81
Martin, Dale B., 46 n. 122, 90 n. 6, 109 n. 89, 187 n. 131, 188 n. 134
Mearns, Christopher L., 16
Meeks, W. A., 46 n. 122, 111 n. 97, 113 n. 107, 122, 126 n. 157, 151 n. 3, 153 n. 7, 161, 163 n. 61
Meggitt, Justin J., 46 n. 122, 110 n. 92, 154 n. 13, 170 n. 82
Mitchell, Margaret M., 2 n. 1, 15, 46, 47, 80 n. 112, 82 n. 115, 171 n. 86, 176 n. 103
Moltmann, Jürgen, 217 n. 50, 227
Morris, Leon, 44 n. 116, 96 n. 33, 99 n. 44, 162 n. 56, 183 n. 122, 184 n. 127, 187 n. 133
Munck, J., 46 n. 123
Murphy-O'Connor, Jerome, 96 n. 32, 97–101, 105 n. 72, 130, 140 n. 19, 154 n. 13, 156, 159 n. 43, 160 n. 45, 162 n. 55, 173 n. 91, 192 n. 2

Newsome, James D., 77 n. 98
Newton, Derek, 154 n. 13, 155, 157, 158, 217 n. 50, 223 n. 70

O'Brien, Peter T., 22 n. 30
O'Day, Gail R., 144 n. 26
Olbricht, Thomas H., 45 n. 120
Oropeza, B. J., 14, 16

Osiek, Carolyn, 157 n. 34, 215 n. 48

Pagels, Elaine, 14, 21, 23
Patrick, James E., 162 n. 55, 164 n. 64
Pearson, Birger, 14, 31, 32, 34, 37, 38
Peterson, Brian K., 2 n. 1, 45 n. 120, 70 n. 66
Philo, 15, 31, 32–38, 53, 111, 111 n. 95
Pickett, Raymond, 98 n. 40, 116 n. 114, 180 n. 115
Piper, John, 22 n. 30
Plato, 63 n. 22, 65 n. 30, 65 n. 36, 66 n. 41, 68 n. 52, 134 n. 6, 135 n. 8
Plummer, Robert L., 96 n. 33
Plutarch, 60, 61, 67–72, 77, 86, 145 n. 34, 249–51
Pogoloff, Stephen M., 2 n. 1, 3, 10 n. 21, 14, 44 n. 117, 46, 51–57, 77, 80 n. 112, 113 n. 104, 115, 118 n. 127, 121 n. 136, 127 n. 159, 128 n. 161, 134, 142 n. 22, 171, 174 n. 92, 176 n. 102, 238

Quintilian, 60, 61, 63 n. 25, 71, 72, 75 n. 91, 76, 79

Reale, Giovanni, 65 n. 34
Richardson, Peter, 43 n. 112, 111 n. 96, 114
Rives, James B., 77 n. 98, 151 n. 2, 157 n. 34, 161, 178, 215
Robertson, Archibald, 96 n. 33
Rohrbaugh, Richard L., 90 n. 7, 91 n. 10, 94 n. 24, 170 n. 80
Rosner, Brian S., 160 n. 45
Rothaus, Richard M., 100 n. 50

Saller, Richard, 90, 91 n. 10, 93 n. 20, 94 n. 21, 95 n. 27, 96 n. 30, 151 n. 3, 152 n. 4
Sanders, Boykin, 185 n. 128
Sanders, Jack T., 46 n. 122, 154 n. 13, 156 n. 28
Schmithals, Walter, 14, 21–23, 166 n. 71

Schowalter, Daniel N., 101 n. 57
Schreiner, Thomas R., 22 n. 30, 117
Schweitzer, Albert, 14, 16
Scroggs, Robin, 15 n. 3
Seifrid, Mark A., 22 n. 30
Seneca the Younger, 71–74, 76, 77, 87, 98 n. 38, 199
Smit, Joop F. M., 2 n. 1, 14, 46 n. 123, 80 n. 112, 154 n. 13, 156 n. 28
Smith, Dennis E., 154 n. 13, 155, 161 n. 47
Stambaugh, John E., 91 n. 9, 92, 93 n. 18, 101 n. 54, 107 n. 78, 111 n. 96, 120, 151 n. 2, 153 n. 7, 186 n. 130
Stettler, Christian, 161, 226 n. 77
Still, Todd D., 183
Strabo, 97 n. 34, 98, 102 n. 61, 250 n. 4
Strom, Mark, 12 n. 23, 109 n. 91, 133 n. 1, 190 n. 1
Suetonius, 61 n. 6, 103 n. 65, 251
Sugirtharajah, R. S., 7 n. 16
Sumney, Jerry L., 45 n. 120, 142 n. 42, 154 n. 13, 156 n. 28

Tacitus, 60, 72, 76, 91, 251
Talbert, Charles H., 14, 21, 96 n. 33, 117, 120 n. 134
Theissen, Gerd, 21, 25, 46, 107 n. 77, 109, 113 n. 104, 115, 116 n. 114, 120 n. 130, 154, 170 n. 82, 183 n. 121
Thiébault, Philippe, 200, 202 n. 11
Thiselton, Anthony C., 14, 16–20, 46 n. 123, 96 n. 32, 112 n. 103, 113 n. 107, 116 n. 114, 134, 162, 171, 183 n. 122, 184 n. 125, 187 n. 133
Thrall, Margaret E., 44 n. 116
Tomlin, Graham, 46 n. 122, 74, 75
Torkki, Juhana, 10 n. 21, 74
Towner, P. H., 14, 16, 34 n. 81
Travis, S. H., 143 n. 25, 145 n. 32

Wallace-Hadrill, A., 93 n. 19
Walton, Steven, 45 n. 120
Wan, Sze-Kar, 174

Wanamaker, Charles A., 55, 80 n. 112
Waters, Guy Prentiss, 22 n. 30
Watson, Francis, 44 n. 119
Watson, Nigel, 192 n. 2
Welborn, Laurence L., 2 n. 1, 10 n. 21, 12 n. 23, 46 n. 123, 80 n. 112, 89
White, Joel R., 162 n. 55
Williams, H. H. Drake, 15, 135, 144
Williams, Michael Allen, 25
Willis, Wendell Lee, 154 n. 13, 155
Wilson, R. McL., 23, 24 n. 41
Winter, Bruce W., 2 n. 1, 12 n. 23, 13, 46–56, 80 n. 112, 95 n. 25, 97 n. 33, 100 n. 50, 103 n. 68, 125, 140 n. 19, 145 n. 35, 147 n. 43, 149, 157 n. 33, 158, 162 n. 52, 165, 166 n. 70, 167 n. 74, 168 n. 79, 174 n. 93, 177 n. 105, 238

Wire, Antoinette Clark, 2 n. 1, 45 n. 120, 80 n. 112
Witherington, Ben, 14, 44 n. 117, 45 n. 121, 46 n. 123, 79, 92, 96 n. 32, 102 n. 61, 111, 113 n. 105, 116 n. 114, 117, 118, 120, 126, 139 n. 14, 149, 158 n. 36, 160 n. 44, 162, 165, 167 n. 72, 171, 178 n. 110, 183 n. 121, 192 n. 2, 235 n. 110
Wright, N. T., 22 n. 30,
Wuellner, Wilhelm, 38, 42, 80

Yamauchi, Edwin M., 21 n. 27, 24
Yeo, K. K., 5, 6 n. 11, 58, 154 n. 13, 172, 209 n. 29, 227
Young, Brad H., 22 n. 30

Zmijewski, J., 143 n. 24

Subject Index

Abraham, 180 n. 113, 215, 221, 234, 244
Ancestors, 13, 86, 87, 157, 164–65, 192, 214–27
Ancestral rites, 214–27
Apollos, 1, 38, 39, 40–44, 52–55, 81, 114, 142, 169, 171, 176, 187, 194
Apostleship, 41, 43, 175, 176
Aristotle, 11, 26, 61–65, 68, 134–36, 199, 251–54

Baptism, 38, 53, 121, 154, 161–65, 167 n. 72, 171, 192, 193, 195
Boasting, 11, 84–88, 142–50, 190

Cicero, 10, 11, 60–78, 249–54
Collegia, 12, 118, 119, 119, 136, 138, 147, 151–69
  collegia sodalicia, 152, 154–61
  collegia tenuiorum, 152, 161–66
Confucianism, Korean-, 9, 10, 13, 19 n. 24, 51, 56–58, 190–247, 255–63
Cross of Christ, 179–81

Discrimination, 1, 19, 57, 111, 130, 159, 168, 169,
Domestic cult, 1, 157, 214–17, 221, 225

Eloquence, 20, 59–87, 133–42, 199, 251
Epicureanism, 74, 75, 251
Erastus, 100, 119–21, 126–29, 172–73

Father (*paterfamilias*), 80, 82, 85, 128 n. 160, 157, 159, 165, 177–78, 184–88, 193
Financial support/ monetary gift, 84, 91, 141, 142, 174–76, 194, 207

Greeks, 43, 47, 105, 115–22
Greco-Roman culture/ society, 3–5, 38, 45, 51, 54, 55, 133, 136, 145, 167, 175, 178, 183, 186, 216

Hellenistic Jewish wisdom, 31–38
Household (*oikos*), 53, 82, 121, 122, 157, 166, 177, 178, 192–95, 201, 215, 218, 219, 220

Idols, food offered to, 16, 29 n. 63, 132, 154, 156, 157, 160, 209, 213, 216, 217, 221
Imperial cult, 13, 36, 44, 95, 103, 104, 125, 131, 152, 157–60, 191, 192, 209–12
Imitation, 61, 87, 129, 145, 185, 196, 199

Subject Index

Isocrates, 11, 61–64, 68, 86
Isthmian games, 100–104, 125, 152, 167

Jews, 2, 22, 41 n. 106, 43, 44, 105, 106, 110–15, 203, 232–35

Leadership, 4, 9, 115–18, 129, 148, 174–75, 196–99, 205, 206–10
Love, 25, 26, 82, 83, 144, 161, 186–88, 214
Lord's Supper, 1, 16, 116, 159, 160

Menial work/ leather worker / tentmaker, 99, 133, 175, 182, 183, 194
Moses, 164, 165, 245
Multiculturalism, 228–36, 246

Opponents, of Paul, 11, 12, 14–54, 87, 112, 114, 136–42, 185, 186
Over-realized eschatology, 16–20

Patronage, 36, 38, 44, 89–104, 118, 119, 125, 136, 142, 158, 212,
  Imperial patronage, 94–95
Peter's party, 38–44
Phoebe, 53, 73, 95 n. 29, 100, 116–19, 129, 172, 174
Philosophy, 10 n. 21, 12, 20, 35, 37, 38, 52, 57, 60–74, 77, 85, 97, 105, 108, 175, 190 n. 1, 199–205, 243, 251, 255–60
Plato, 61–66, 68, 134, 199, 251, 252
Power of God, 15, 36, 42, 43, 50, 54, 104, 140, 141, 147, 150, 169, 175, 179, 180, 181, 208,
Proto (or incipient)-Gnosticism, 21–30

Resurrection, 16, 147, 162, 163, 166–69

Rhetoric, 2, 45–55, 59–64, 78–88, 133–50
  Rhetorical analysis, 2–4
  Rhetorical conventions, 45–54
Romans (ethnicity), 47, 60–64, 76, 104–6, 123–30, 163–65, 250
Roman Citizenship, 75, 92, 93 n. 20, 94, 127, 128, 149, 193

Schisms/ factions, 1, 17 n. 15, 19, 25, 47, 69, 79, 131, 165, 169–79, 181, 195, 226
Shinto Shrine worship, 8, 198 n. 1, 209–28
Slave, 7, 92–97, 105, 108–11, 149, 232, 235
Social status/class, 4, 27, 48, 51–59, 87–100, 119–52, 168–208
Stephanus, 53, 100, 101, 121, 122, 195
Stoicism, 10, 74, 251

Temple, 100, 101, 102, 103, 154–55, 157–60, 166, 169, 191–92, 213
T'oegye, 5, 10, 13, 56, 199–203, 217, 243, 255–63

Unity, 6, 160, 169, 178, 188, 193, 195, 213, 214, 226, 228, 230, 236, 237, 242, 246

Wisdom (*sophia*), 10, 11, 22, 31, 64–67, 133–42, 148–50, 181, 190, 199–209, 243–44, 260–63
  Wisdom of God, 12, 15, 22, 23, 32, 34–36, 42, 43, 57, 67, 75, 79, 81–84, 88, 104, 132, 135, 137–43, 147, 148, 150, 181, 190, 200, 203, 208, 209, 241, 244
  Human/ worldly wisdom, 57, 67, 79, 81, 82, 134, 135, 138, 140, 150, 175, 200, 103, 139

www.ingramcontent.com/pod-product-compliance
Lightning Source LLC
Chambersburg PA
CBHW061429300426
44114CB00014B/1600